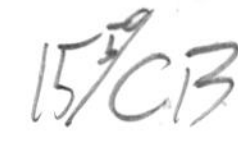

Instant Graphics

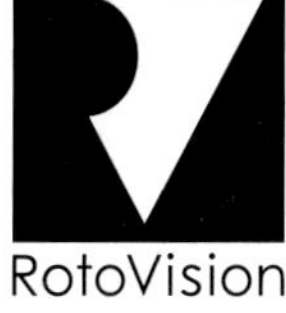

A RotoVision Book

Published and distributed by
RotoVision SA
Route Suisse 9
CH-1295 Mies
Switzerland

RotoVision SA
Sales and Editorial Office
Sheridan House, 114 Western Road
Hove BN3 1DD, UK

Tel: +44 (0)1273 72 72 68
Fax: +44 (0)1273 72 72 69
www.rotovision.com

10 9 8 7 6 5 4 3 2 1
ISBN: 978-2-940361-49-6

Art Director Tony Seddon
Design by Studio Ink

Reprographics in Singapore by ProVision Pte.
Tel: +65 6334 7720
Fax: +65 6334 7721

Printing and binding in Singapore by
Star Standard Industries (Pte) Ltd.

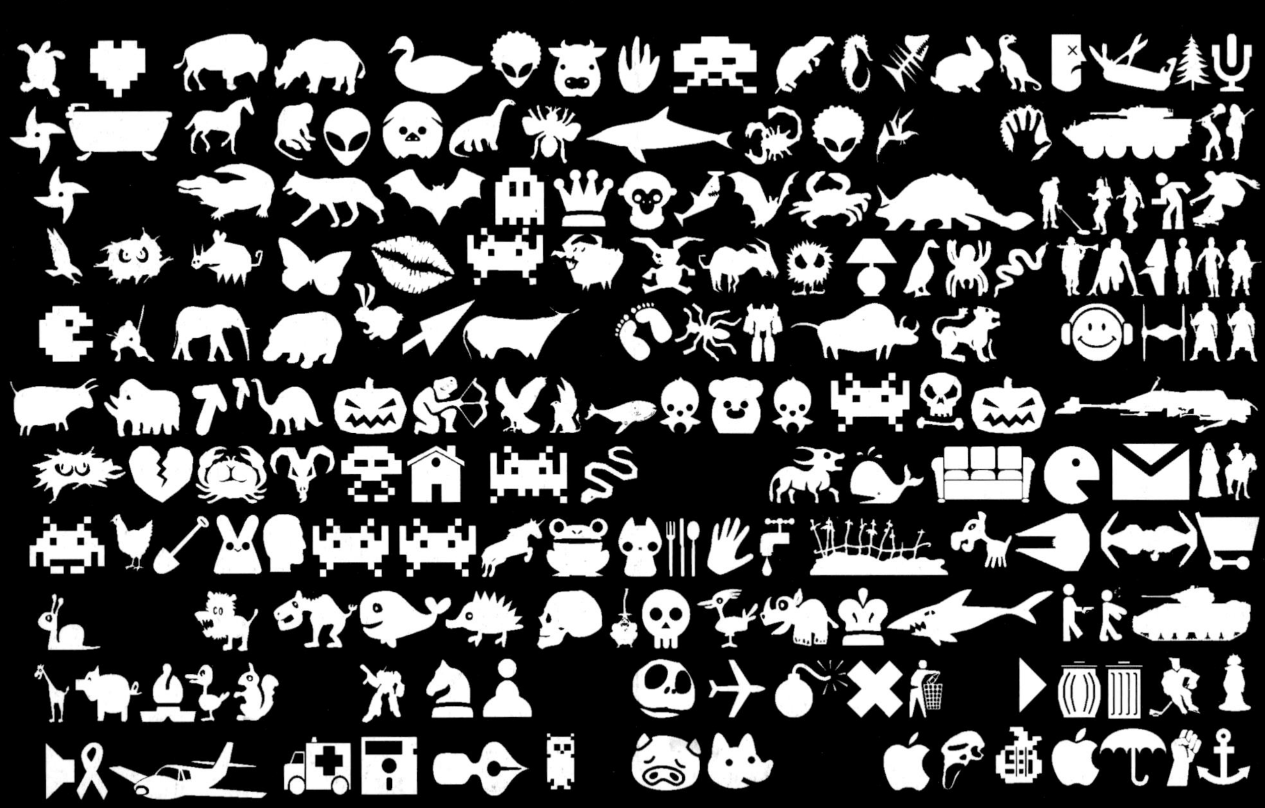

Instant Graphics

Source and Remix Images for Professional Design

Text by Chris Middleton,
images curated by Luke Herriott

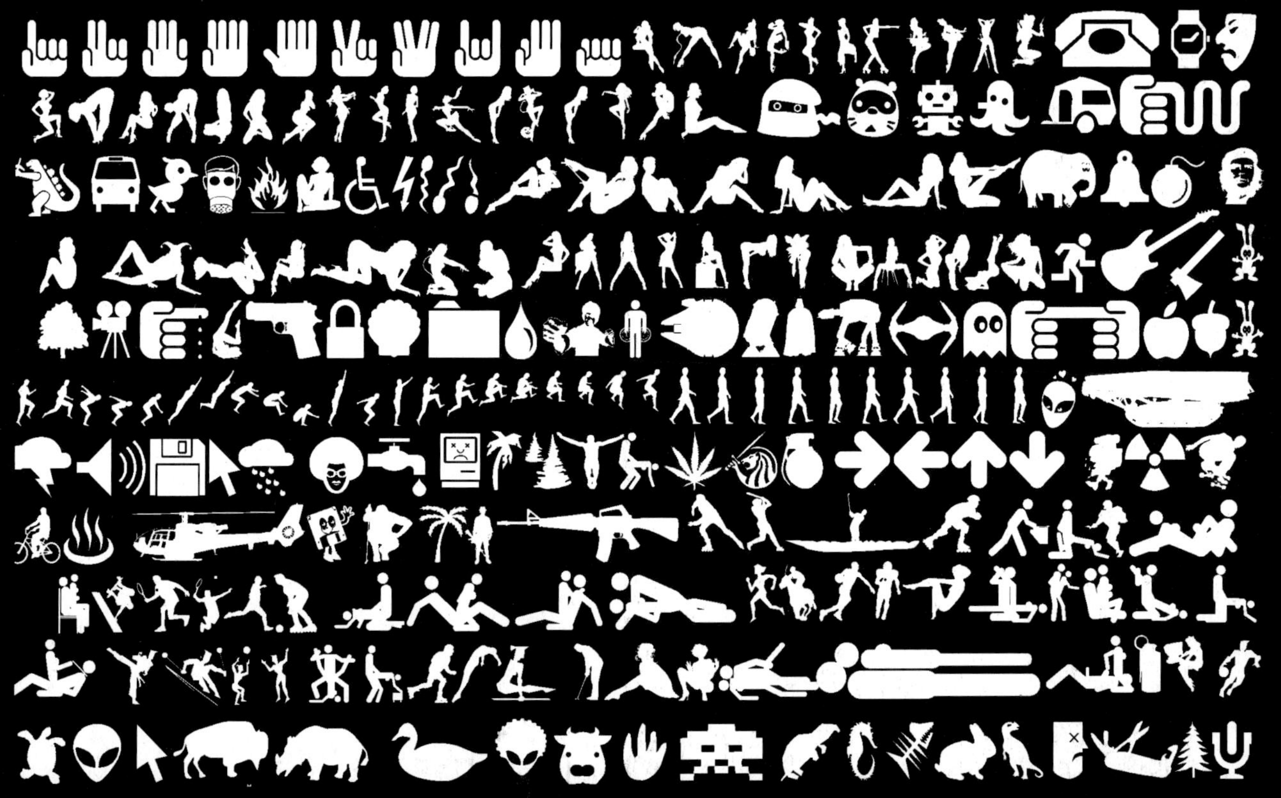

Contents

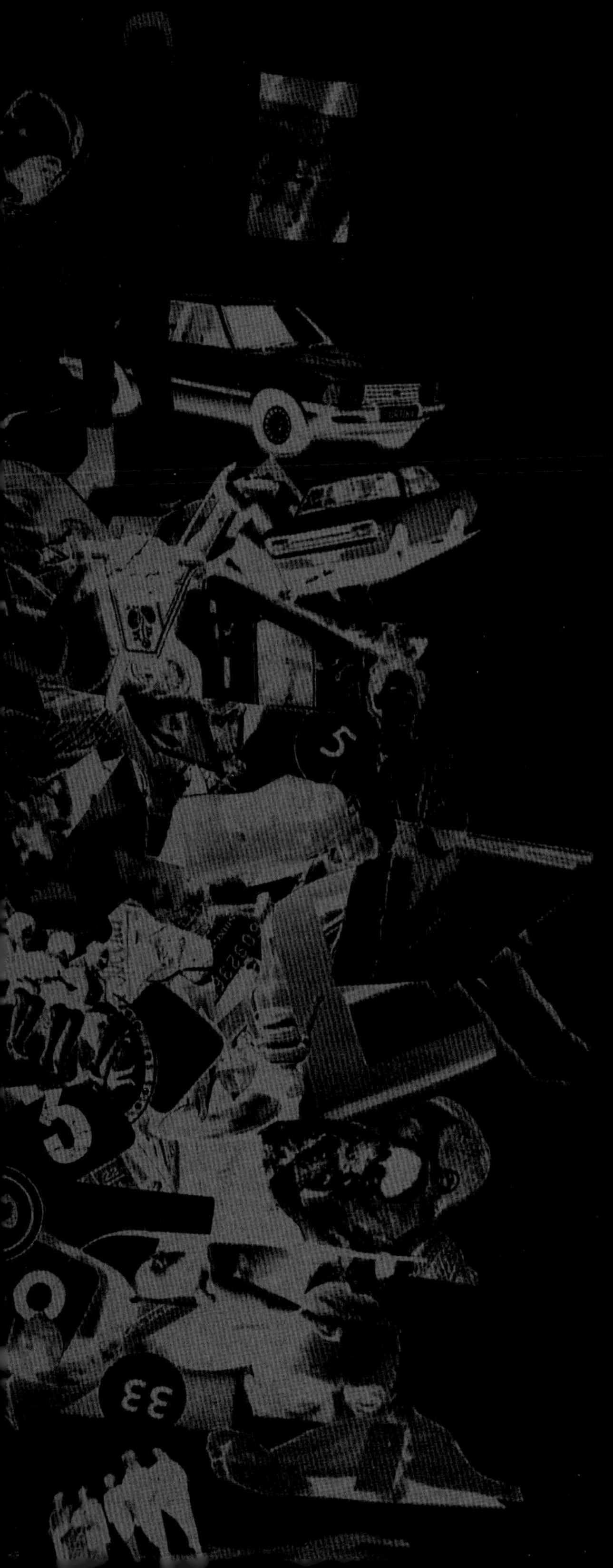

Chapter 1: Celebrate clip art

Chapter 2: Hints and tips

Chapter 3: Case studies

Chapter 4: Appendix

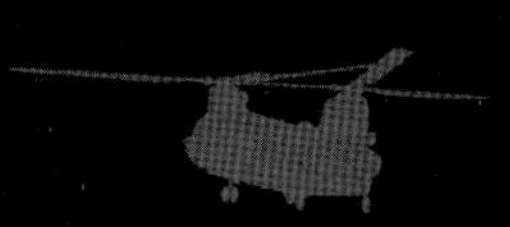

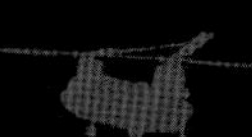

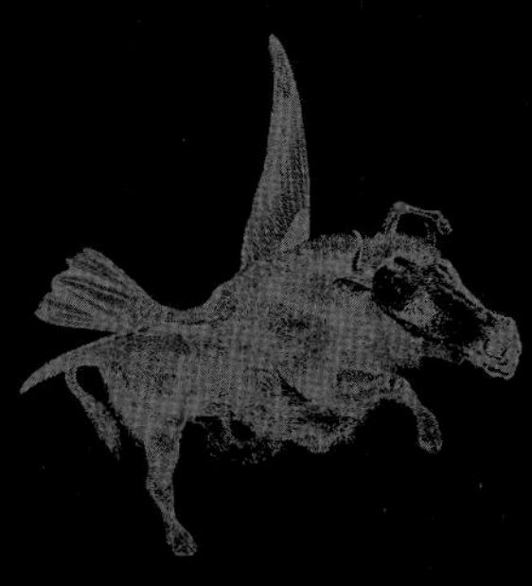

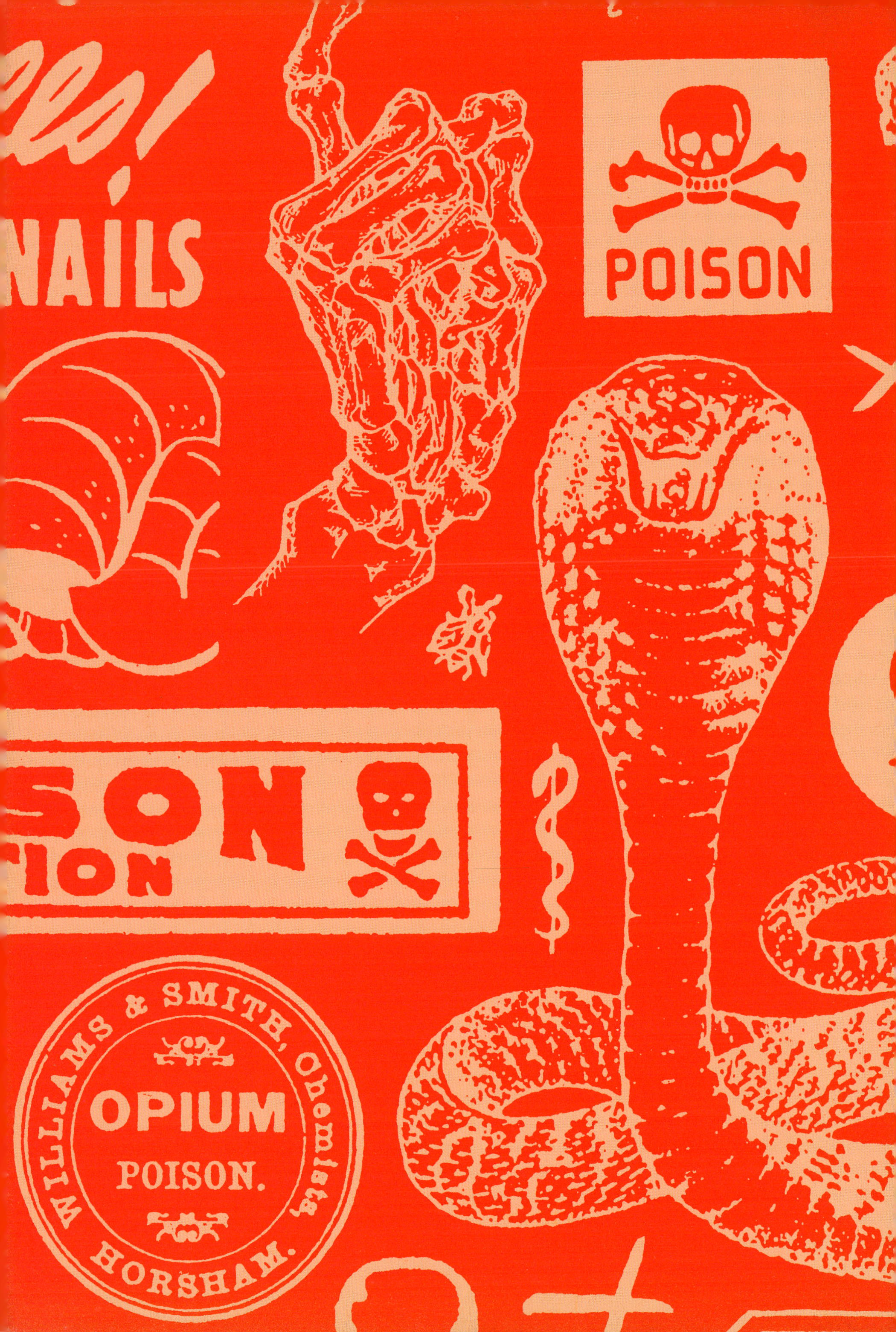
NAILS
POISON
WILLIAMS & SMITH, Chemists
OPIUM
POISON.
HORSHAM.

Chapter 1

Celebrate clip art

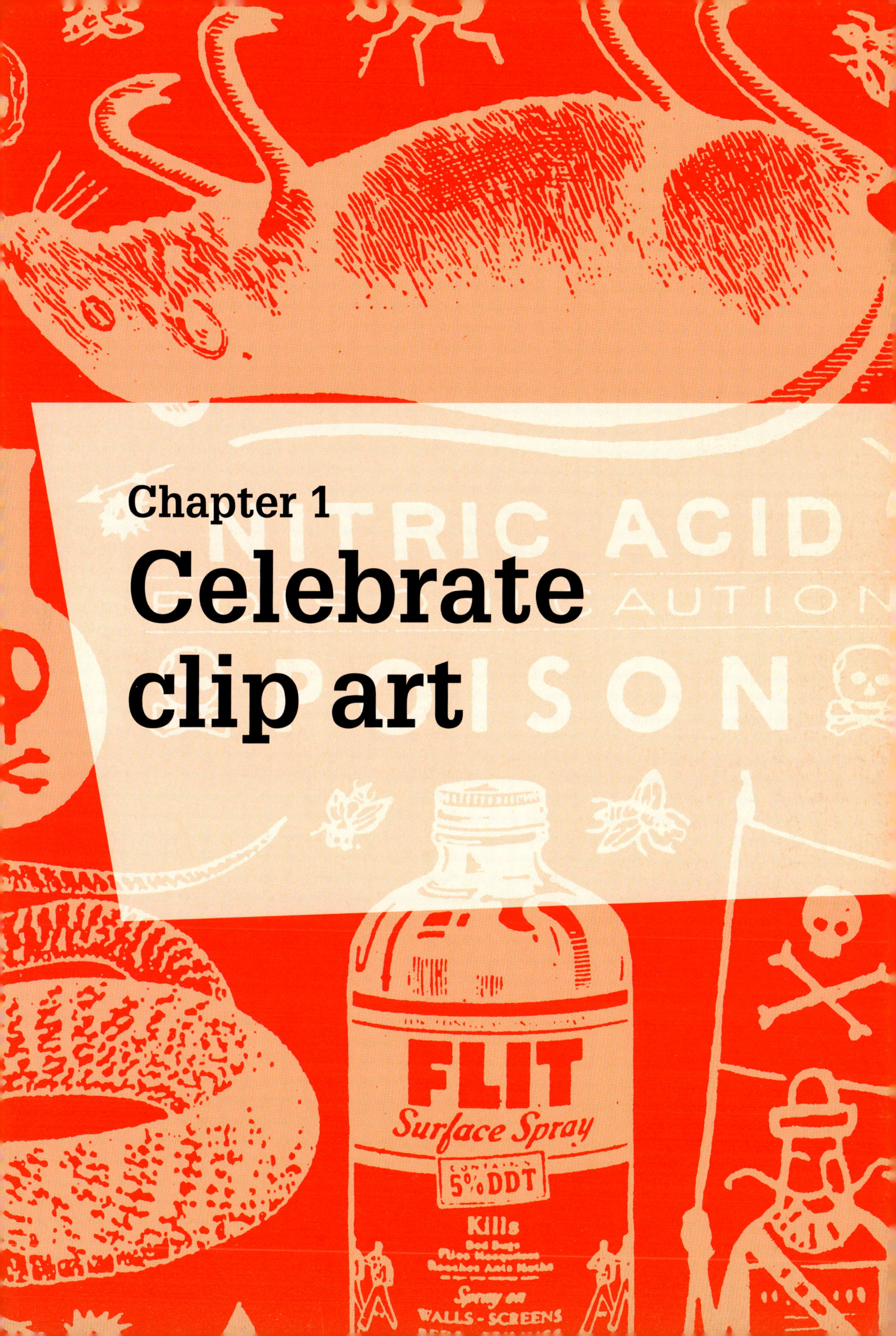

Clip-art culture

Clip art in professional illustration and design, like sampling, cutups, and cut and paste before it, has ceased to be the preserve of the amateur, the cheat, or the lazy. For many of today's designers, understanding and recontextualizing image sources has become as important a creative pursuit as the ability to make something from scratch.

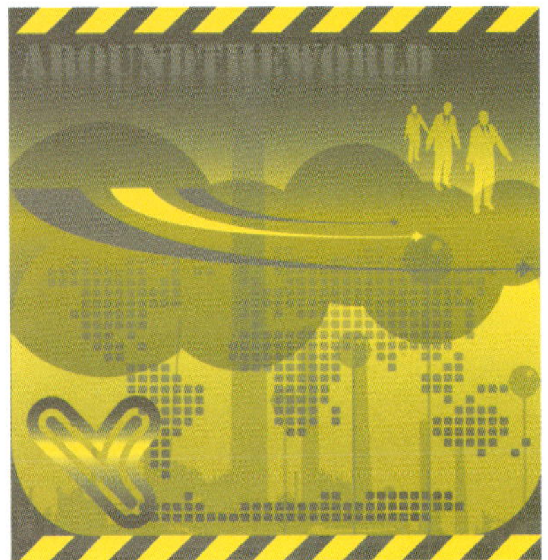

⬆ Around the World, a vector piece from the personal portfolio of Nicole Andujar. Arrow, people, and map of the world clip art were sourced from the Freewave book at www.fontmonster.com.

➡ Martin O'Neill's Con Ghiacco poster, uses just a tiny fraction of the artist's vast, physical archive of found imagery and clip art collected over many years, here recontextualized in a traditional collage to create new layers of meaning and collisions of ideas.

Instant Graphics is a book about clip art, sourced, and found imagery, in the context of the best in contemporary graphic design and illustration. It is a book about sampling and remixing images—one featured designer, Erich Brechbühl calls himself "Mixer," acknowledging that definitions of the designer are fluid, amorphous, ever-changing. Indeed, many of our contributors click the link between the sampler/DJ and the designer and illustrator in a wired and wireless world. "I believe the same process goes into creating music and designing," says Nicole Andujar of ChixInk studio.

Instant Graphics is about graphics that have been duotoned, flipped, colorized, and cut out; images that have been drawn, resampled, rasterized, and silhouetted; pictures that have been shot by the designer, screenprinted, cut out and arranged by hand in collages, scanned into Photoshop, and imported into a publication as a flattened illustration. For "instant graphics" read instant inspiration, instant raw material, and instant play—that most underrated and essential of creative pursuits.

In the context of the me-me-me world of online communities such as YouTube, Facebook, Bebo, MySpace, and Second Life, this book is about the rise of what you might call the "Museum of Me" as designers become curators and collectors of imagery, finding new life, new work, and new money from within their collections, archives, abandoned roughs, and picture bins. For example, our profile of Martin O'Neill reveals just one of many illustrators working today who has begun mining his vast archives of imagery, offcuts, and rejected ideas to produce new pieces that are as much about the original images as they are about making new work.

➡ Erich Brechbühl sourced images of soundwaves in an audio editor from a Google image search, and repeated and layered them to build up a faux-grayscale image of musician and live-sampling vocal artist Bruno Amstad for this concert poster.

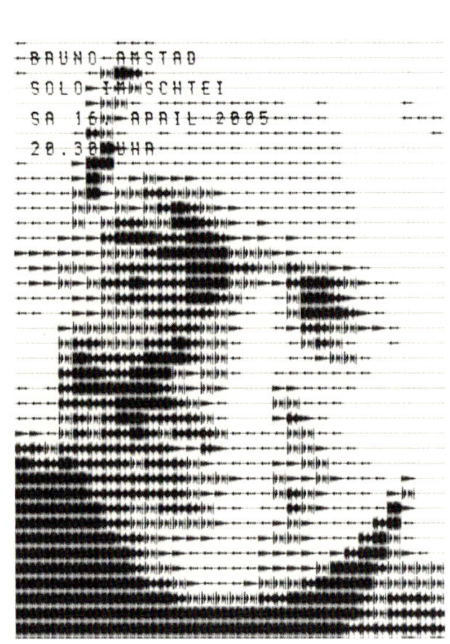

SOURCE IMAGES

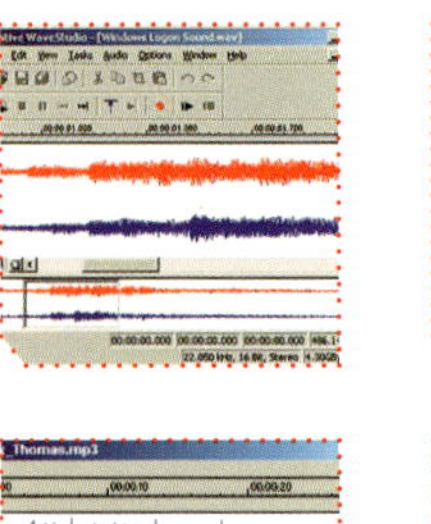

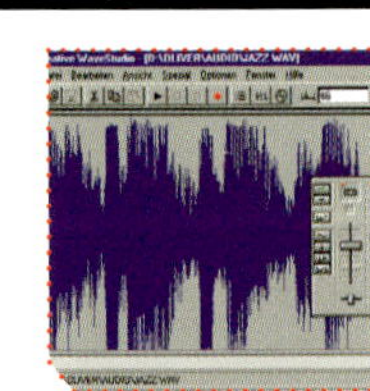

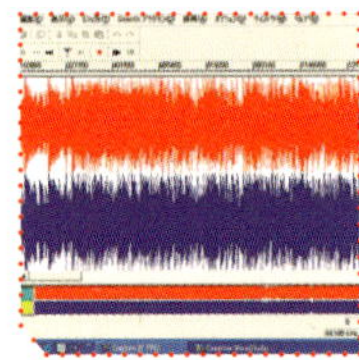

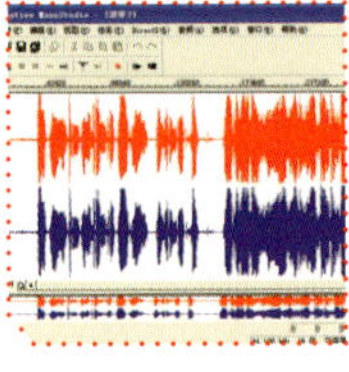

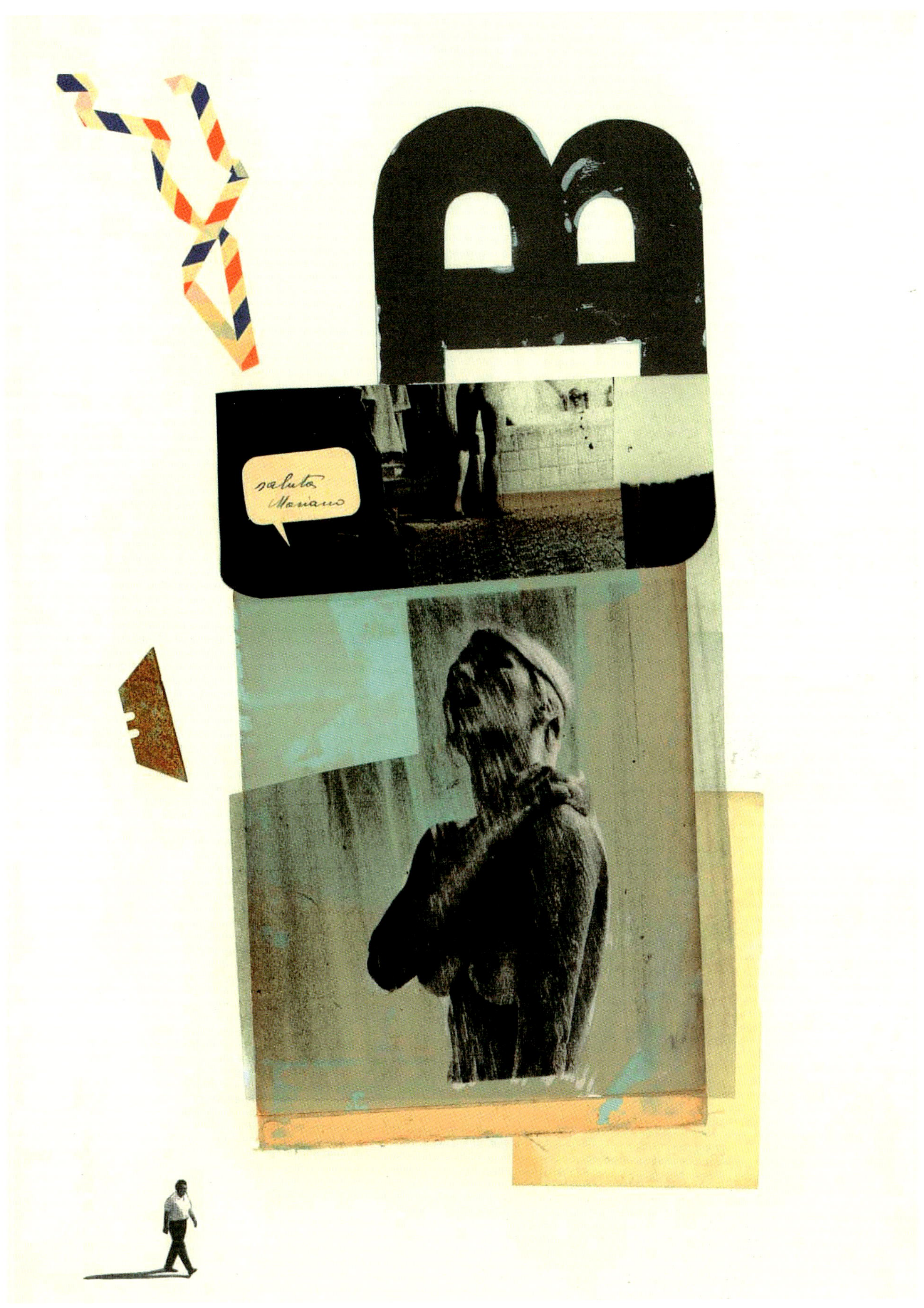
B
saluta
Mariano

Clip-art culture

Professional designers have become expert filters of information, because the same pictures are available to everyone through vast corporate portals such as Getty Images, photosharing sites such as flickr, and low-cost resources such as iStockphoto.

That said, and more than anything, *Instant Graphics* is about a passion for pictures and how the once derided notion of clip art has been recontextualized and reinterpreted in the era of shareware, tagging, and peer-to-peer filesharing.

In the background, the familiar questions rage about copyright and ownership in a digital culture driven by the free and unfettered flow of information (by the desire to share and create) and yet still economically underpinned by the intellectual property wars of big business. *Instant Graphics* will tell you what designers and illustrators think about it, and how they work within a legal framework that is decades behind the technology and the culture, and perhaps a century behind what most people want.

Niall Sweeney, cofounder of Pony, says, "Perhaps the world is so saturated with images that it seems rude to keep making new ones. So clip art could be seen as a kind of recycling. Take haute couture fashion designer John Galliano. He takes direct samples from disparate cultures and times, and collages them together to create something new. He is basically a clip artist."

For many, this is what it is all about. Clip art, sourced, and found images can be used directly or ironically in their original form, or as a jumping-off point for creating work that pays homage to its roots, original contexts, and inspirations. They can also expose the passions, hobbyhorses, and hang-ups of the designers and illustrators who use them.

For many designers, this is precisely the point: using clip art and sourced and found imagery isn't cheating, it's a way of adding depth and meaning to graphical work, just as for many musicians it's important to reveal their sources, passions, and processes for the approval of their most knowledgable peers.

Plan-B Studio's clip-art portrait of Pink Floyd, renowned as pioneers of the use of found sounds and tape loops, for a retrospective feature in *Billboard* magazine.

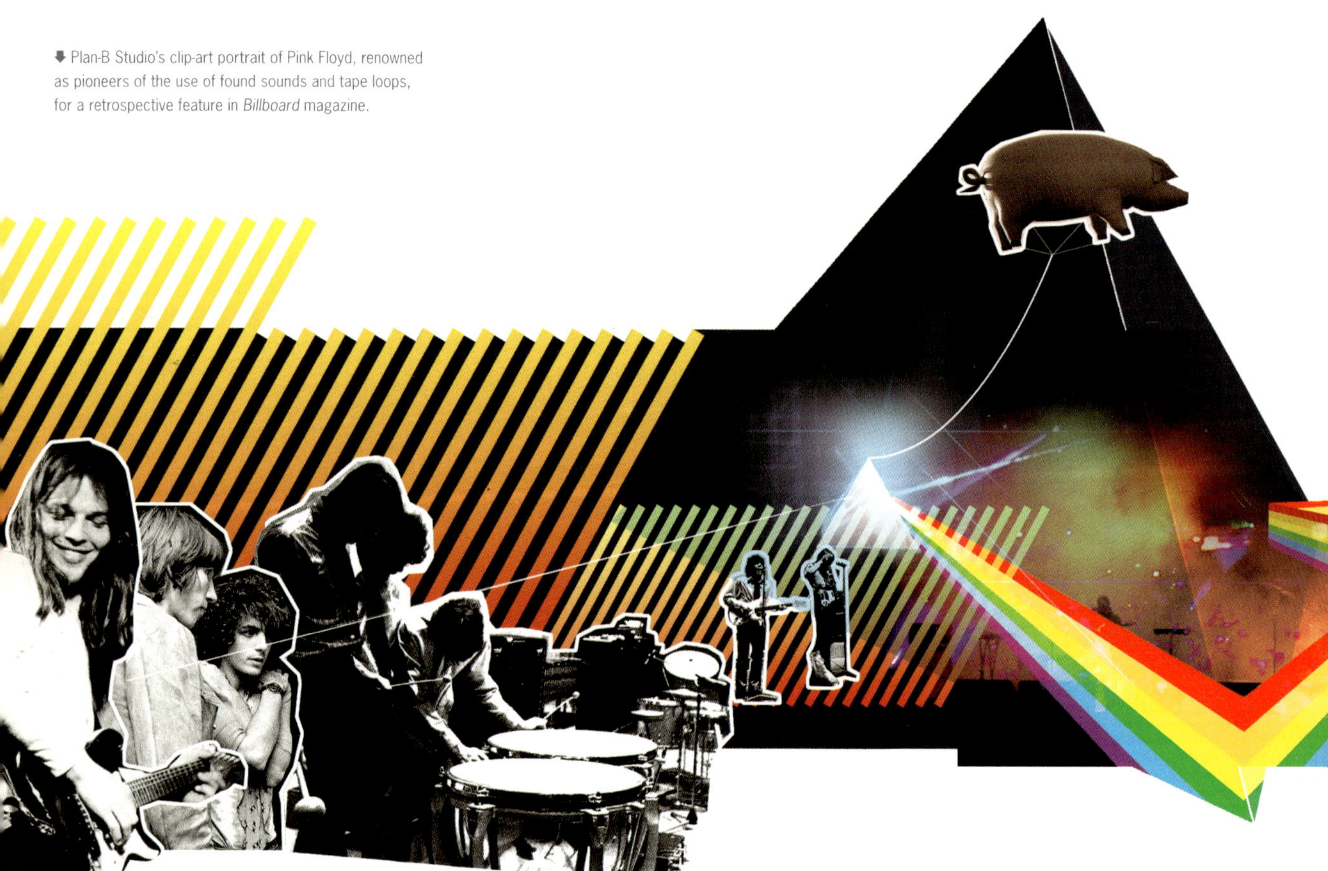

Needless to say, it's also a way of producing work quickly and within slashed budgets and timescales. Either way, the roles of designer, creative director, and illustrator are merging and taking on new forms and creating a mash-up of skills.

This book is about the creative repercussions of democratizing both technology and the availability of information; it's about what happens when you enable the mass exchange of ideas. In this context, using clip art, sourced, or found imagery does not reveal a paucity of original ideas (as it might have done 20 years ago); quite the opposite. When so much raw material is up for grabs—there are more web pages than there are people on the planet—and the means to sample it and remix it are in everyone's homes, then good ideas come at a premium, and the lure of the scarce, the handmade, and the authentic becomes stronger. But then, the true faker is often the best-informed and most passionate artist of all. For the archivist, building a personal collection of imagery is the straightest route toward authenticity. The old economy was built on scarcity and exclusivity, so in a new economy where information is valued by the speed at which it moves, the real prime movers are visual ideas that are strong, original, direct, and exquisitely executed, or which communicate quickly and effectively to the right people. And that surely is what good design is all about. Take the work of KesselsKramer, Peter and Paul, or Plan-B Studio: all exemplars of the winning concept and the choice of found imagery, as much as the clarity and beauty of the design. When raw material is so freely available, then depth of knowledge and skill about how to use that material is what sets apart the great designer and the inspired illustrator, from the merely competent or good.

Many people will say that the debate about fair usage (what constitutes fair use of existing or copyrighted material) began with the work of conceptual artists such as Marcel Duchamp, who famously signed a urinal and declared it a work of art. Yet found objects in art have a lineage as long as the history of art

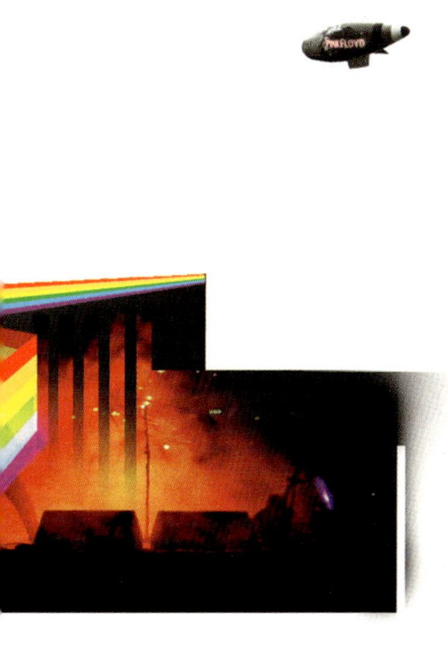

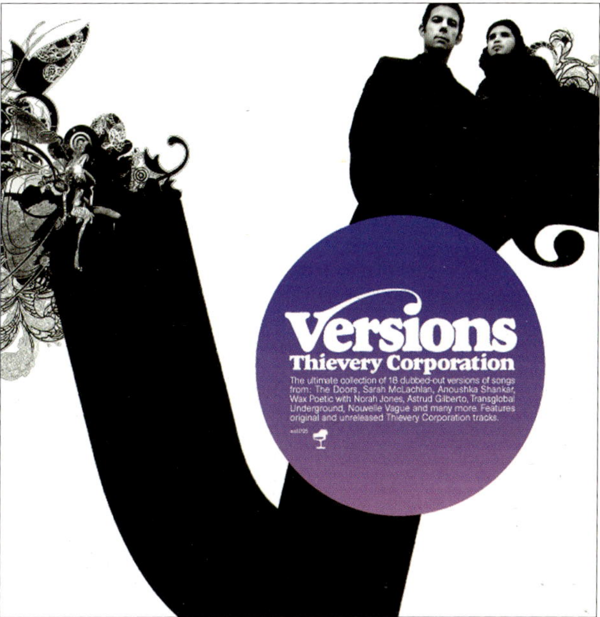

Ashby Design's relationship with Thievery Corporation shows the power of a strong design aesthetic applied to music. It also pays homage to The Beatles' *Revolver* cover, and to the colorized clip-art covers of Led Zeppelin's albums I and III.

itself, from Picasso's use of bicycle parts in sculptures of animals back to the first person who whittled a graven image of an animal from a fallen branch. Historically, copying the Masters was considered to be a part of a painter's training. Contemporary artist Glenn Brown paints detailed canvases copied from commercial illustrations and book covers. He also lifts images by Auerbach and Dali, but is taken very seriously in the art world as an artist in his own right.

With the written word, many will tell you that cut and paste dates back to the Beat Poets, and to William Burroughs' and Brion Gysin's experiments with cutup texts; and yet both were inspired by T.S. Eliot's *The Wasteland*, who was in turn inspired by, among many others, William Shakespeare—perhaps the most famous of all remixers of other people's ideas.

In music, today's DJs are influenced by users of the first digital samplers in the 1980s, and yet those musicians were in turn inspired by Kraftwerk, Can, and the tape-loop experiments of Pink Floyd in the 1970s, who were themselves influenced by avant garde composer Karlheinz Stockhausen. Arguably, the inventor of the sampler was Thomas Edison, the progenitor of recorded sound in the 1890s, and yet before him dozens of classical composers collected folk songs passed down through the generations and incorporated them into their compositions.

Clip art can also be performance: DJs such as Coldcut remix clip-art graphics live and synchronize them to their performances, while designer Kanardo has created a live act out of sourcing clip art from free font sites, printing them on sticky paper, and arranging them into giant images onscreen.

Today, as design, illustration, motion graphics, video, music, games, sound, and interface design all merge, subversion is perhaps the most useful tool a designer can bring to the use of raw material. But in design, the successful sample is the one that shows the greatest understanding of the source material, or the most innovative spin on an old theme.

We hope you enjoy this book.

Chris Middleton

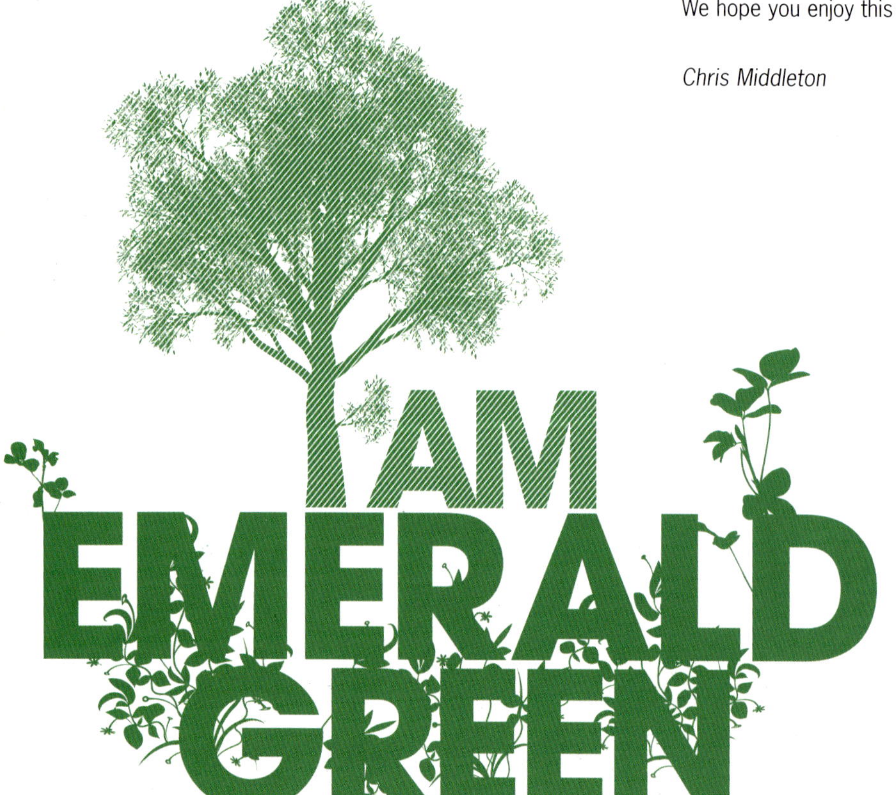

Green is good for Joe Maguire Design, adding a human polish to nature's work, and playing with expectations and the very concept of color by combining and colorizing clip-art sources into a simple, impactful graphic.

A characteristic collision of images and cultural artifacts mark out the work of designer and illustrator David Joyce.

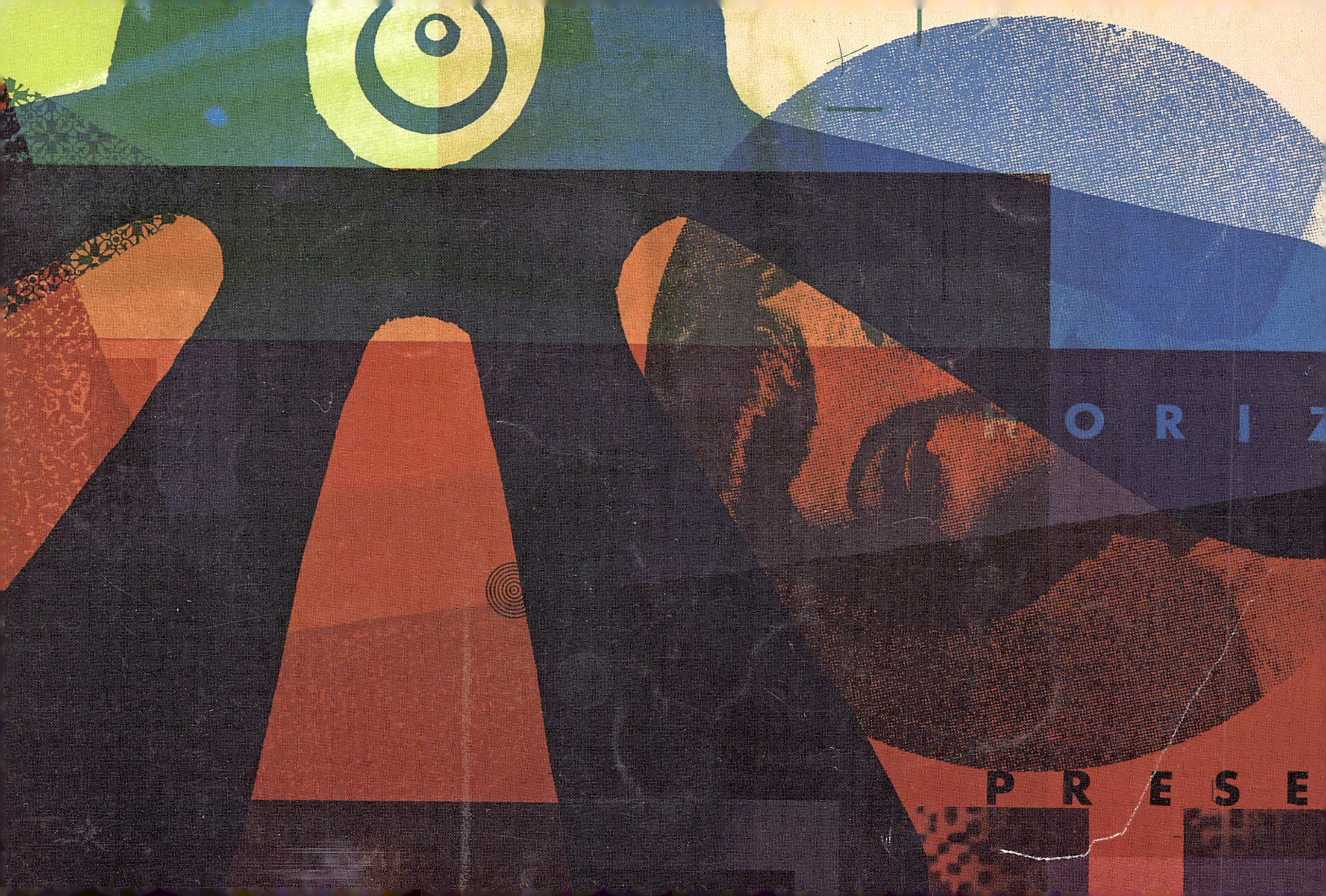
ORIZ
PRESE

Clip art in contemporary design showcase

Sampling and recontextualizing are woven into the fabric of contemporary design and illustration. Often, many of the images that form the elements of contemporary collage are freely available clip art, found images, or serendipitous designs that have been remixed to match the brief. Here is a selection of some of the best in international print design.

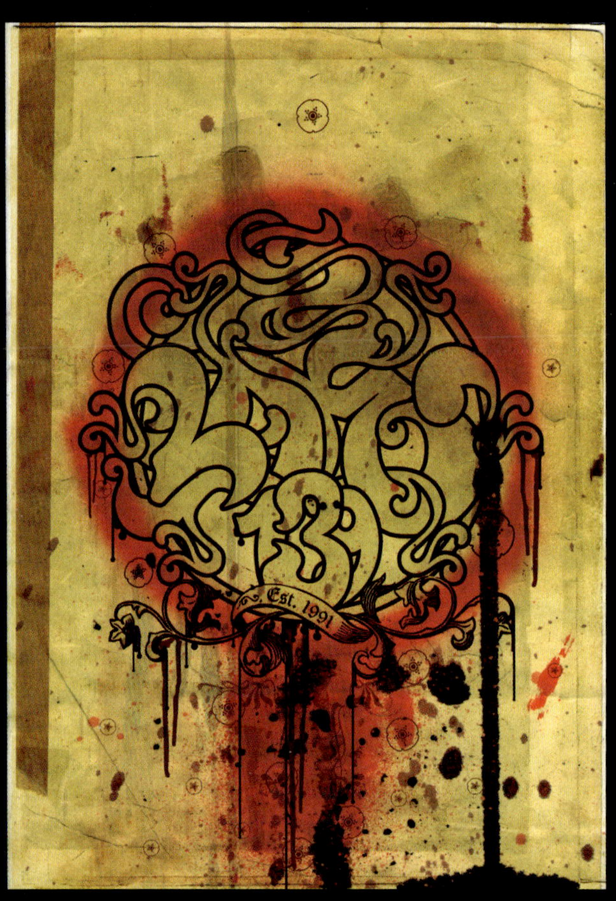

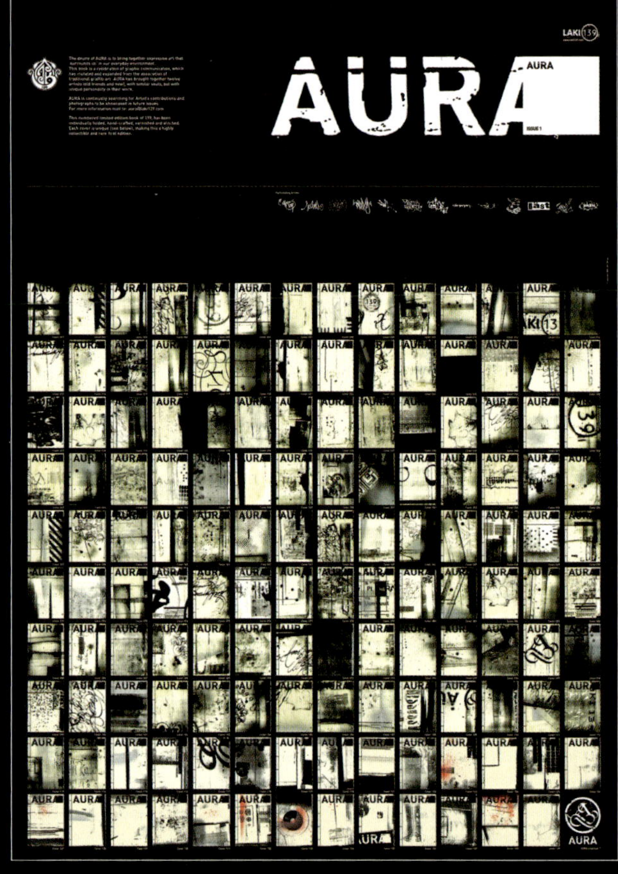

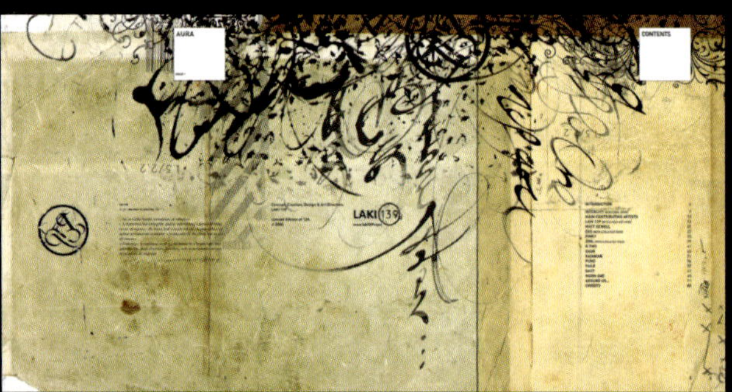

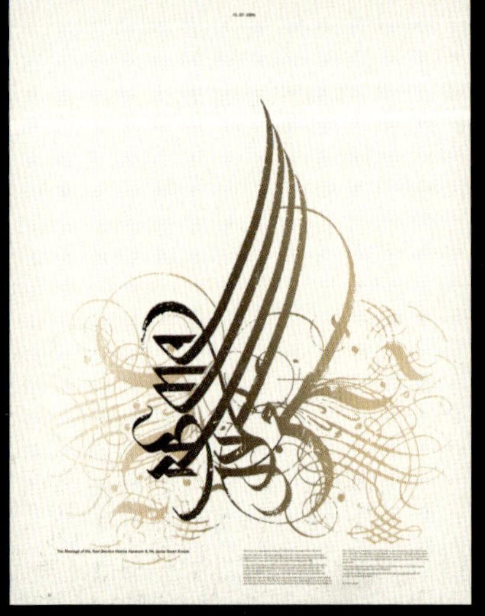

⬆ ➡ Simon Slater of Laki 139 art directed these pages of graffiti journal *Aura Magazine*, and (top right) this poster, using found images and clip art from a Pepin Press book. (Bottom right) Laki 139 Wedding poster, using found images from a Charles Snell alphabet.

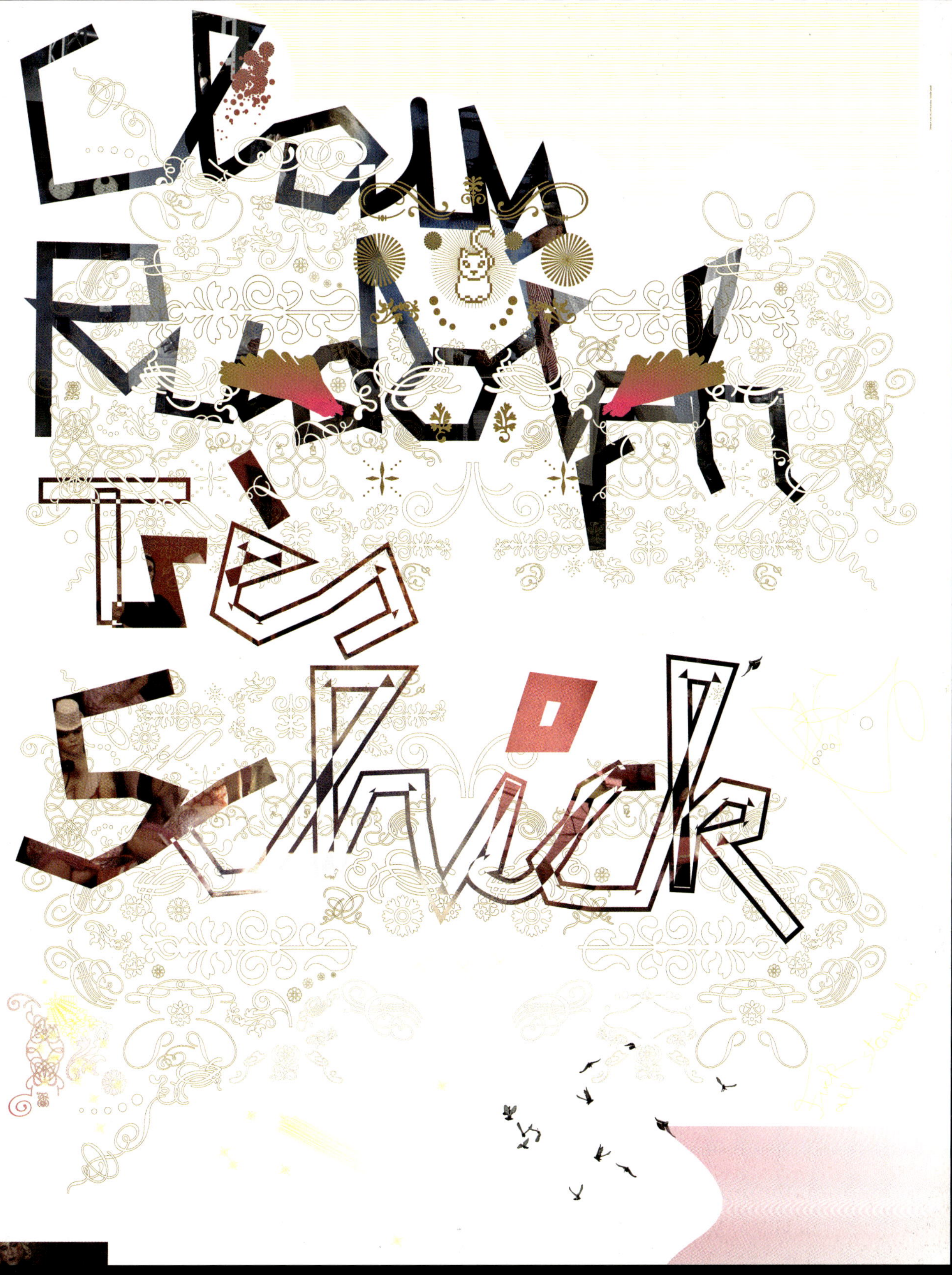

Nicole Jacek created this poster, among others, for a etrospective on the artworks of Claus Rudolph, using both raditional and digital collage techniques.

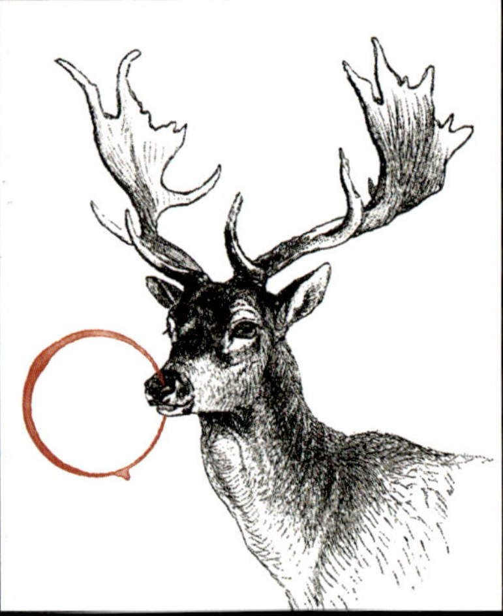

⬆ Design studio The Joneses made this Christmas card for Wine Intelligence—a business specializing in research for the wine industry—by combining a clip-art reindeer, sourced from a clip-art CD, with a Photoshopped wine glass ring.

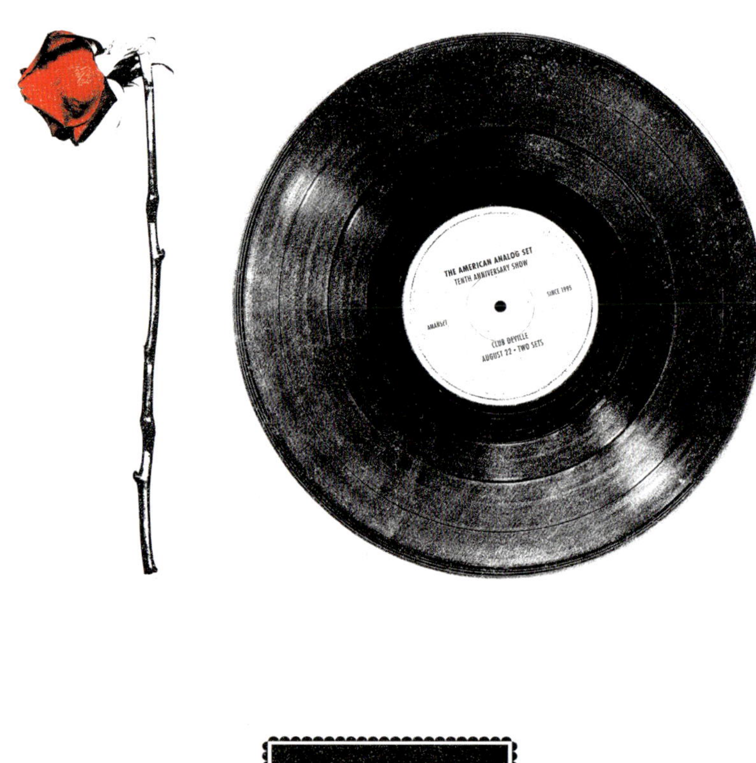

⬆ In a similar style, The Small Stakes created this 10th anniversary poster for the American Analog Set using monochrome art clips of a rose and a vinyl record. Many of the studio's works freely sample clip art from Dover Books.

➡ Sinister, low-fi monochrome clip-art collage from Alex Williamson for this poster, which has the energy of a graffito, while recalling a 1970s photocopier-artwork.

Professional designers and clip art: a lifelong relationship

Many designers' relationships with clip art, sourced, and found imagery are longstanding ones, forged at school, college, or in the earliest years of their professional careers.

Frederic Vanhorenbeke of Coast Design says, "I started using clip art in 1991—my first year at art school." On some of the designs he has art directed or created himself, Vanhorenbeke employs clip art and sourced imagery "as is" from royalty-free CDs, seeing huge creative potential in recontextualizing and subverting the often staid, conservative, or familiar images he selects.

For example, for Coast's design for Swirl People's 12" single, "(I'll be a) Freak for You," Vanhorenbeke chose an image from a DigitalVision CD called CEOs and simply inverted it, cropping closely in on the image of a sharp-suited female executive to create strong diagonals within the frame. This leaves the viewer—and listener—to explore the relationship between title and image in their own minds (the viewer's task of reconstruction).

The lesson here is that even a familiar stock shot, vector drawing, or icon can be raw material to any designer bold or imaginative enough to make a strong statement with widely available imagery—to imbue it with new meaning, to make us look at the source material anew. Often designers feel that if an image is overly familiar or too easy to find then it no longer has inherent value. If that were true, then Andy Warhol would not have had a career. As musician and producer Brian Eno once remarked, "Don't be afraid of things because they are easy to do."

🡇 Coast Design's cover for Swirl People's "(I'll Be a) Freak for You" used images sourced from a DigitalVision CD called CEOs, remixing familiar, corporate image library shots with a mischievous twist.

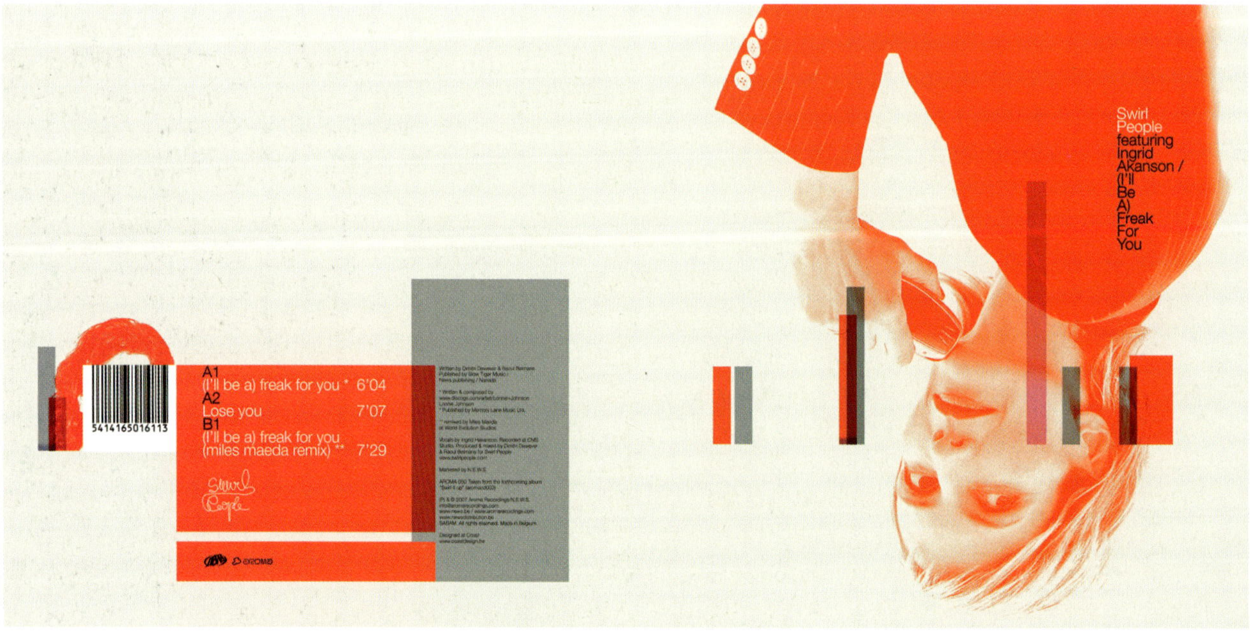

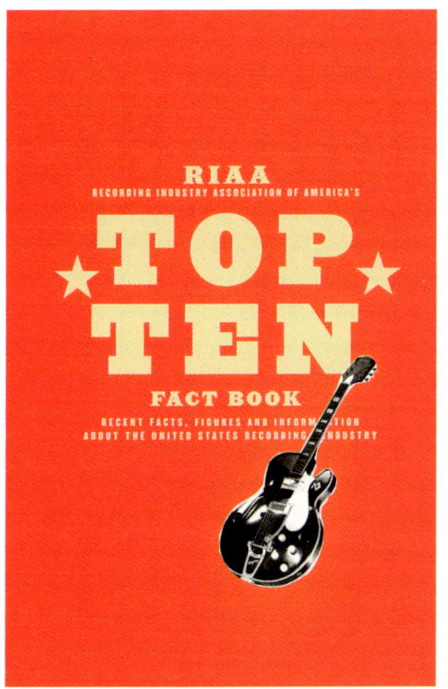

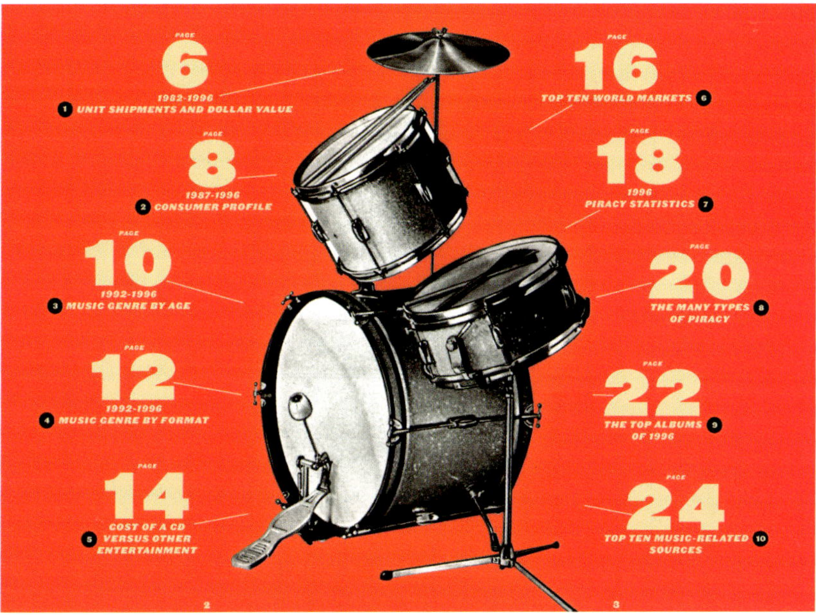

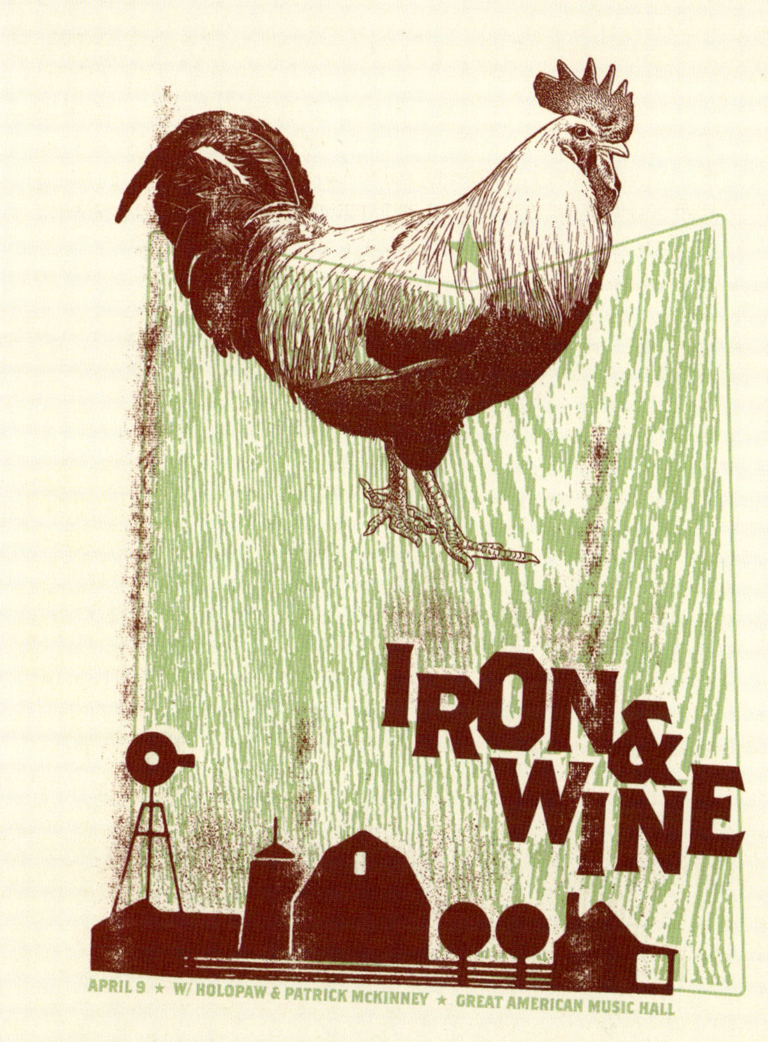

⬆ Ashby Design used clip-art images of instruments from old Sears catalogs for the *Top Ten Fact Book* for the Recording Industry Association of America.

⬅ The Small Stakes' Iron and Wine poster for the Great American Music Hall mined Dover Books resources for the source clips of a farm and a chicken.

⬇ Erich Brechbühl sampled images from Transport for London and modified them in Freehand for this party poster that had the theme "underground."

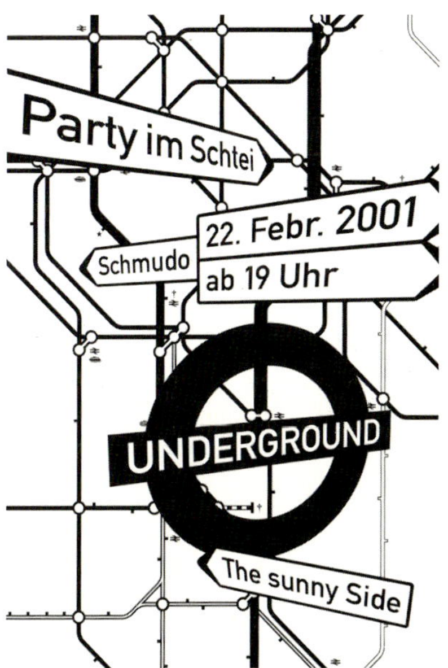

Professional designers and clip art: a lifelong relationship

For many designers, this placing of images in new contexts or using them as raw material to sample, paste, tile, and remix is the unique creative challenge of instant graphics. Graphic designer Erich Brechbühl (a.k.a. "Mixer") says, "The first time I started using found images was about six years ago. I noticed that you can play around with the knowledge of the viewer, if you use images that he knows." On occasion Brechbühl has lifted entire public domain images such as subway maps, which he then vectorizes and modifies in Freehand.

Marie-Joe Raidy of Raidy Printing Group says, "When I became a designer, but wasn't yet in the commercial and corporate world, I initially boycotted clip art, and only used original artwork done by other illustrators/designers and myself. There then came a time when I joined the corporate world, and this is when, with less time to design and more work to do, I began to go back to clip art and found images that I could use, get inspired by, transform, or distort. Sometimes, I have clients that specifically ask me to use clip art, especially for Middle Eastern youth magazines."

Scott Witham of Traffic Design Consultants has produced stunning designs for environmental groups, including a series of arresting posters for the Carbon Neutral campaign. He admits that as much as 70 percent of the elements for the posters he art directed, and which were designed by Stephen Kelman, were sourced from clip art, stock imagery, and found images, combined with hand-drawn elements that they scanned in. Beautiful results from often ugly elements: an apt, inspiring message.

"From day one!" says Witham when asked how long his studio has been playing with clip art. "It's an essential part of the creative process, finding things, manipulating them, and so on. It's always been there—it's just easier to get hold of images now due to the internet."

➡ Traffic Design Consultants' collision of clip graphics creates a beautiful pile-up, out of which Design Director Scott Witham hopes an inspiring idea will grow.

⬇ Raidy Printing Group's seasonal gift box is an idea within an idea within an idea. The box design uses clip elements, and within the completed box is a digital card containing a high-res clip image of a magnifier. Blowing it up onscreen reveals the hidden message.

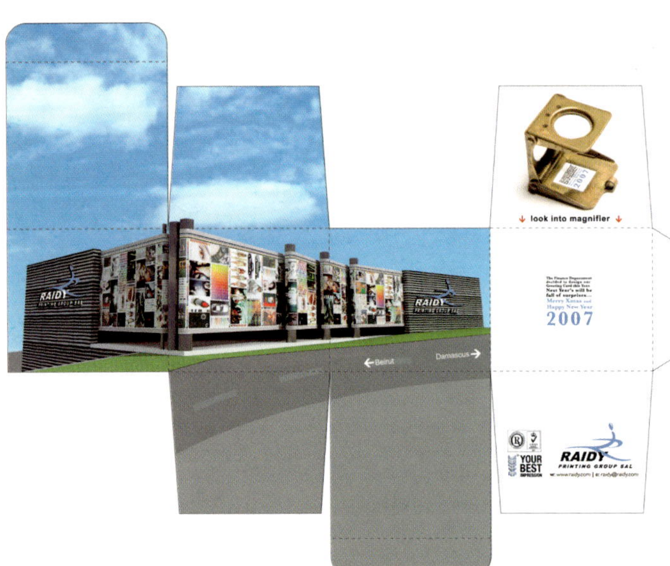

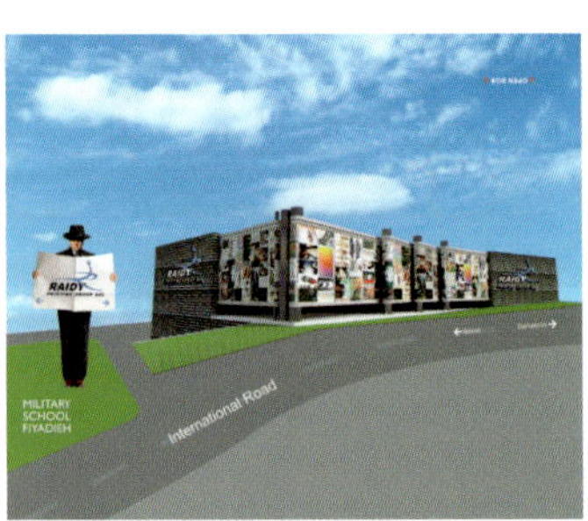

SOURCE IMAGES

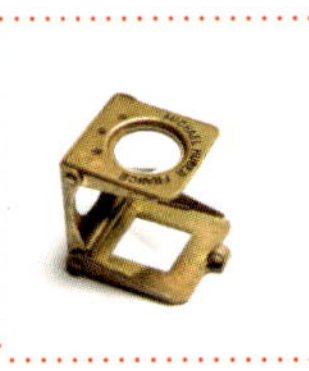

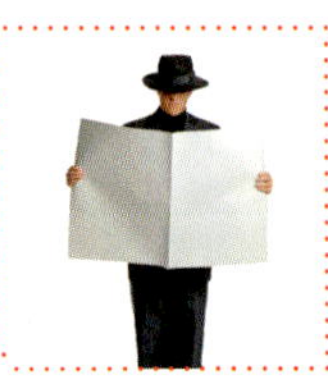

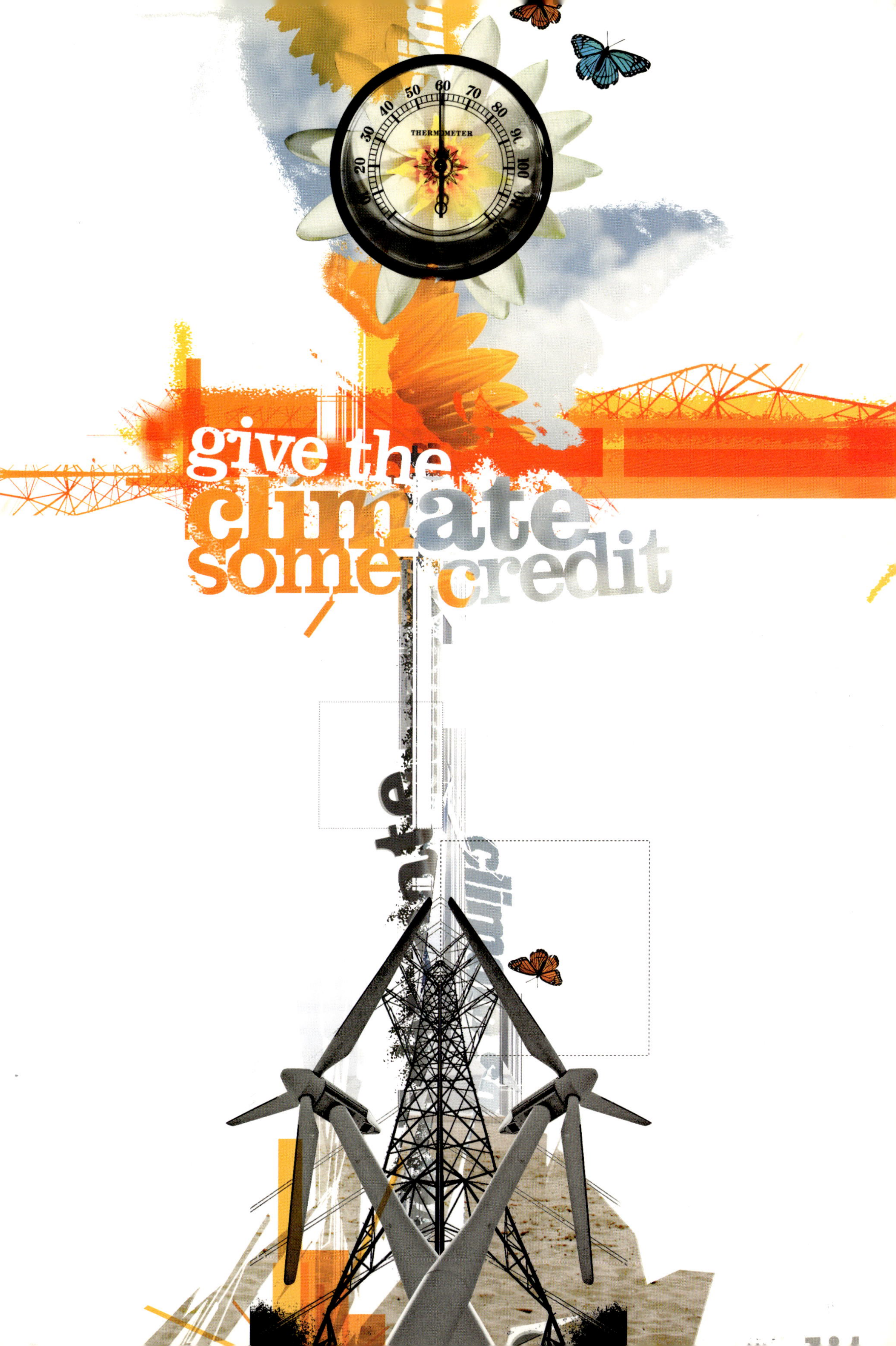
give the
climate
some credit
THERMOMETER

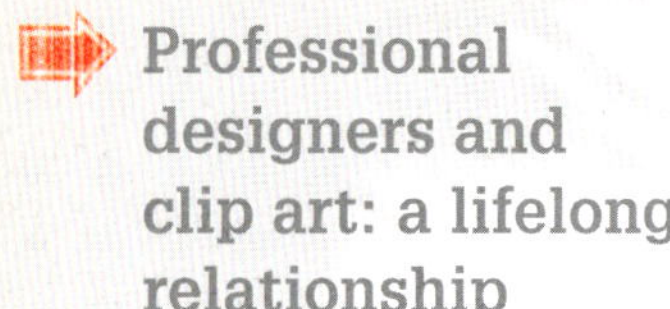

Professional designers and clip art: a lifelong relationship

CityAbyss' Beatta Szczecinska says, "I had been using clip art already during my studies, starting with collages. I used to glue them together, often adding other hand-drawn elements to create a brand new value. At that time I also started to draw from my own photographs. More serious and broad 'digging' in search of samples began a couple of years ago."

For many working designers, clip art and found imagery are core to the creative process, just as a palette of colors is to a painter—after all, with Photoshop and the Adobe Creative Suite, any pixels can be cloned and applied with a brush, including pixels cloned from clip art and found imagery, and applied as textures, wallpapers, or patterns.

For example, some of CityAbyss' work includes pixel samples from the work of nineteenth-century Japanese woodblock artist Hiroshige, which has then been subsumed into a larger illustration combining traced stock drawings, clip art, and samples from *Vogue* and post-Stalinist Polish art magazines. Indeed, for many professional designers, their first use of clip art coincided with using digital systems in the design process for the first time.

CityAbyss mashed-up stock imagery from some startlingly different sources—*Vogue*, Hiroshige woodblocks, and Polish art. However, each component image has a shared graphical identity, suggests Beatta Szczecinska.

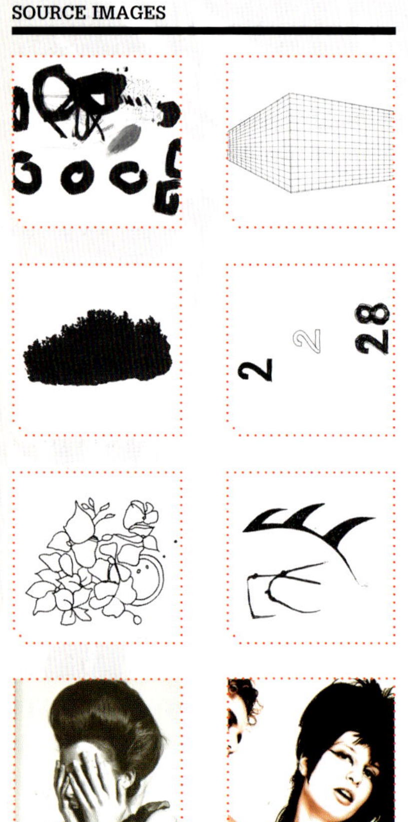

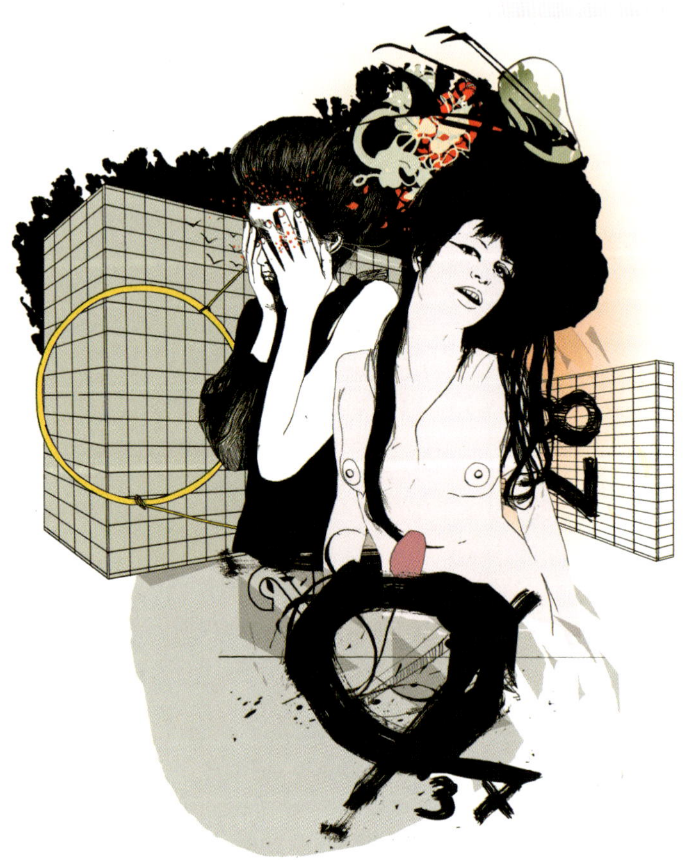

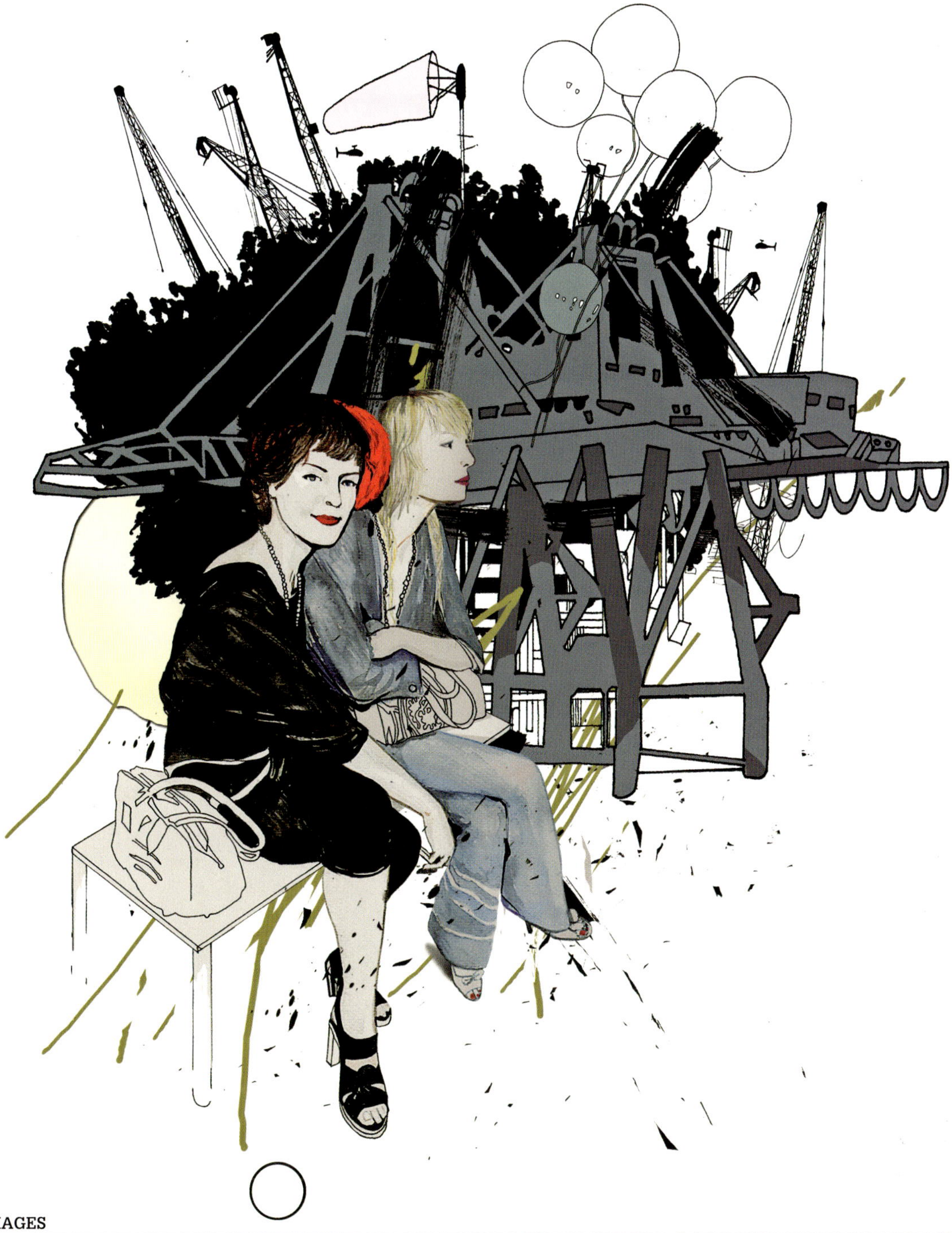

SOURCE IMAGES

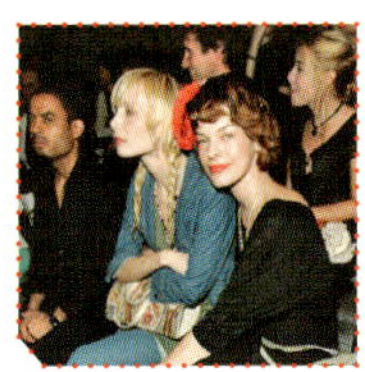
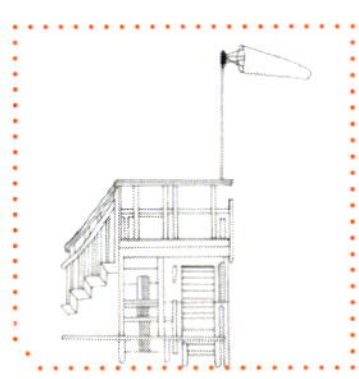
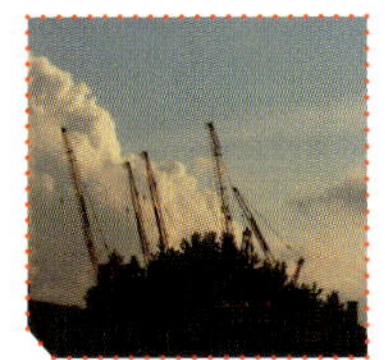
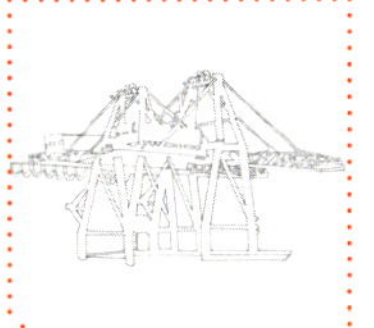
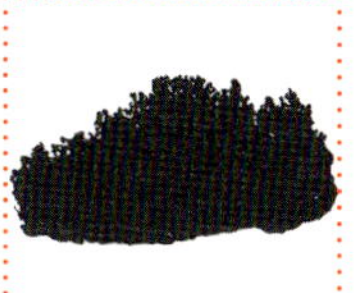
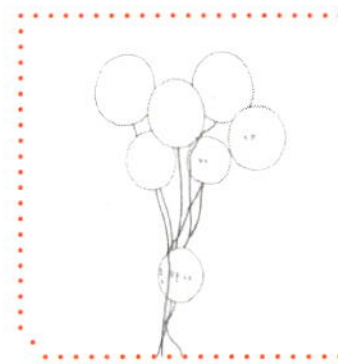
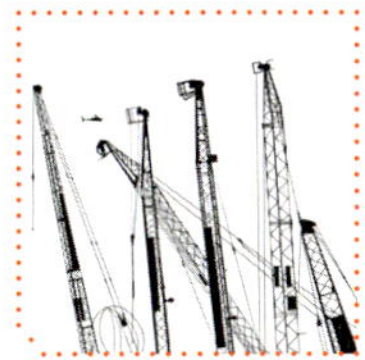

⬆ CityAbyss' work here suggests the modern world is the scene of a crash between past and present, from the wreckage of which we are free to pick and choose what we like. Layered drawings made from scanned photographs.

The designer as collector and curator

Perhaps the twenty-first century has made us all collectors, as, in a big world of pictures, you have to choose what you like and hang onto it. Certainly, we have become image sound filters, and technology exists to filter things for us based on our previous choices: too boring for some, too cool for school for others. Meanwhile, some designers like to keep things small...

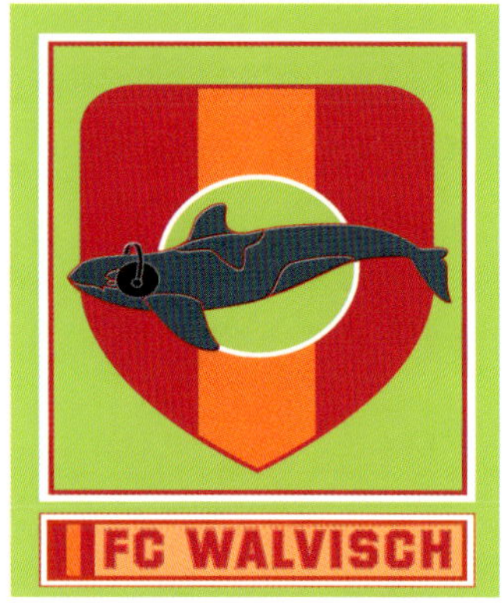

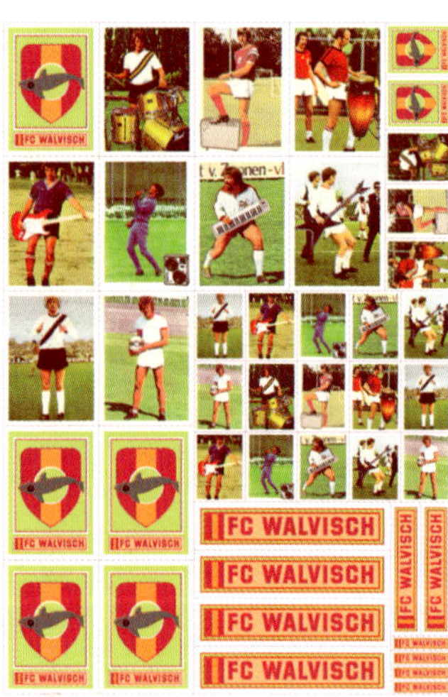

⬆ ➡ KesselsKramer's work is all about the idea of the designer as conceptual thinker and joker. What makes its work stand out is the clever execution of a single idea—a good joke well told. The studio has also made its name by seeing value in the discarded image: by making us look at it again, we question the value systems that threw it away. For this house identity for music studio FC Walvisch (which means "whale"), Karen Heuter combined 1970s-style soccer cards with instruments to create a visual identity for the soccer-mad studio owner that is funny, stylish, and every old schoolboy's dream.

Many designers and illustrators are explorers and archivists of their immediate environments, scouring the city streets, parks, river banks, gardens, markets, and even their own studios, for objects, textures, and source material that they can scan in and use in their palettes, or incorporate into freehand collages and assemblies of objects.

Whether or not they use digital techniques to manipulate such raw materials and create their final designs, many designers inevitably find themselves becoming collectors and/or curators of certain types of imagery or objects—insects, sports cards, magazine clippings, old catalogs, engravings, or prints. Some develop a fascination with a specific type of image or object—perhaps from an accidental find—and set about actively researching and building collections of them, which, in turn, begin to influence their subsequent work.

Says Neal Ashby, Creative Director of Ashby Design, "I collect mostly old catalogs, like Sears, Montgomery Ward, or JC Penny. Old magazines are a great source of inspiration too: *Life* magazine in particular. I have a library of catalogs that I reference from the 1920s to the 1980s.

"I think to be a great designer you have to have a frame of reference for your work and its place in the continuum of decorative arts and design. To do this, it's important to at least have a certain level of knowledge of the past. If not a curatorial level of knowledge, then at least an awareness."

Beatta Szczecinska of CityAbyss says, "I think that collecting is a natural process for every artist. If it comes to artists who become curators, they are people with experience and knowledge and maybe that is why they are focused more on artists' needs—as distinct from curators who do not create their own art (although there are always some exceptions).

"I build my own library of clip images—more samples I would say—but do not think it will become a new strand of business for me. I wouldn't like to use it in any other way except for the way I am using it now, which is as an inspiration."

Nevertheless, particularly in a world of mass inexpensive storage on the average desktop, such personal collections can rapidly take on a life of their own, and become a valuable commodity—even a currency. And as designers and makers collect more and more material, to be tagged and stored away, it can begin to add greater depth to a body of work over the course of a designer's career and begin to inform it, or take on a contingent relationship with it.

Nicole Andujar of ChixInk says, "If I don't use a piece of clip art or an illustration, I will archive it and use it later. It becomes part of my library under separate labels. It has always been a standard for me as I keep creating, and the workflow leads to that.

"I don't know how important it may be for other designers, but speaking for myself, I do collect books and pieces of clip art as much as I can because again, they are things which help me in my work and they also inspire me to try new techniques and do things I have never thought of."

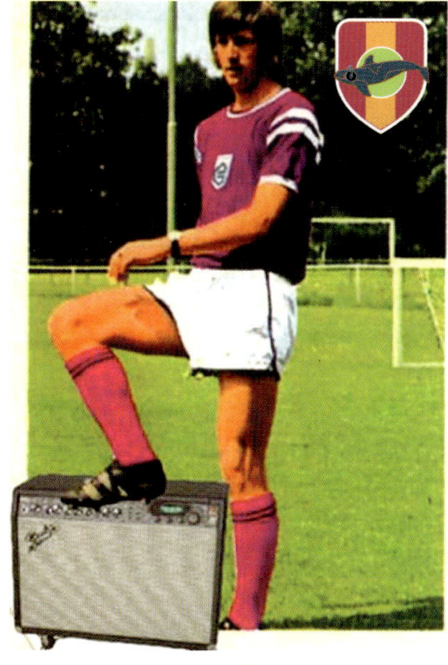

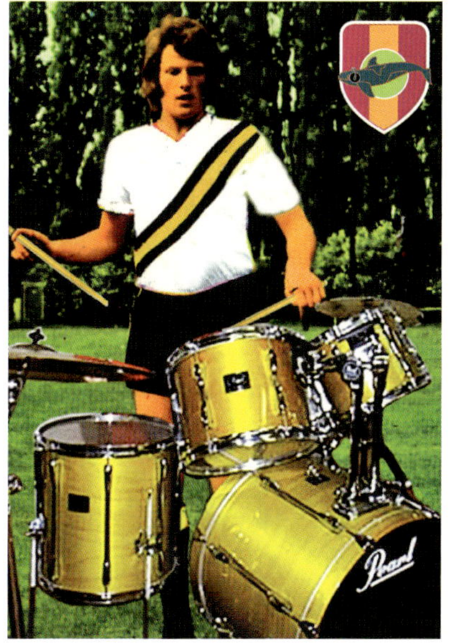
Pearl

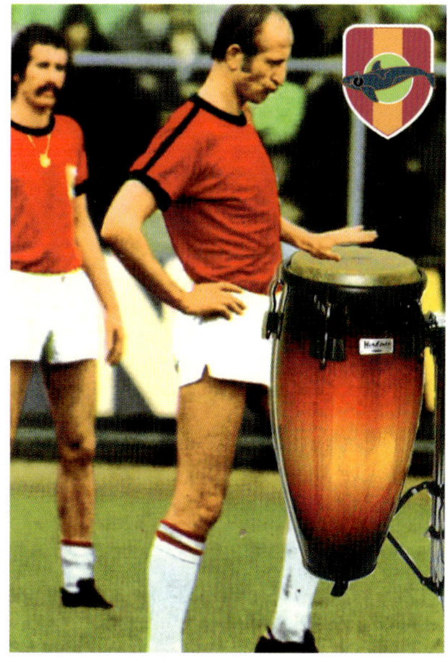

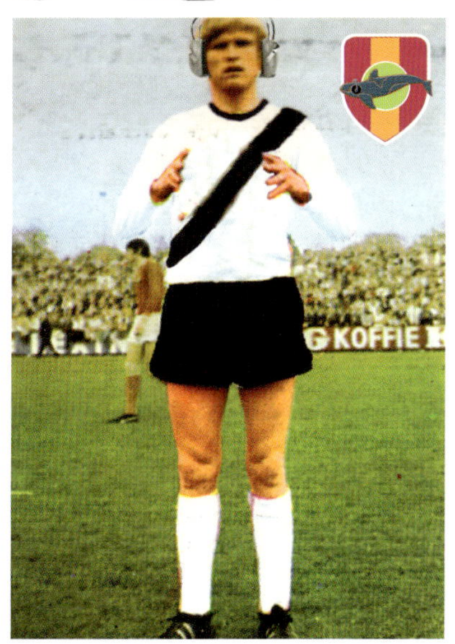
KOFFIE

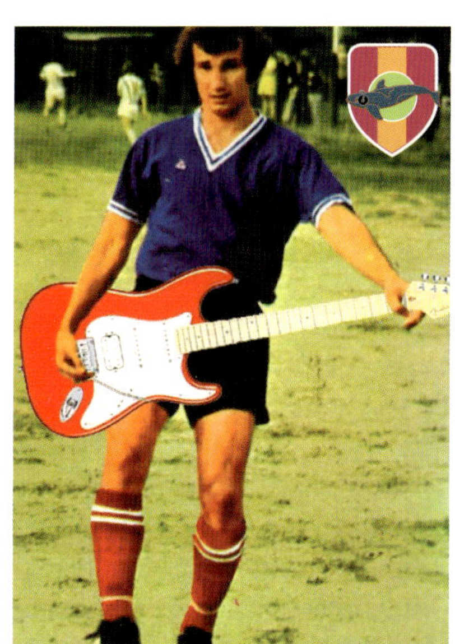

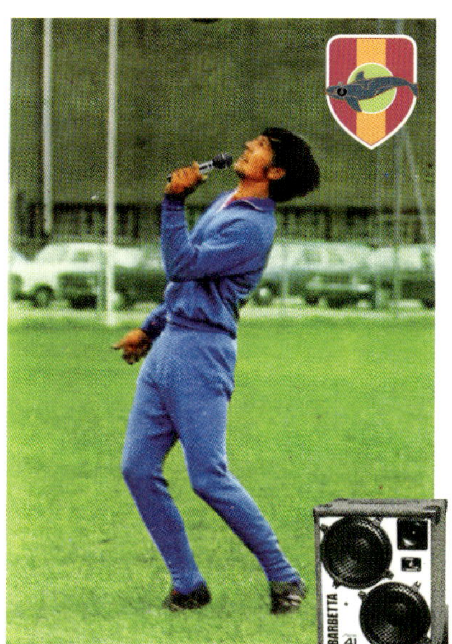
BARBETTA
41

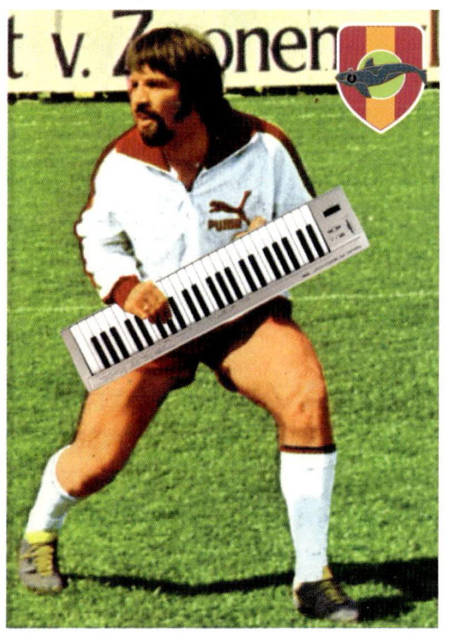
PUMA

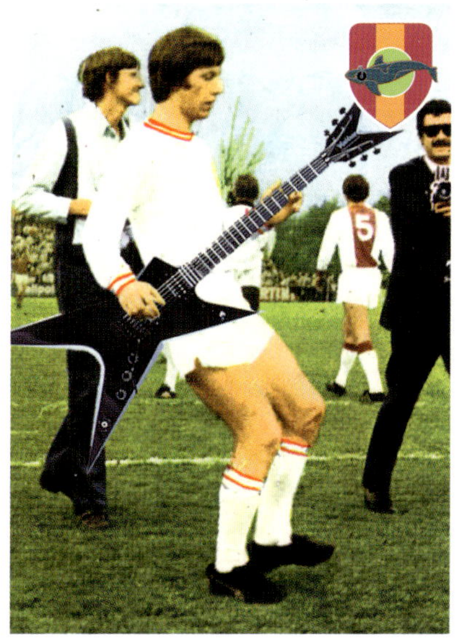

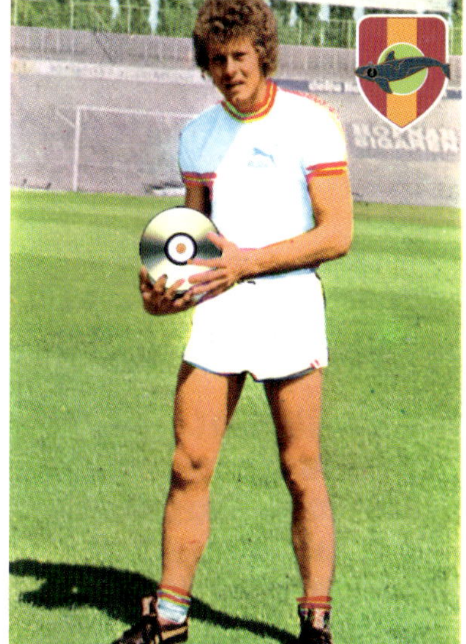

The designer as collector and curator

Often at the research stage of any design or illustration—and in the creation of mood boards and subsequently rejected designs—designers and illustrators research, collate, and compile enormous amounts of material around particular subjects, moods, and emotions. Each collection is a road untraveled in terms of the final commission, perhaps, but it remains an invaluable expression of alternative ways in which the brief can be met, and the aims, emotions, and mood of the project expressed. As such, it may take on greater value later, and find new potential uses within other design work.

"It is vastly important to me that I keep collections of photographs, typography, drawings, writing, music, books, objects, and a multitude of other ephemera," says David Donohoe, Creative Director of Studiomime. "I have always been a collector and this informs the way I think about design.

"For many years I have taken photographs, kept notebooks, sketchbooks, and scrapbooks. This is a source I constantly maintain, almost acting as an extension of my brain in many ways. It is invaluable to me as a very tangible library, which I consult frequently and which informs many of my design decisions."

Erich Brechbühl created this poster for jazz band Elliott by googling the word and seeing what images came up in his search: an accidental collection of Elliotts to illustrate the band, from which he made a curator's selection.

SOURCE IMAGES

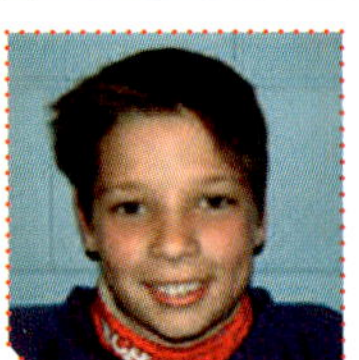
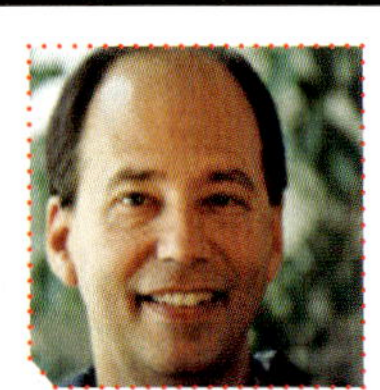
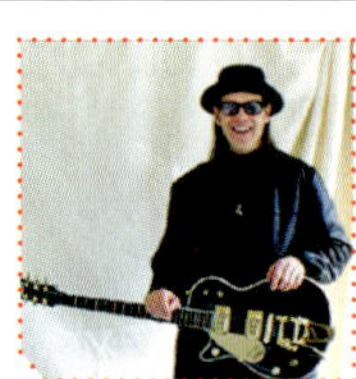
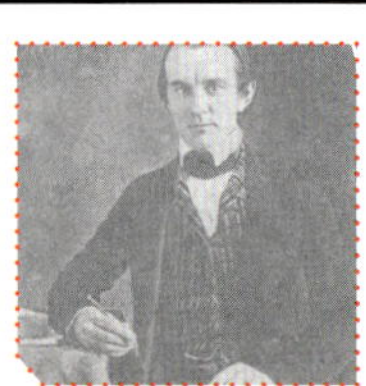
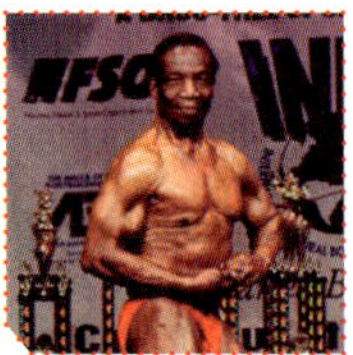
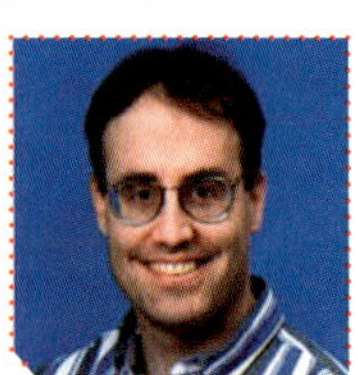
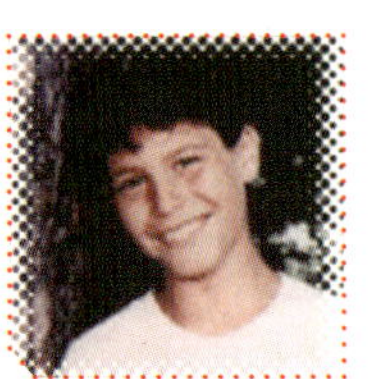
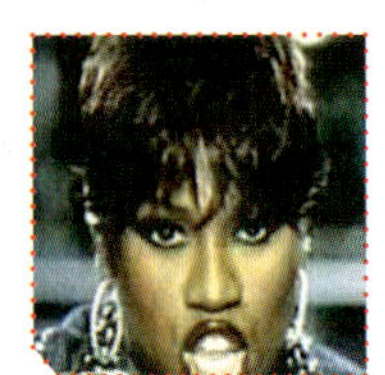
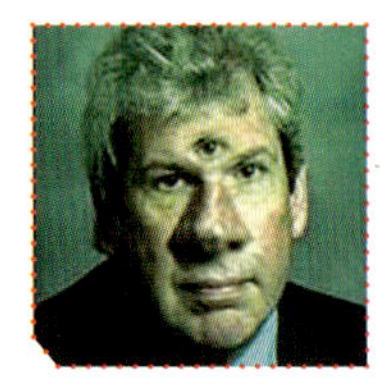
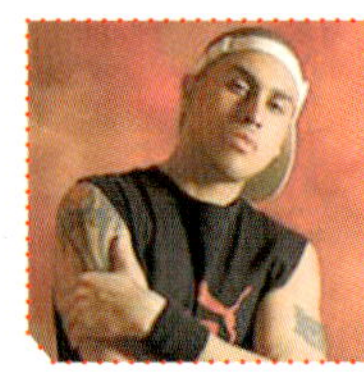

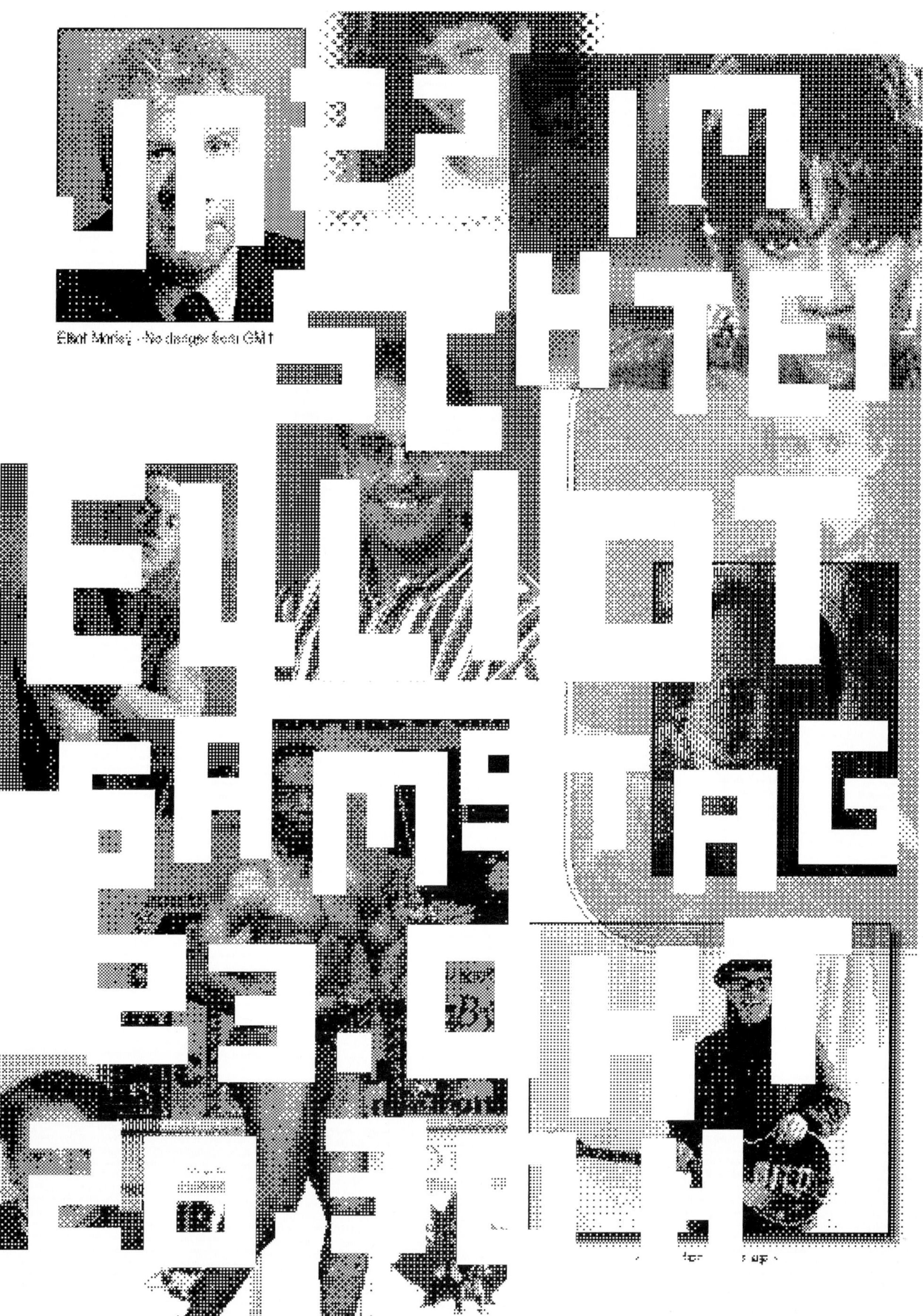

The big question:

sourcing images

We pitched a small number of big questions at a range of professional designers and illustrators worldwide, to see what size answers came back: small and incisive; big and all-encompassing; personal and local.

Q: How difficult is it to source original clip art, or "found" images to use in your work? And where do you source them from?

"It can be tough if the image needed is very specific, but the search function in Getty Images works quite well. But even if you can find the images you like, sometimes it might not fit into the final artwork. Therefore, it takes trial and error. Start layering, masking, and merging, and then stop. Take a look the next day, and start improving again until satisfied. For personal work, I recommend sources like Creative Commons images or Stock.xchng. For commercial work, I use Getty Images."
Sean Tan, Archizen Creative

"It depends on what I'm searching for. Sometimes it's enough to search in Google and take the first pictures it shows me. Sometimes I have to go to the library to find what I need. My most used source is Google Images. Otherwise I keep my eyes open in everyday life."
Erich Brechbühl (Mixer)

"It is hard for me to answer this question, I use a vast array of things, from well-known magazines to ordinary newspapers. Often I receive 'accidental' magazines from people I know. Once I got a cocktail catalog, which later inspired one of my works. It is similar with the internet. I don't have any fixed source, just try searching the web with the 'word' I'm interested in. It is not difficult for me at all, as I do not use images the way they were created or used before. In my art everything that I use becomes my own transformed drawing or creation."
Beatta Szczecinska, CityAbyss

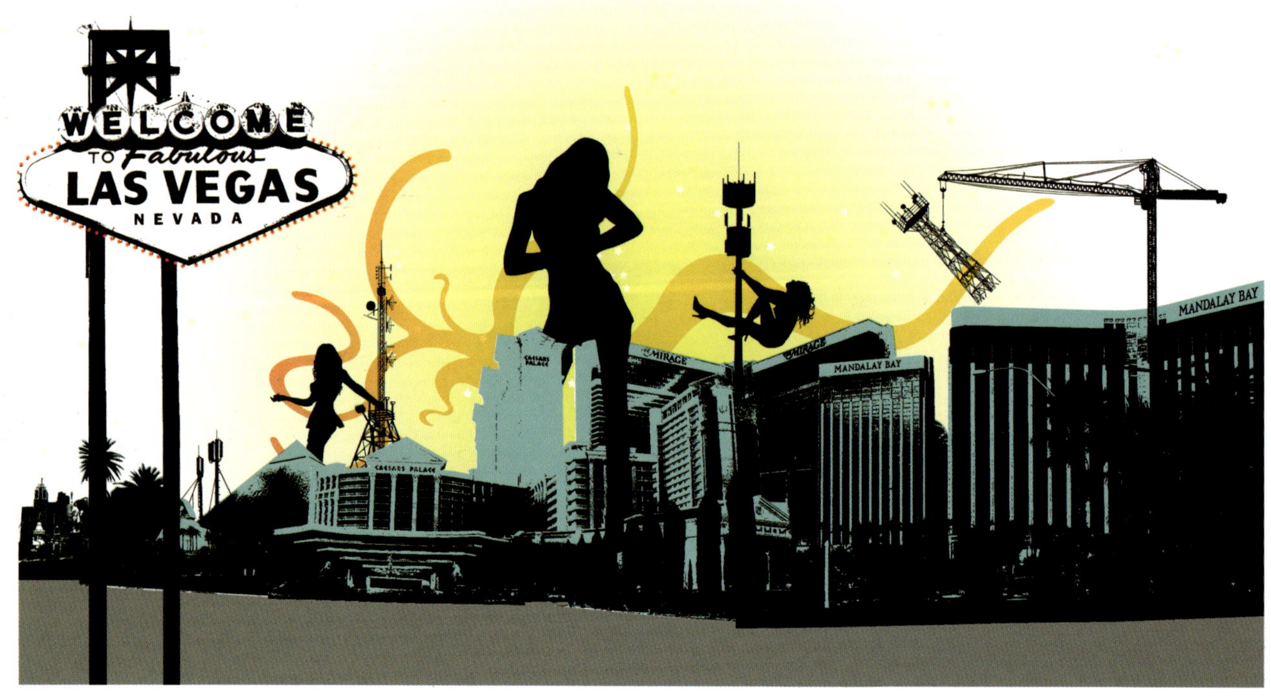

↓ Every element of Plan-B Studio's designs for *Radio Billboard* magazine's feature on Nevada radio is clip art that has been cut out, bitmapped, modified, and/or redrawn.

"It's not difficult at all. Just press Return."
Coast Design

"I often use iStockphoto or You Work For Them, as well as Freewave. I don't think it's difficult. If I already have an idea of what I want to design, then I look for specific images and search until I am happy with them and if I am not, I keep looking for ones that will work. This also depends on the timeframe one is given to finish a design. When you are pressed for time, you usually can't find exactly what you want and you have to either compromise the design or do it as best as you can even though you may not be 100 percent happy with it."
Nicole Andujar, ChixInk

"I've used Dover Books, old catalogs, and such that I pick up at flea markets. I also tend to use a lot of natural objects that I pick up when I'm out walking to the store, like leaves and other plants. If you use Dover Books or other source imagery that is easily accessible, there may be a chance you'll see that image in someone else's work, but the context could be totally different."
Jason Munn, The Small Stakes

"iStockphoto, Google Images, photo-lab trash bags, charity shops, and long attentive walks. The closest thing I use [to a regular source] is iStockphoto, admittedly only rarely. I sourced the photography for my album *Statuesque* there. In this instance I knew I wanted images of swans and wasn't confident that I could get what I wanted myself in the field, so I checked iStock. I was amazed when I came across Mark Stokes' excellent photographs. They were infinitely better than I had expected to get. Aside from the obvious cost advantages of this site, I think the originally amateur nature of it allows for some approaches and ideas that wouldn't neccessarily be found in some of the mainstream, higher budget sources."
David Donohoe, Studiomime

"Books. *Scan This Book: Three* and *Official Signs & Icons 2*."
Tom Varisco, Varisco Design

"Google, Flickr, and A9, basically."
Mariana Bukvic

Red Design is one of the most high-profile design studios to have incorporated clip art and found imagery into its signature designs.

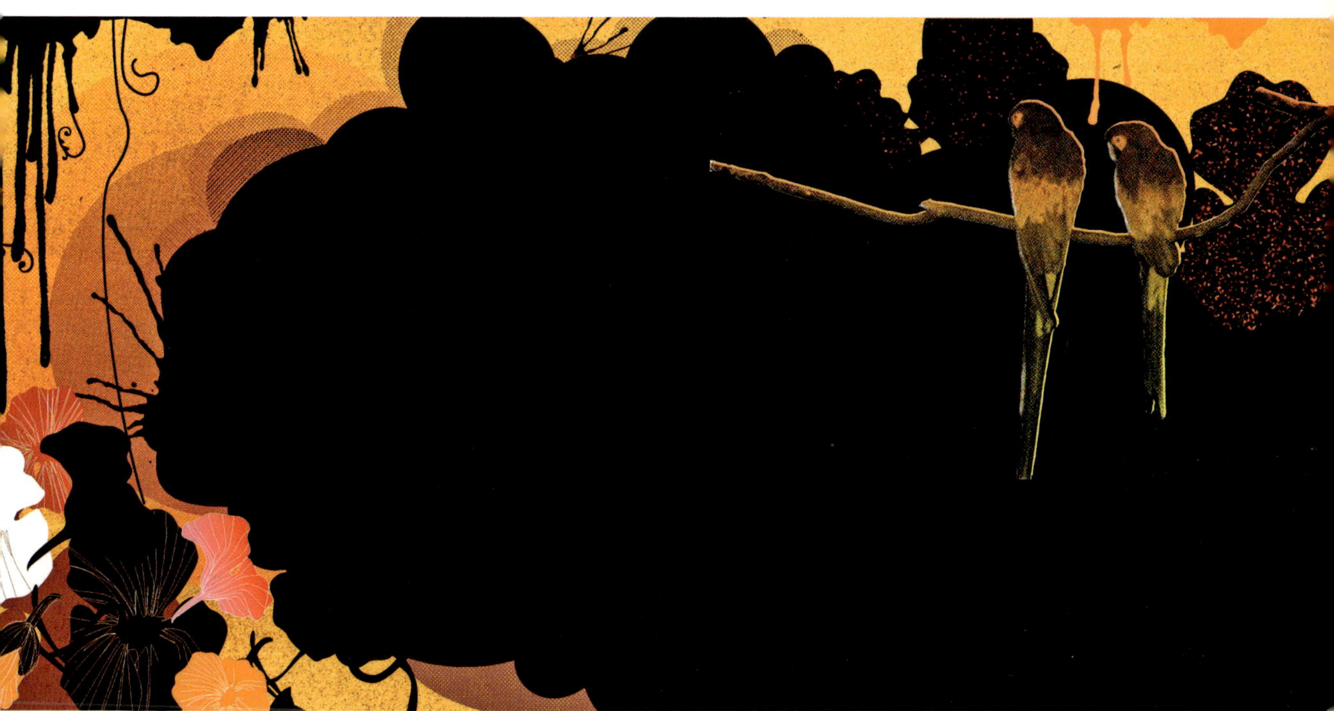

The designer as collector and curator:

Martin O'Neill

Illustrator and graphic artist Martin O'Neill has built an international reputation by being so defiantly old-school, analog, hands-on, scissors, and paste that he appears almost avant garde: a man among mousemats.

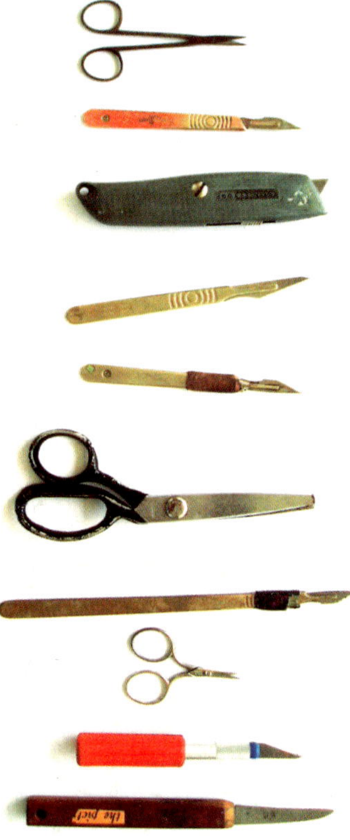

So used are the design community to poseurs and fakers in their midst that the idea of a charming, unkempt man on a bicycle who assembles pictures using scalpels, scissors, overlays, and glue seems like the most outrageous radical manifesto. When he stands his bicycle in the window of his junk shop seafront studio, some of the more urbane, self-consciously chic passersby often pause and appraise it, assuming it must be an installation. What's his angle? he sees them thinking. The answer is simple: making beautiful pictures using clip art.

For O'Neill, found imagery is root and branch of his work; found imagery in the sense of tens of thousands of clippings, photos, old magazine articles, catalogs, engravings, single characters cut out of newspaper headlines, cigarette and sports cards... the list is ongoing, and largely in his head. He has been collecting items such as these for nearly 15 years, both to use in specific projects, and simply because he likes them or thinks they might be useful one day.

However, as his collection has grown organically and haphazardly, being crammed into whatever drawers and available containers have been to hand, O'Neill has begun to see all manner of new, serendipitous, and unusual connections between the thousands of clips in his image archive.

In short, O'Neill has found himself the curator of a living work of art, a collection that has become something other than what he originally intended, and it has started him thinking about all the new things he might do with it.

"In 1994 I returned from a three-month study at Hochschule Pforzhiem in Germany with two suitcases of found paper," he says. "Since then this has grown into a vast collection of pictorial and textural reference material. Commercial deadlines left less time for rifling through piles of paper, so the archive has slowly been divided and subdivided into what is now over 200 vessels, a mismatched series of containers comprising plan chests, multidrawer filing cabinets, cigar boxes, tins, and paper bags."

This is not a precise filing system in any sense of the word and almost anything could be found in any section, he explains. Each group is an assortment of images and ephemera cut from their original context lying with other loosely related elements awaiting their appearance in a collage. "These individual items move and migrate around the studio depending on the themes I am gathering together, getting regrouped with a bundle of component parts in a separate pile or tray for the duration of a particular project," he explains.

"The hand-doodled titles of these vessels are a mixture of word association and my own rhyming slang, drawn over and retitled when the contents change. They work hand in hand with my visual memory and are more of a clue than a definition as to where to find something. With titles like Squint Westwood, Crayons and Death, Cutlery and Religion, and Inbred Bin, they are only really designed for me to understand. Part of my research for a project called *Catalog* involved creating a written document to accompany the archive. Entitled *Dogs and Dice*, this works as a sort of directory of my haphazard indexing system."

↑ No, not clip art (originally) but O'Neill's creative tools... although by the time you read this, he has probably cut the pictures out of this book and filed them in his collection. Why not scan them and use them in your next piece?

◆◆ A small part of the collection that started as a personal filing system, became an archive, and then a living, breathing, functional work as unique as its creator. Proof, in fact, that the old office adage of having a filing system everyone else can understand (along with a tidy desk) is not the sign of an organized person, but usually the sign of a dull and uninspiring mind.

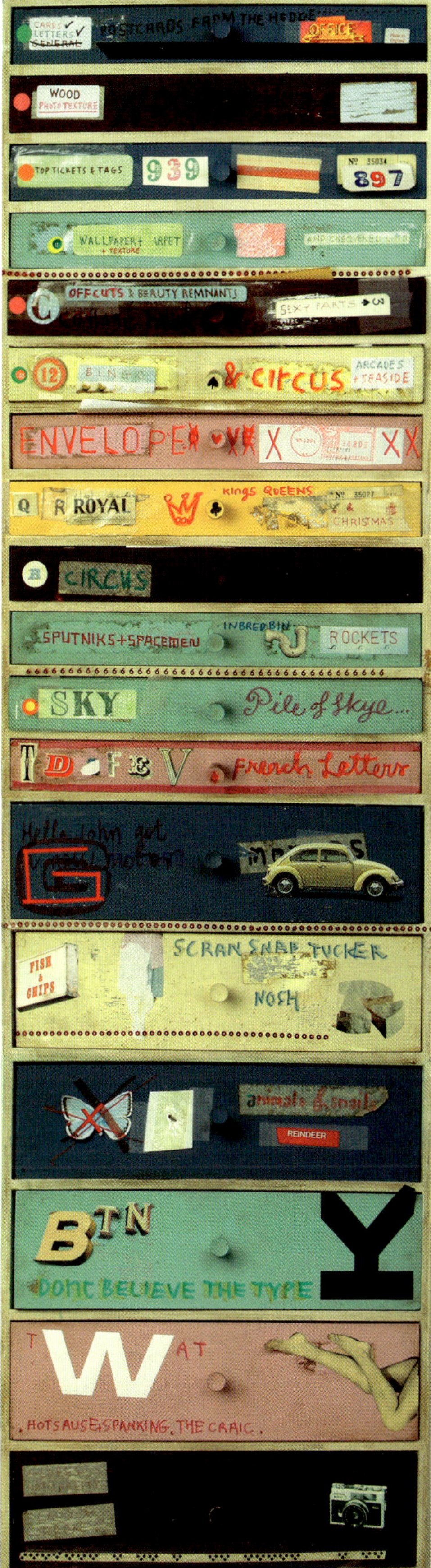

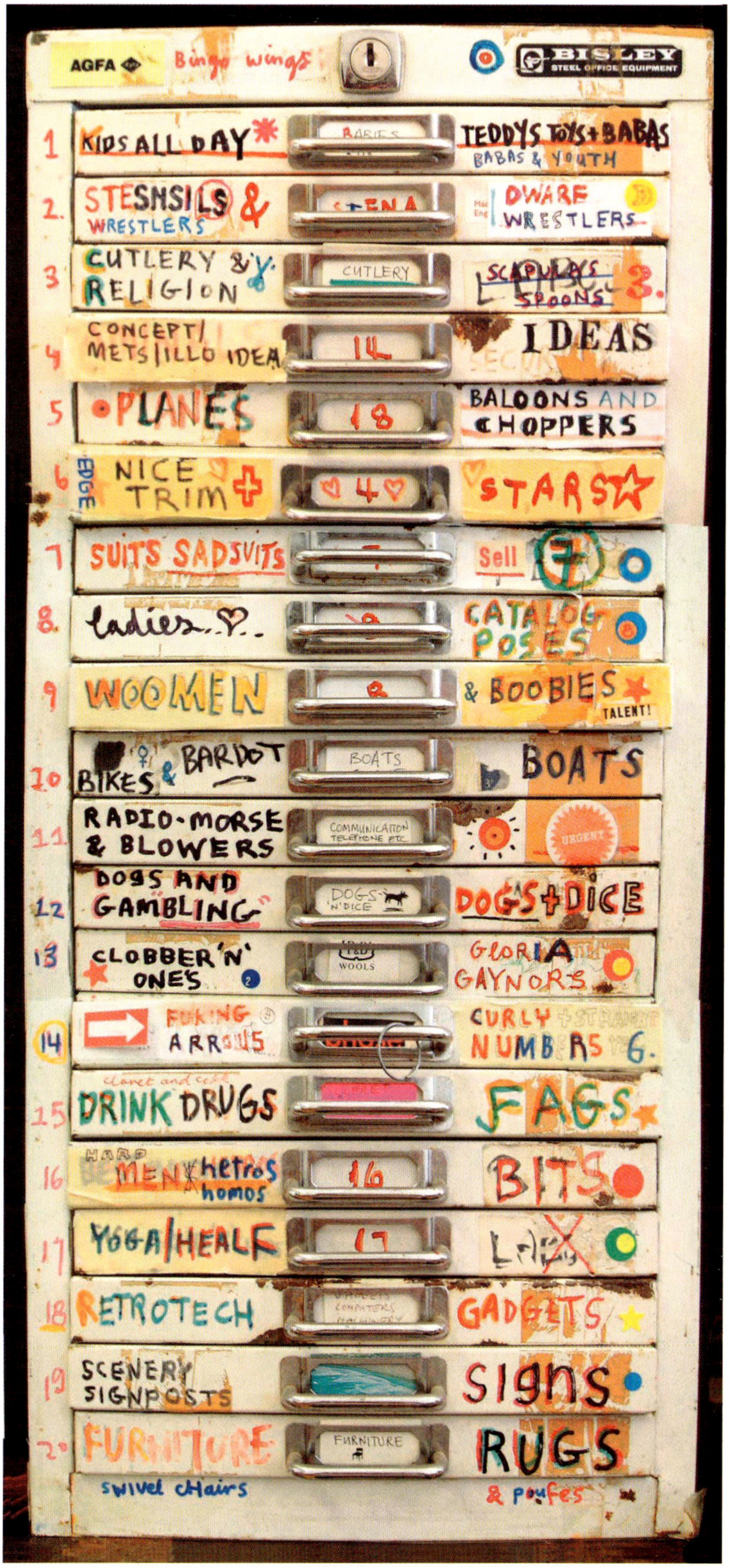

The designer as collector and curator: Martin O'Neill

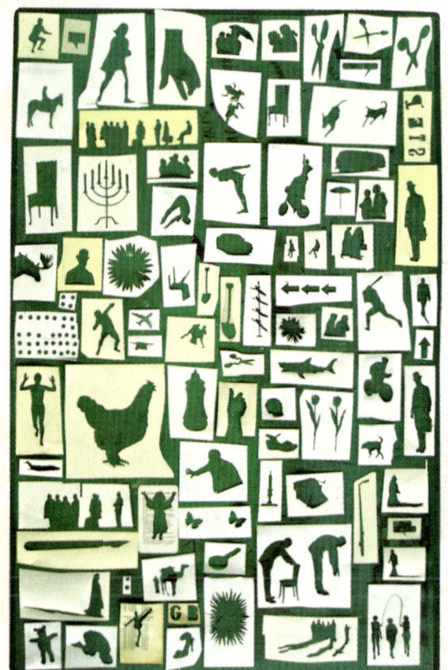

⬆ Not silhouettes, but anti-images or negative cutouts; O'Neill has even collected the leftover paper from his meticulous cutouts, which become images defined by their absence. Placed together on a board, they are a fascinating work in their own right, full of whatever meanings you wish to read into the absent subjects. What you discard is as important as what you keep.

Formally analyzing his "cataloging" process of collecting and editing in this way has made O'Neill aware of the tens of thousands of decisions he has made in more than a decade of image making. "The process seems to have been a subconscious piece of work in itself," he says. "I've begun to see my studio as a living, evolving object or an artwork in its own right—a sort of 'super collage,' a scruffy mothership, not just a tool for my commercial output. The collection is a balance between my personal and professional practice and the *Catalog* exhibition brings unseen elements into the public view for the first time.

"This raw collage material is a crucial factor in my image-making process. Manipulating the individual elements and changing their context is what excites me. This 'changing' is essentially 'hands-on' cut and paste—by taking elements and physically shaping them, cutting them out with a scalpel and gluing them down, creating juxtapositions and hierarchies between the parts, moving backward and forward between textural elements and pictorial ones—the crude and the refined. It leaves the viewer free to create their own narrative framework between each visual fragment.

"By working in this way, I have been able to construct new works that investigate and represent the individual elements, the categories and their links. I developed a series of nine posters from 55 new collage sketches created while I was researching my own archive. It felt like time to do it, a spring clean, a stock take: a new starting point."

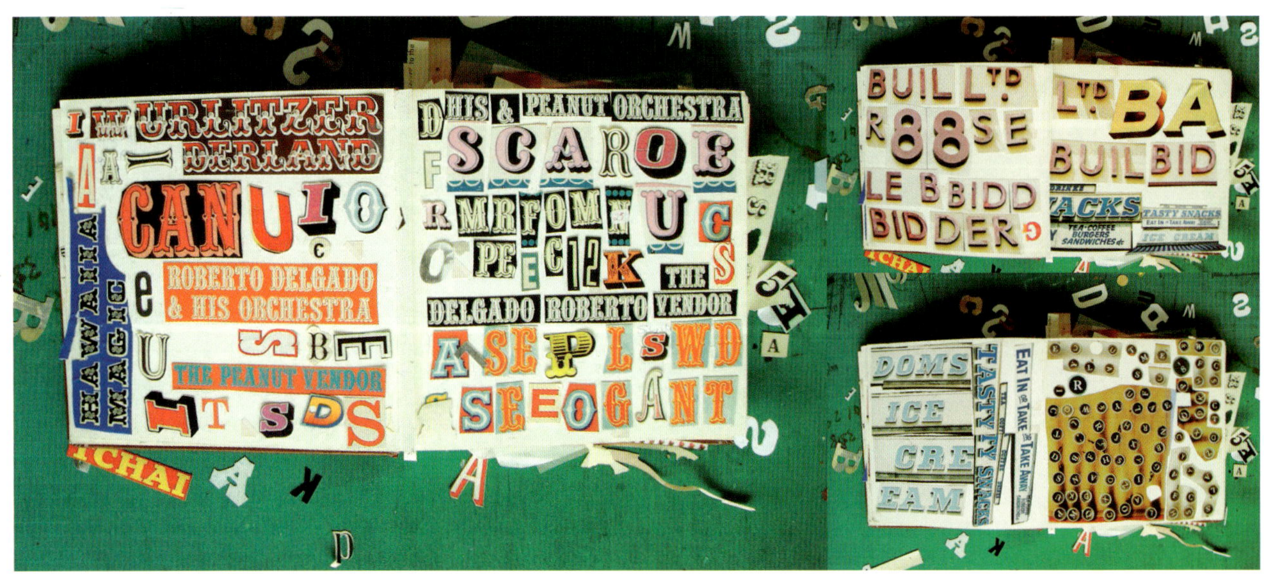

⬆ Black Dog Book. A Burroughs-like text, a typographer's collection of letterforms and fonts, a scrapbook of snippets collected on unknown journeys, or none of the above? To anything that appears to have design, the human eye and mind ascribe a meaning; even on the act of collecting itself.

➡ A collage of collages, a storyboard, or a series of new perspectives, with each one informing the ones before and after it? Every clipping tells a new story when placed in a new context. O'Neill seeks out ephemera and gives it, what? A home, a sadness at its passing, a sense of fun, a celebration? You decide.

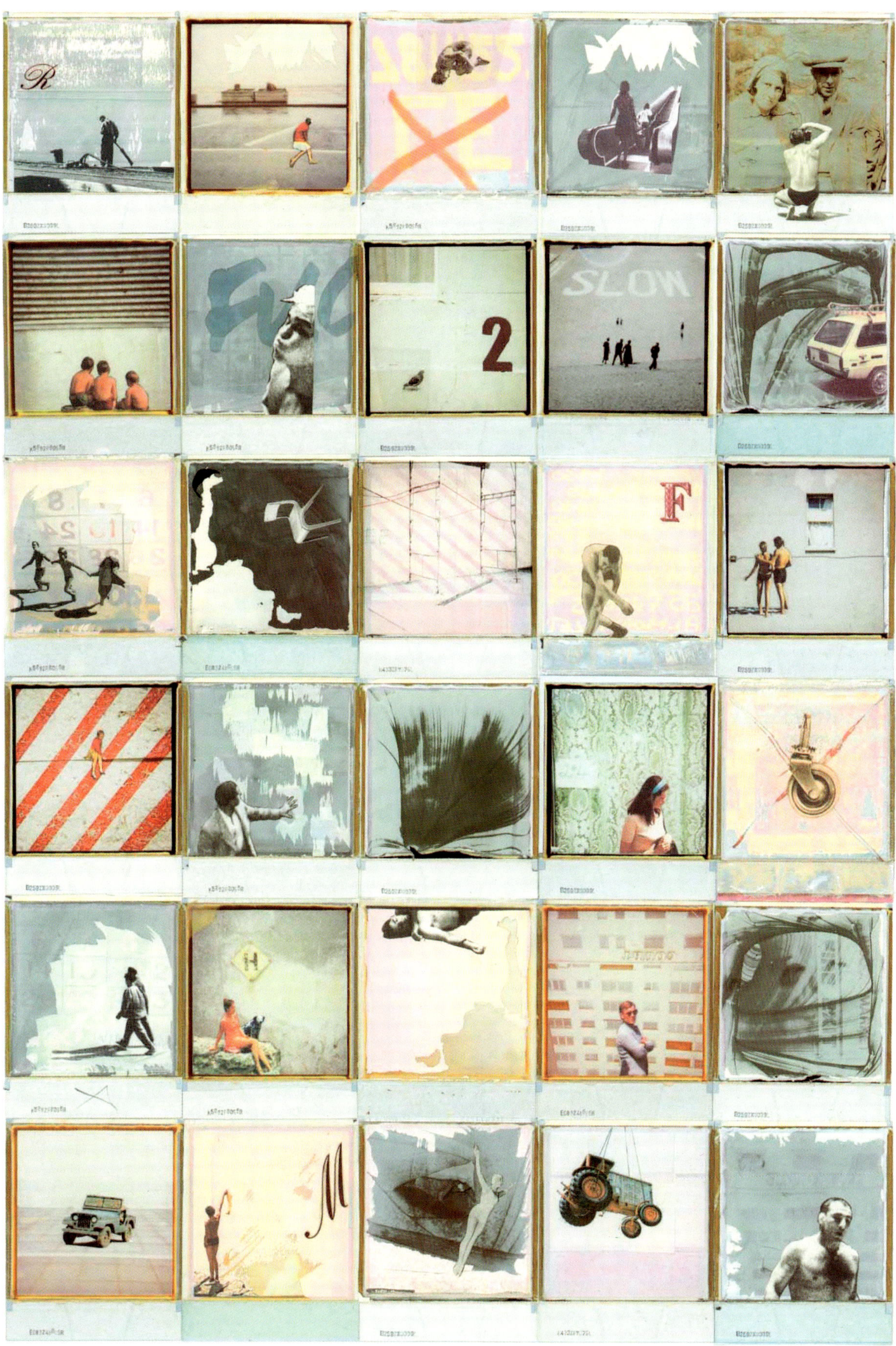

The designer as collector and curator:

Corridors of My Mind

John Finnell of Corridors of My Mind is a graphic designer, illustrator, and multimedia menu designer, for whom clip art, found images, and remixed graphics are a common factor linking much of his work, from hardcore metal T-shirts, to designs for New York bars, to website menu designs for movies such as *Constantine* and *The Perfect Man*.

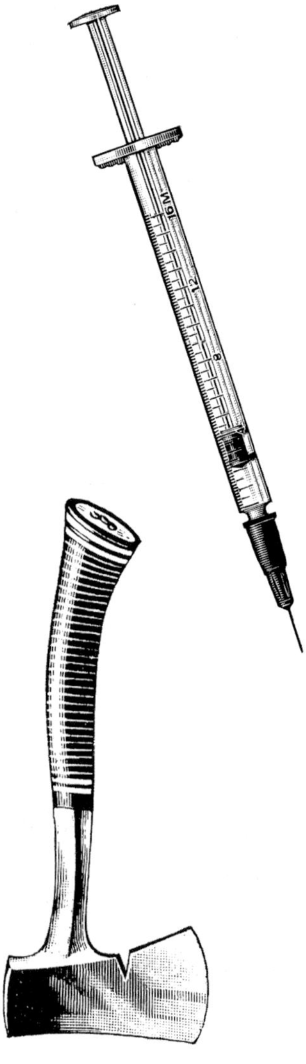

John Finnell is an avid collector of clip art, both for his personal projects and passions and for his client work. So when did he start using clip art, found images, or source imagery in his designs and illustration work, and what inspires him?

"Sometime in 2004 I believe," he says. "I was shown the Dover Books collection by my Art Director at the time. From there I started collecting them every time I found one that struck my interest.

"In terms of inspiration... that is an ever-changing question and answer for me. Anything that is emotional or has depth in the following categories: music, books, intellectual movies, friends, women, any form of art. Also, Buddhism, peace, my journal, looking within, nature, supernatural stories, war, happiness, sadness, living... it's really everything that is in front of me, and the decisions I choose to make that ultimately bring new and exciting events into my reality... which in return create inspiration."

How much of a factor is cost in his work? "For my collage art outside of the computer, I'm somewhat cautious of how much I spend. Some of the old magazines and books can add up [in terms of cost], but most of the time they are really cheap and I only have to worry about quantity making it too expensive. If it's a little bit over my normal spending, but something I can't live without and think it would be great in a piece, I will definitely buy it.

"As for client work, budget is usually not a factor with source imagery. I can either spend the money beforehand and have it in my collection, or I buy it during the project. Stock art and photography is usually cheap enough to not worry about money being a deciding factor. And, if I can't afford it, there are tons of creative solutions to come up with using free imagery found on Google or in magazines. As long as I manipulate it enough, I'm OK.

"Not all imagery for client work needs to be copyright free. Sometimes it will be for a pitch or the image will be used as a temporary solution and replaced or bought later. I think doing really big projects like sculptures, or a book, or printing lots of posters, is when the cost of creating becomes a concern to me.

"I am constantly building my library of source imagery, it's a very important aspect for me to have at hand when doing art. I'm collecting old books and magazines like crazy these days. I'm building a library of my own art photography. I'm also constantly building a digital library for my client and digital artwork. I definitely don't see it as a new strand of business. It's a part of it. I steal images wherever I can. There can never be enough meaningful art in the world. So, it's probably more important for designers and illustrators to *do* personal art."

⬆ Some of John Finell's clip-art collections, which are also works in their own right. Entitled Modern Man, Finnell describes these pieces as "a reflection of mankind past, present, and future." The images were sourced from Dover Books' *Heck's Pictorial Archive of Nature and Science*, and other royalty-free illustration books. From these and other sources, Finnell collects images to remix and manipulate for T-shirts, web menu designs, and more.

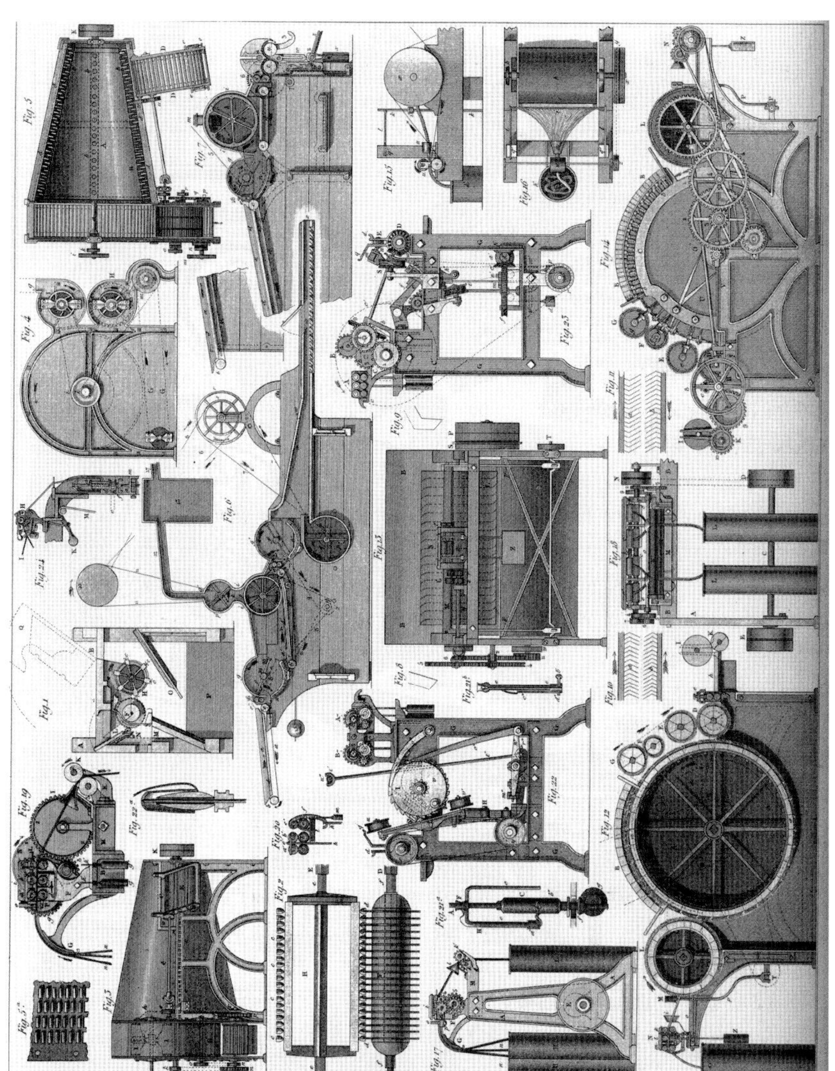

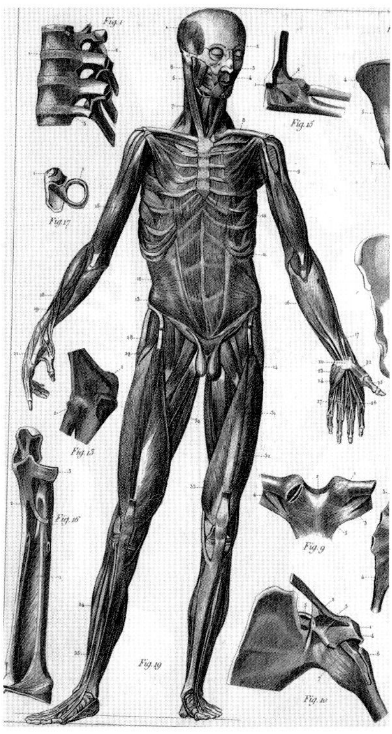

⬅ ⬆ More of Finnell's clip-art collections, sampled from Dover Books and other sources, and interpretable as a scrapbook collection of similar shapes and forms, or as artworks in their own right that invite us to explore what a collection is, and what it means in terms of identifying "Modern Man." These are images of images of objects, here reprinted again... a sample of a sample of a sample.

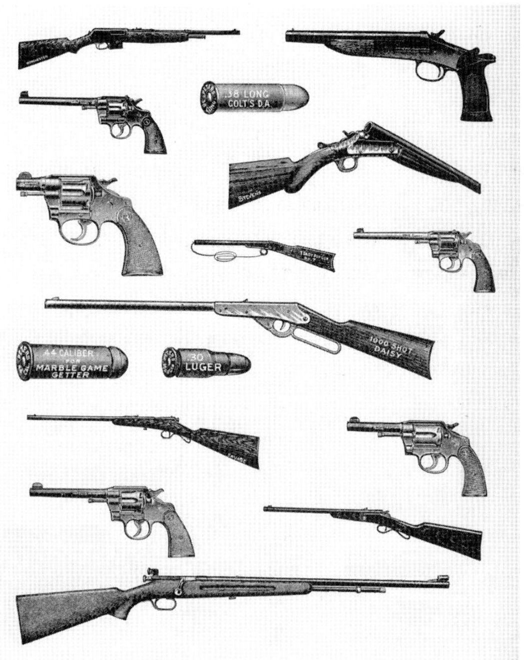

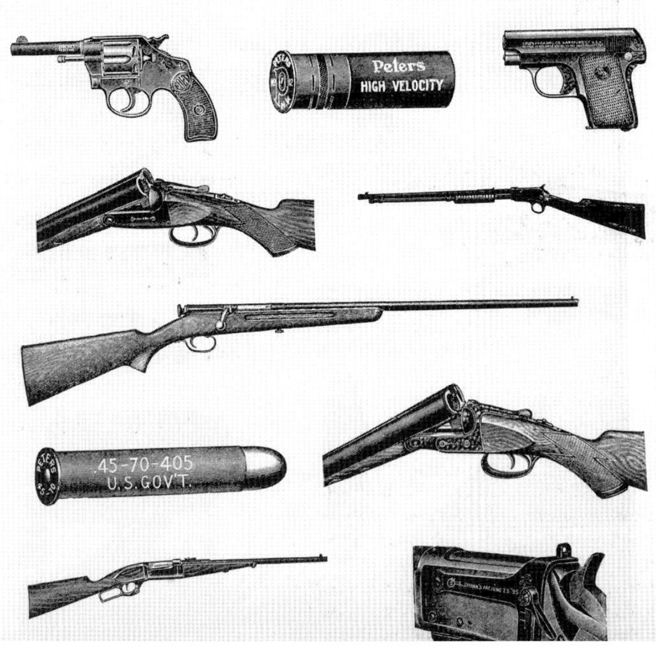

So much to do, so little budget

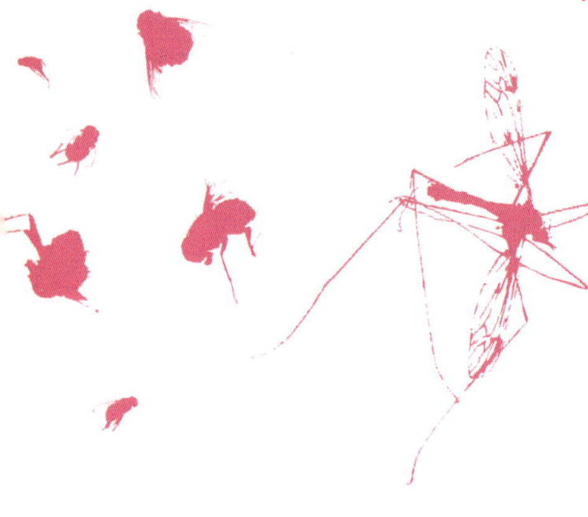

In a multimedia, multichannel market for graphic design (within which work is often valued by the speed at which it moves as much as by its inherent design or informational value), it is no surprise that many graphic design commissions take place in the context of shorter timescales, tighter deadlines, and often punitively restrictive budgets.

Indeed, as many designers are all too aware, this is especially (and ironically) truest when working for clients whose inherent kudos for a designer's portfolio means they can drive down external design fees.

How budget relates to quality

Sean Tan of Archizen Creative is philosophical about the relationship between budget and quality of work, "Budget-wise, money will always affect the whole design process. It doesn't mean the higher the budget, the better the design work. It might turn up vice versa." While this may not in itself be the most profound insight into the design process, it is a prelude to a familiar debate for any creative person. For designers specifically in such a market, clip art, sourced, or found imagery can often represent a shortcut to inspiration and a fast track to hit a deadline, as they offer designers a chance to strip out the expense of time-consuming, in-house illustrative or photographic work.

But that is not to say that using sourced imagery is "cheating"—far from it; its use can give designers the opportunity to be truly playful once they have sourced raw images that, in themselves, go some way toward satisfying the brief. In this instance, design becomes a partly curatorial process; one that involves bringing together and spinning a story out of whatever images are to hand, or can be found at low cost—or within the designer's own environment.

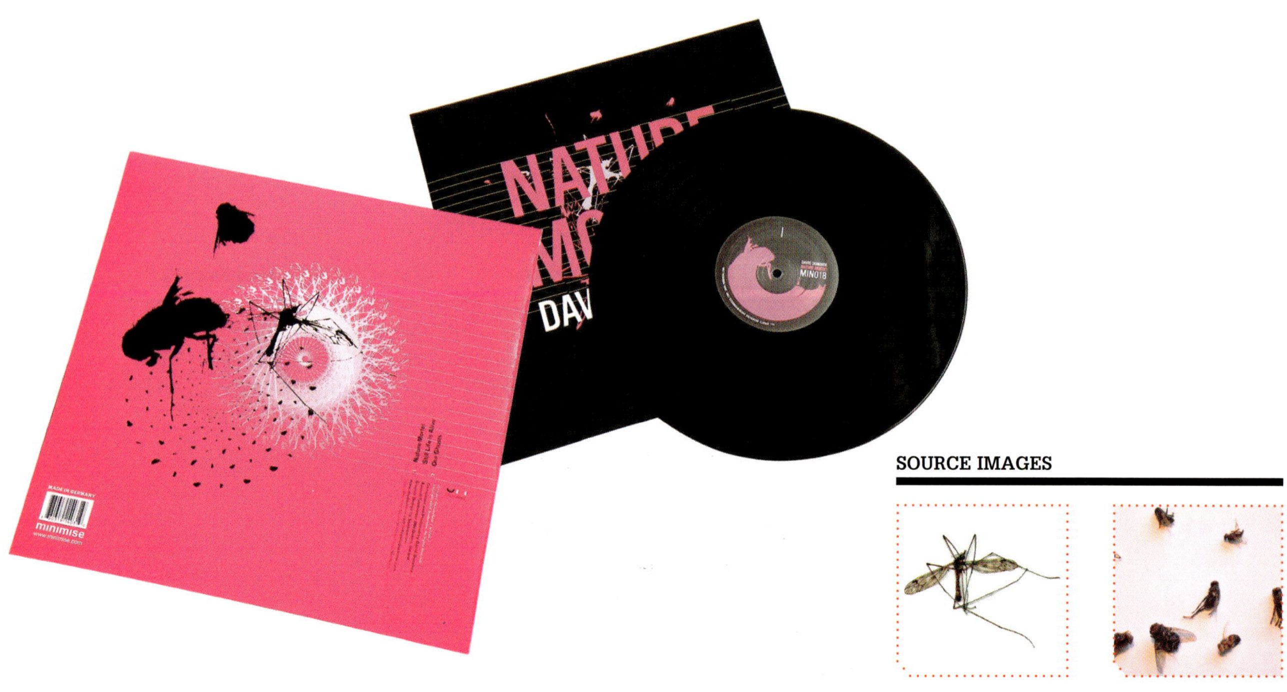

🠗 Studiomime, run by the multitalented David Donohoe, created the artwork for Donohoe's own recording using found objects and images from the studio.

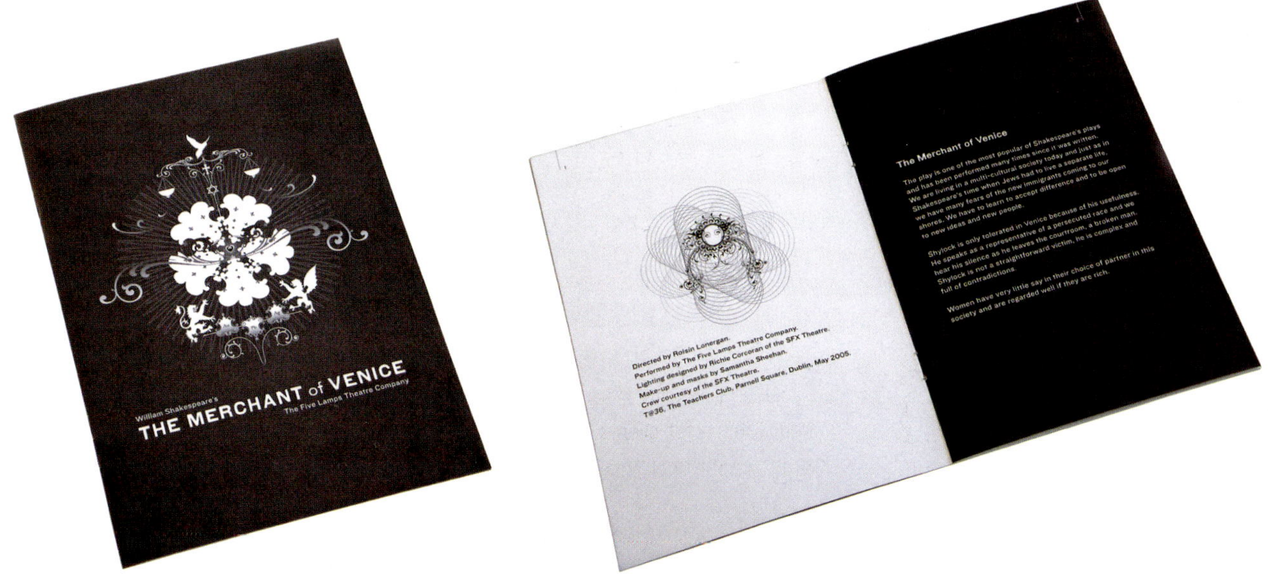

SOURCE IMAGES

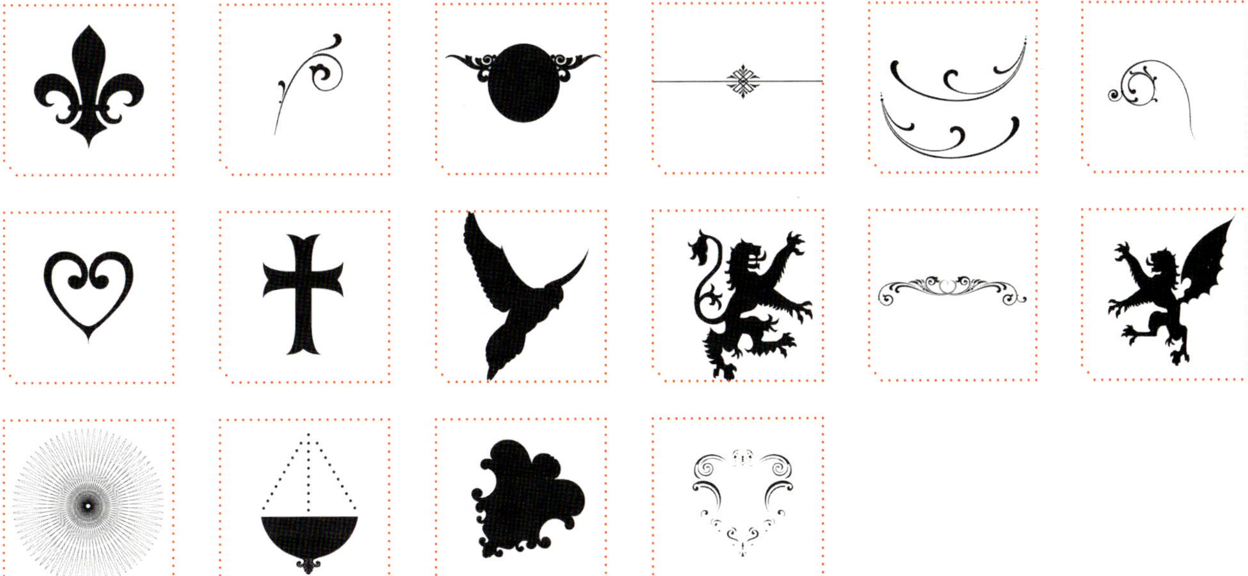

For other designers, the situation is rather different: they simply do not have the financial luxury of being able to commission external illustrators and photographers. However, many of those same designers relish that kind of challenge.

David Donohoe is both a creative director, graphic designer, and musician, who releases his design work under the moniker Studiomime. "I typically find myself working with relatively small budgets, but I wouldn't say that I ever find this a hindrance," he says. "My natural decision making tends to be based more on working within limitations. I try to do as much of the work on a project myself not simply to save costs, but because this is my craft." For Donohoe, much of the found imagery in his work is a conflation of clip art from low-cost image banks or Creative Commons-licensed work, together with sketches that he makes all the time in notebooks (and then subsequently mines for inspiration and illustrative raw material), plus observational photography from his own, immediate world, namely that of his design studio.

⬆ Studiomime's beautiful artwork, top, for a Shakespeare performance is a sublime combination of the simplest monochrome clip-art elements, shown above.

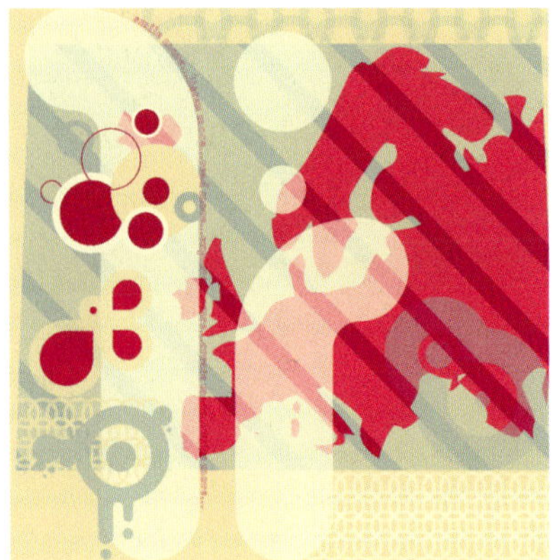

Nicole Andujar's Fuscia World is an exhibition piece shown at the Design District of Miami's Culture Kings event. Many of the original elements are taken from the Freewave book at www.fontmonster.com.

KesselsKramer produced a range of clip art and source image-derived pieces for the design identity of the Hans Brinker Budget Hotel in Amsterdam. The idea is an inspired joke on the concept of a "no frills" hotel, as typified by these examples of signs and information graphics.

For example, the sleeve design for his own CD, *Nature Morte!*, mixes clip art, scanned notebook drawings, and digital photos of insects that he found dead in his studio over the course of one hot summer. The latter were not so much "found images" (in the conventional sense of samples, cutouts, tear sheets, or cutups), but digital images of found objects from within his own creative space—creatures that had presented themselves to his enquiring and documenting lens. Some of these raw images were blended in Photoshop, while others were redrawn in Illustrator.

Away from the improvisational world of designers such as Donohoe, a great deal depends on whether a designer can go back to the client and secure a budget for paid-for illustration work, or for photography, which might be either bespoke; sourced from a high-cost commercial image bank, such as Getty, Corbis, or PA Photos; or downloaded from lower-cost services such as iStockphoto, which also sells vector illustrations and graphical icons.

Eric Kessels of KesselsKramer has produced some inspired designs where the concept of "zero budget" was part of the brief. For a series of posters for a budget hotel, he sourced images from luxury hotels and subverted them. He explains: "The Hans Brinker Budget Hotel is based in Amsterdam. This campaign borrows the swanky photography from high-class hotels around the world to tell, in an honest way, exactly what the Hans Brinker Hotel does not have (a lot) instead of telling what the hotel does have (not a lot)!"

Not all designers agree that budget is one of the prime movers behind any decision to use sourced/found imagery or clip art. Nicole Andujar of ChixInk says, "It depends on the design. If it calls for source imagery and the client is willing to pay for the import, as well as if the client is happy with the image, then it will be used. As far as personal designs, it depends on how much it will help finalize the design or what is the timeframe, because if the time allows, I can create a custom illustration or image myself with the tools I have." Including, Andujar admits, images created using clip art.

Of course, even if budgetary constraints do throw a creative cordon around a design commission, the prime, overriding consideration for the use of found or sourced imagery or clip art remains an aesthetic one, and not one of how much money is slapped on the table from the design's financial patron.

CityAbyss's Beatta Szczecinska says, "I use only 'free' sources. If I want to use something that is more widely 'known,' or 'recognized,' then it will lose its [immediately recognizable] identity through my interference, my transformation."

Scott Witham of Traffic Design Consultants puts it more simply: "If it's not as close to free as possible, we may as well do it ourselves."

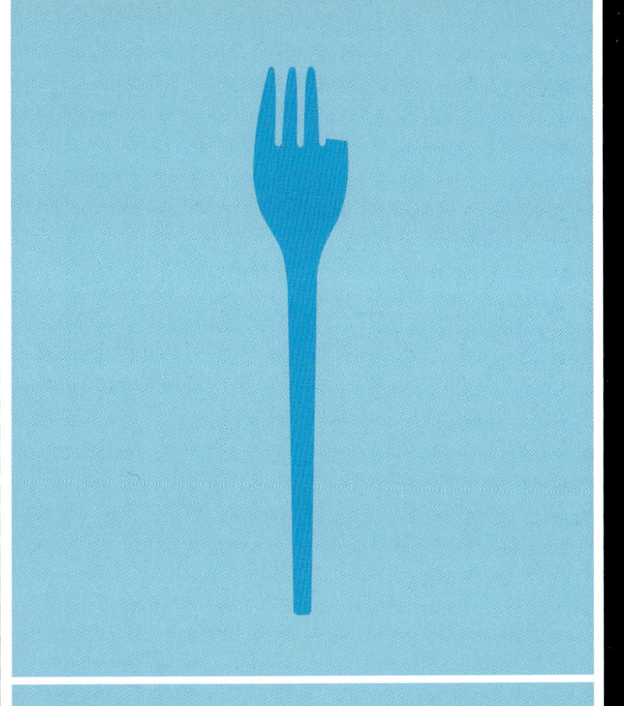
Unique Design
HANS BRINKER BUDGET HOTEL, AMSTERDAM
+31 (0)20 622 0687 hans-brinker.com

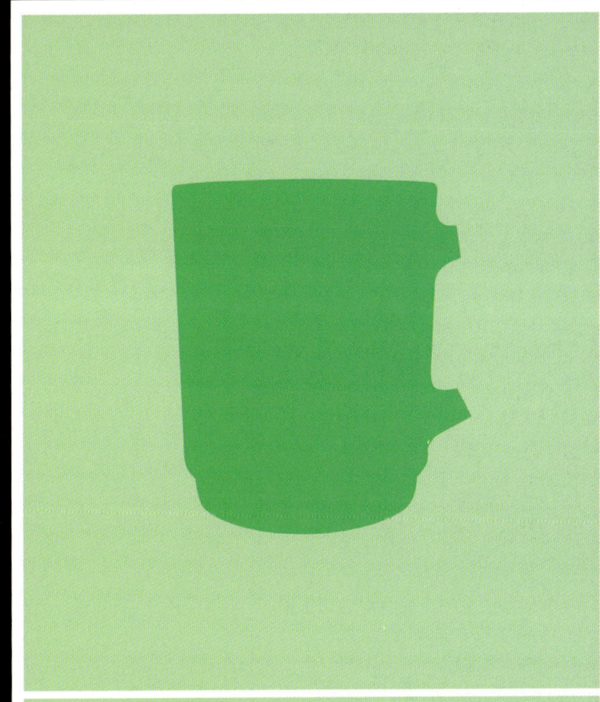
Unique Design
HANS BRINKER BUDGET HOTEL, AMSTERDAM
+31 (0)20 622 0687 hans-brinker.com

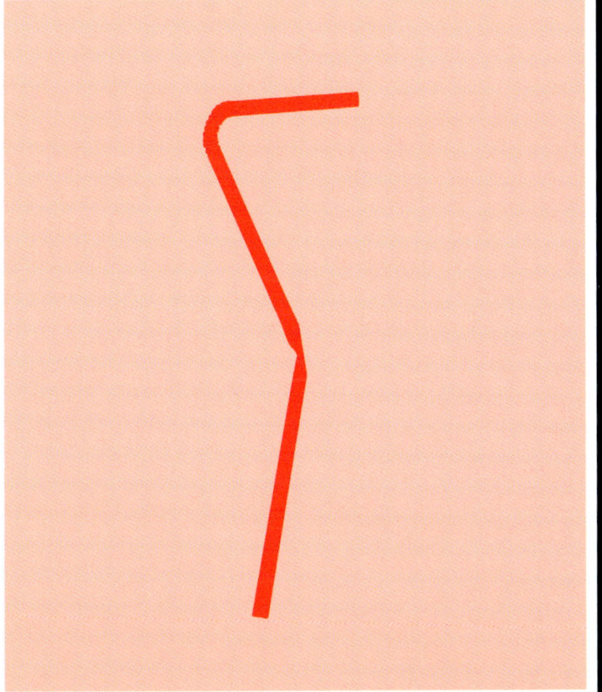
Unique Design
HANS BRINKER BUDGET HOTEL, AMSTERDAM
+31 (0)20 622 0687 hans-brinker.com

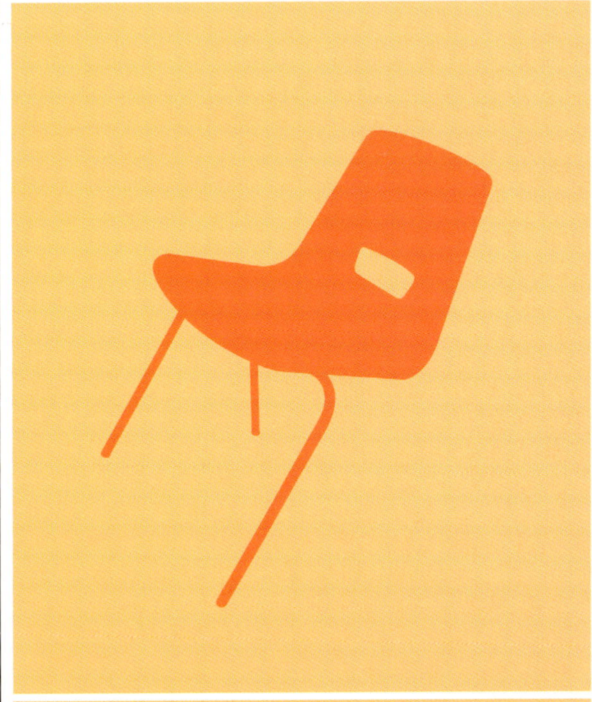
Unique Design
HANS BRINKER BUDGET HOTEL, AMSTERDAM
+31 (0)20 622 0687 hans-brinker.com

Creative dossier:

Aboud Sodano

Sometimes tight deadlines, a tighter budget, and a demanding, high-profile client with "portfolio kudos" is a recipe for clarity of vision and the imaginative use of the simplest elements, as Aboud Sodano found when working with Paul Smith.

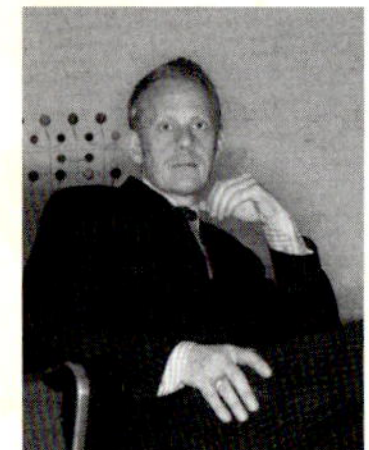

Studio: Aboud Sodano
Designers: Alan Aboud, Sandro Sodano, Chris Bedson
Client: Paul Smith

Conceptual thinking about the client and the values of a brand translates into the three Fs—formative, functional, and funky design—far more than the flashy, ostentatious, or pretentious use of graphical elements. This is never truer than when the client's brief is to create work that is all about maintaining a unique brand relationship with its customers in an overcrowded and "noisy" market.

College friends Alan Aboud and Sandro Sodano formed Aboud Sodano in 1989. Their creative partnership combines Aboud's art directional and experimental typographic skills with Sodano's photography. The company's main clients are in the fashion industry—the designer Paul Smith has been coming to them since the duo left college. Other clients include Levi Strauss, H&M, and R. Newbold.

The commissions from Paul Smith were all on extremely tight deadlines that necessitated a prompt response and swift solutions—hence the decision to use clip art. Says Aboud: "Budgets, or lack of them, always come into it, as so many clients withdraw any sense of generosity or reality with regard to budgets. Levels have slowly risen, but they are still too low to merit commissions for creative images."

"With the advent of digital technology, designers are increasingly having to become photographers, just as in the late 1980s when we all had to become typographers and artworkers with the advent of the Apple Mac," he adds. "So clip art, in these times, is a financial necessity."

Invitation to Paul Smith's Japanese show. These elements all came from clip-art resources, so it was important to make the right choices to illustrate the brand. For a designer label such as Paul Smith—whose name is associated with classic fabrics, but contemporary cuts—Aboud Sodano's clip-art-based design suggests that Paul Smith has stamped his contemporary aesthetic onto a traditional device.

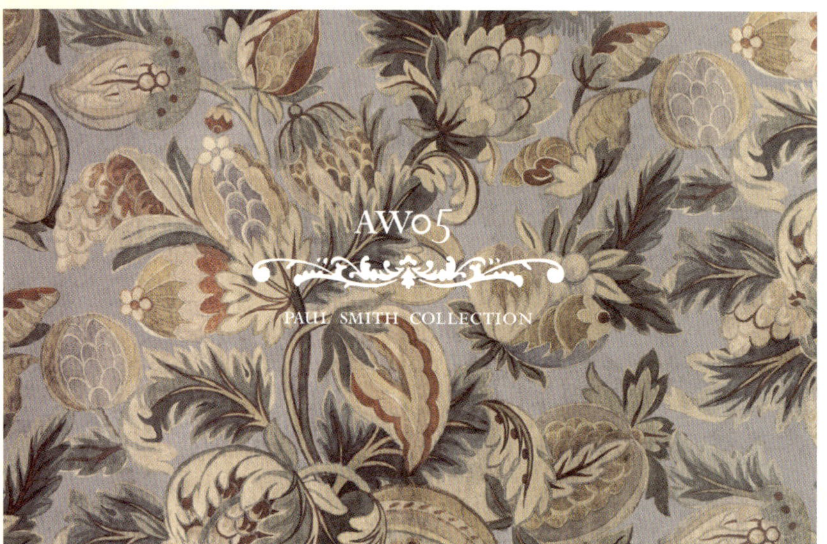

SOURCE IMAGES

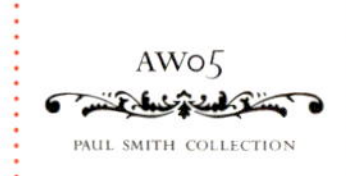

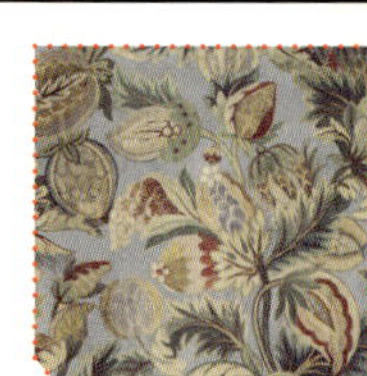

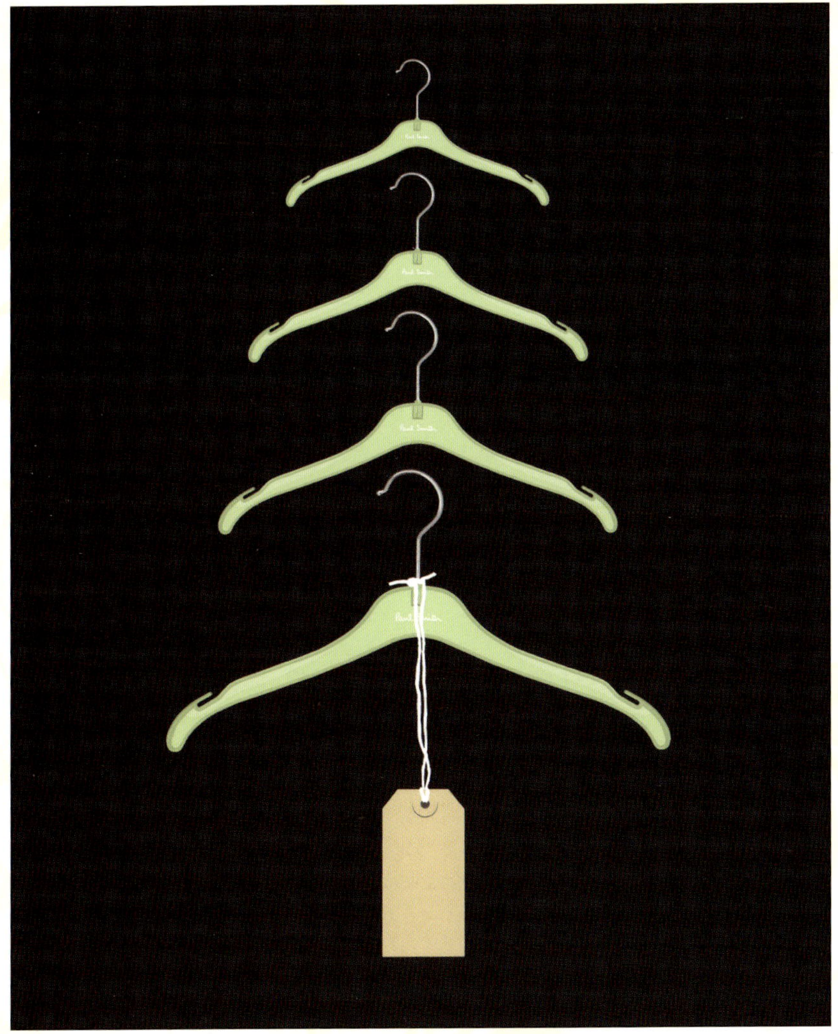

SOURCE IMAGES

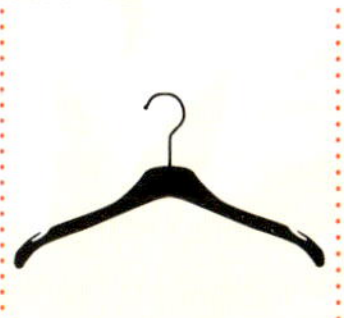

Paul Smith Christmas card. A simple idea for a Paul Smith Christmas card, but one that is both smart and amusing. As well as being a visual pun, the design also stamps a strong personality on a drab and impersonal set of clip-art images—an average clothes hanger, and a plain parcel label. This speaks volumes about the strength of the brand.

Aboud Sodano's greetings card. The decision to make a familiar piece of clip art into the central message creates work that stands out from the crowd—when combined with the right choice of materials. In a graphic design market that is trend-driven, clip art can have the reverse effect of seeming timeless.

Aboud admits there is always a concern when a piece of art or design is in the public domain, as designers may feel they are not being creative or individual enough. This is why Aboud personalizes and adapts clip art.

For the invitation to designer Paul Smith's Japanese show, Aboud Sodano played on the theme of the show, which was the works of writer Evelyn Waugh. The white woodcut decoration was sourced from a Symbols font called Adobe Woodcuts, and the only creative change that was made was to recolor the font white.

For Paul Smith's Christmas card, which featured an abstract Christmas tree constructed from coat hangers, clip art was again the obvious choice. The image was constructed from line art clip originals, which were then rendered in 3D.

Says Aboud Sodano designer Chris Bedson: "Christmas cards always have a fast turnaround so there was no time to draw or shoot anything. For our studio Christmas card, we wanted to use an old-fashioned woodcut-style image, so clip art again was an obvious choice. We found the source in a book of tree woodcuts at a local bookshop."

The stump and ground were from a separate image from that of the tree, and the two were comped together. The image was also debossed, which was tricky because the image itself was too detailed for a deboss, so the team did a rough trace which became the template for the final work.

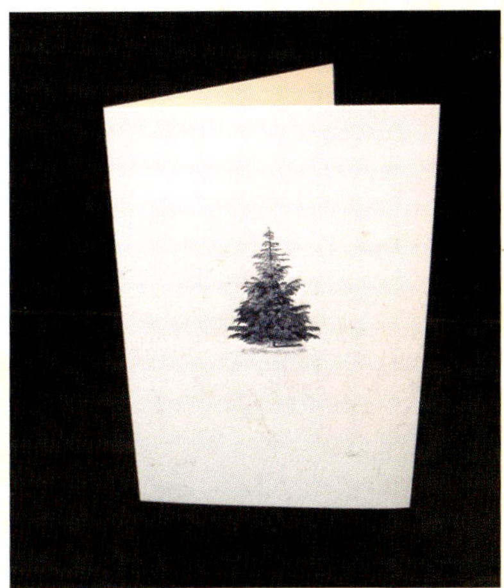

SOURCE IMAGES

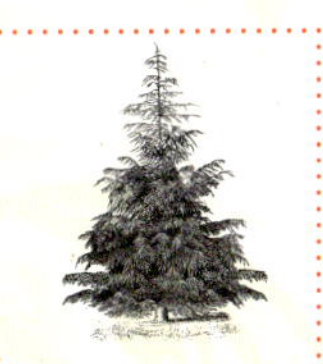

The big question:

inspiration

Now we present part two of our big questions pitched at a range of professional designers and illustrators worldwide. Our designers were given no more specific brief than "answers, please, at whatever length you feel appropriate."

Q: Who or what inspires you in your designs and use of clip art, found, and sourced imagery?

"There's a lot of things that inspire me. From films to astronomy to music. In the modern design industry, it would be works from Psyop and Joost Korngold from Renascent. Their work is just awesome!"
Sean Tan, Archizen Creative

"I'm influenced by everything—stories, conversations, spirits and ghosts, pookas, calligraphic marks, type, love, death, songs, drawing, myth, fables, fairy stories, throwing salt at the fire, making the sign of the cross at the front door in the sand with your feet. I'm influenced by where I am and who I'm with. Also imagination and folklore, raised on songs and stories, heroes of renown passed down and exaggerated, and what does it mean today, if anything, where does it live in the urban domain. I'm heavily influenced by where I live and have a real sense of place. I studied in London and all the time I was there I was homesick. My work at the time was all about home. Lost and found and all that jazz."
David Joyce

"I am inspired by art in general, trying to follow all its domains from architecture, music to fashion, furniture design, and so on. I am interested in anything new and exciting that I haven't seen before. In addition, in my work I am trying to admonish [sic] a human being surrounded by this new reality and see how he is coping with it. If it comes to who inspires me, it would definitely be Howard Hodgkin (late period), Benjamin Savignac, Cleo Sullivan, Sophie Toulouse, Werke, and many more people—also from the world of music."
Beatta Szczecinska, CityAbyss

"I am inspired by everything that surrounds me. It could be an object on the street, some random color combination I come across, or a beautiful object I see. I visit many art fairs and art exhibitions to see the latest techniques fine artists use, and seeing beautiful things also inspires me."
Nicole Andujar, ChixInk

"Streets, magazines, life, people, books, shapes, details, a line treatment, a color brush, a word, a bug. Inspiration lies in everything I see, breathe, or experience."
Marie-Joe Raidy, Raidy Printing Group

"I'm inspired by a lot of designers who combine found imagery or objects with their own work and create something new. One of my favorite designers is Dirk Fowler, who letterpresses all of his posters and sometimes uses found objects in his concepts and printing, like using a vinyl record in his design, but also using the record to apply the ink to the paper. Really great work."
Jason Munn, The Small Stakes

"My main drive is the need to record, document, and produce. I think I just need to be designing, photographing, writing, making music, drawing, etc. In order to feel alive. I am inspired by limitation, structure, texture, method, tradition, craft, stillness, belief. Lots of stuff. I am very influenced by natural life systems and as such my attitude to work is very holistically detailed."
David Donohoe, Studiomime

"Inspiration comes from anywhere: movies, books, looking around, visiting New York or other cities; other designers like Henry Wolf or Paula Scher."
Tom Varisco, Varisco Design

➡ The Gherkings by Erich Brechbühl. Block goes rock in this simple combination of traditional found images—a gherkin and a king—for this concert poster for a local band, combined with some well-researched script.

ORIGINAL IMAGES

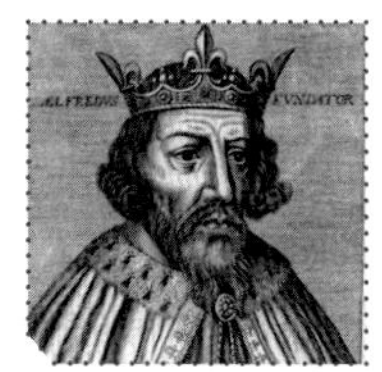

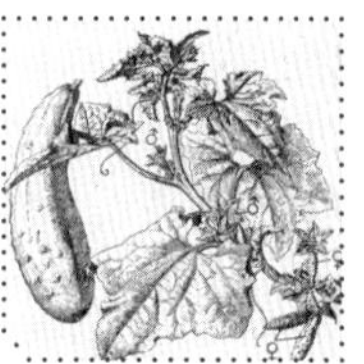

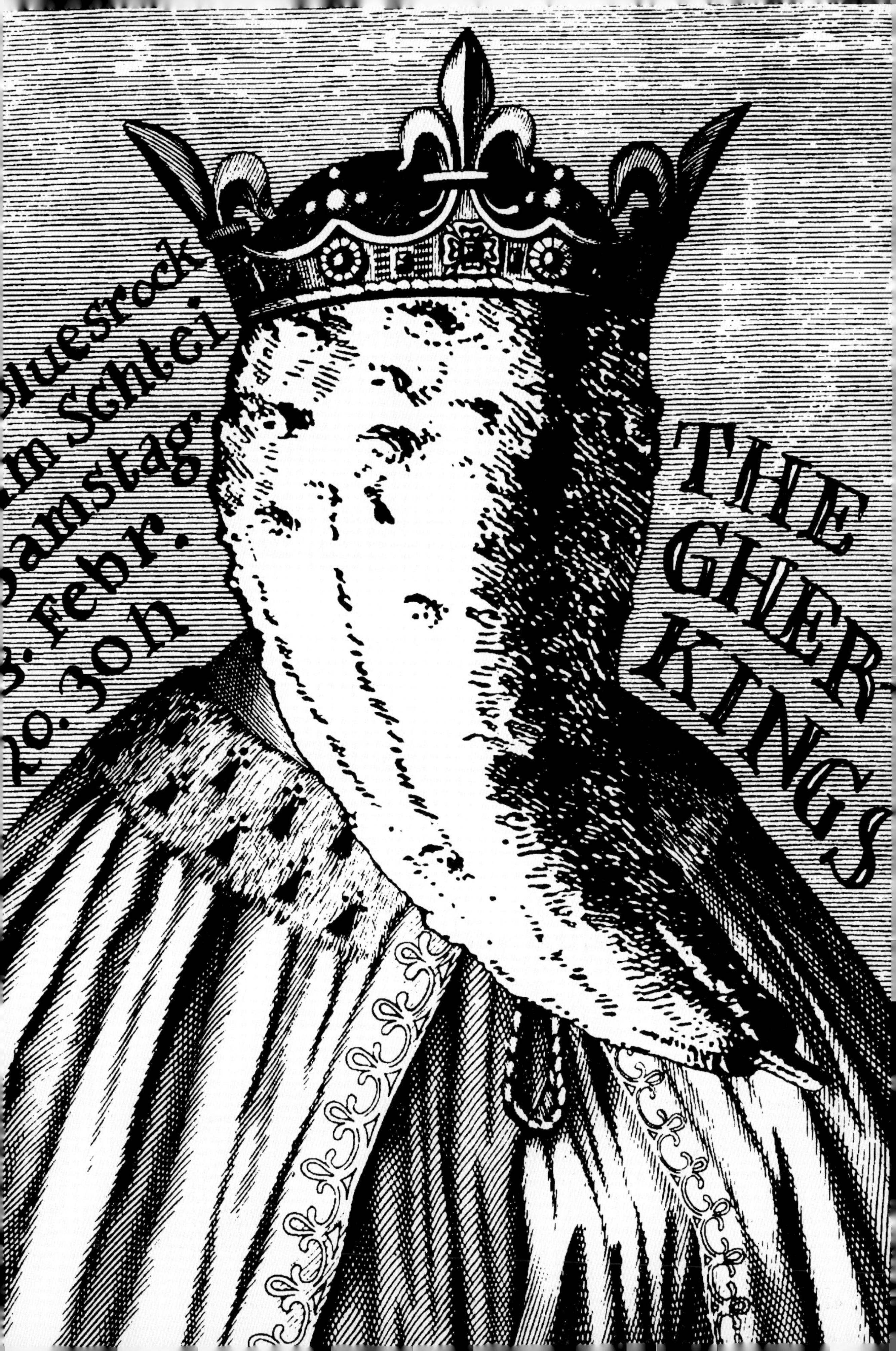
luesrock
im Schtei
Samstag
3. Febr.
20.30h
THE GHER-
KINGS

Sampling, remixing, and the law

"Fair use is not a doctrine that exists by sufferance, or that is earned by good works and fair morals... it is a right that is necessary to fulfill copyright's very purpose, 'to promote the progress of science and the useful arts.'"
US Judge Dennis Jacobs, 2004

What constitutes the fair use of digital material, including images, texts, and artworks has been at the forefront of international debate since the internet became mass-adopted in the mid-1990s. It is also at the forefront of an internal debate for designers every day: those who use clip art, sourced, and found imagery; who reference familiar or iconic pieces in their work; or who clone pixels from digital photos.

"Fair use," explains Sean Tejaratchi, founder of clip-art zine *Crap Hound*, "is the only legal acknowledgment we have that copyright controls can, indeed, equal censorship of free speech and free expression if permitted total and unrestricted reign. The problem with fair use as it stands is in its interpretation with regard to art reuses."

Tejaratchi argues for a redefinition of fair use. "Because art is not defined as a business, and yet some art must compete for economic survival in the marketplace, we think certain legal priorities in the idea of copyright should be revised to uphold artistic imperatives in commercial contexts," he says.

The arguments surrounding the rights and wrongs of fair use, filesharing, and the associated issues of piracy and illegally copying work are not as new as many imagine. The Great, or Royal, Library of Alexandria—most likely founded in the third century BC—has become synonymous with lost learning; a great repository of human

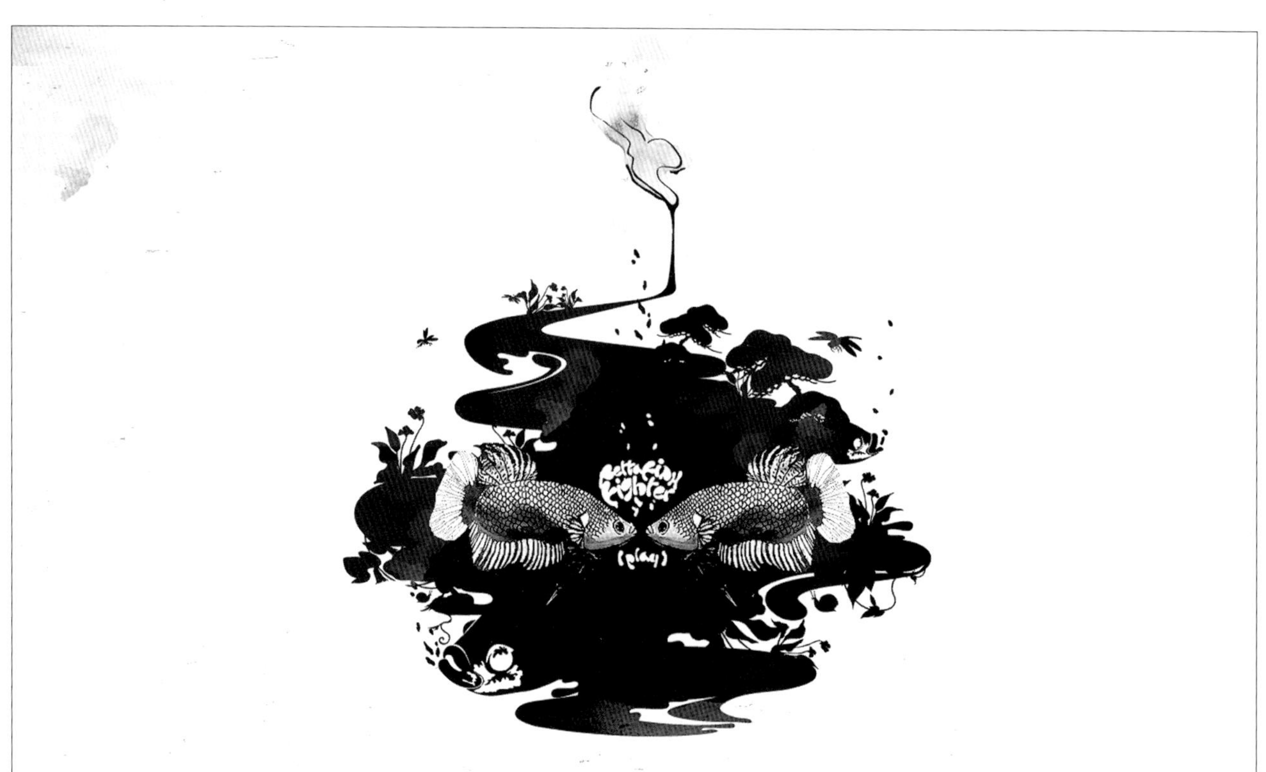

Beta Design produced the Beta Fish Fighter Game for one of its own teaser campaigns. The game was part of a series of minisites based on Beta illustrations to promote the company in Brazil. Clip-art originals were sourced from a variety of sources, including Japanese clip-art sites, and were modified in Illustrator.

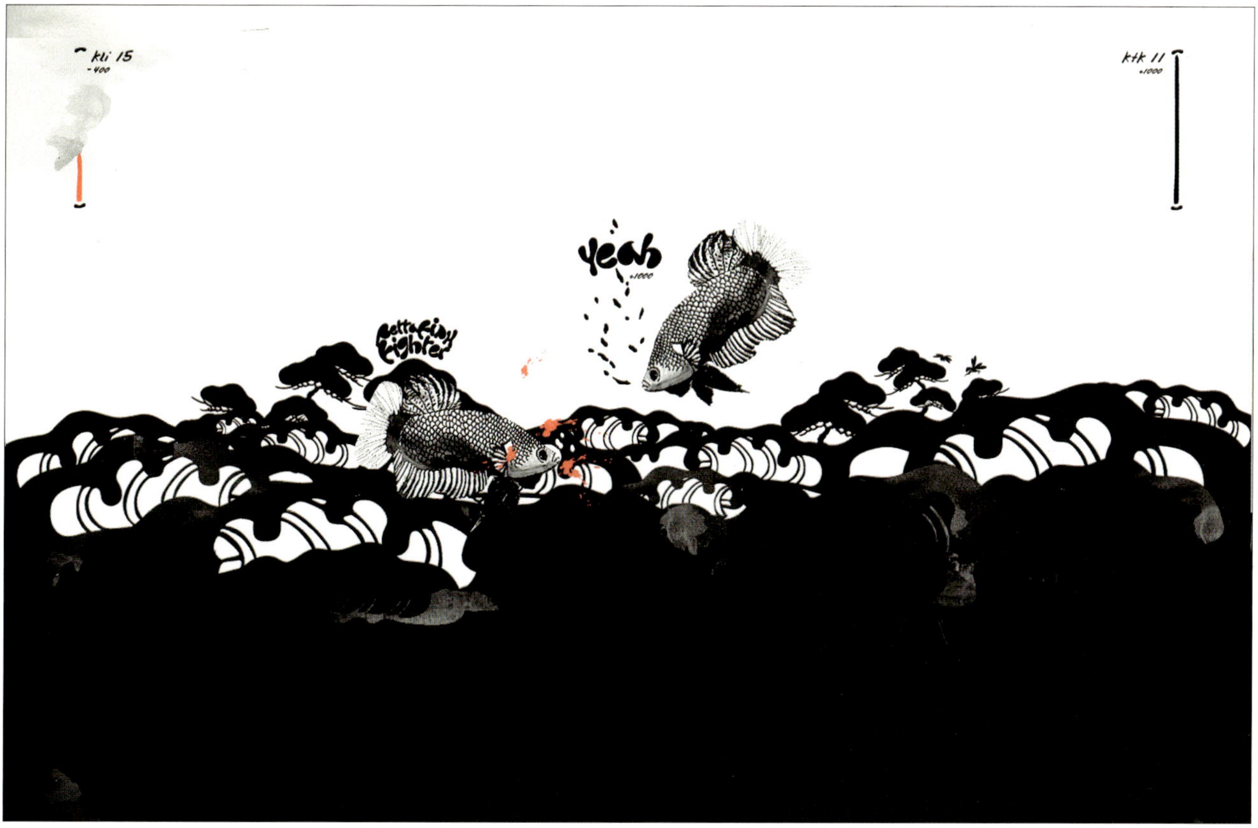

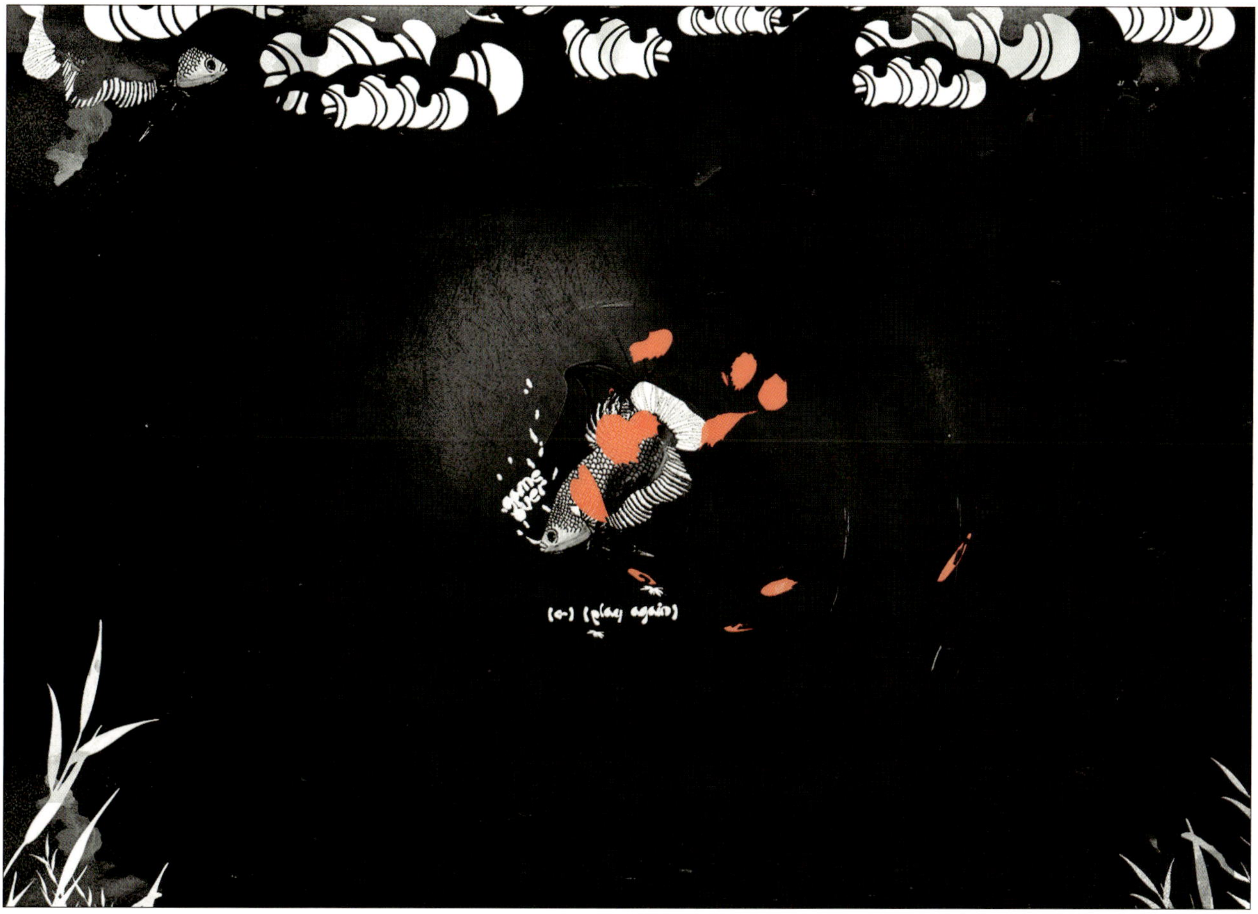

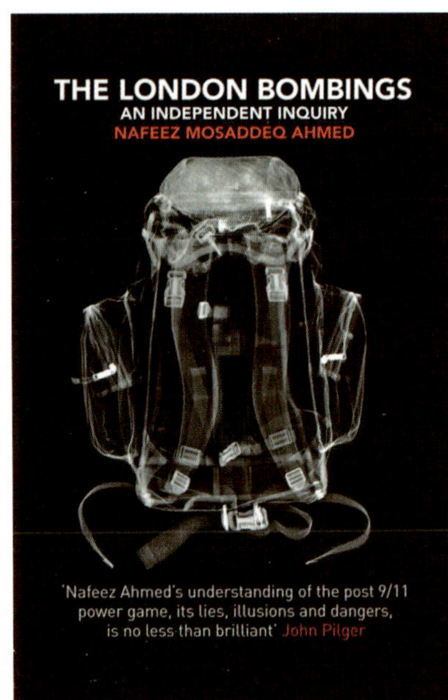

compoundEye's cover design for this bleak publication was chosen from a series of possible designs, all of which used sourced clip art and stock imagery, compiled in Photoshop and InDesign.

knowledge, art, and philosophy that was the privilege of an educated elite and later destroyed by fire by one invading horde or another. It is a romantic idea; too romantic, in fact. Today, few are aware that the library's shelves were stocked with parchments (text and pictures) pirated from passing ships. However, the artifacts were appropriated on behalf of a privileged elite, rather than the general populace, giving it the veneer of cultural respectability that ancient history allows.

Historians are still arguing over who is responsible for the Library's apparent demise, with stories pinpointing its destruction at four different times over nearly a thousand years. Who was to blame? Arguably, whoever wasn't writing the dominant history of the day; it was always the other guy.

And so it is in the twenty-first century. Two cultures battle it out over today's repository of knowledge, the internet, with each blaming the other for burning down the house. To oversimplify the debate, on the one hand are people who believe in asserting the moral imperative of intellectual property in every case (hard to do in a hypertext, cut-and-paste culture), while on the other are those who believe in the free flow of ideas and knowledge as an absolute, and who have come to regard publishers, multinationals, and top-down distributors as fair game.

The battleground is fair use: the ability to share content, such as an illustration, digital photo, video clip, text, or sound file, that has been legally sourced and paid for (by copying a file to consume on a different device, for example), together with the legal issues surrounding whether aspects of that content can be sampled in a different context as part of the creation of something new.

As designer, clip art collector, and prime mover of *Crap Hound*, Tejaratchi is forthright about the false conflation of "piracy" and fair use in the creation of art, design, and other creative pursuits, using digital sampling techniques. "It is delusional to try to paint these new forms of fragmentary use and sampling as economically motivated theft and piracy. These terms must be reserved for the unauthorized taking of whole works and selling them for one's own profit. Artists who routinely appropriate are not attempting to profit from the marketability of their sources. They are using elements, fragments, or pieces of someone else's created artifact in the creation of a new one for artistic reasons."

"It is a minefield, but I try not to concern myself with it too much," says John Finnell of multimedia design studio Corridors of My Mind. "It all depends on the image. I try to stay away from ones that I know will get me in trouble, and if I manipulate something enough then it is completely legal to use. So, don't be afraid... just manipulate it enough and don't blatantly rip someone off. We all have feelings and put lots of energy into our personal work. But really, I've always hated copyright issues and any laws that slow or stop the process of art. Art is good for humanity. Let's keep it good and free and flowing and not put too many barriers on ourselves. Make art! Have fun! We need it!"

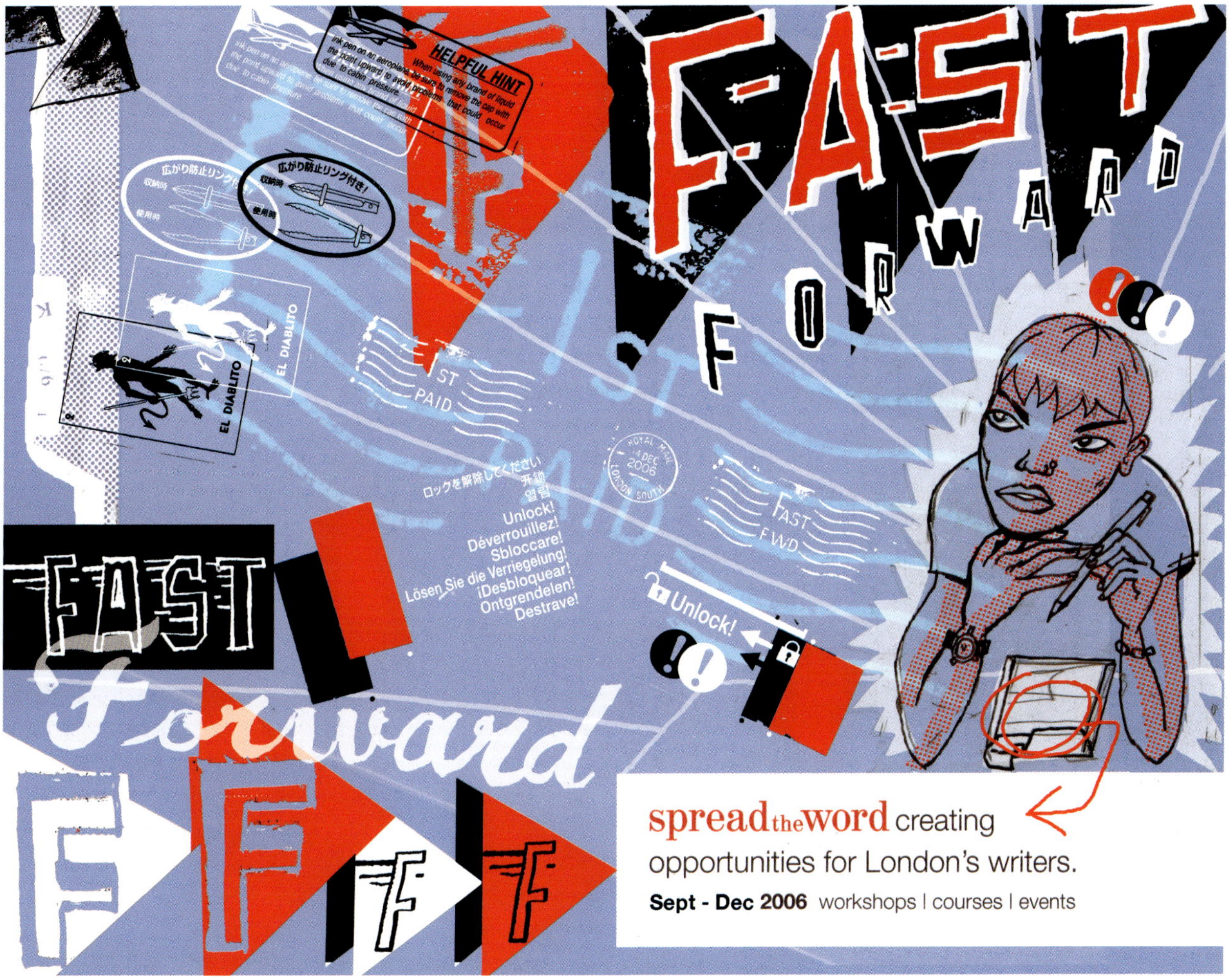

FAST FORWARD

HELPFUL HINT

Unlock!
Déverrouillez!
Sbloccare!
Lösen Sie die Verriegelung!
¡Desbloquear!
Ontgrendelen!
Destrave!

FAST Forward

spreadtheword creating opportunities for London's writers.

Sept - Dec 2006 workshops | courses | events

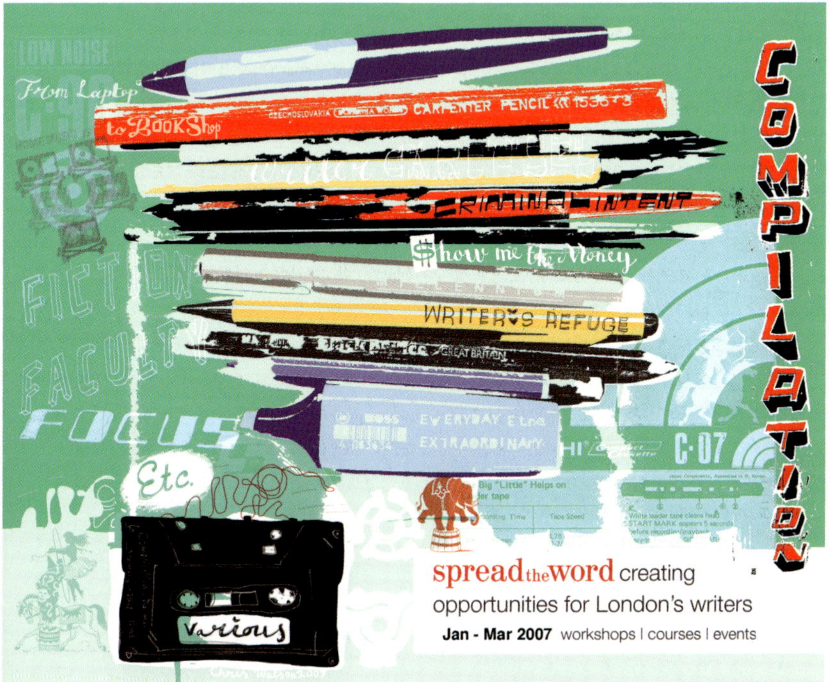

Two illustrations produced using clip art, collected, and found images by Chris Watson: Compilation (left) and Fast Forward (above).

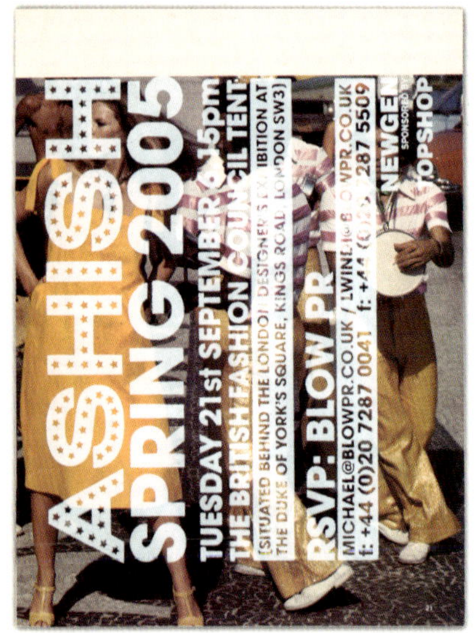

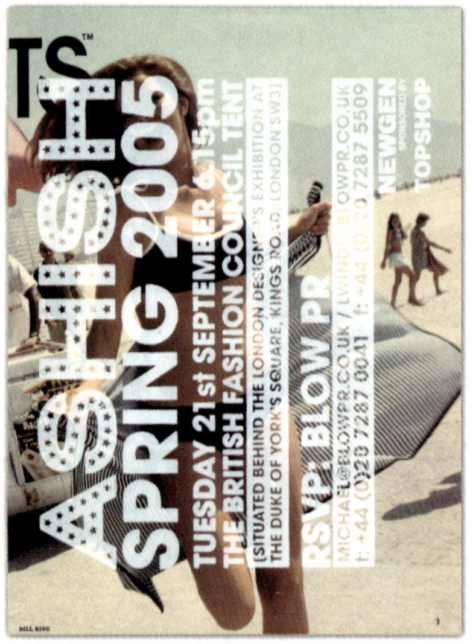

Byboth created designs for fashion designer Ashish for his London Fashion Week catwalk show. Each invitation was an original screenprint onto page torn out of 1970s fashion magazines and mail-order catalogs, says Byboth's Jay Hess.

"An artist's product is his reputation," says Sean Adams of AdamsMorioka. "Taking someone else's work and using it without permission in a way that was not originally intended can only harm the reputation of the creator. As creatives, we should recognize this and get all permissions and clearances possible."

But is it as simple as that? Not in a collage culture. Both sides of the debate ascribe value to content, but one is essentially interested in financial value, while the other says it is concerned with education and enlightenment (others like free content). Unlike the days of antiquity, today both sides are documenting the history of our times: the publishers and the self-publishers. Both sides have a point, however: if a great painting or photograph is owned by a nation state, or is so identifiable that it resides in the "public domain of the mind," then what right does a software company or news agency have to all of the income from its reproduction? The counterargument is because it has bought that right, and that the image may not have been in the public domain of the mind in the first place had it never been commercially printed and distributed. The issue becomes more complex, however, when we talk about sampling and collage.

Today an image can be shared from peer to peer worldwide with a click. There is no middleman, other than the vast corporations and the billionaire owners of YouTube, MySpace, and flickr: proof positive that, even in the infinite share-and-share-again world of the internet, a good idea is still worth vast amounts of money, especially one that facilitates unlicensed consumption (along with the voluntary sharing of creative work, social networking, and so on). It's free in the sense that people can use the services, but the concept is worth billions.

Photography and music have always been shared, and always will be because that is what they are for, but some of the counterarguments hold true there as well. Except that what few on the multinationals' side of the equation choose to acknowledge, is that filesharing drives and increases paid-for legitimate sales, while also allowing companies to resell, with zero packaging and distribution costs, material that had languished in their vaults for decades. Few renegotiate outmoded contract terms with those artists.

All this is relevant to design and illustration that uses clip art and found imagery because they are in the realm of derivative works, collages, and sampling. Says Tejaratchi: "Collage's reused elements may remain identifiable, or they may be transformed to varying degrees as they are incorporated into a new work, where they may join other fragments, all in a new context and forming a new whole. This becomes a new original, neither reminiscent of nor competing with any of the originals it may draw from. Direct referencing of something old within something new does not equal the generally accepted term of 'copying,' yet both whole-work copying and fragmentary appropriation in new work are still treated equally as theft in copyright law."

A derivative work is one that is not a counterfeit of another work, or passed off as the original (intellectual property), but one that has sampled it in order to create something new. Whether the sample, found image, or art clip, is the root of the work, or merely an element of it, is the core of the problem. Should the sampled artist be paid, even if the original work is unidentifiable and subsumed into a newly created piece? If the sample has been well disguised, does that make it better than a poorly reworked one?

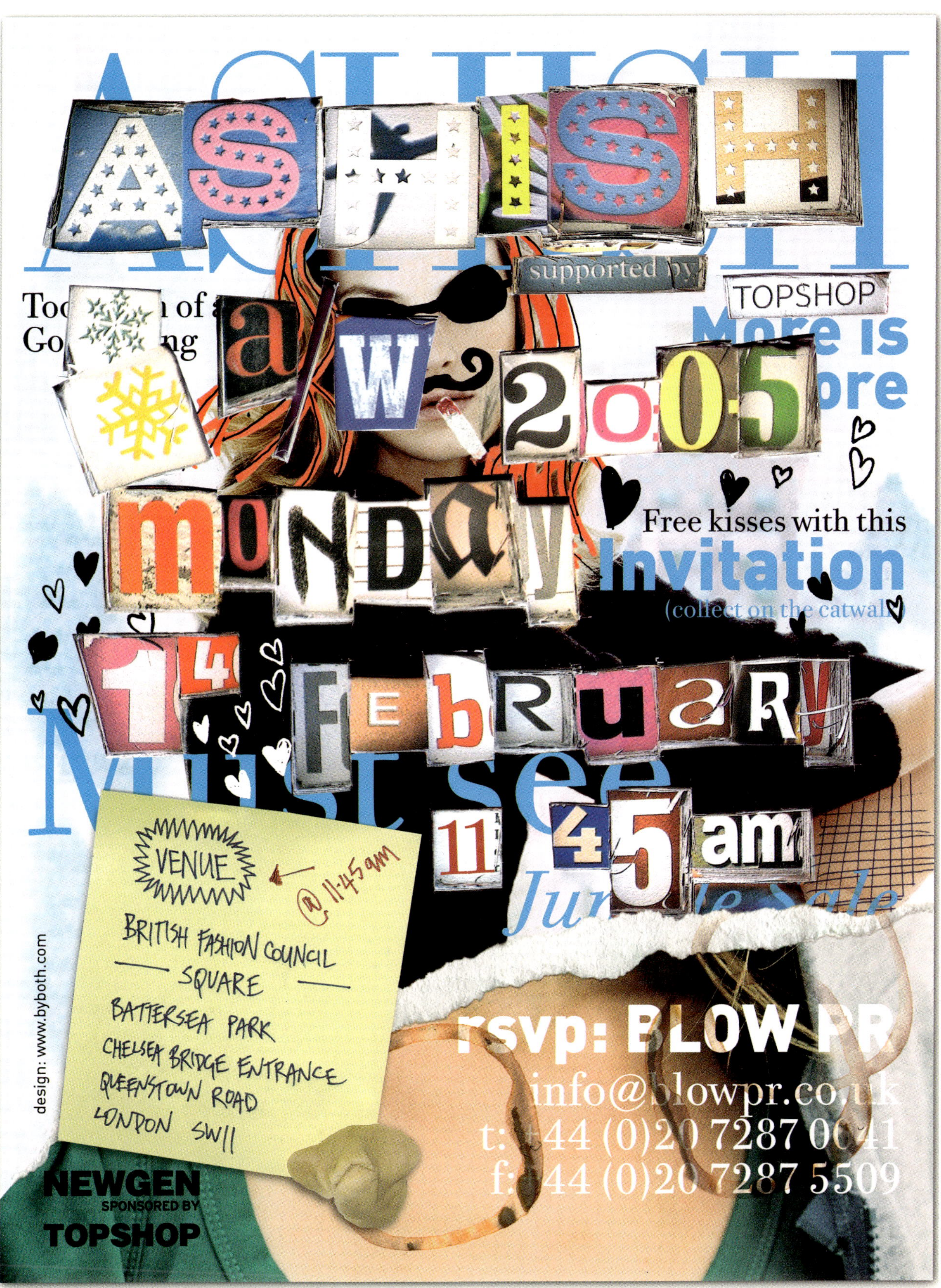
ASHISH
supported by
TOPSHOP
a/w 2005
monday
14 February
11 45 am
More is more
Free kisses with this
Invitation
(collect on the catwalk)
Must see
VENUE
@ 11.45 am
BRITISH FASHION COUNCIL
SQUARE
BATTERSEA PARK
CHELSEA BRIDGE ENTRANCE
QUEENSTOWN ROAD
LONDON SW11
rsvp: BLOW PR
info@blowpr.co.uk
t: +44 (0)20 7287 0041
f: +44 (0)20 7287 5509
NEWGEN
SPONSORED BY
TOPSHOP
design: www.byboth.com

Sampling, remixing, and the law

In a working example of cultural appropriation, some of Tejaratchi's opinions have been sourced from his multimedia publication for music collective Negativland, entitled "Negativland: No Business," which explores the concept of fair use and derivative works. For more about the project, and Negativland themselves, visit negativland.com. For their own part, Negativland describe "No Business" as being "all about stealing music, filesharing, the supposed collapse of the music industry, and a nice piece of pie. Taking famous and not so famous music from the whole array of show business, Negativland recompose it all to make a project of thoroughly unoriginal music and dialogue they hope to copyright themselves." To test the limits of their theories, we have freely sampled one or two of the textual elements here.

"When collage uses existing works, the result is what some copyright scholars call a derivative work. The collage has a copyright separate from any copyrights pertaining to the original incorporated works. Due to redefined and reinterpreted copyright laws, and increased financial interests, some forms of collage art are significantly restricted.

"The copyright status of visual works is less troubled, although still ambiguous. For instance, some visual collage artists have argued that the first-sale doctrine protects their work. The first-sale doctrine prevents copyright holders from controlling consumptive uses after the 'first sale' of their work. The de minimis doctrine and the fair use exception also provide important defenses against claimed copyright infringement. The Second Circuit [US] in October, 2006, held that artist Jeff Koons was not liable for copyright infringement because his incorporation of a photograph into a collage painting was fair use."

The above two paragraphs are from Wikipedia, and I have cut and pasted them into this document. I am, however, not claiming them as my own work; their appearance here is fair use of someone else's material, with an acknowledgment. That said, it is material that has been posted there free for the world to share. I might not have acknowledged the source and simply rewritten it, in which case, at what point would the text have become "mine?"

"All claims that collage is simply out to resell its sources are absurd," says Tejaratchi. "Anyone familiar with actual examples of collage understands that the internal snippets present within a work in no way duplicate or compete with the appeal of those original sources in their entirety. This fragmentary selecting and combining

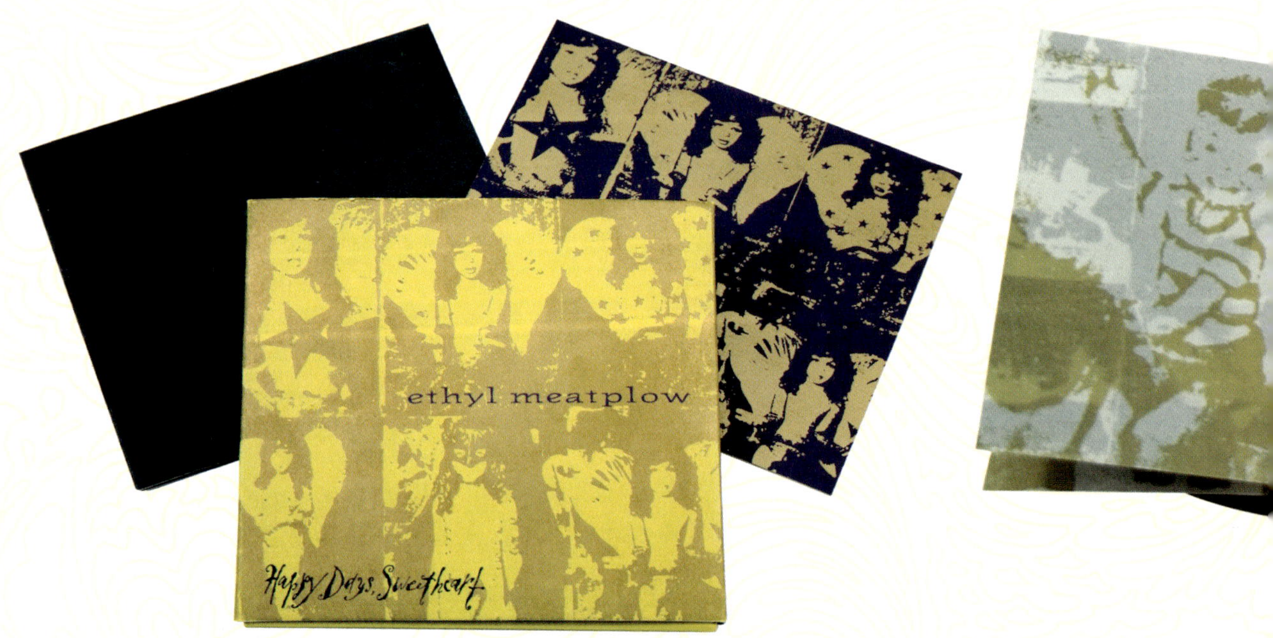

(which creates an entirely new effect) puts the references in a new context. It may even be partially dependent on the recognition of that fragment as part of the expression."

The solution, says Tejaratchi, is a straightforward redefinition of copyright law to accept the principal of free fair use for most forms of collage, or sampling that recontextualizes the sample. "If the work is judged to significantly fragment, transform, rearrange, or recompose the appropriated [sampled] material within a new work, then it should be automatically seen as a valid fair use—an original attempt at a valid new creative work."

"The connections between collage in illustration and design, and sampling in music are manifold," says Neal Ashby. "Music is becoming more of a collage stylistically, and design is becoming more lyrical. There is a nice reciprocity that is happening between the two art forms."

To a degree it is about acknowledging sources and knowing "where we have come from." Today's designers and illustrators need to know what is going on in art today as well as what has happened in the past, in the broader (or longer) history of art.

David Donohoe of Studiomime is well placed to explore the connection: "As it happens I am also a recording musician and do use sampled sound in my work. There is obviously a similar process at work in the reappropriation of artifacts toward an end product, be that a design or a piece of music. There is a huge amount of crossed thought, emotion, and intention for me in media in general. I am often struck by just how similar my work processes are regardless of which media I am working in."

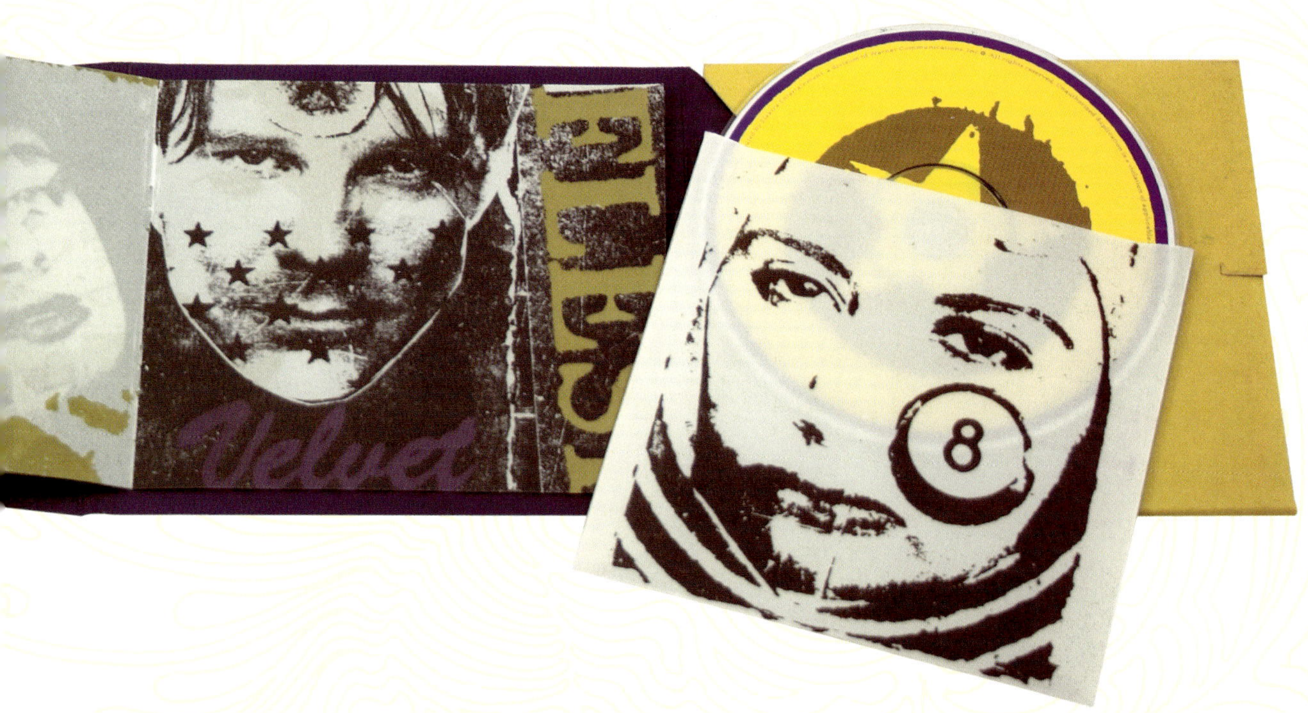

Creative Commons

In a culture of share and share alike, the legal system surrounding copyright protection is perhaps two decades behind content usage models, and moves slowly and in local markets (as opposed to the global reach of the net).

➡ Creative Commons' licenses are hugely popular with many designers, illustrators, photographers, videomakers, writers, and musicians, and can cover just about any licensing scenario in both local territories or worldwide. However, some online portals through which digital content can be accessed, downloaded, or legally purchased do not know how to handle the licenses, or overwrite their own contractual or intellectual property terms, meaning that the creator's stated licensing preferences are effectively disregarded by the site's owners. This has yet to be tested in law. Despite this, Creative Commons licenses are becoming the lingua franca of the legal filesharing community and many creative self-publishers. By consuming content released and protected under Creative Commons terms, users agree to the creator's licensing restrictions, which may allow them to use the content free, but not to produce derivative works, for example.

www.creativecommons.org

Put another way, the internet, and the ways in which many designers, illustrators, researchers, students, musicians, and writers use it, threatens "old economy" concepts of content ownership and licensing to the extent that many copyright owners—including the big businesses that own image banks such as Getty and Corbis—have often sought to impose restrictions on the way content can be used and shared that have simply never existed before. Meanwhile, the impetus behind the way the public uses and wants to use the internet is manifestly about sharing, copying, and self-publishing, and not locking up content in proprietary boxes with "do not use" stamped all over them.

The problem is a deep one and full of built-in tensions and contradictions, because in an information economy, rights ownership is akin to land ownership or oil reserves, and yet everyone wants to roam on the land for free and share the free flow of that oil.

It was inevitable, then, that the internet would throw up an alternative licensing framework, developed and maintained by artists and other creative people. Creative Commons is an organization that aims to create a layer of "reasonable copyright" within licenses under the principle that "some rights are reserved." Creative Commons aims to encourage the sharing of different types of material, including artworks, photography, and illustrations, together with music, scholarship, literature, coursework, and even recorded speech, but within reasonable licensing restrictions that do not neglect the creator of the work.

In other words, content creators—such as photographers, illustrators, and designers—can elect to release their content under Creative Commons licenses, which have become a lingua franca of the connected, online world—a community that is inherently resistant to what they see as legal or technical barriers to sharing, such as digital rights management (DRM) schemes.

In this way, the organization forms a philosophical bridge between the opposing forces of the proprietary copyright industries and the "copyleft" community, which believes that the notion of intellectual property has no place in an online world.

The organzation says, "We use private rights to create public goods: creative works set free for certain uses. Like the free software and open-source movements, our ends are cooperative and community-minded, but our means are voluntary and libertarian. We work to offer creators a best-of-both-worlds way to protect their works while encouraging certain uses of them—to declare 'some rights reserved.'"

Creative Commons says that it hopes to "build upon and complement the work of others who have created public licenses for a variety of creative works. Our aim is not only to increase the sum of raw source material online, but also to make access to that material cheaper and easier."

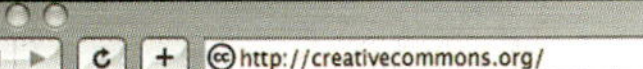
Creative Commons

http://creativecommons.org/ 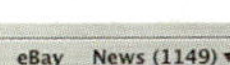

Auto Trader UK eBay UK Google UK2.NET Friday-Ad Router Admin Apple .Mac eBay News (1149) Apple (179) yousendit.com

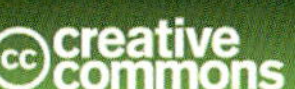

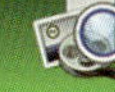 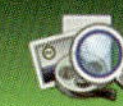 Find CC Licensed Work

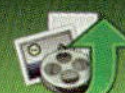 License Your Work

Search Site | Worldwide Select a jurisdiction

Share, reuse, and remix — legally.

Creative Commons provides free tools that let authors, scientists, artists, and educators easily mark their creative work with the freedoms they want it to carry. You can use CC to change your copyright terms from "All Rights Reserved" to "Some Rights Reserved."

We're a nonprofit organization. Everything we do — including the software we create — is free.

Learn More Support CC

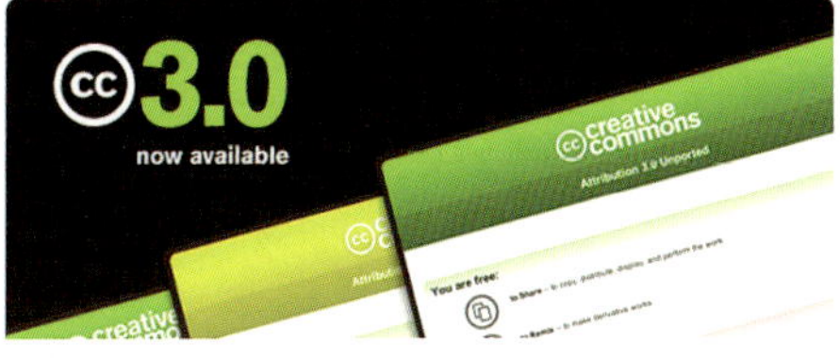

Featured Projects

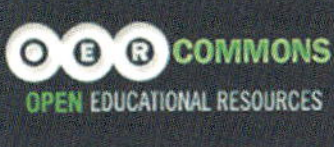

OER Commons

OER Commons provides open educational resources for teaching and learning that are freely available on-line for everyone to use, whether you are an instructor, student, or self-learner. OER Commons uses Web 2.0 features such as tags, ratings, comments, reviews, and social networking in order to create an on-line experience that engages educators in sharing their best teaching and learning practices. OER Commons is a project of ISKME, and it encourages users to use any Creative Commons license except No Derivatives.

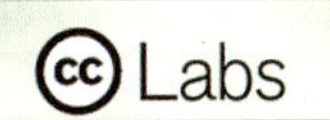

Home
Weblog
About
FAQ
Contact
Press Kit
Policies
Privacy
Sitemap

Explore
Audio
Video
Images
Text
Education
Software

The Commons
Science Commons
iCommons
ccInternational

Latest News

Job: Administrative Assistant

Mike Linksvayer, April 9th, 2007

Creative Commons has an opening for a full time administrative assistant in its San Francisco office. See the job description and how to apply.

Also see our other openings.

Vote: NetSquared Innovation Awards

Mike Linksvayer, April 9th, 2007

Voting for the NetSqaured Innovation Awards, previously blogged here, runs today through April 14.

You must register and vote for five to ten social enterprises. Twenty winners will receive expenses for two staff members to attend N2Y2 and participate in the NetSquared Technology Innovation Fund.

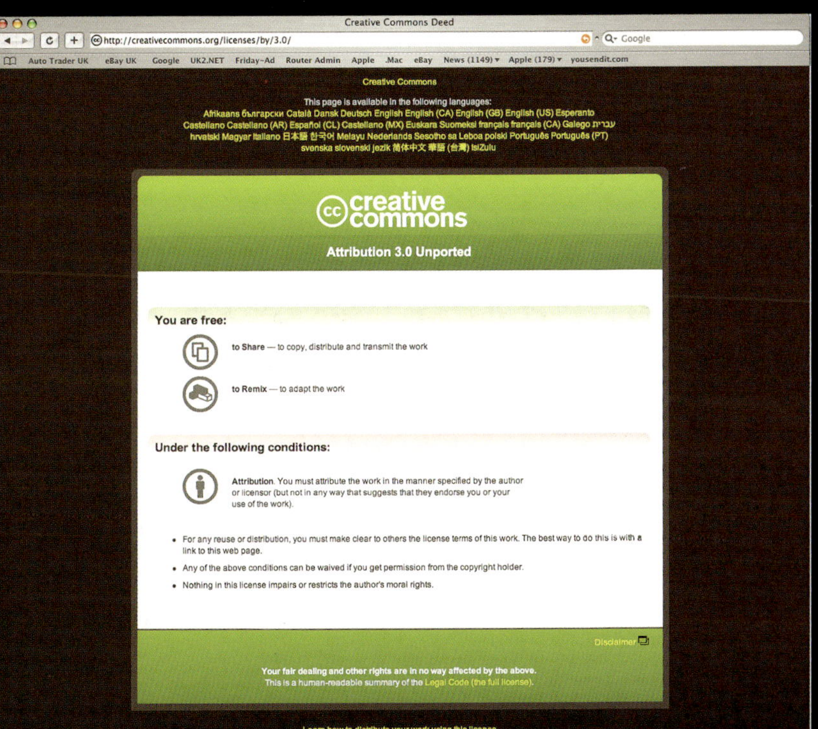

➡ MySpace has become a publishing phenomenon, with tens of millions of unknowns and wannabes rubbing shoulders with famous names.

➡ Video-sharing site YouTube is perhaps the most important news hub in the world, as videos can be posted as soon as an event happens without restrictions. However, only a tiny proportion of content hosted on the site is original, and much of it is there illegally, or without the permission of the originator. That said, the tens of thousands of viewers of some of the videos could be argued to be keeping many a career alive, and bringing new consumers to old content, reenergizing markets without any financial outlay for the original publisher.

⬇ flickr, the photo and image sharing portal has redefined the concept of the image bank, making millions of tagged images available free under Creative Commons licenses, and throwing down a gauntlet to major commercial portals, such as Getty Images and Corbis. Now anyone can be a professional image-maker simply by sharing their work.

To this end, the organization has developed metadata (data about data, more commonly known on sites such as flickr and YouTube as tags) similar to the rights descriptions used within many copy protection schemes, which can be used to associate creative works with the license to use it in a machine-readable manner.

Creative Commons adds, "We hope this will enable people to use our search application and other online applications to find, for example, photographs that are free to use provided that the original photographer is credited, or songs that may be copied, distributed, or sampled with no restrictions whatsoever. We hope that the ease of use fostered by machine-readable licenses will further reduce barriers to creativity."

Among the 11 different types of license that can be associated with content for online or other forms of digital distribution are:

— **Attribution:** *where a creator's content is available for use as long as the creator is credited*

— **Non-Commercial:** *where content is freely available as long as any work based on it is not produced for commercial gain*

— **No Derivative Works:** *where a creator's work is freely available in its existing form only and is not permitted to be used in derivative works*

— **Share Alike:** *where derivative works based on licensed content have to be distributed under an identical license*

Graphic designers and illustrators—together with art editors, creative editors, musicians, and so on—can actively search for Creative Commons licensed work through the organization's website, and be directed to sites such as flickr, MySpace, and YouTube from where they can download the content and use it within the terms of the above licenses. These rights can be global or local, and can give designers and illustrators the voluntary means to use clip art, images, photographs, and so on legally, as long as the creators of the work are acknowledged.

Many of the works featured in this book feature elements sourced through Creative Commons searches and licenses.

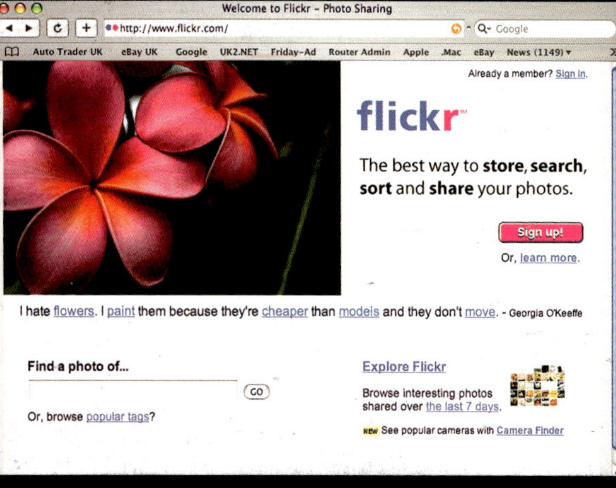

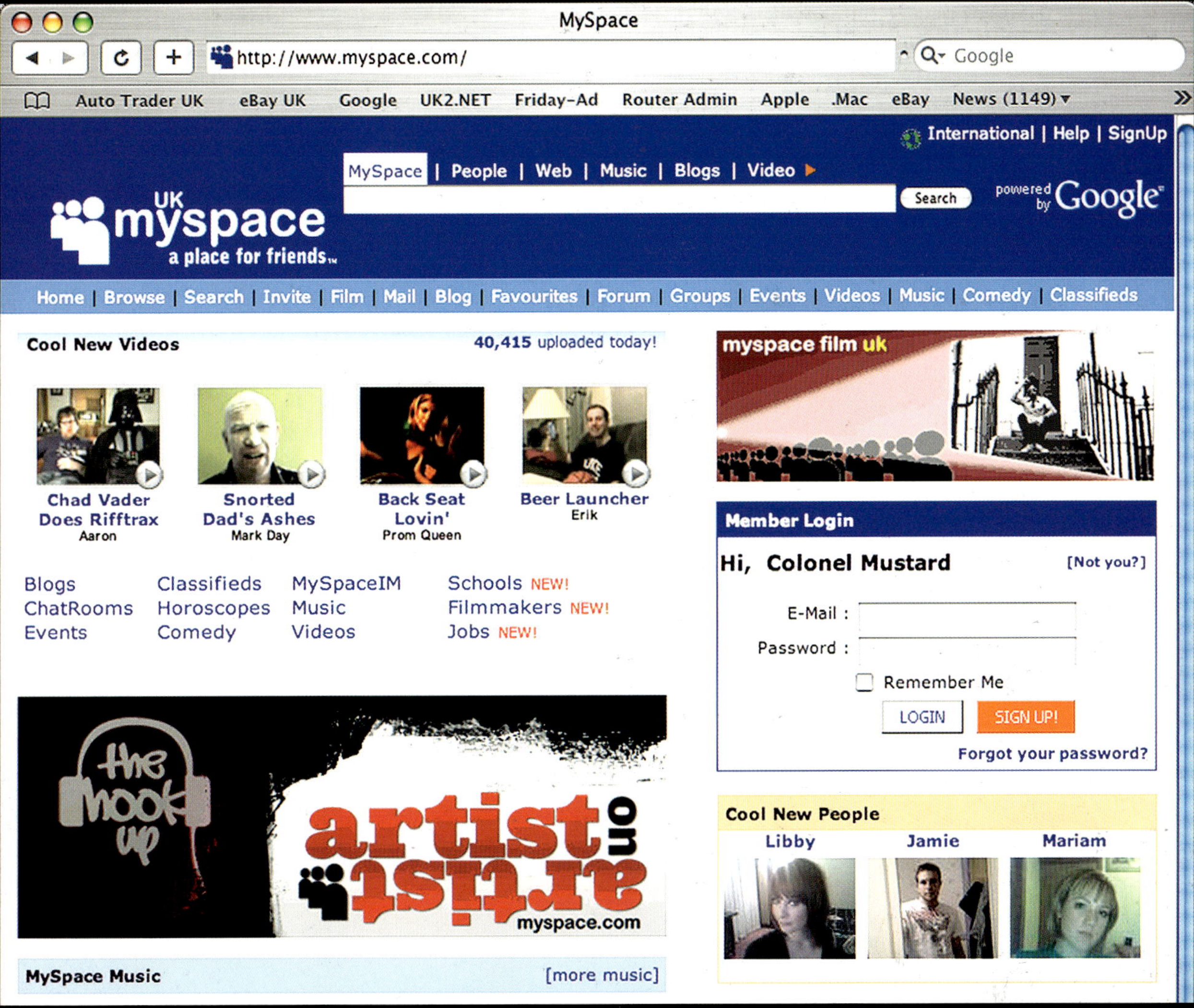

MySpace
http://www.myspace.com/
Auto Trader UK eBay UK Google UK2.NET Friday-Ad Router Admin Apple .Mac eBay News (1149)
International | Help | SignUp
MySpace | People | Web | Music | Blogs | Video
Search
powered by Google
UK myspace a place for friends
Home | Browse | Search | Invite | Film | Mail | Blog | Favourites | Forum | Groups | Events | Videos | Music | Comedy | Classifieds

Cool New Videos 40,415 uploaded today!
Chad Vader Does Rifftrax — Aaron
Snorted Dad's Ashes — Mark Day
Back Seat Lovin' — Prom Queen
Beer Launcher — Erik

Blogs ChatRooms Events
Classifieds Horoscopes Comedy
MySpaceIM Music Videos
Schools NEW! Filmmakers NEW! Jobs NEW!

the hook up
artist on artist
myspace.com

MySpace Music [more music]

myspace film uk

Member Login
Hi, Colonel Mustard [Not you?]
E-Mail :
Password :
Remember Me
LOGIN SIGN UP!
Forgot your password?

Cool New People
Libby Jamie Mariam

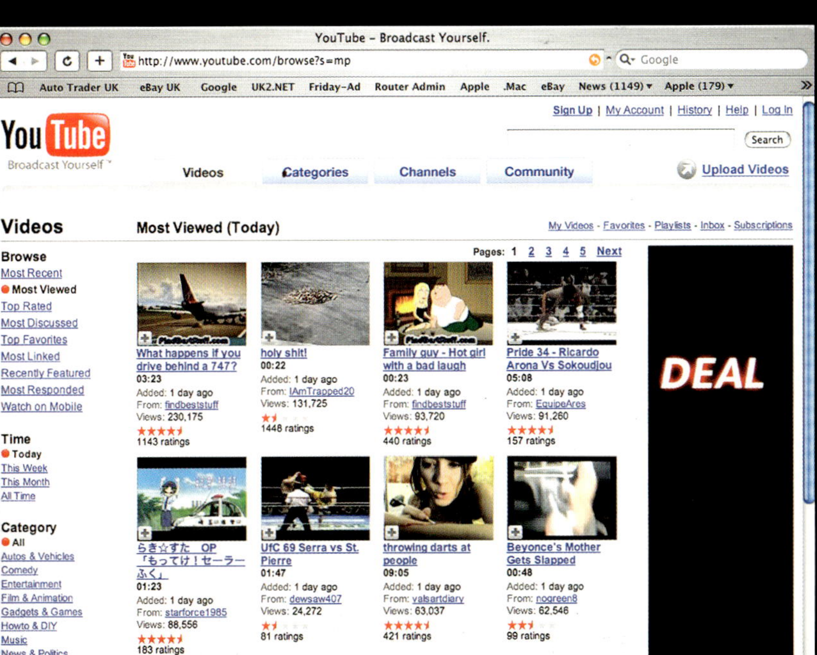

Digital cameras

The wide availability, ease of connection, and low cost of usage of digital cameras has made them matchless image gatherers for professional designers and amateurs alike, especially since cameras' inclusion in cellphones and other devices. Here are tips for using your camera to make and share your own clip-art resources.

Create your own clip-art archive

With cellphone manufacturers now the biggest camera manufacturers in the world, the digital camera truly is everywhere, from the high-end SLR or medium-format camera with a digital back, to the compact, point-and-shoot, to the ever-burgeoning megapixel count of the average cellphone.

In many ways this is another golden age of photography, and it is a boon for designers and illustrators. However, the real bonus for image-makers seeking to build up clip archives of their own to sample, cut, paste, remix, and recontextualize in their work, is the fantastic opportunity to get creative.

SELECTING OBJECTS TO SHOOT

— *Many illustrators and designers like to use silhouettes, strong shapes, and lines in their work. Try shooting both complex objects and natural forms—bicycles, trees, plants, tools, and decorative objects—as well as subjects with perhaps simpler lines—animals, people, buildings, etc.—in order to build up a useful library of source imagery that you can recontextualize.*

— *Shoot against neutral or non-detailed backgrounds, so that the object can be better isolated and cut out later on in Photoshop.*

— *Make sure you shoot images at a high enough resolution to ensure crisp lines in the source image. This is particularly true if you are shooting on cellphones, where motion blur is far more of an issue than on many other types of camera.*

— *Shoot a library of natural textures—leaves, petals, bark, rocks, wood grain, waves, sand, grass, etc. Use these as background textures or details within your work.*

— *Also shoot man-made surfaces and forms—concrete, bricks and building materials, textured glass, metallic surfaces, plastics, rope, along with man-made surfaces that have been weathered by nature.*

— *Shoot letters, typefaces, and symbols, for example, newspapers, magazines, and promotional material. These may prove to be a treasure trove of image clips for your later work.*

— *Shoot signs and posters, especially when traveling abroad, to get a truly global library of letterforms and designs.*

— *Remember: compact cameras with long digital (rather than optical) zooms can create clarity issues when zooming in on distant objects.*

— *Also be careful when shooting objects close up, that lens distortion does not occur.*

➡ Just a handful of examples of the many things you can shoot to build up your own digital image archive.

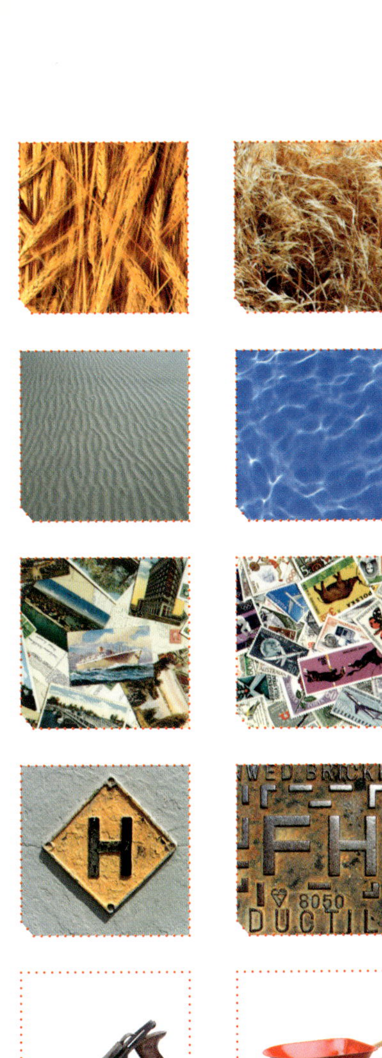
H
FH
8050
DUCTILE
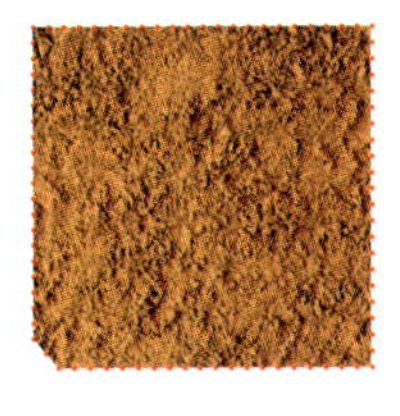
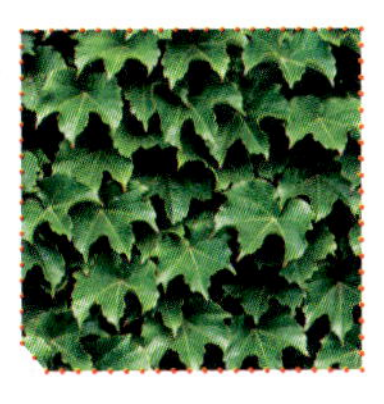
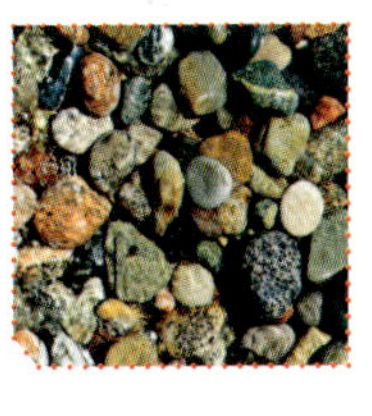
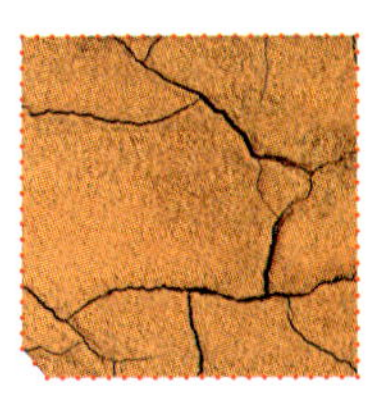
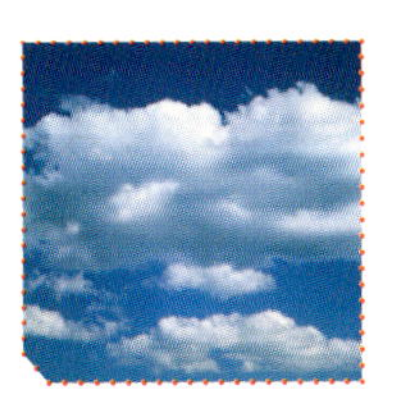
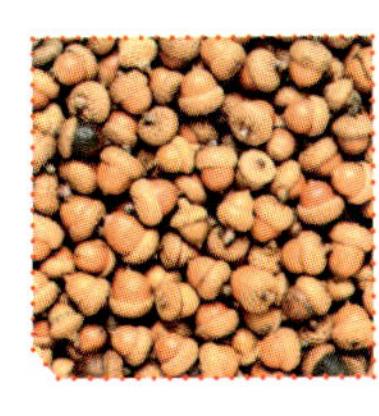
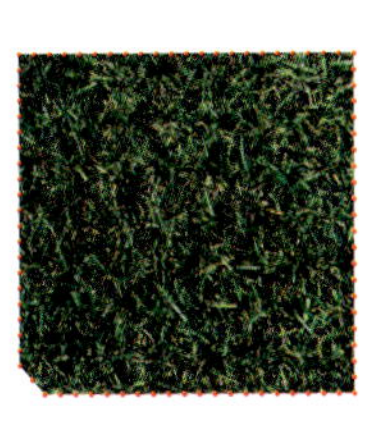
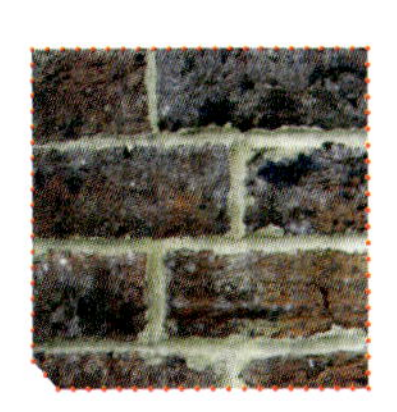
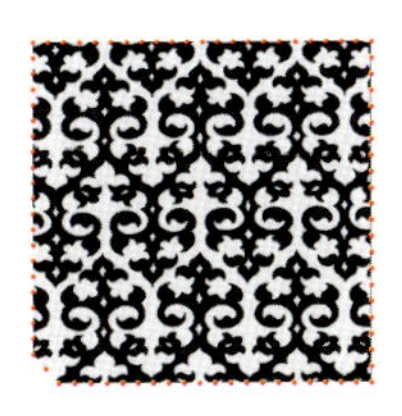

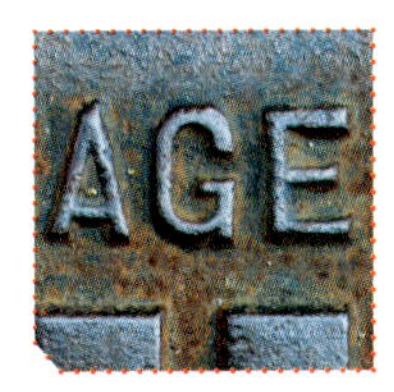
AGE
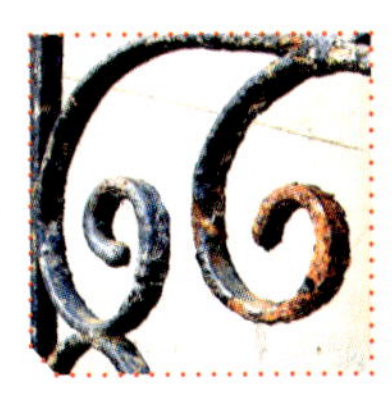
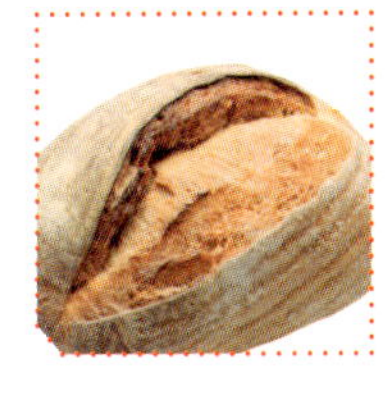
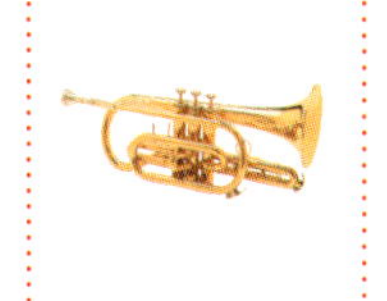
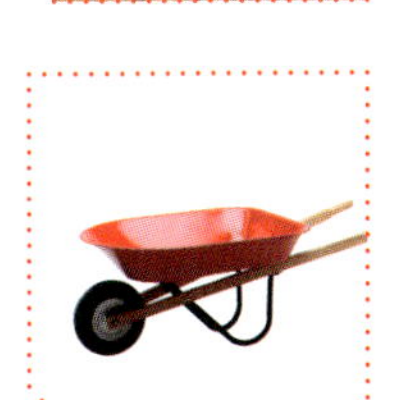
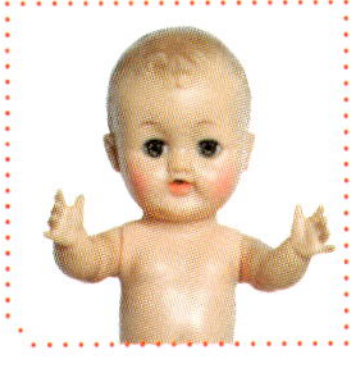
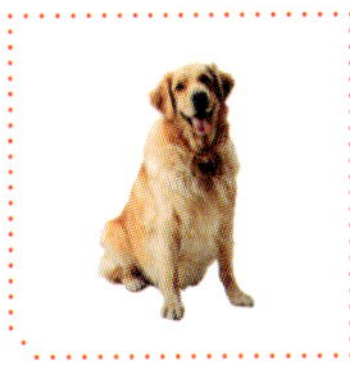

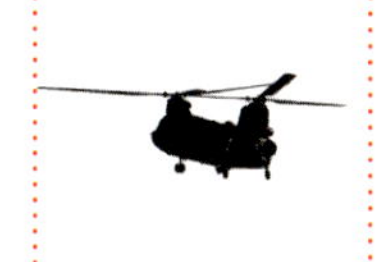
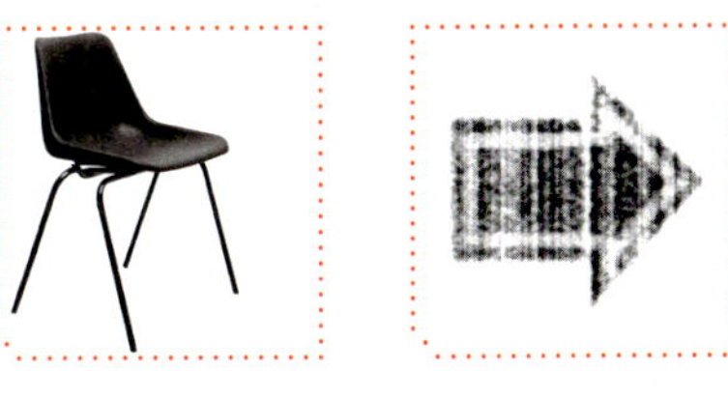
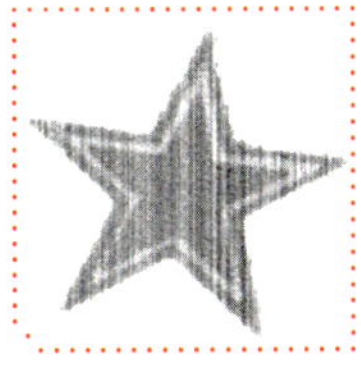
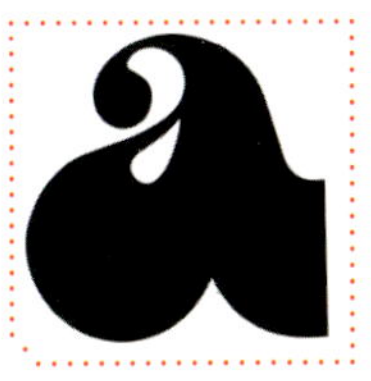
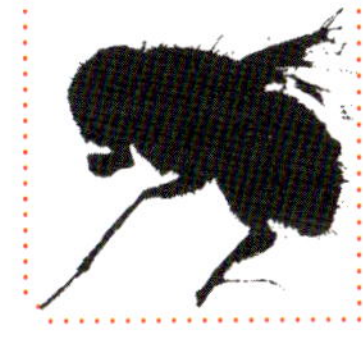
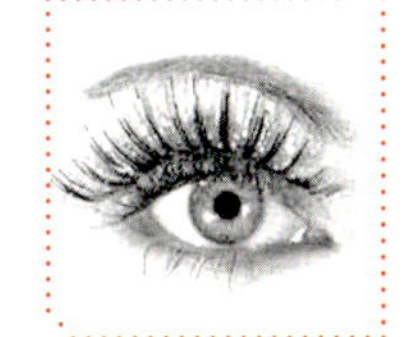
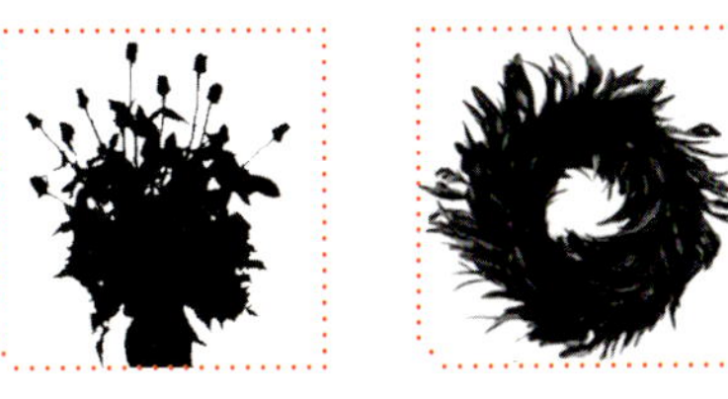
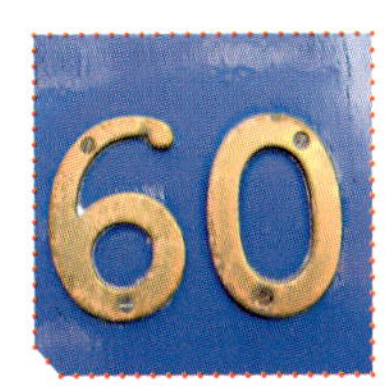
60
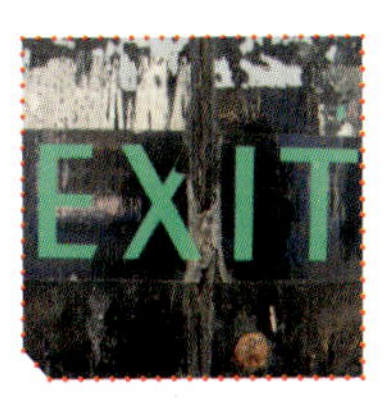
EXIT

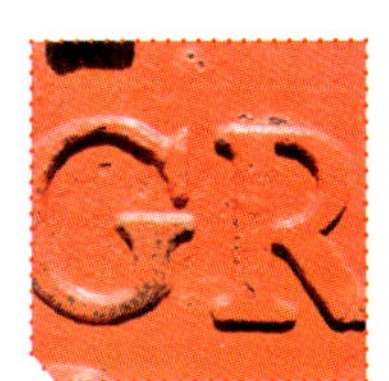
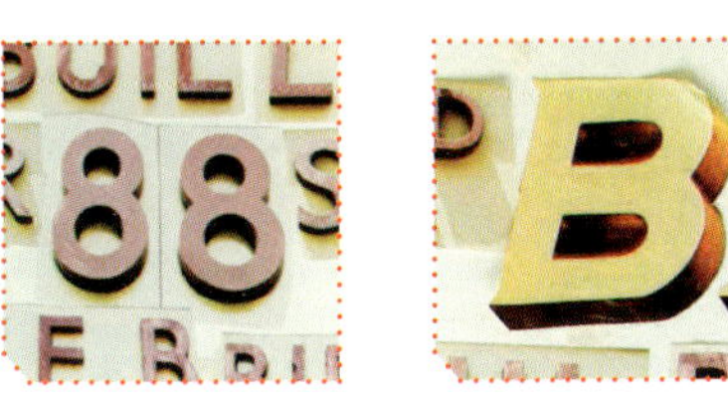
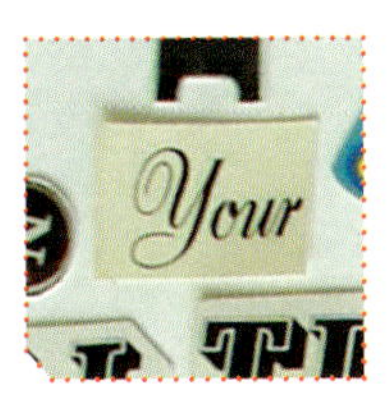
Your
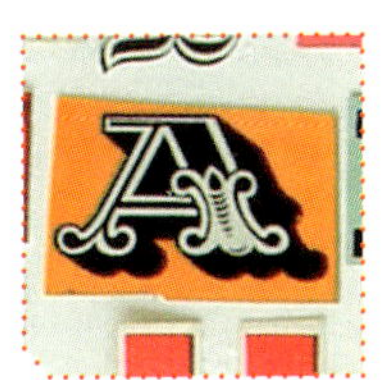

22
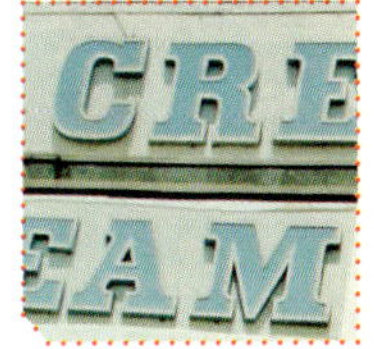

Nondigital techniques

Most designs and illustrations that make use of multiple sources and then recontextualize the parts are essentially a form of collage (from the French coller, to stick). This is a method of creation that is as much about assemblage and having a good eye for source material and its malleability and usefulness, as it is about origination.

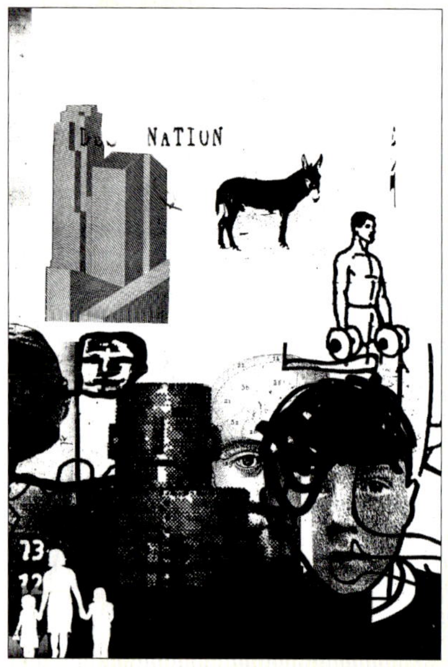

⬆ Alex Williamson uses clip art from all manner of sources, combined with technologies old and new to create work that here comments on the media used to create it, and the millions of images competing for our attention every day.

➡ Russell Warren Fisher scoured junk shops and markets for source images and clips for a retrospective look at the career of theater group Theatre du Complicité, mapping their journey in the performing arts from their earliest days with ephemera (top left). Images from Fisher's sketchbooks and from old manuscripts were used in the brochure designs for the Tiggy Twilight store (top right and below).

However, it is also about making something new, but in this case from found materials, textures, other materials, newspaper clippings, ribbons, portions of other artwork, photographs, and so on.

Many of today's designers and illustrators have returned to this more plastic and manual technique as a means of differentiating themselves from their digital-only peers, or because it is more satisfying. Meanwhile others mix and match their media to create work that is truly unique: assembling collages by hand and then scanning them, and combining them with digital elements, or tweaking the overall levels of the assembled work in Photoshop.

John Finnell of Corridors of My Mind is one designer who has crossed over, as it were, from the wholly digital to the more manual techniques of physical collage. "I used to only work digitally," he says. "But lately I've found collage to be my favorite medium. I have been meaning to play around with silkscreen for T-shirts and posters with a friend of mine. I'm planning on working with this medium very soon. I would also love to do sculpture work with found objects and other material, in the future. For now, it's mainly collage and photography, and every now and then I get back to some digital stuff. Although, having the digital knowledge is a super useful tool."

Collage made from photographs, or photographic elements, is more commonly known as photomontage—both the process and result of creating a composite image by cutting and joining a number of other photographs. Of course, the principal is central to working in Photoshop too, which layers image upon image and then flattens them to produce a single composite.

However, many professionals still make use of manual photomontage and collage techniques, sometimes also distressing the image physically, and adding in new elements and materials on overlays to get a sense of how the light strikes it, and how it interacts with the real world. Creators such as Alex Williamson, Martin O'Neill, and David Newton are in this category, although they may resort to digital techniques later on in the process.

Designer Russell Warren Fisher developed some designs for theater group Theatre du Complicité and explains that he "scoured junks shops, antique markets, ephemera, found objects, and his personal sketchbooks for the designs that explored the history of the group and celebrated their journey as a theater company."

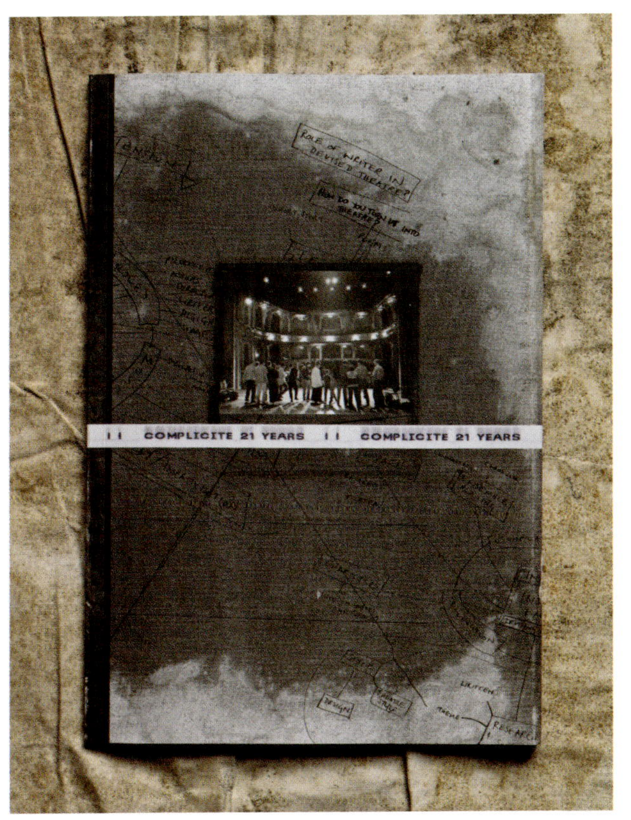
COMPLICITE 21 YEARS
COMPLICITE 21 YEARS

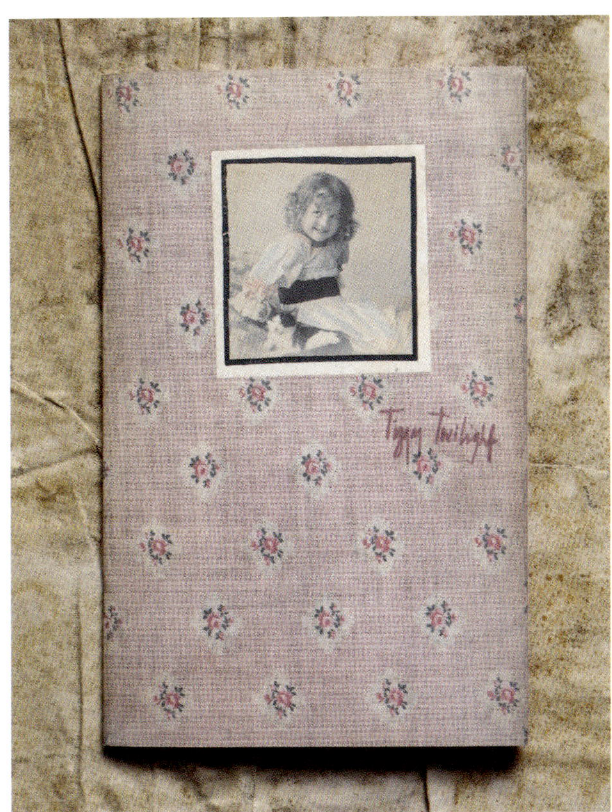
Tiggy Twilight

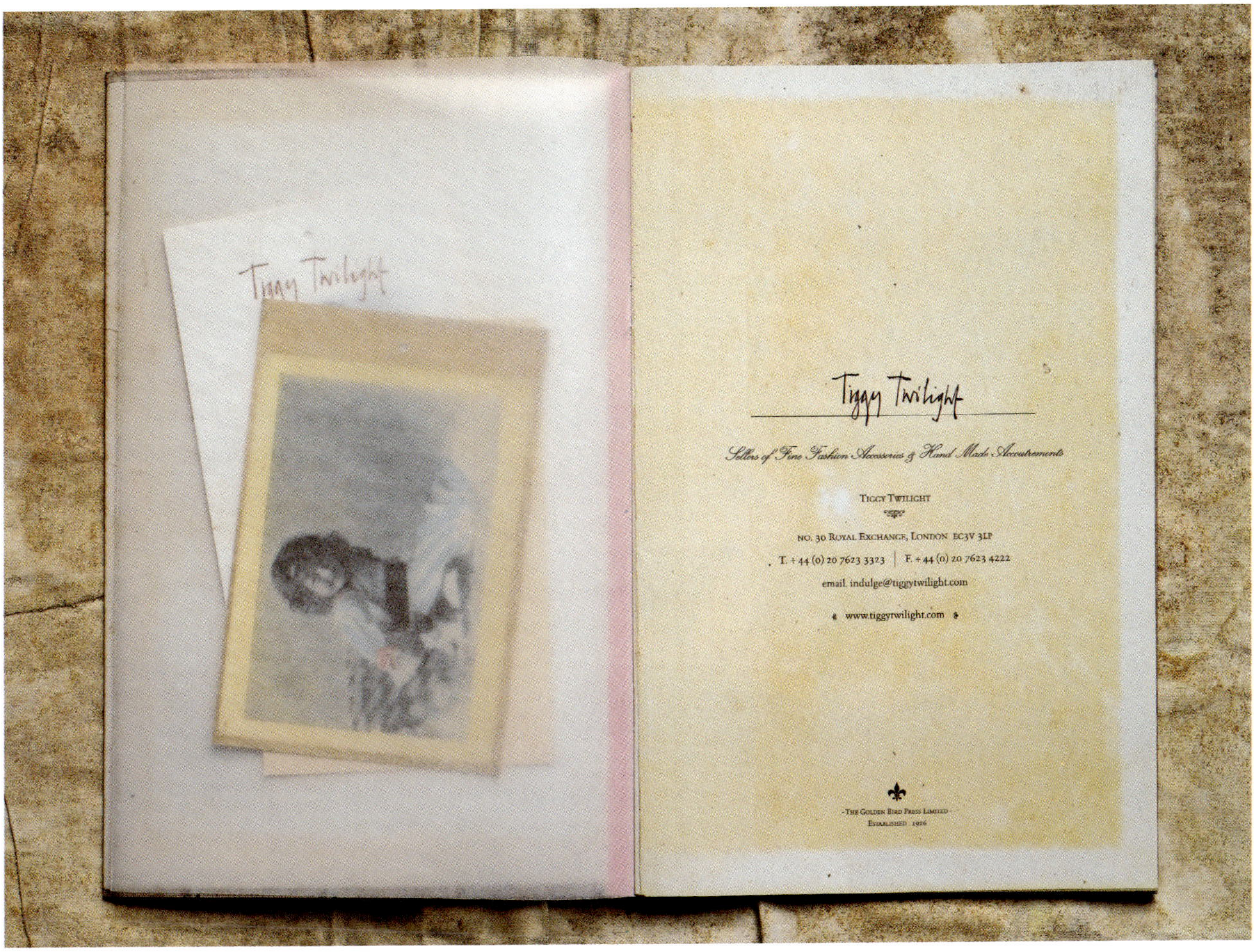

Tiggy Twilight
Tiggy Twilight
Sellers of Fine Fashion Accessories & Hand Made Accoutrements
TIGGY TWILIGHT
NO. 30 ROYAL EXCHANGE, LONDON EC3V 3LP
T. +44 (0) 20 7623 3323 | F. +44 (0) 20 7623 4222
email. indulge@tiggytwilight.com
www.tiggytwilight.com
THE GOLDEN BIRD PRESS LIMITED
ESTABLISHED 1926

IMAGES USED

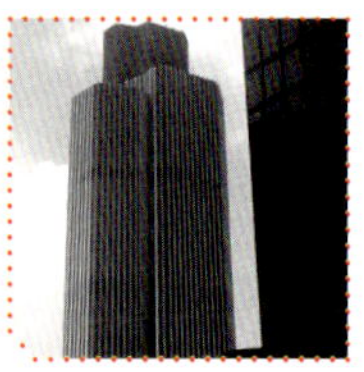
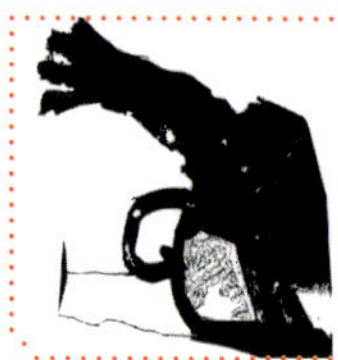
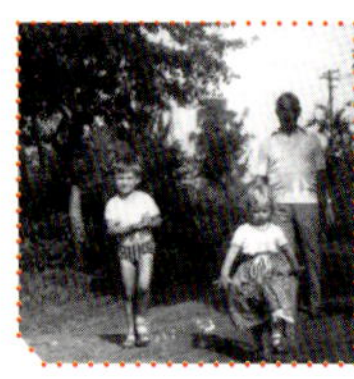
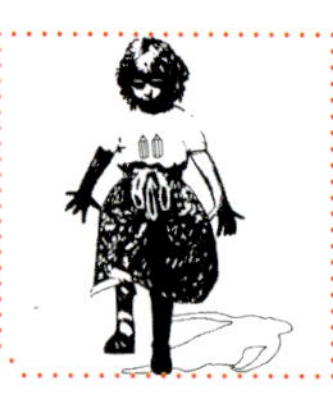
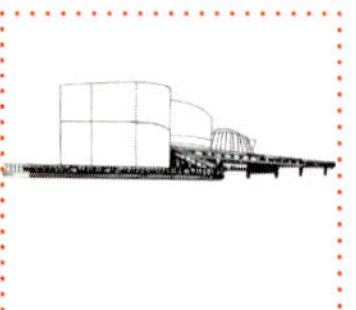
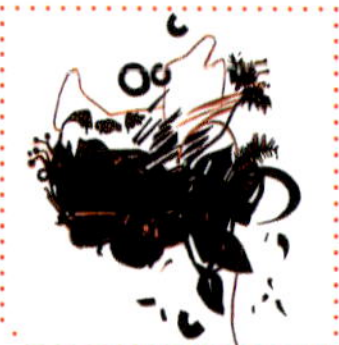
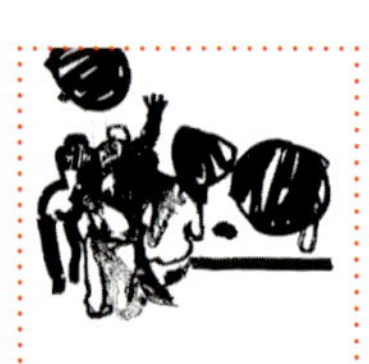

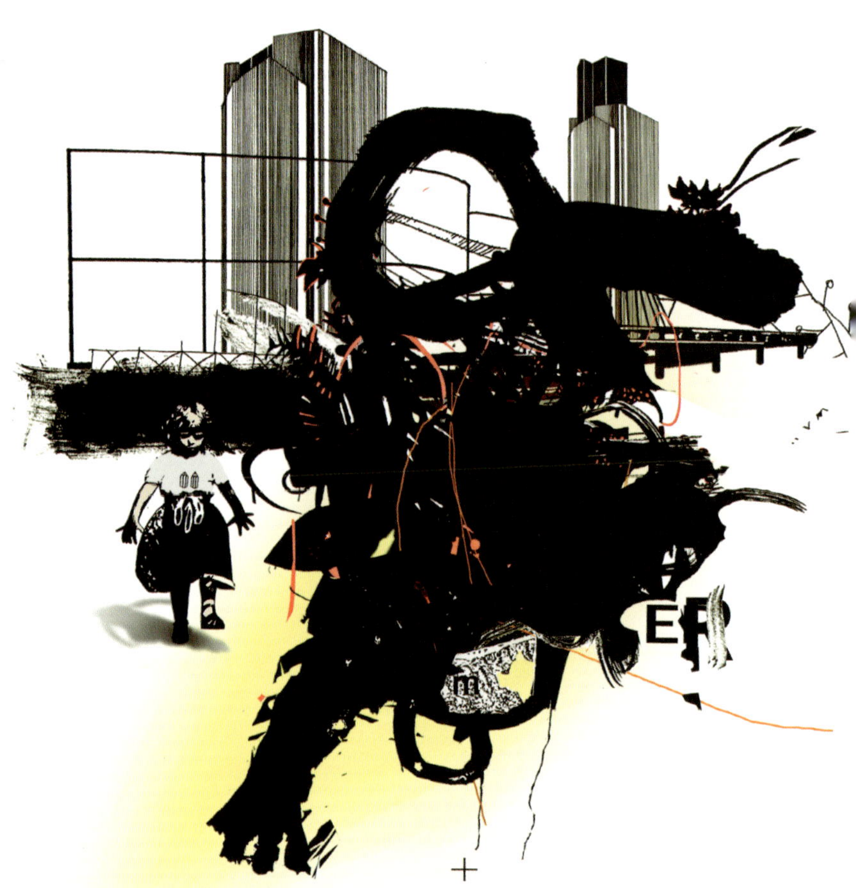

⬆ CityAbyss produced this lifestyle study of urban space from clip art and stock photography, including linocut prints. Photographic elements were redrawn by hand.

➡ A limited-edition print from the *Catalog* research project by Martin O'Neill entitled She Paid With Her Life. This collection was inspired by 1950s true crime magazines.

For others, it is an option, rather than the alpha and omega, or a Canut-style stance against the digital wave. Says Sean Tan of Archizen Creative, "Sometimes I might need to shoot my own images to get the right elements. For example, in a recent job my idea was to create something with very abstract movement, so I tried to pour a kind of liquid into a glass of water and let it spread and take photo after photo of the movement of it. Then merge that digitally into the artwork. So it really depends on what the final result is intended to be."

StudioMime's David Donohoe concludes: "I mainly work digitally in the assembling of my ideas into a final piece of work, but the constituent parts of the work will often come from many different sources; photographs, scans, video, drawings, sketchbooks, craft, artifacts, and so on."

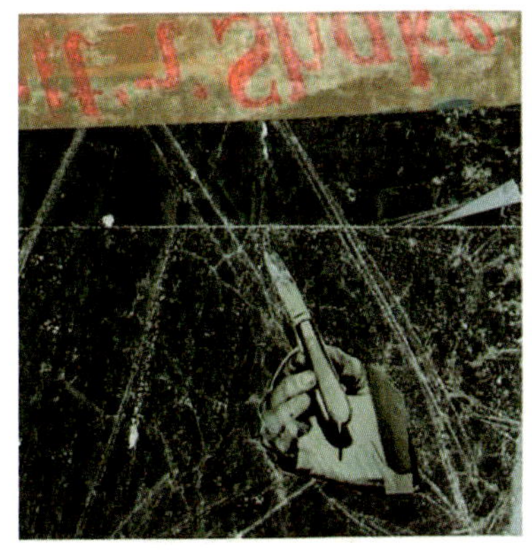
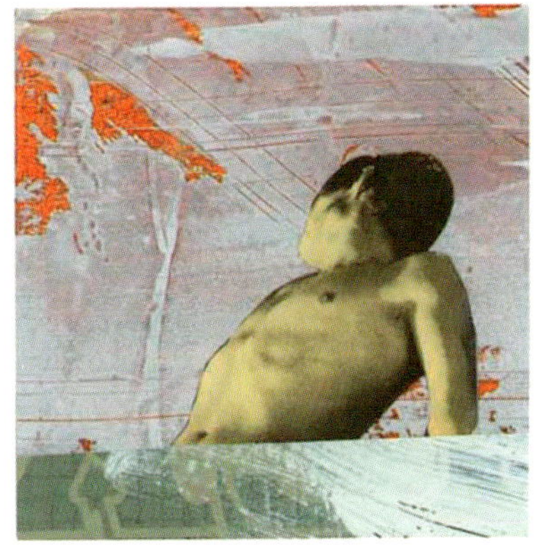
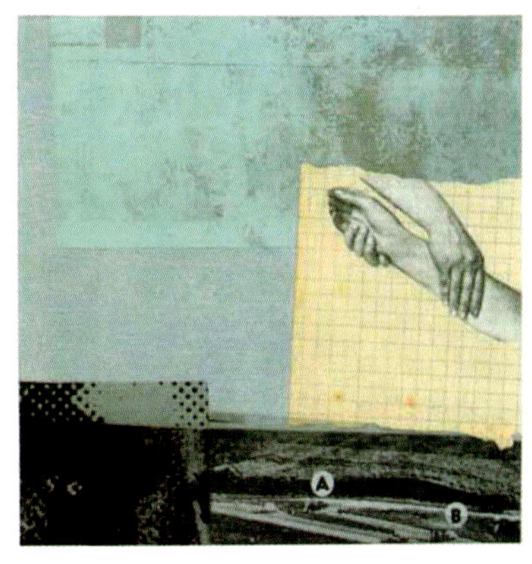
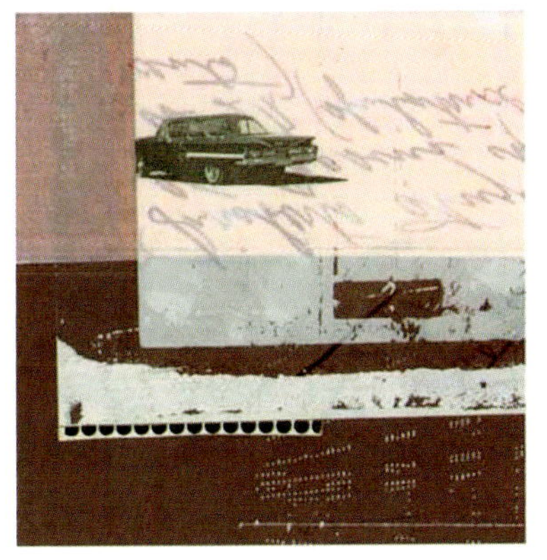
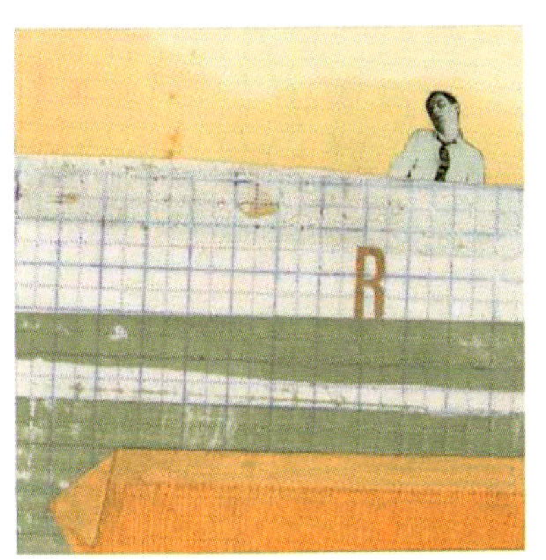
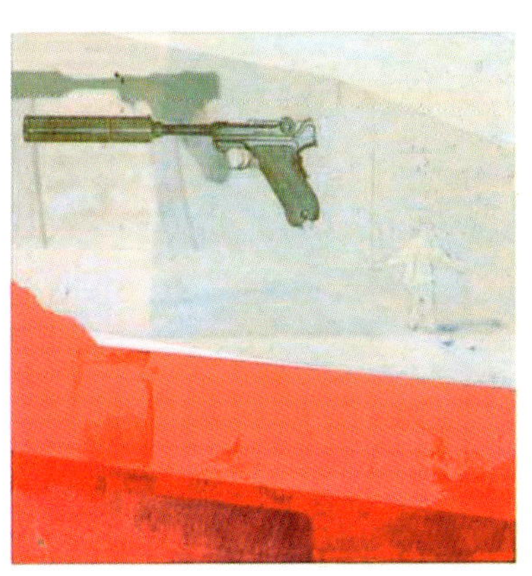
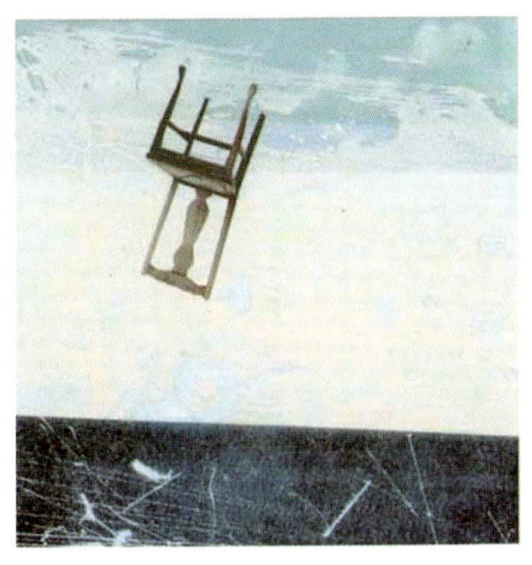
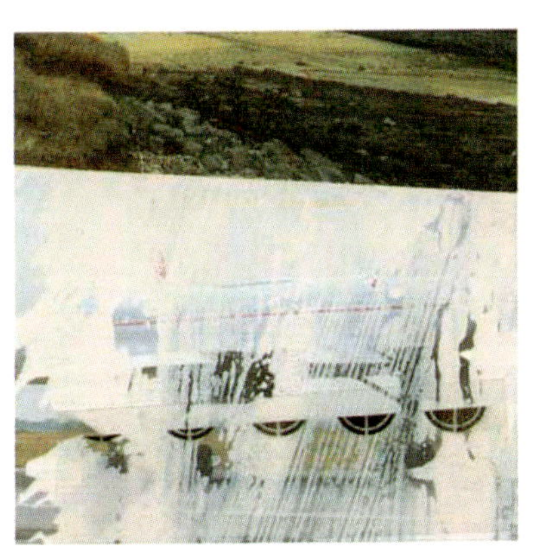
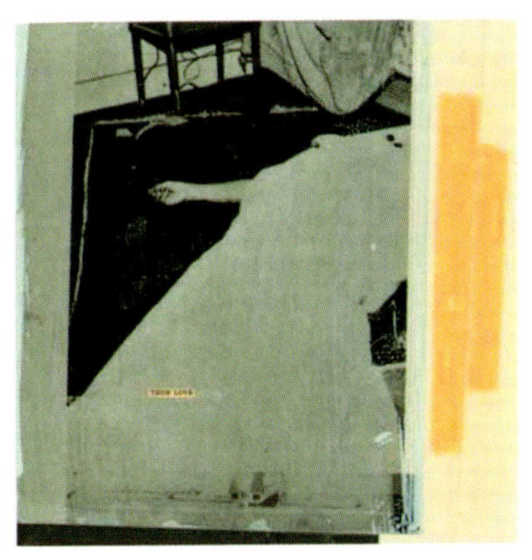
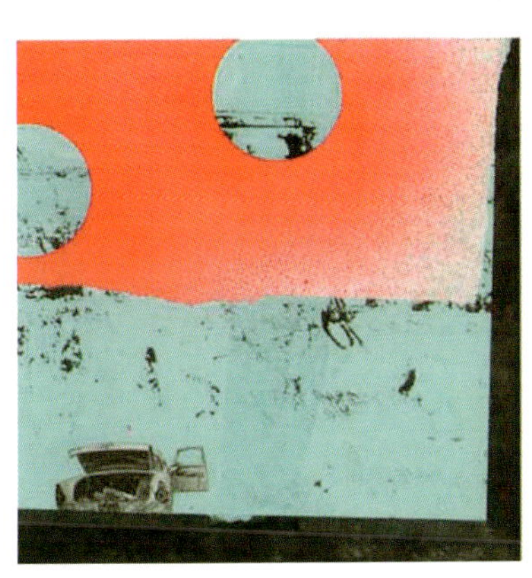
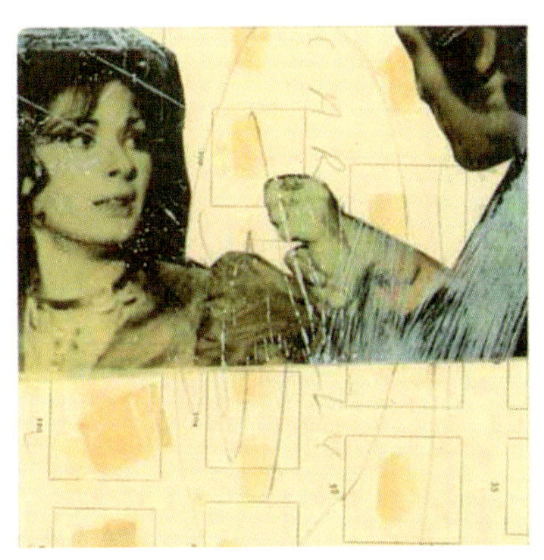
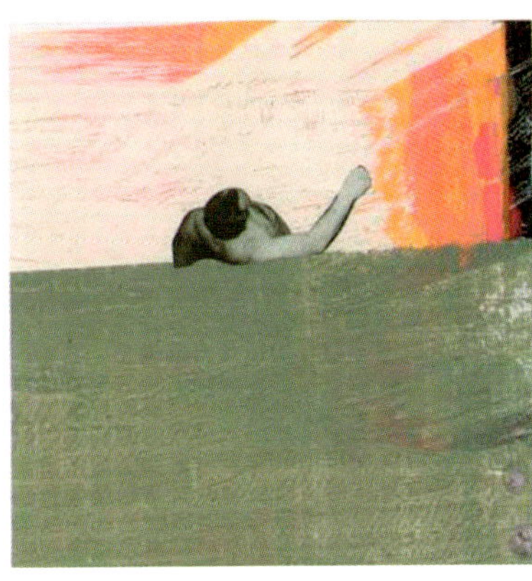

Creative dossier:
Archizen Creative

One of the functions of this book is to lay bare the creative process and to showcase some great designs and illustrations. Here Sean Tan of Archizen Creative deconstructs one of his illustrations and lays out all of the disassembled images and image elements, and acknowledges his sources.

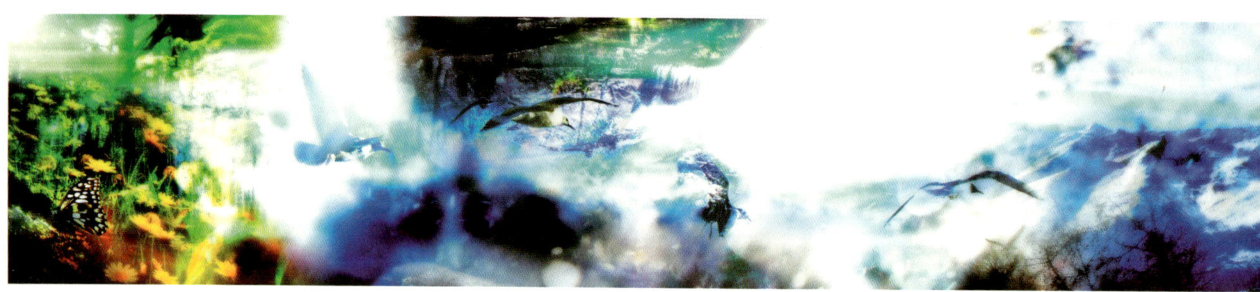

Studio: Archizen Creative
Designer: Sean Tan
Project name: Luna

Project description

"Luna is a personal experimental project using photomontage. It is about the transition of life and the beauty when life is shared. Everything is linked together and we can only see the beauty when we start appreciating it. The beauty of sharing." The project itself was built using shared elements, and will itself be shared, says Tan. All of the images were found using a Creative Commons search. The images themselves all came from flickr and were used under a Creative Commons Attribution 2.0 license. Says Tan: "I use these beautiful images shared by their respective 'owners' and combine them all together."

Techniques

The image was constructed mainly using Adobe CS2. Says Tan: "I gathered all the images in separate layers and masked them together layer by layer until I achieved the desired outcome."

COMPONENT IMAGE NAME / FLICKR AUTHOR NAME

Electric flower / LaserGuided
Full cast jump / OpenCage
Cherry Blossoms 6 / maveric2003
Snow Flakes 4 / chrisWhite
Silver / katia BR
IMG_2245.jpg / Joe in DC
sakura 04 08 – 04 / itchys
Bald Eagle (immature) / dobak
DSC_4658 / dboy
FishingHellesdonMill10_05ddd / Chylandra
IMG_3865 / cyancey
BUTTERFLY / blamfoto
AURORA / Bistrosavage
DSCN0389 / angela7
on the rocks / angela7
seagull. / withoutyou.
Waterwall / No7
SunSet / No7
Verdant Mountain in the Clouds / TheLizardQueen
View from Pointe de Renod / MGSpiller
Sweet embrace / sjoe
Flowing to the Sea / nelgallan
sunburst / nelgallan
Orange Iguana / wjklos
Untitled / whiskymac
Untitled /whiskymac
IMG_1301.jpg / Montana Wangden
clouded / utnapistim
Forest in Burgundy / tinken
021 Hocking Hills 120704 / szuppo
Luna / ~srozekrans

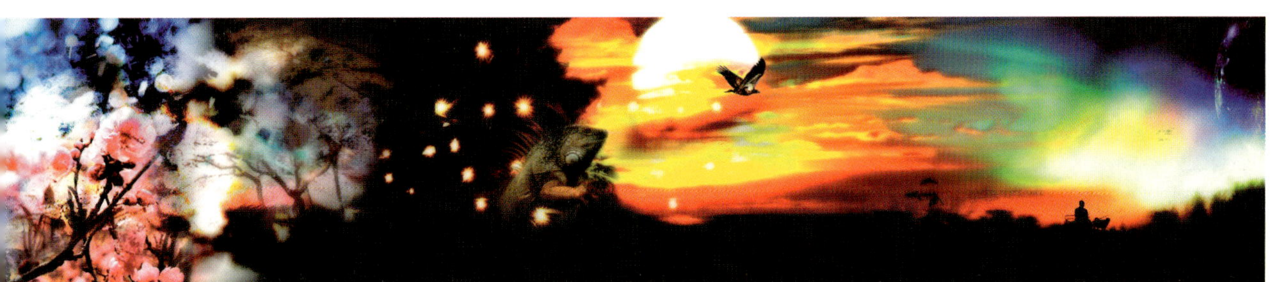

ORIGINAL IMAGES

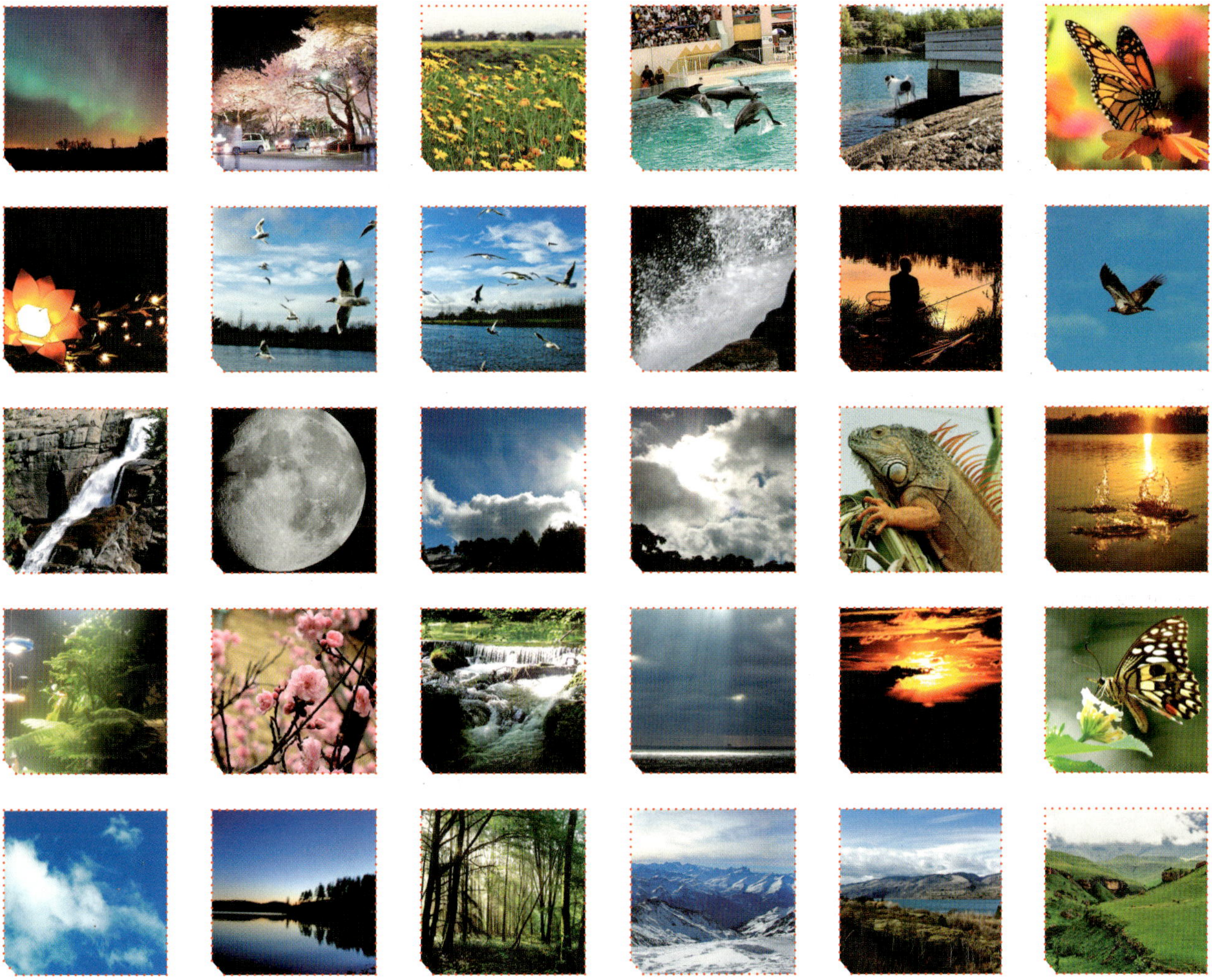

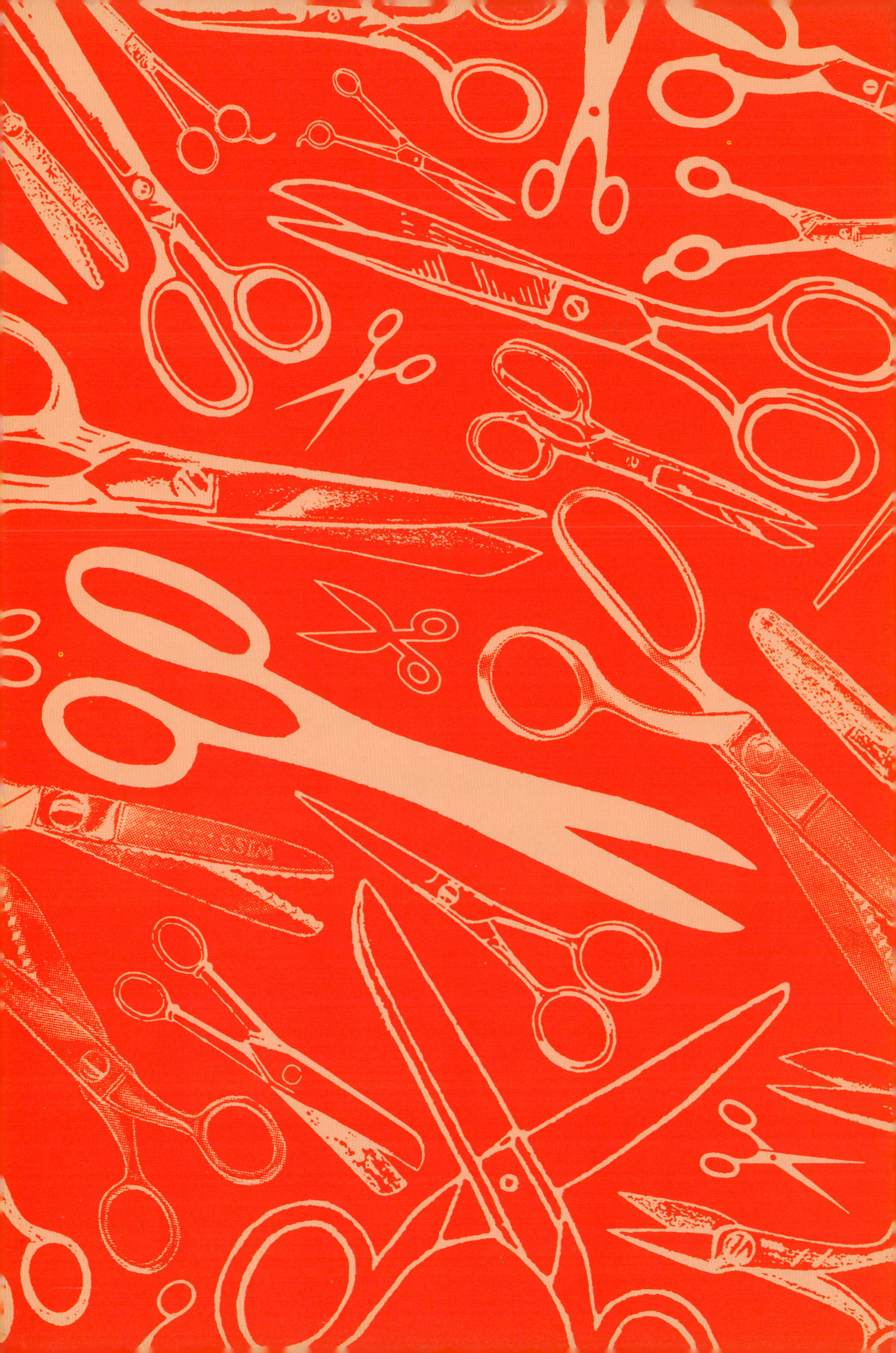

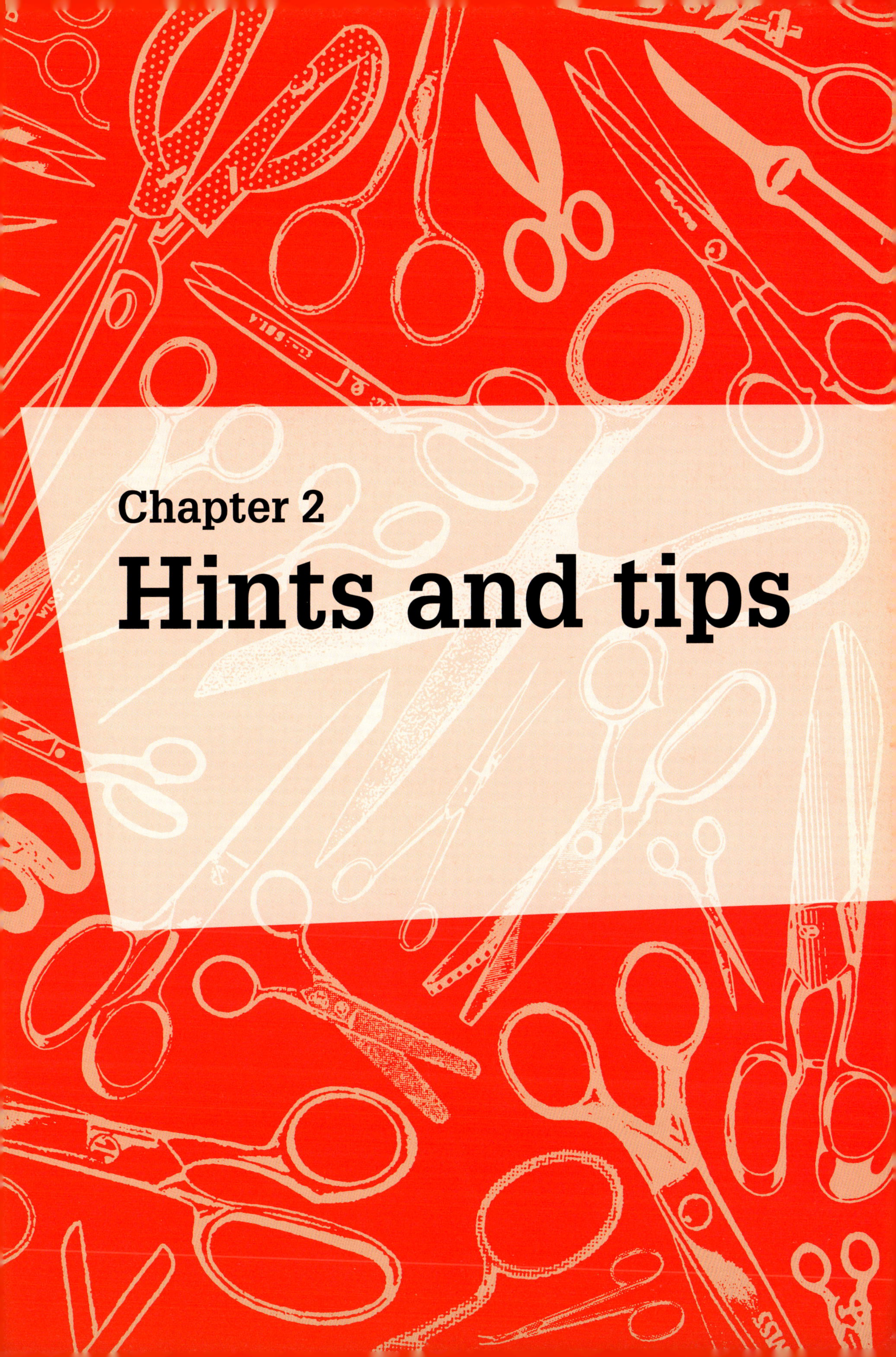

Chapter 2

Hints and tips

Introduction

For many designers using clip art in its original form means an aberration of taste and a denigration of their design skills, but, as we have already seen, it should never be overlooked as a would-be design source even in its rawest form, if you have the conceptual imagination, or sense of mischief, to pull it off.

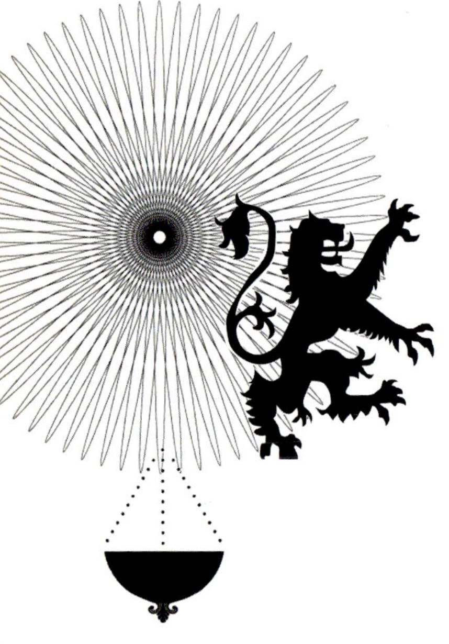

⬆ Some people see clip art as a low-grade source of cut-and-paste images for amateur design, but as we have seen it can form the basis of stunning pieces of design and illustration. Even assembling three clip-art images, icons, or font characters on the page, as here, can spark ideas for patterns, shapes, assemblies, and compositions.

➡ A page from an edition of *Crap Hound*, the legendary self-styled "zine of found and stolen popular imagery," maintained by designer and cultural commentator Sean Tejaratchi.

⬇ Music videos, interactive menus on DVDs, and Flash-based websites increasingly make clever use of clip-art images, clip animations, and other free image sources.

Clip art is an inexpensive or free source that can be manipulated, colorized, and comped beyond recognition—physically and digitally—into an illustration or a piece of design that has become unique due to the way it has been imaginatively customized.

For many designers, cut and paste, customization, and personalization form the bedrock of their business, and paying homage to your sources is all part of the process; in some cases, such deep, contextual knowledge of where imagery comes from has replaced manual dexterity and skill with design tools. It's all about the big idea; or, it's all about choosing the right source or knowing its provenance. Maybe it's also about choosing something you like.

But still many designers don't like to admit to using clip art or found imagery at all (even if they obviously do), as they feel it is somehow demeaning—in spite of the huge amount of graphic design around us that demonstrably uses clip art, or, at least, looks as though it does. And as we have explored in these pages, neither Picasso nor Warhol found it demeaning. We approached dozens of designers and illustrators who very obviously use clip art, and many of them denied it, or declined to be associated with it.

Perhaps the issue here lies in the terminology we use to make distinctions and spurious claims for different value systems: "clip art" is something made by someone else, artlessly, for commercial gain; whereas a "found image" implies personal discovery and uniqueness—even if you are simply recontextualizing a picture.

No one embodies this argument better than Sean Tejaratchi, progenitor and prime mover of underground clip-art zine *Crap Hound*. Tejaratchi has made a career of being a "crap hound"—collecting and sampling images and picture elements from thousands of sources. He then publishes selections of them en masse in periodic editions of his zine as a scannable or photocopyable royalty-free resource.

In this way, the images have been stripped of their cultural contexts and become simply raw material to either look at, enjoy, or appropriate. He leaves that decision up to you. The risk and responsibility, then, are his (such as they are), but his cult status makes designers feel that Tejaratchi's found images have an underground kudos, a feel-good factor that somehow seems better than any other magazine cover disc.

Wherever you stand on the use of clip art in professional design, it is undeniably an influence on the look and feel of many of today's graphics. We are so surrounded by samples that even an original article often looks or sounds like it may be a copy of something, or has been morphed beyond all recognition. That playfulness, after all, is the fun part.

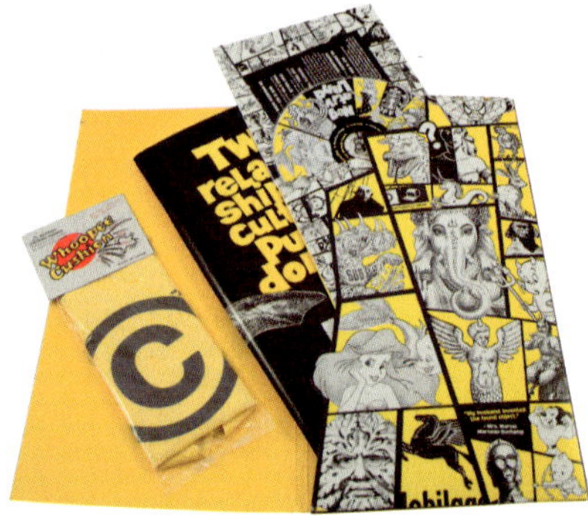

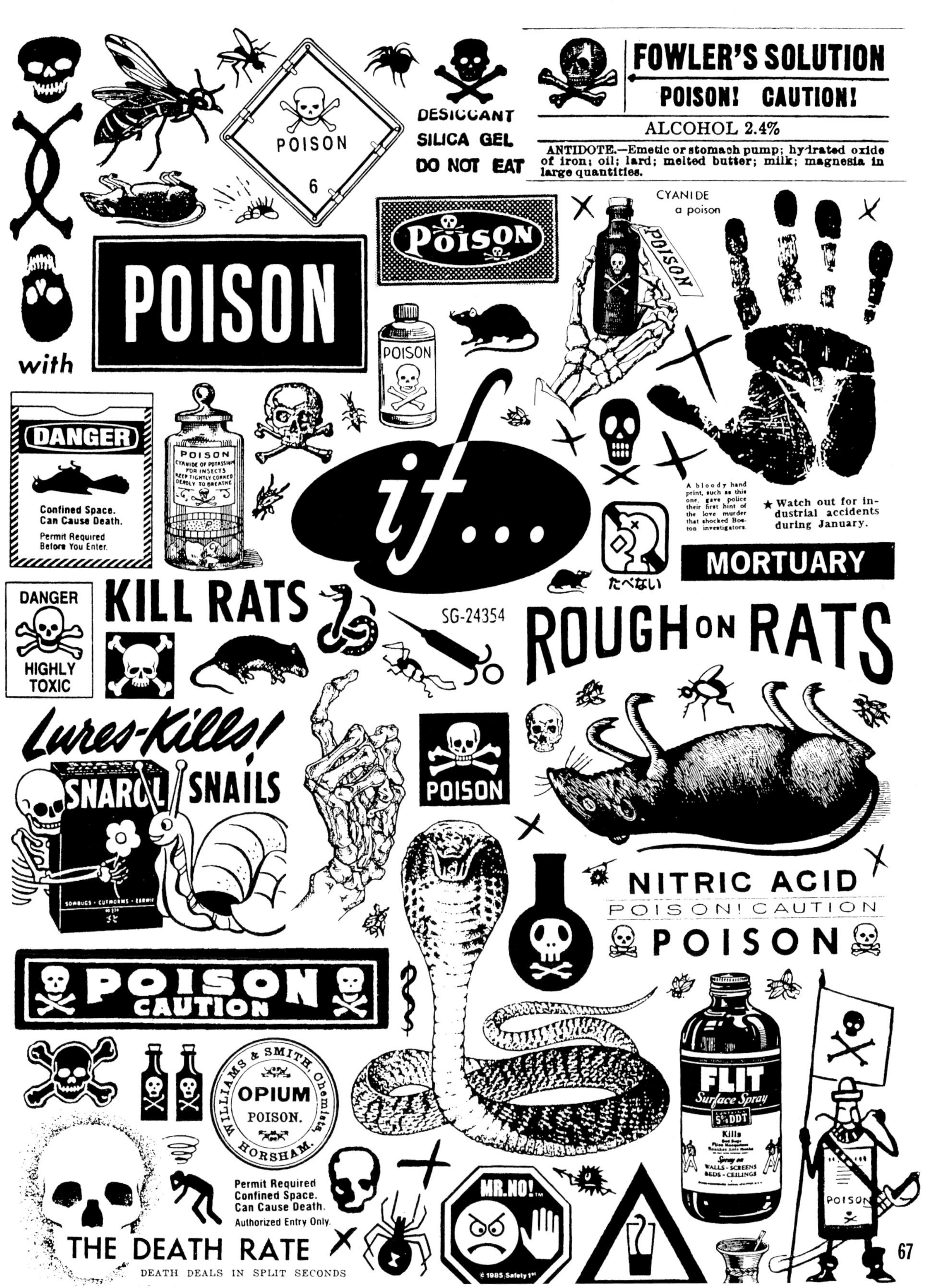
FOWLER'S SOLUTION
POISON! CAUTION!
ALCOHOL 2.4%
ANTIDOTE.—Emetic or stomach pump; hydrated oxide of iron; oil; lard; melted butter; milk; magnesia in large quantities.
POISON
6
DESICCANT
SILICA GEL
DO NOT EAT
POISON
with
POISON
CYANIDE
a poison
POISON
POISON
DANGER
Confined Space.
Can Cause Death.
Permit Required
Before You Enter.
POISON
CYANIDE OF POTASSIUM
FOR INSECTS
KEEP TIGHTLY CORKED
DEADLY TO BREATHE
if...
A bloody hand print, such as this one, gave police their first hint of the love murder that shocked Boston investigators.
★ Watch out for industrial accidents during January.
MORTUARY
たべない
DANGER
HIGHLY
TOXIC
KILL RATS
SG-24354
ROUGH ON RATS
Lures-Kills!
SNAROL
SNAILS
POISON
NITRIC ACID
POISON! CAUTION
POISON
POISON
CAUTION
WILLIAMS & SMITH, Chemists,
OPIUM
POISON.
HORSHAM.
FLIT
Surface Spray
5% DDT
Kills
Spray on
WALLS - SCREENS
BEDS - CEILINGS
Permit Required
Confined Space.
Can Cause Death.
Authorized Entry Only.
MR. NO!
© 1985 Safety 1st
POISON
THE DEATH RATE
DEATH DEALS IN SPLIT SECONDS
67

Introduction

Today, for many designers and illustrators, clip art is one of the foundations of both the process and the visual identity of graphic design, and a natural extension of the culture in which we live where sampling and personalization are twin tracks of many mainstream creative processes.

It's fair to say that for increasing numbers of creative people across different disciplines formulating a satisfying creative process is at least as important—and for many, more important—than the finished piece, and part of the reason for this is the increasing homogenization of design processes around the desktop, laptop, and the Creative Suite.

For many designers, sabotaging the predictability of the design process is one way of personalizing it. We live in a cut-and-paste culture, and so a lot of graphic design reflects a cut-and-paste, pixel-packing aesthetic. In terms of process itself, abandoning the desktop and physically engaging with manual skills rather than simply referencing them onscreen can seem like an act of rebellion.

In this section, we'll explore some work-throughs and practical examples of how clip-art originals can be (and have been) morphed and manipulated by designers and illustrators who are not ashamed to admit to it. Some of the tricks of the trade will be showcased and explained in the following pages.

⬆ Clip art can be decorative or thematic; help define space, layout, and form; it can create depth and context for text and image elements when used as a background, as well as be the raw source material for the type of work we have already showcased in this book.

⬇ ➡ Even an apparently random selection of images, including some of the elementary images from within the designers' work featured in this book, can be recontextualized and used to create new works, rather than obviously derivative works that infringe people's intellectual property rights.

EXAMPLES OF CLIP-ART ORIGINALS

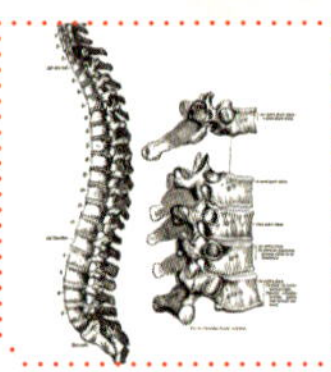
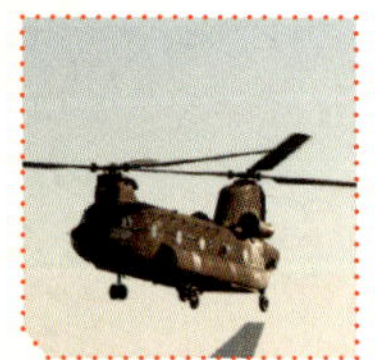
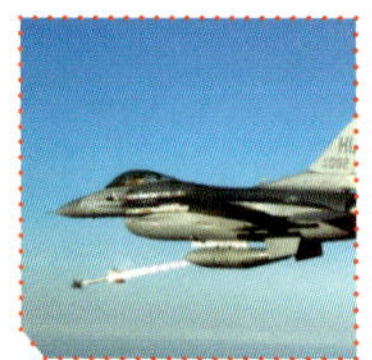
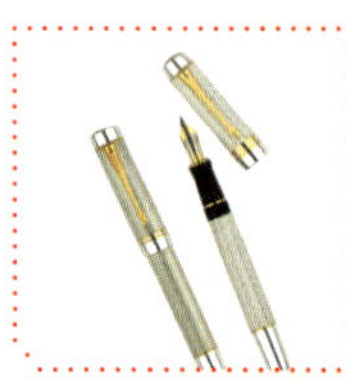
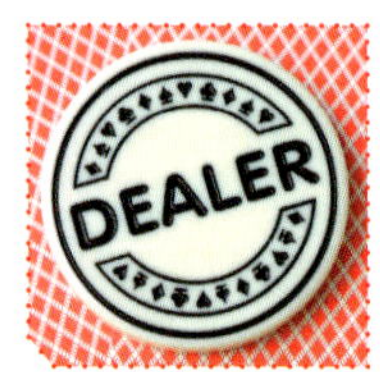

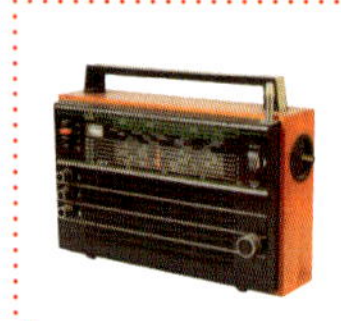

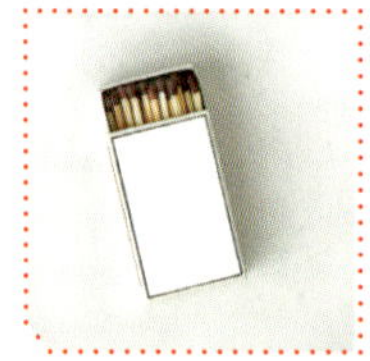
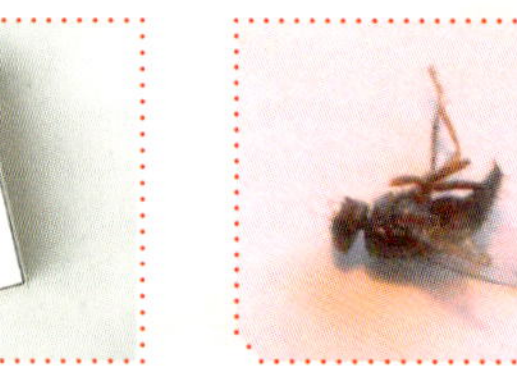
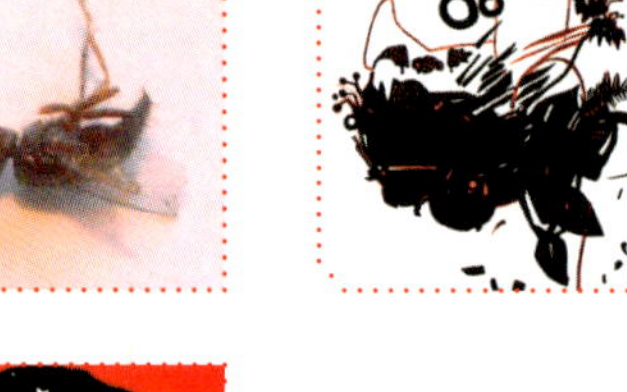
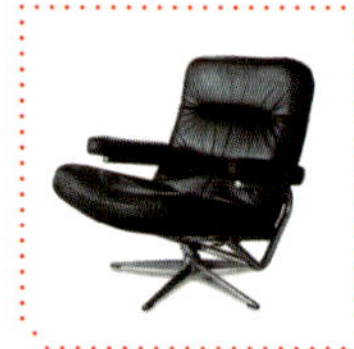
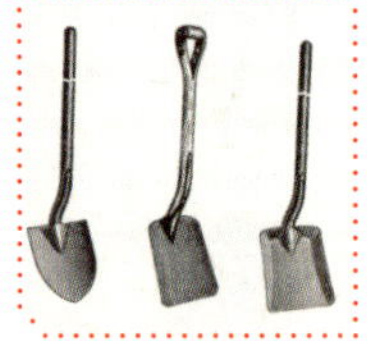

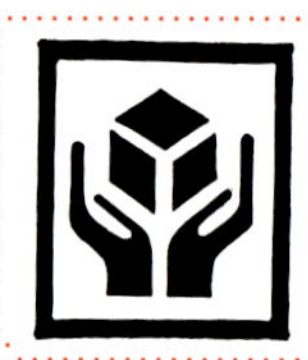
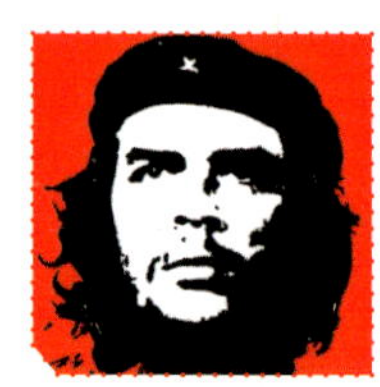

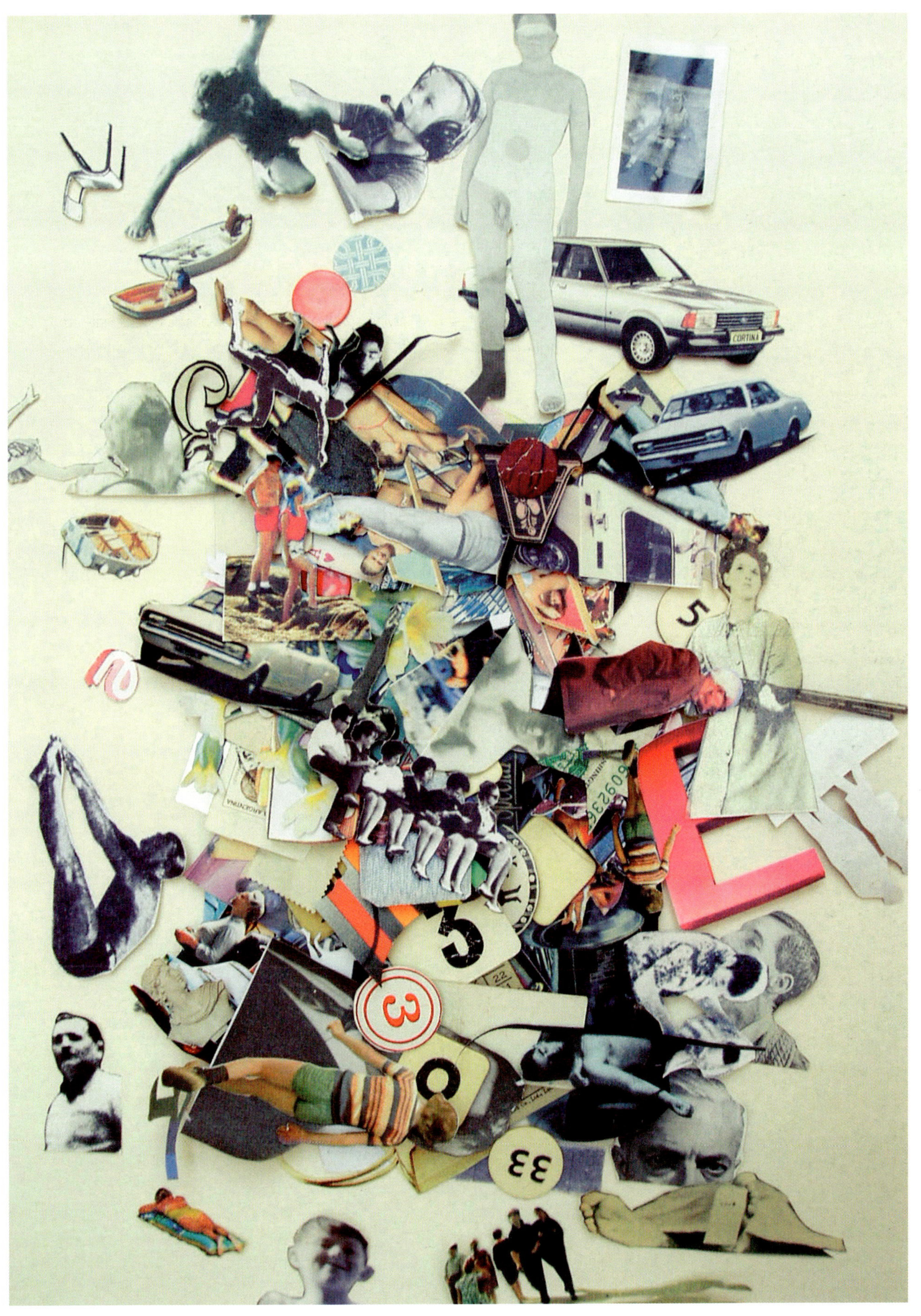
CORTINA

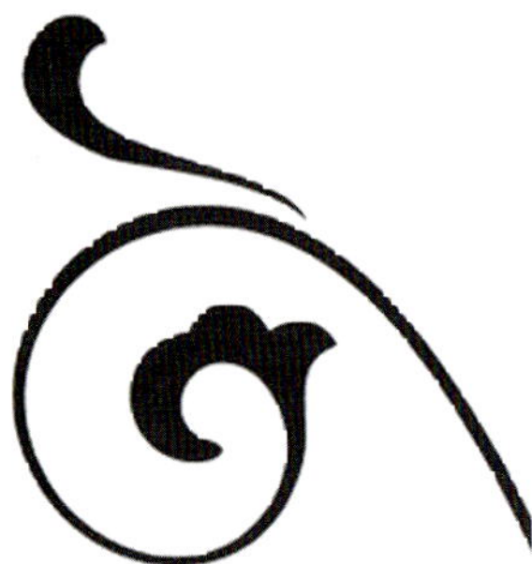

Avoid being a follower

Often one popular stock image or clip appears in ads and layouts for a number of clients. The key, as many designers and art directors recognize, is to ensure that their work stands out among the plethora of advertising and design messages that consumers are bombarded with every second. If you are selecting clip art from popular clip-art packages or free collections on the web, then the likelihood is that the same images will be appearing elsewhere—perhaps even on the opposite page to the design you've created, or on the same shelf as a rival brand in the supermarket. However, simply recontextualizing an image can change its meaning forever.

Crop it

Selecting a piece of clip art doesn't mean that you have to use it "as is." Cropping the image can simplify it or alter the meaning. Taking the art apart and using bits of the image can also add a different significance and, by regular use, can ensure continuity throughout the design, document, or campaign.

Tailor it

Combine separate pieces into one or break up the images and simply use elements of the original piece. Stretch, shrink, flip, rotate, colorize, and recolor. Unite bold shapes into unique images and use plug-in filters and graphics software to boost or warp source art. When modifying clip art, use an image editor or illustration program to experiment and discover the best way to rotate or resize graphics in a page layout application.

Using stock photos from the client and clip art from a letterpress type book, design studio Fullblast created this wedding invitation, complete with scanned handwritten letters from the couple's courtship, and a perforated response card.

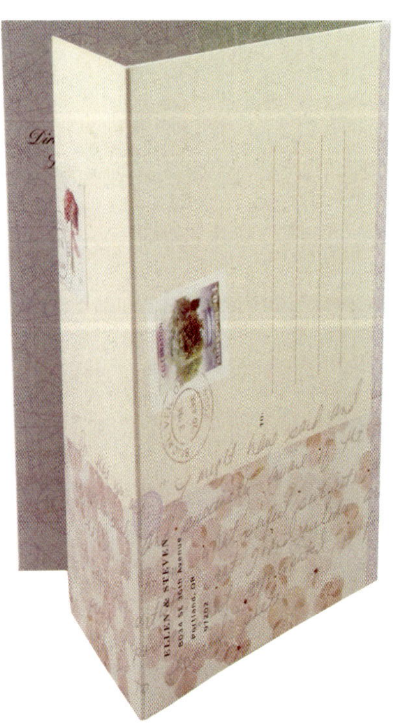

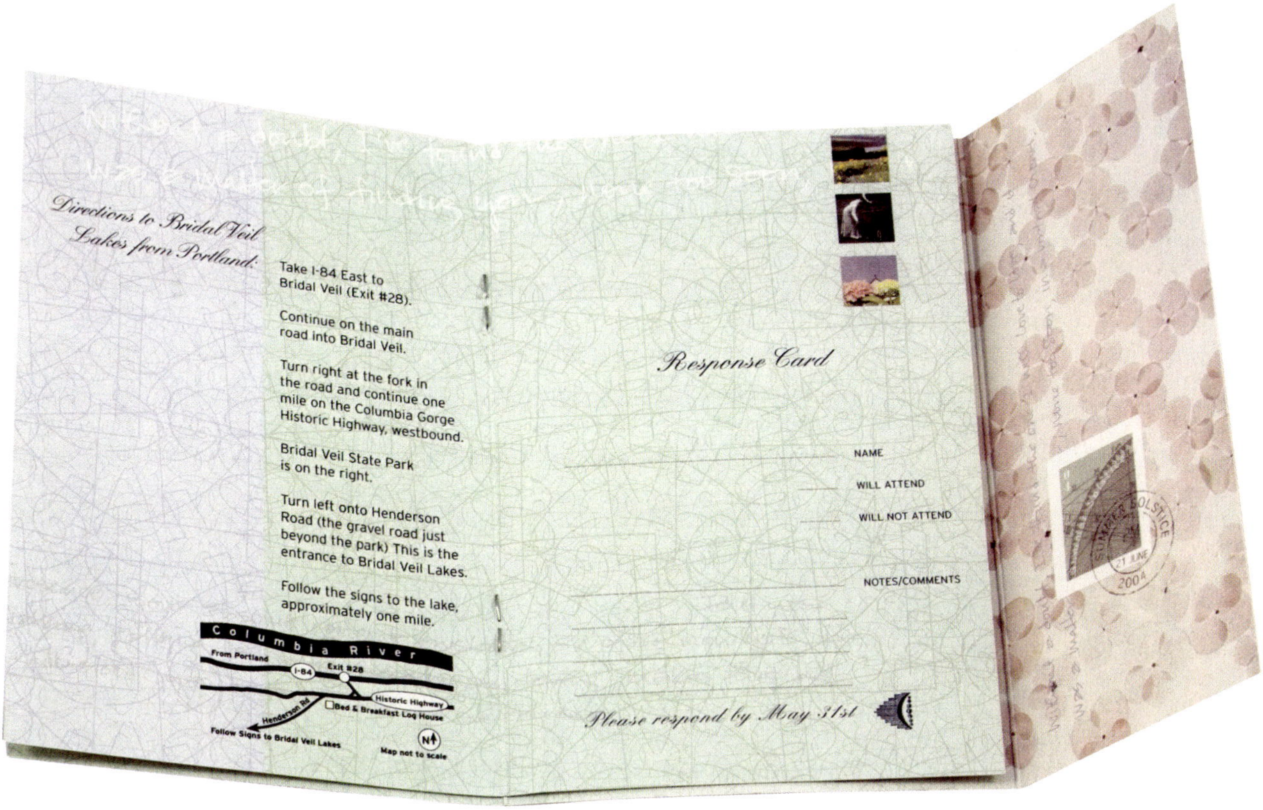

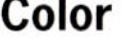

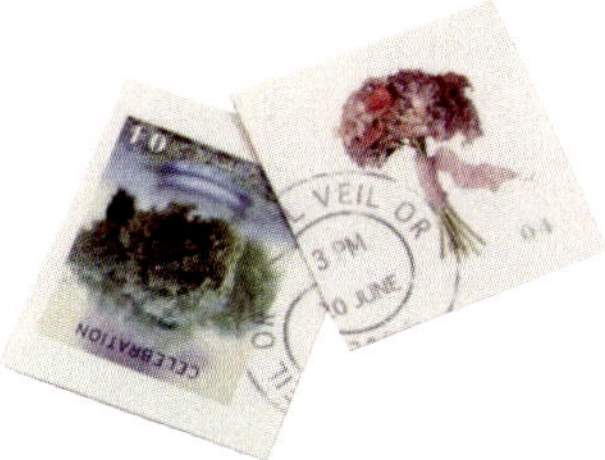

▲ The central spread of this beautifully designed wedding invitation by Fullblast. The studio's Todd Skiles says that each clip-art element was scanned and converted to bitmap, with colors then added in InDesign. Note the customized stamps included as a finishing touch.

Color

Converting color clip art to grayscale bitmap renders the colors in shades of gray and increases the usability of the images. Monochrome clip art is ideal for publications that need to be printed on printers with a low dpi.

Multiple images

Remember Andy Warhol's Campbell's soup cans paintings when using clip art and take a single piece of art and make several duplicates—recurrence of an image reinforces the message, provides consistency, and creates familiarity. Arguably, it can also take away its meaning or invite us to explore new meanings. Was Warhol commenting on mass production, celebrating a design he liked, or asking us to look at mass-produced items and appreciate their beauty? Broken-down elements of the art, for example, can be used to introduce sections of text or differentiate between points. Use duplicates of clip art in varying sizes and colors; make a single image stand out in color.

History/trends

As with fashion, illustrative styles and imagery go in and out of mode. So instead of opting for in-vogue images, search back to art associated with other eras, such as etchings, retro graphics, or Victorian papercuts and contemporize them in software. It's only a matter of time before an old style is rediscovered, reappropriated, and presented as the next big thing.

Multiple images

One of the challenges of creating illustrations and graphics using found images and clip art is not just sourcing the right image (although many designers and illustrators create valid and exciting work simply by making us look at a single image, or juxtaposition of images, in a renewed or radical context), but sourcing multiple images and creating successful graphic design from them.

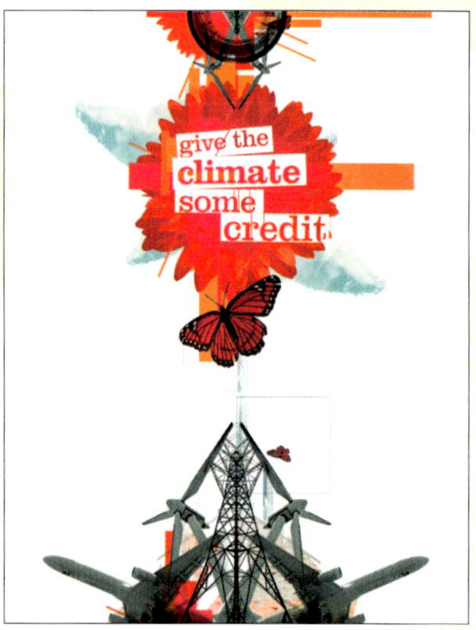

⬆ Traffic Design Consultants' environmental campaign posters create beautiful forms out of multiple, often ugly, images: an idea that is both simple, elegant, and high concept.

⬇ Plan-B Studio takes a similar approach on this low-carbon campaign, here creating a whole world out of layering multiple clip images.

A sound creative tip used by many leading graphic designers and commercial illustrators is to build up the roots of the piece from a selection of found images—either in collage, or replacing scissors, paste, and the camera-ready board with sampled and cloned pixels.

Using multiple images has several advantages: it makes the use of any one piece of clip art less overt or obvious, which can make the image more exciting visually, as curves, lines, shapes, or word forms, and the spatial relationships between them take on a more fluid and organic form.

The concomitant of this is that the design becomes more exciting conceptually, revealing multiple collisions of ideas, associations, connections, and inspirations. Just as any one of us will associate a variety of very personal images with overly familiar briefs, such as "classic," "fun," "youth," "nostalgia," or "romantic," so this type of design reveals the creator's own inspirations. In many senses, this is a mood board approach, where the mood board becomes subsumed into the design itself; it exposes the creator's process, his raw materials—even his environment, if he has sourced images from his immediate world. Of course, it can also be just for the hell of it.

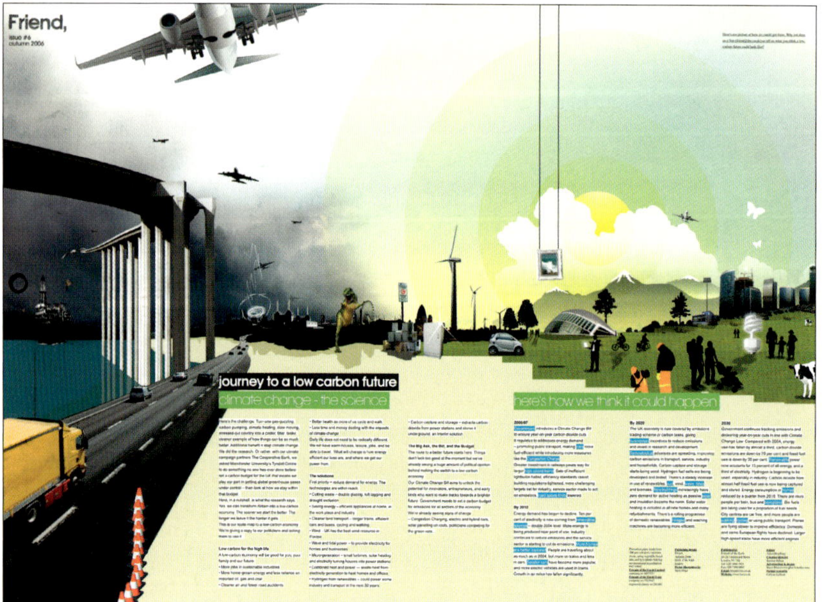

CREATIVE HINTS AND TIPS

— *Have fun with it and play: use Photoshop to arrange, layer, and merge images together. Cut and paste images either by hand and scan them, or slice, dice, destroy, and remix within Photoshop.*

— *Consider using multiple images to populate a single, larger image and position them to create depth, distance, and context for the viewer.*

— *Think about the creative DNA. Create a single object or form out of multiple found, clip art, or cutup text elements and explore the relationships—if any—between each of the component objects and the larger form.*

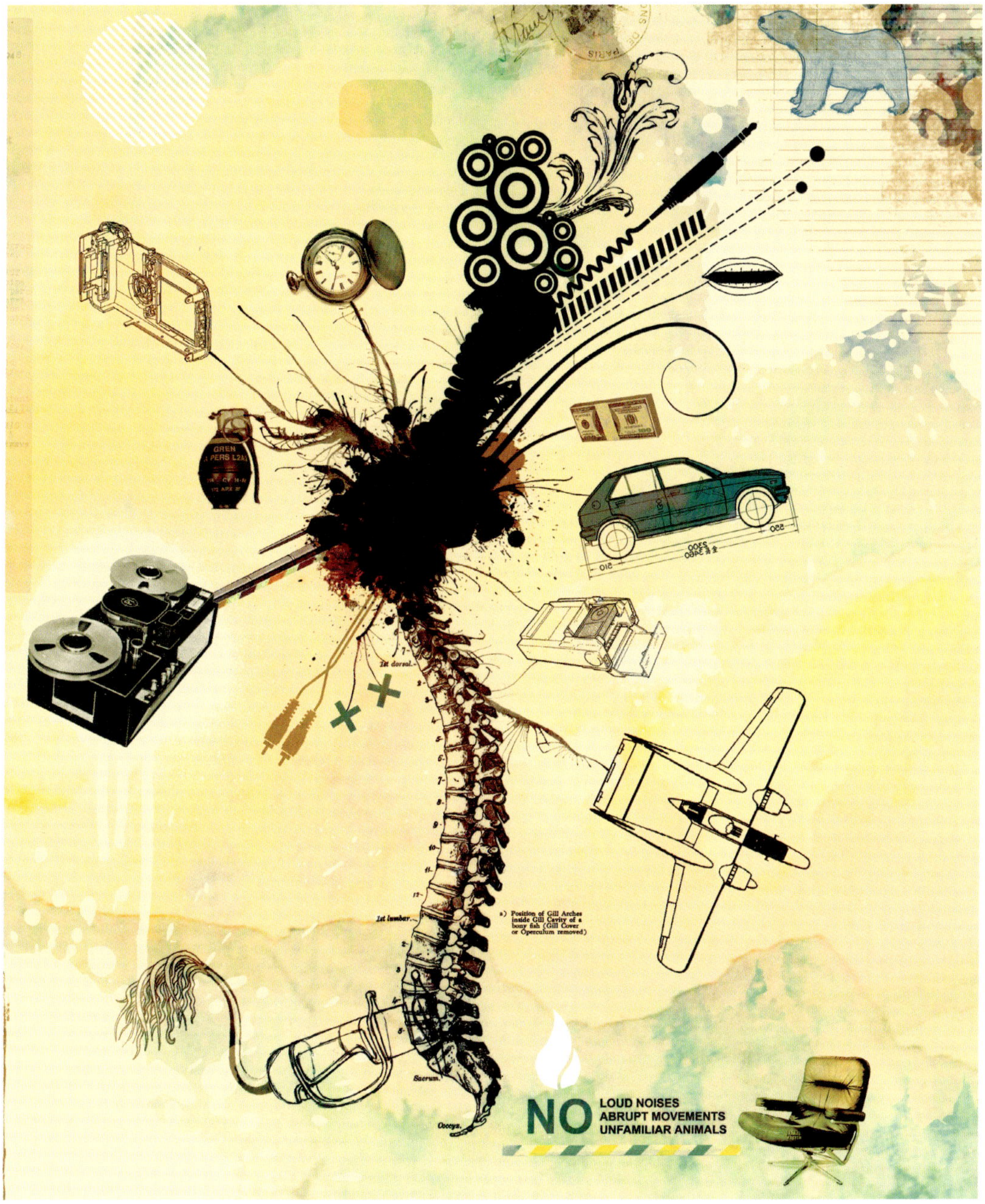

Wiretrap Studios' maledreamcodec is a wonderful composition that encodes and decodes the male subconscious with a beautiful assembly of clip-art elements.

ORIGINAL IMAGES

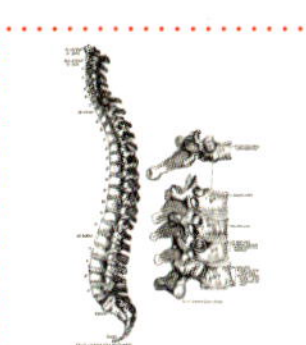

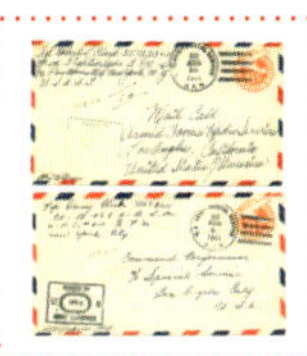

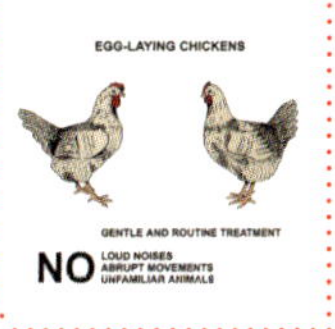

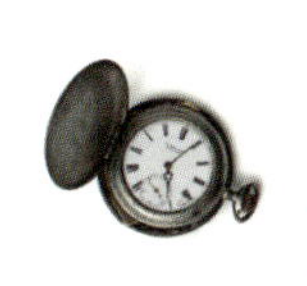

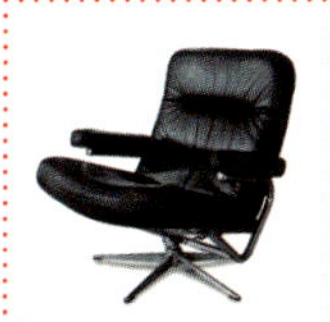

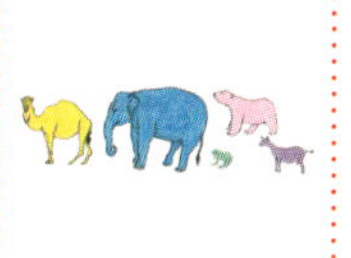

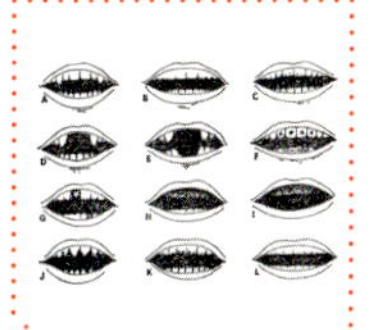

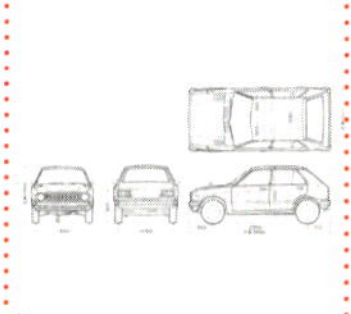

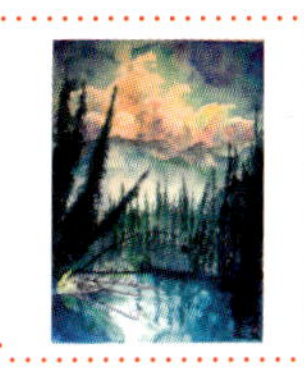

Silhouettes

Silhouettes and shadow forms challenge and amuse us and play with our knowledge of, and familiarity with, an object or person. They objectify the subject, turning living things or inanimate objects into graphical devices, or into tiles in a pattern that can be colorized, rotated, inverted, duplicated, or mirrored.

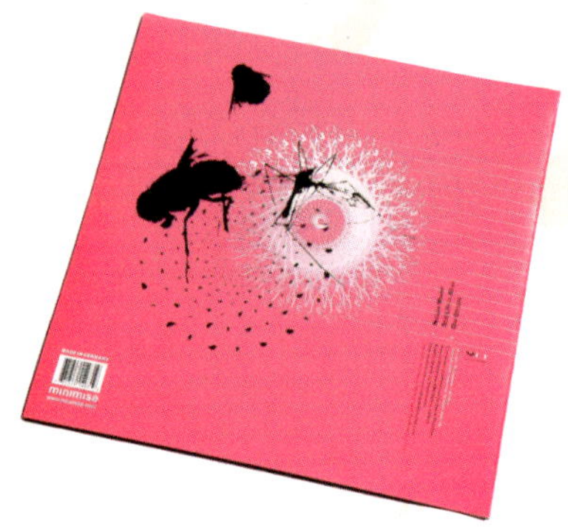

⬆ Studiomime sourced images from within the design studio itself and then silhouetted them to create this cover design.

As graphical devices, they can also evoke a mood, a movement, a mind-set, a genus. As such, their importance to graphic designers and illustrators cannot be underestimated. Consider: movie director Alfred Hitchcock and silent movie legend Charlie Chaplin were stars as people, but their silhouettes became graphical icons on merchandise that remains successful to this day. Mickey Mouse was a graphic to begin with, but he becomes an icon when shown in silhouette. Billions of dollars have been made from merchandising just the familiar shapes of those ears, which originated with circles on a sketchpad.

Silhouettes ask questions of the viewer: do you recognize that person from their body shape or profile? Is that familiar silhouette the actual person, someone dressed in the same way as them, their shadow, or simply a graphical representation of him or her—a featureless cartoon? Is that silhouette of a girl on a beach at sunset, or that boy in a field, a specific person, a simple drawing of an "everyperson," a cutout shape, or intended as an evocation of a mood? Has the silhouette been hand-drawn, is it a piece of clip art, or has it been traced from an original photograph and filled in by hand, or

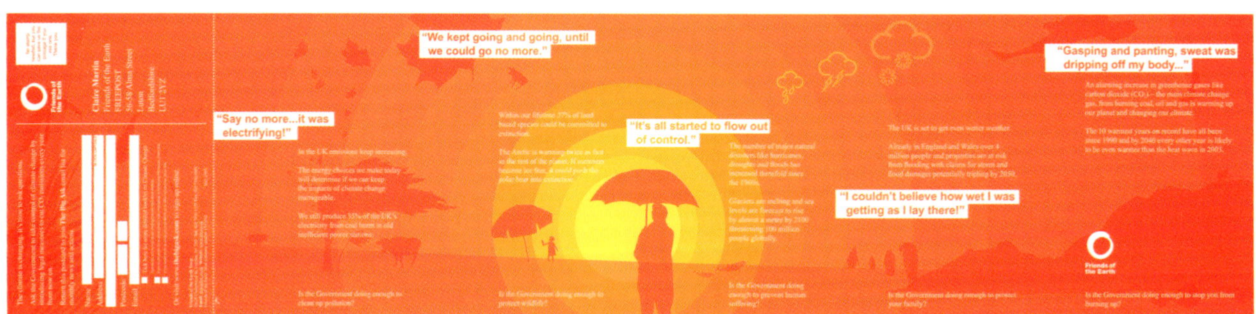

ORIGINAL IMAGES

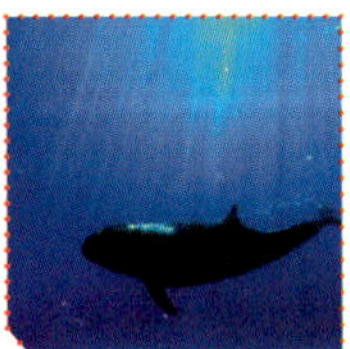
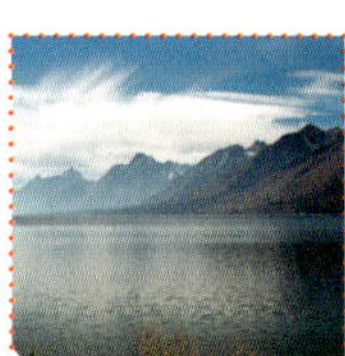
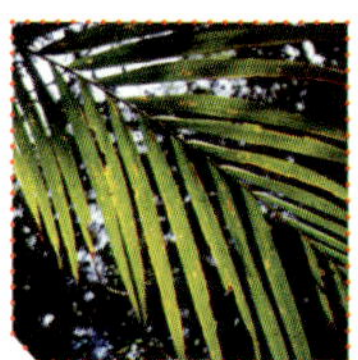
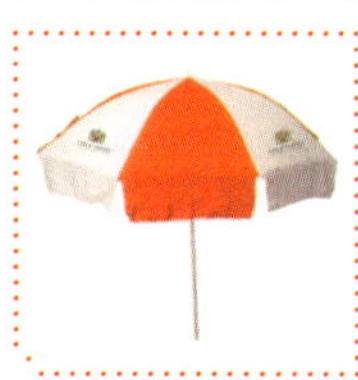

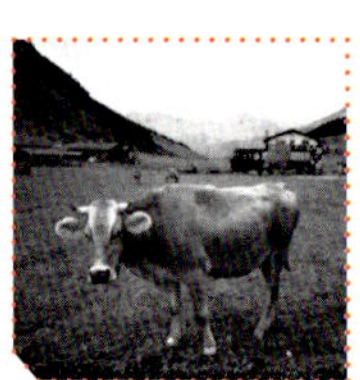
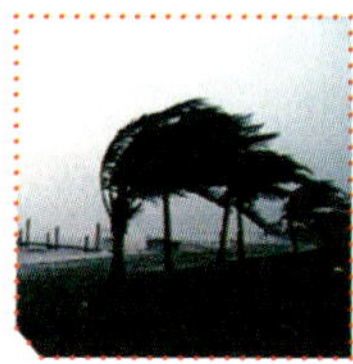

⬆ Plan-B Studio continues its environmental campaign design for Friends of the Earth with the intelligent but simple use of silhouetted images. Silhouettes do not have to be black to create their monochromatic impact; they can be part of the overall colorway, or be filled with pattern or other image elements. Think imaginatively about how you might use silhouetted image clips in your work.

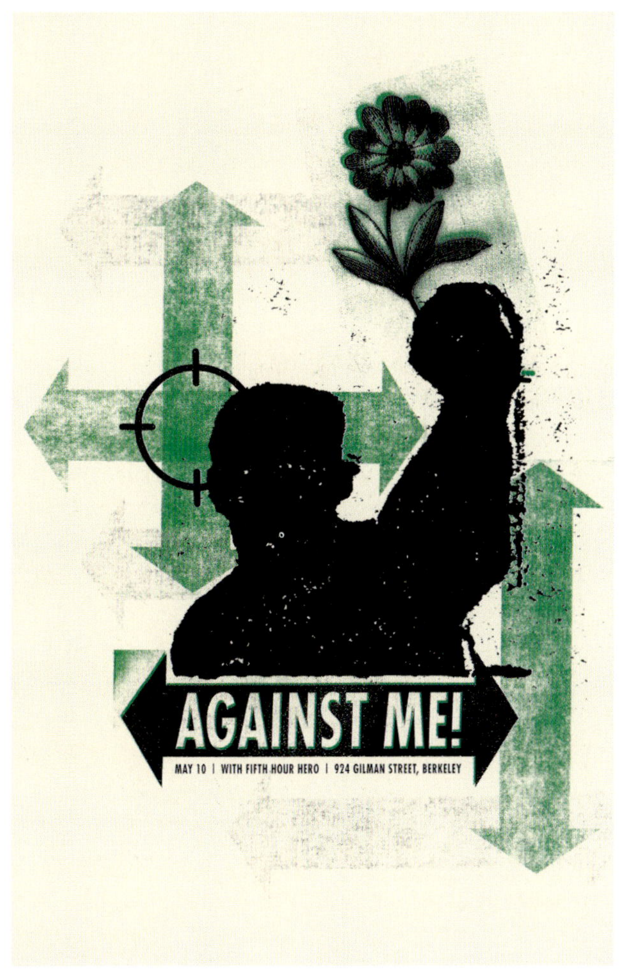

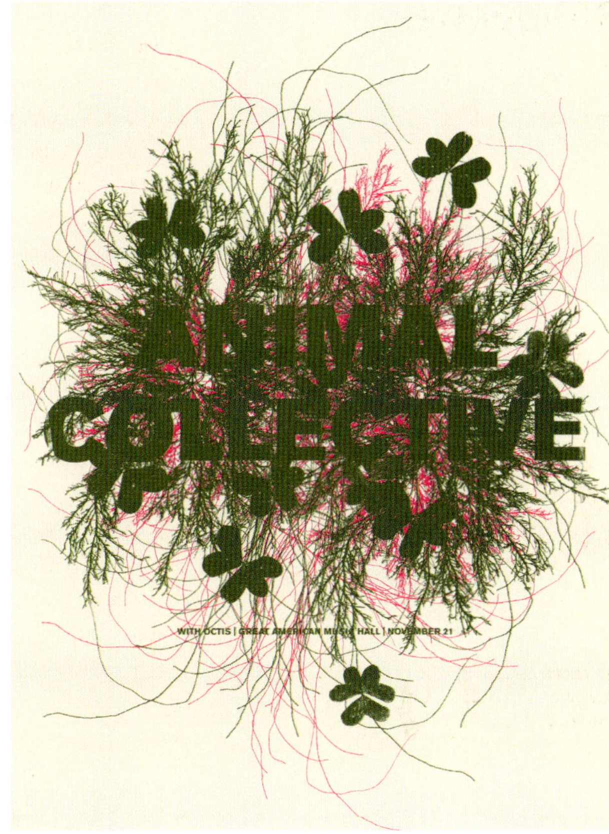

Concert posters by The Small Stakes. For the Against Me show, the poster combines a Dover Books flower clip image with an old advertisement, while the Animal Collective poster layers scans of Jason Munn's pressed flower collection.

in Photoshop? Is that silhouette genuinely of the object you think it is, or is it a visual joke, a trompe l'oeil that has conned your perceptions?

Questions such as these are invaluable to any visual artist or designer, and any one of them can form the basis of a creative strategy: like play and experimentation, asking questions is an underrated creative strategy, but one that is used by all successful designers and illustrators.

The conceptual side of using silhouettes is yours to play with and contradict, but making silhouettes can be easy. Scan or import your original into Photoshop or Illustrator; you can create silhouettes in a number of ways, and use them in many more.

CREATIVE HINTS AND TIPS

— *Try adjusting the brightness and contrast, making the image very dark and the background very light. The Levels palette will give you greater control.*

— *Trace the image and fill it with a single solid color.*

— *If you have a hard-copy original, you could fill it with black ink by hand, and then scan it. This will give you a useful hand-drawn quality.*

— *Output and photocopy the image, adjusting and pushing the contrast as you go. You can do this over and over again to obtain different results.*

— *Colorize the silhouette.*

— *Tile it and create patterns with it.*

— *Combine multiple silhouettes into a larger pattern, graphic, or letterform. Create wallpapers and engraving-style illustrations.*

— *Use silhouettes within images of real environments.*

Play with color

One of the more obvious creative strategies when incorporating clip art and found imagery into your design or illustration is to convert or change the original color(s) and subvert representational, naturalistic elements by making them into graphical components through the transformational use of color.

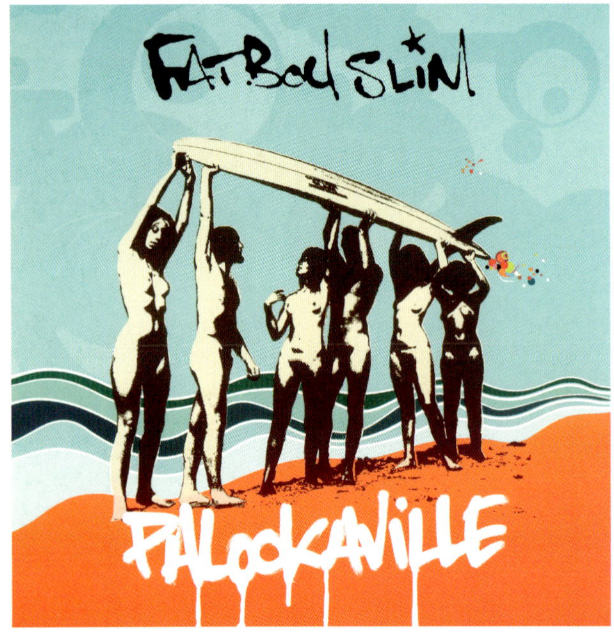

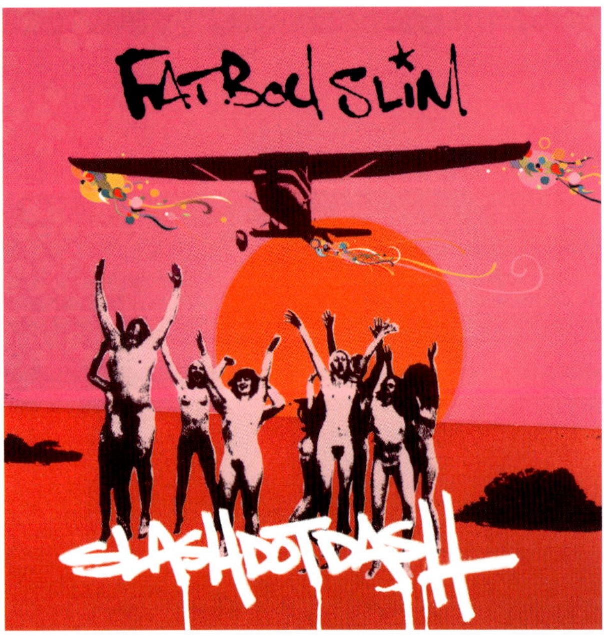

⬆ Red Design's well-known collaboration with DJ and musician Fatboy Slim combines low-fi clip art and tear sheet images with a striking use of color and composition. A perfect match with Fatboy Slim's music.

CREATIVE HINTS AND TIPS

— *Make a four-color image into a monotone, duotone, tritone, or quadtone, creating images that have a strong graphical punch, or which make discrete use of a second or third color to create subtle highlights and nuances in the image, or to accentuate or isolate a second color within an otherwise monochrome picture.*

— *By using the Hue and Saturation palettes in Photoshop you can create unusual color combinations.*

— *Experiment with reducing the color palette to one or two colors. Try substituting colors.*

— *Change or add in a flat background color.*

— *For more radical effects, try inverting the image—essentially creating a negative color image and reversing the tonal values.*

— *Explore the use of color channels, either singly or in new combinations. This can produce some stunning results when working with photographs, even when using black-and-white originals.*

— *Colorize black or line images—when using cutouts or silhouettes, for example.*

— *Overlay color washes over monochrome images.*

— *Overlay colors across multiple images and explore the transparency of the wash and each object.*

— *Sample or match colors from other images—for example, from found images or clip art, and then reuse those colors within other elements of the design.*

— *Alternatively, sample colors from the design and digitally match the colors within your clip art or found images to them.*

— *Subvert the iconography of familiar images by altering their colorways.*

— *Burn in or dodge colors to explore their relative intensities.*

— *In Photoshop, select areas and Fill with a solid flat color.*

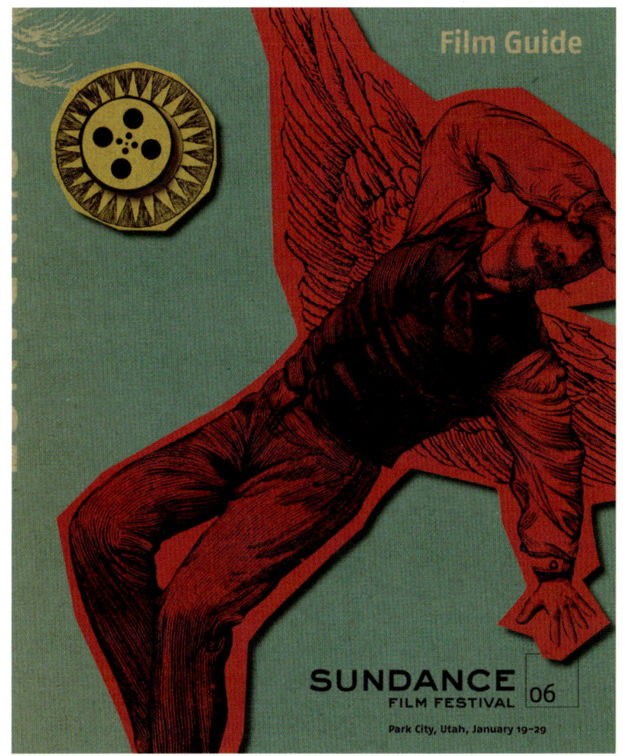

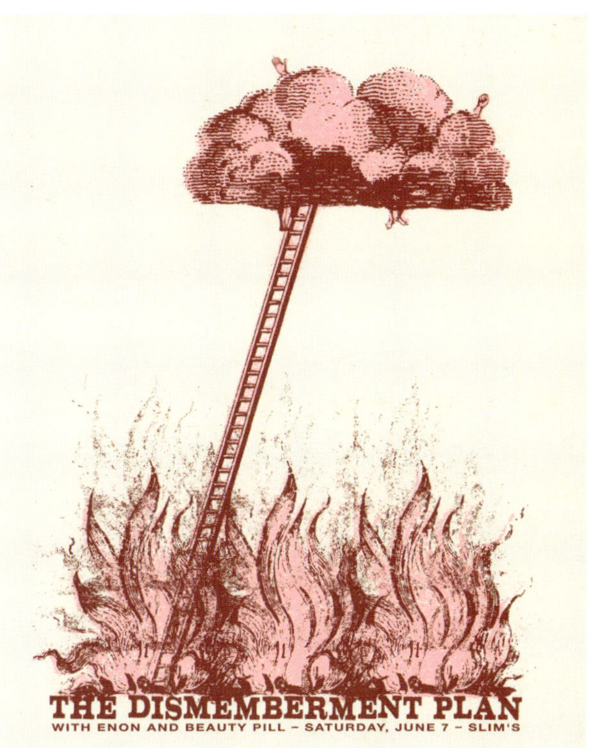

↑ AdamsMorioka's wide-ranging collaboration with the Sundance Film Festival revolves around creating graphics that pay homage to the festival's all-American heritage while appearing sophisticated yet inexpensive, thanks to the intelligent use of color and texture.

↑ This Small Stakes concert poster is at once old-fashioned and strikingly modern, thanks to a strong color approach that is still easy on the eye.

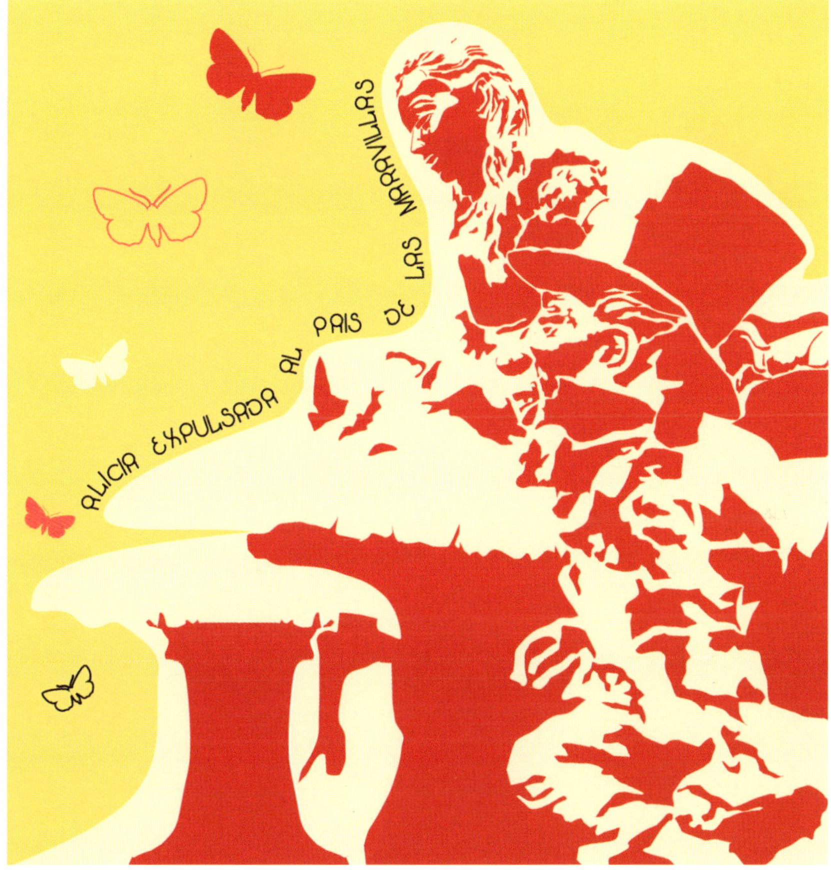

← Nicole Andujar of ChixInk demonstrates that color choice is one of the bedrocks of successful design using clip-art elements, bringing the composition to life and binding the clip sources together.

Layering

Layering is one of the prime techniques within any piece of visual design, creating a three-dimensional chimera in the resolutely two-dimensional world of most graphic design and illustration.

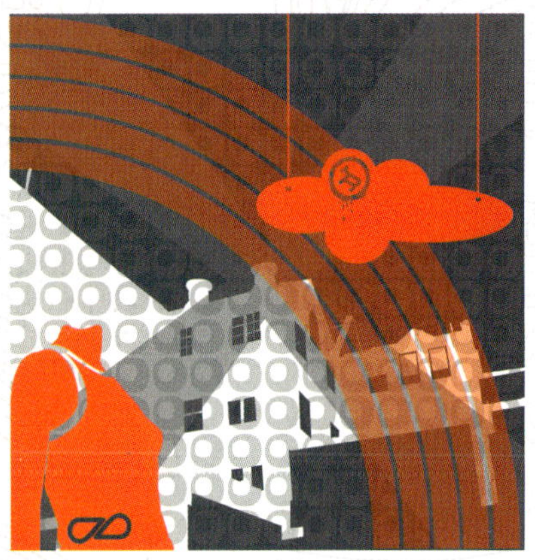

⬆ Nicole Andujar creates a dynamic design by layering clip-art elements and picking them out in different colors to create a design that has real depth and movement.

⬇ Ashby Design's work with Thievery Corporation is all about layering influences, samples, and clip elements to create designs that are rich and absorbing.

Layering creates depth and visual flair, but is also the main component in collage techniques within which dozens, perhaps hundreds, of component images, including clip art, sourced, and found imagery, can be combined into a larger, coherent whole. However, with Photoshop, it can have a subtly different meaning, as any image imported into an open file will appear on its own layer—a seamless overlay at one with the images above and beneath it.

Layers can tell a story within a piece of design or illustration, by combining and—as is so often the case with clip art and found imagery—recontextualizing images from different times, eras, locations, or media, and using them to create a "big picture" of the subject, which can then be seen simultaneously from different viewpoints.

But the use of layers can be devoid of this kind of context, and simply be used to construct beautiful images, patterns, and striking graphical compositions that play with form, color, line, texture, and tone, while still conveying the right message.

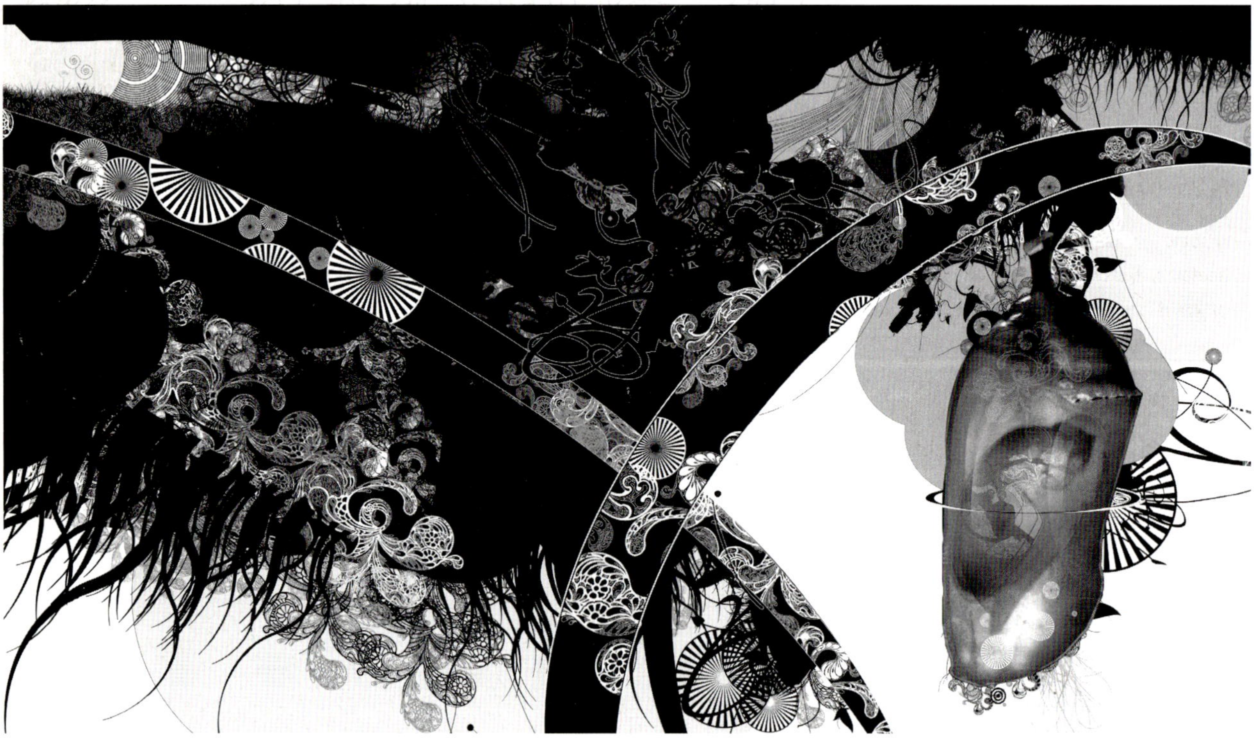

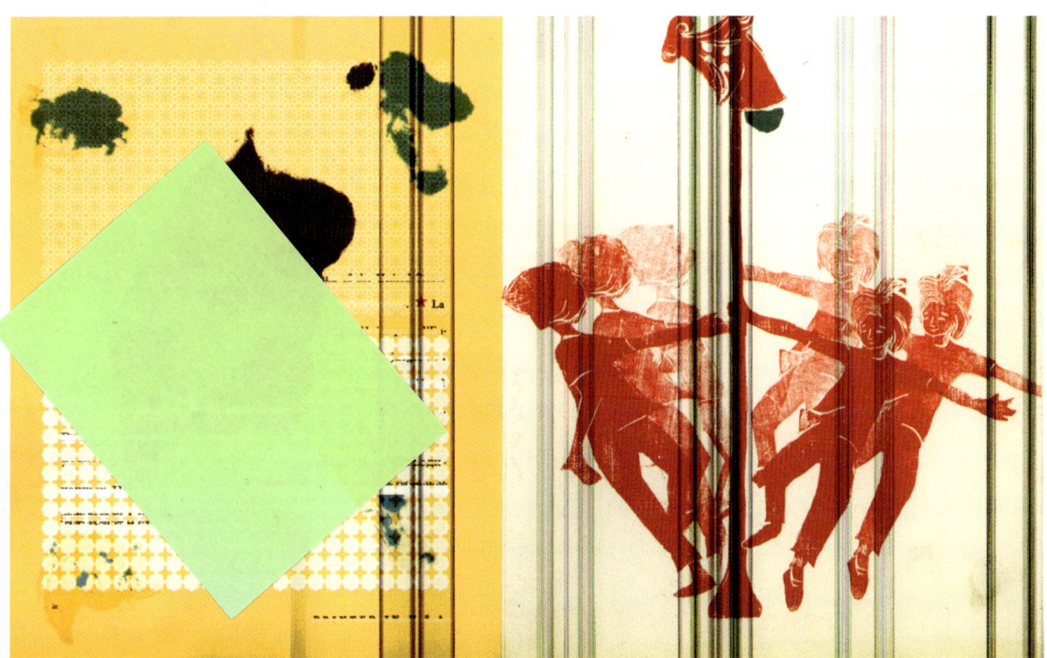

David Joyce creates a ghostly beauty from layering multiple repeated images and combining them with texture and color.

CREATIVE HINTS AND TIPS

— *Create interest by layering multiple images.*

— *Import a number of images into Photoshop, allocating each its own layer. Remove any backgrounds and unwanted details.*

— *Play with the composition to create visually arresting shapes and collisions of images.*

— *Use different levels of transparency to suggest depth and create intrigue and excitement.*

— *Similar effects can be achieved using a manual, old-school hands-on approach with collage, cutups, cutouts, scissors, scalpels, and paste.*

— *Photocopy images onto different papers and acetates, and onto materials with different levels of translucency.*

— *Find and recycle imagery from transparent packaging, cartons, etc.*

— *Get more hands-on still by using stencils to overlay type or graphical devices and icons.*

— *Motion graphics designs, such as on DVD menus, make exemplary use of digital collage and layering techniques. Consider using a similar approach for print-based design.*

Martin O'Neill's signature style is rooted in layers of clip images combined in a traditional collage that has a Modernist feel in this fascinating example.

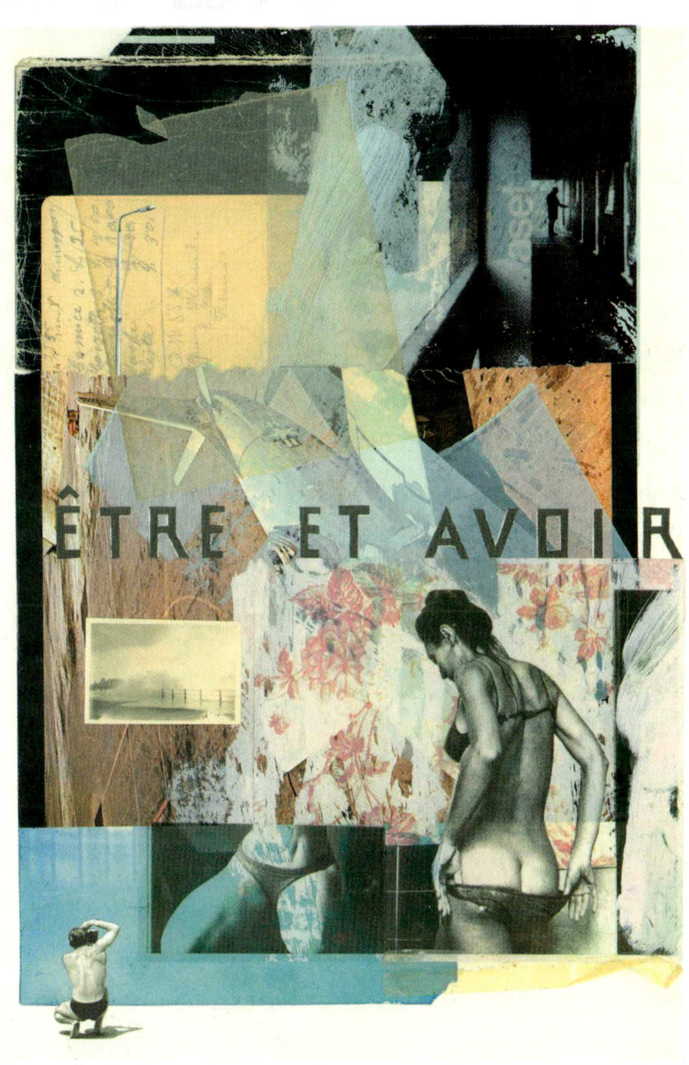

Merging images

This is similar to layering, but with the emphasis on creating specific shapes or graphical devices. Often designers make silhouettes of images first before joining them together to create new forms rather like shadow puppetry. Again, doing so can subsume your source images into new, more complex forms and hide the origins of your raw material.

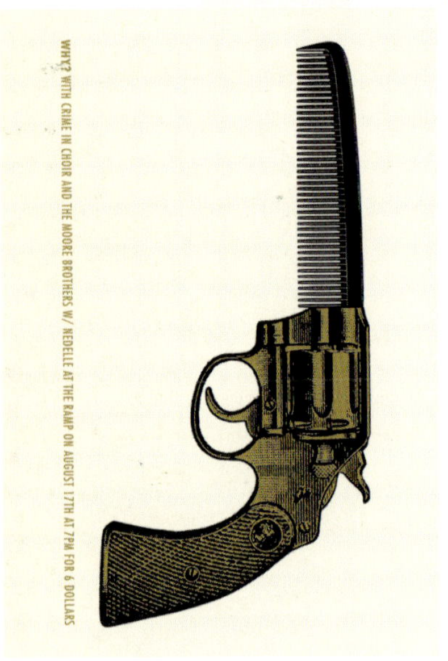

↑ The Small Stakes work for the band Why? finds the studio creating a finely groomed image. Wild West or Italian barbershop? You decide.

CREATIVE HINTS AND TIPS

— *Overlay and merge images to create new shapes and forms.*

— *Take individual images out of context to create something unique and startling. Doing this can create jarring juxtapositions, but can equally find common forms between apparently disparate images.*

— *Experiment with scanning continuous-tone images, such as color or black-and-white photographs, and then posterizing them or creating solid graphics from them, before combining them into a single graphic or illustration.*

— *This can all be done in Photoshop, Illustrator, or by hand with a scalpel.*

↓ Turning street photography into clip art, the illustrator Jonni combines graffiti-style tags, Right Bank hauteur, and Left Bank nous for this image that seems part Punk, part Agit Prop, and all Parisian. The end result is a piece that appears deliberate and typeset, rather than entirely composed of combined images.

ORIGINAL IMAGES

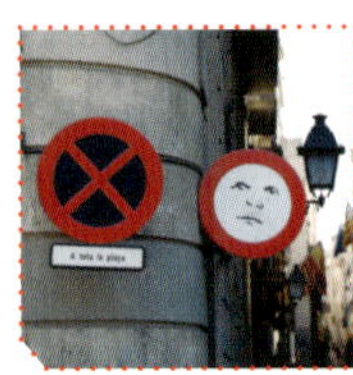
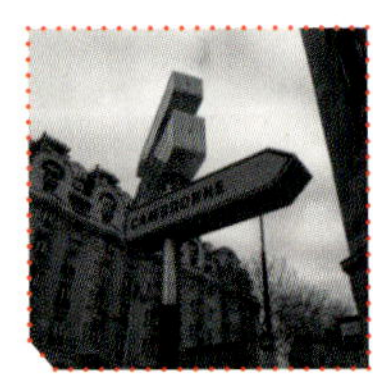
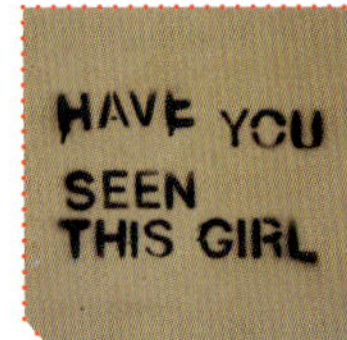

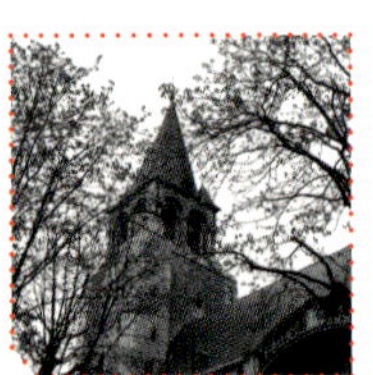
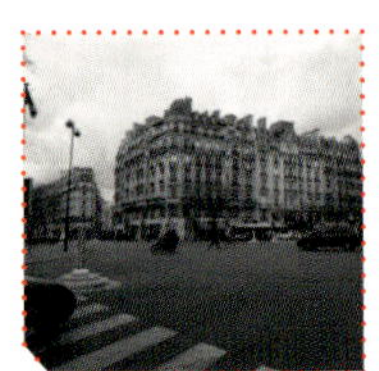
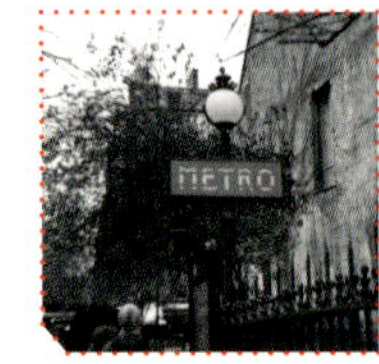

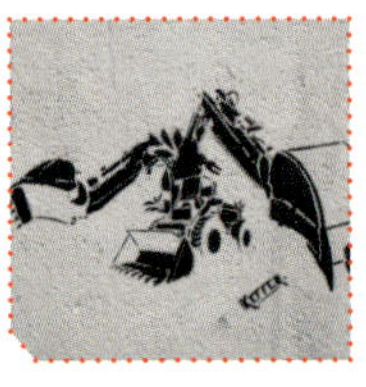
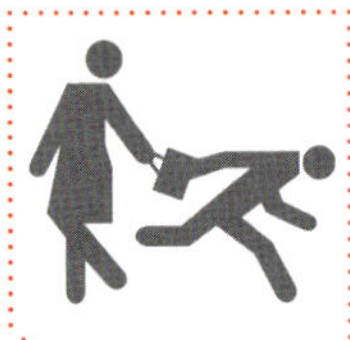

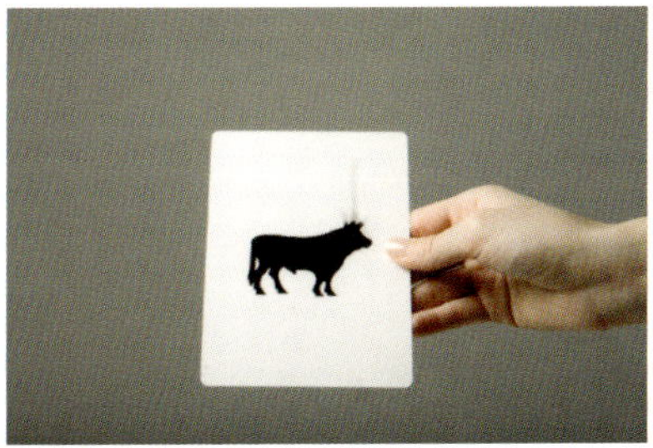

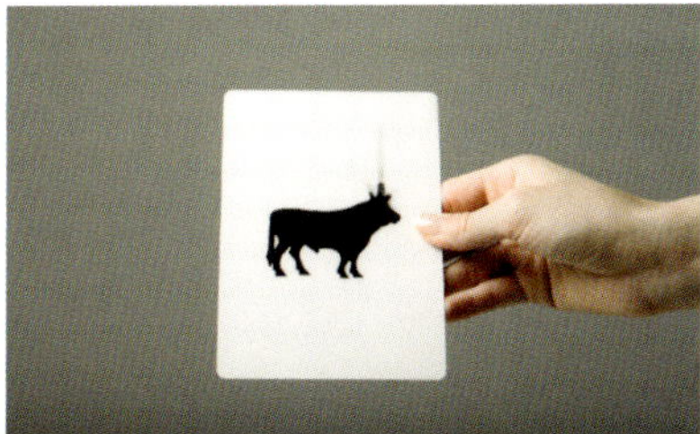

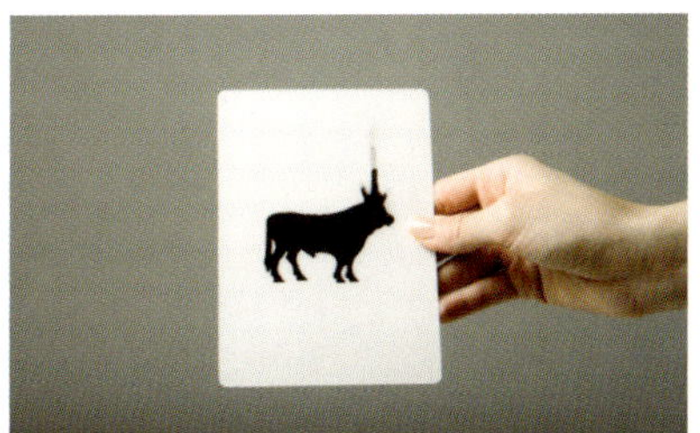

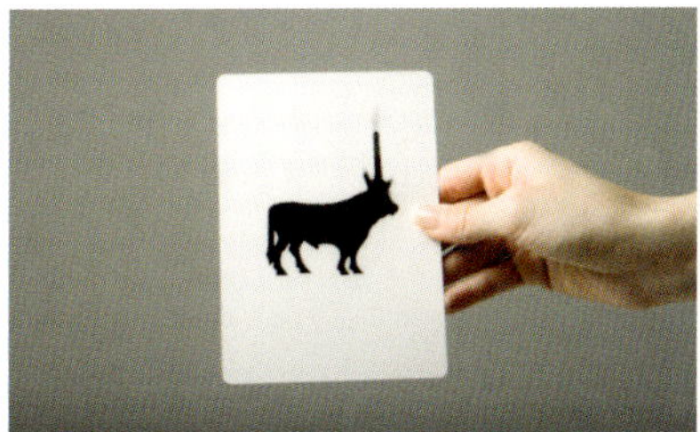

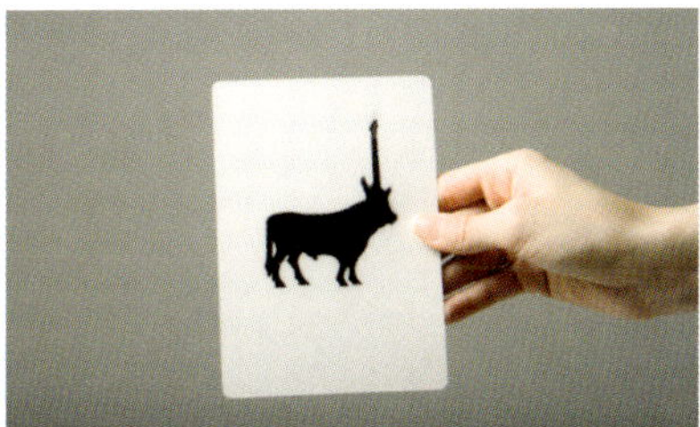

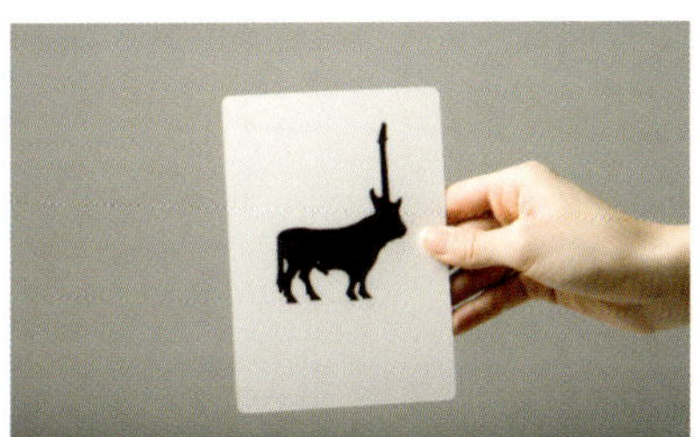

⬆ Nicole Jacek combines a cow with a guitar for this lenticular-printed music festival flyer that merges the two images with a tilt of the hand, turning horns into a guitar.

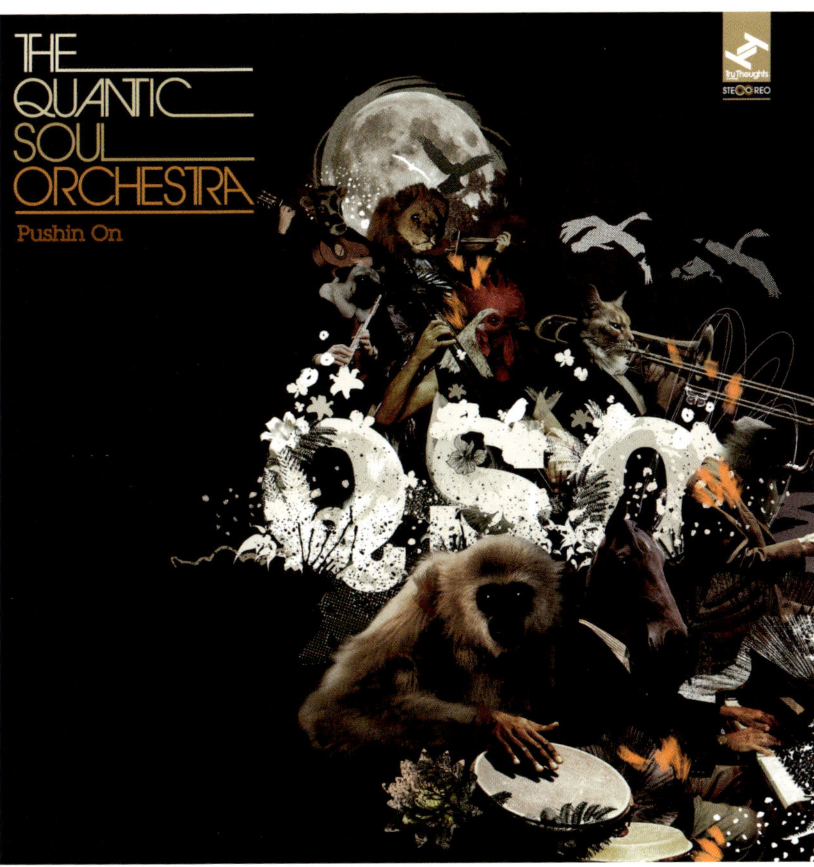

⬆ Red Design amps up its low-fi clip-art approach to a more hi-fi level by combining dozens of clip images into a rich composition that turns each viewer into a potential listener. "What does this music sound like?" asks the design, and the only answer is to play it and find out.

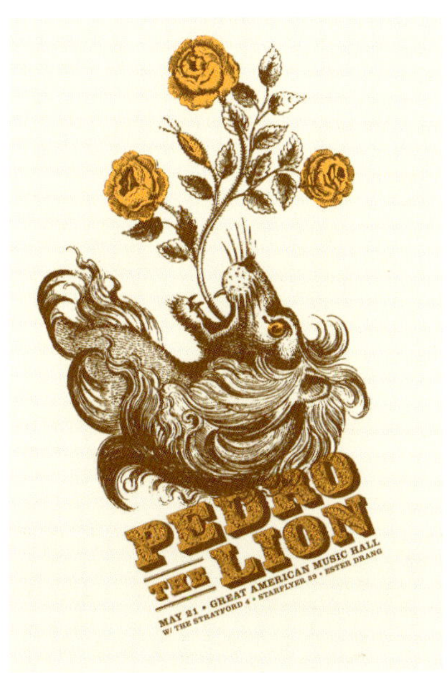

⬆ The Small Stakes produces another signature music event poster showcasing a combination of clip images with subtle color selection.

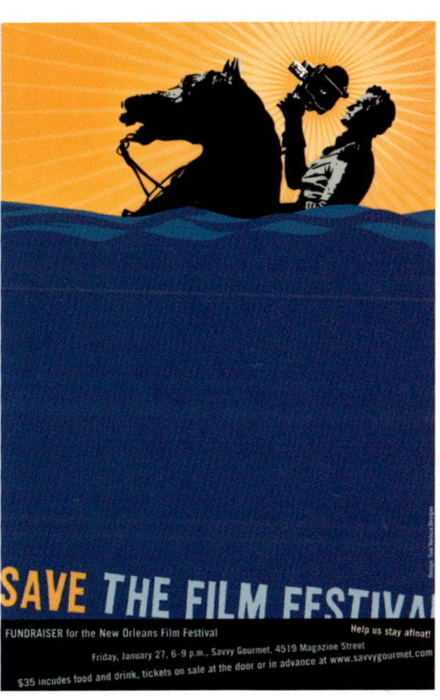

⬆ Tom Varisco Design's poster is an object lesson in the graphic impact of intelligently combining clip art and found image elements with strong color composition.

Hands-on and mixed-media techniques

Among the most exciting and traditional ways to use clip art, sourced, and found imagery is to collage it, and also to source physical objects and to experiment with the means of creation and production. In this age of the widespread availability of advanced digital software and hardware, the most successful professional designers and illustrators are often set apart by having evolved the most original creative processes.

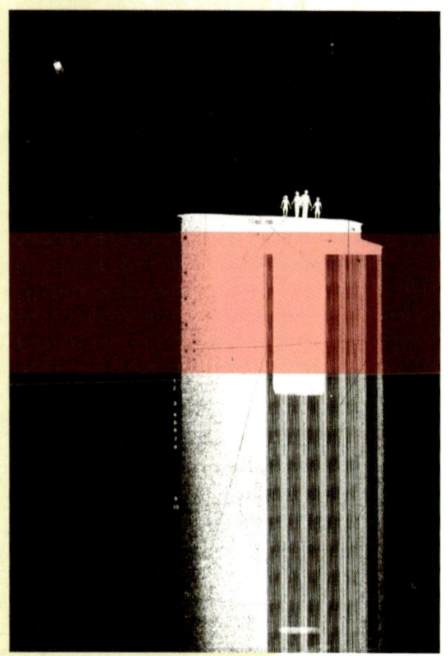

Of course, many also blend old and new hands-on techniques: as ever with sourcing images, everything is grist to the creative mill; everything is raw material for the creative eye and the enquiring mind.

As we have already explored in the section on nondigital techniques, collage-like techniques have existed since the advent of paper in China over two millennia ago, and the technique became increasingly widely used a thousand years later among wandering Japanese priests, who began to explore the effects of paper textures when using brushes to write haiku poems.

The practice took off with the rise of both popular photography and travel, which gave way to scrapbooking, but it swiftly found its greatest expression by being absorbed into the epochal art of such twentieth-century artists as Picasso and Braque, who finally coined the term "collage."

In a time where we are saturated with web-available images and computer-generated art, not to mention photosharing via cellphones and other digital devices, many designers are creating cutting-edge work by finding and sourcing printed matter that can be cut up, scanned, photocopied, painted on, and manipulated in much more experimental ways.

⬆ Alex Williamson's dark and sometimes disturbing work is visually rich and arresting, but also suggests the primitive, dirty output of old photocopiers and laser printers.

➡ David Joyce's work mixes photocopying, drawing, scanning, sampling, and notebook elements, and sets out to challenge and provoke the viewer.

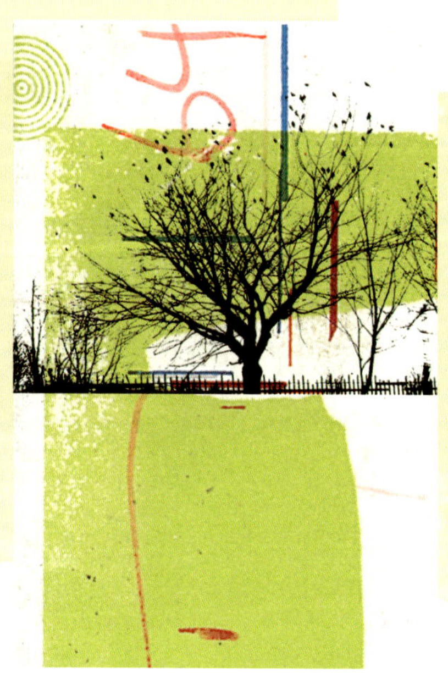

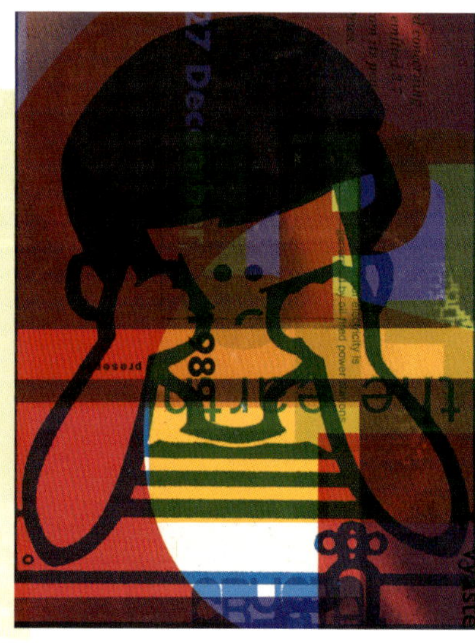

CREATIVE HINTS AND TIPS

- *Try mixing digital and nondigital techniques. Perhaps trace or sketch a photo/image and use that as the basis of any farther computer manipulation.*
- *Take a back-to-school approach and use charcoal, pencils, or other soft media to take rubbings from stone and other surfaces, and then scan the results into Photoshop.*
- *Acquire found images or objects via your scanner and import into Photoshop. Trawl markets, thrift stores, and building clearance sales to find unusual objects and fragments.*
- *Also scan found materials, graphics, packaging, etc. Try placing objects on your scanner, like pebbles, hands, feathers, and insects, and then importing the images into Photoshop.*
- *Experiment with scale: scan large objects and use them very small as details within your work; conversely, scan small objects and blow them up very large and explore the creative potential of image degradation and lower resolutions. Can you sample a texture from this and use it in your work?*
- *Scan at different resolutions to see what effects you can achieve.*

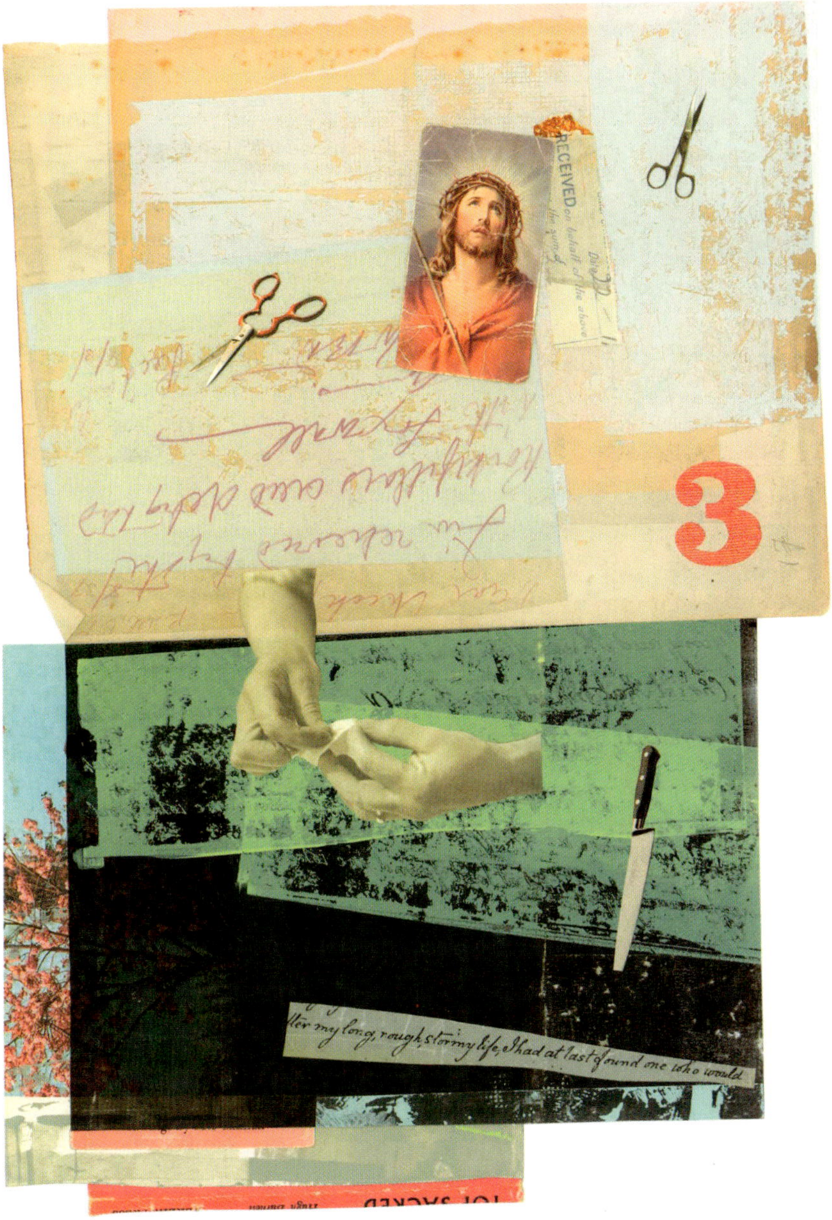

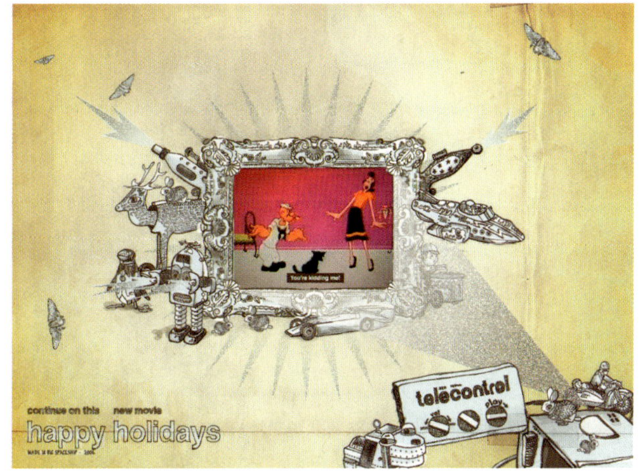

⬆ Martin O'Neill's instantly recognizable style is hands-on at every stage, rarely involving digital editing techniques except to scan or make color corrections.

⬅ Beta Design's mixed-media work is like a postcard from the future sent back to an earlier, more innocent time: a barrage of clip elements, scans, drawings, and samples.

Using pattern

One avenue that has truly been opened up by digital techniques is making and sourcing patterns, and using them as raw material within graphics and illustrations.

Take care, however: certain patterns are easily identifiable, and many are the intellectual property of their creators, some of whom (fashion houses, especially, but also some private individuals) can be extremely, and successfully, litigious.

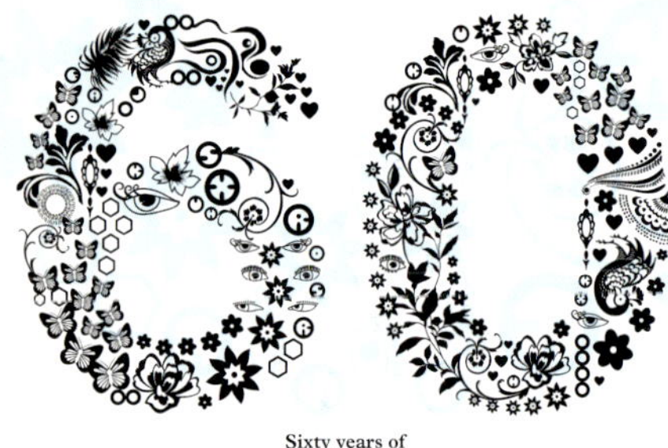

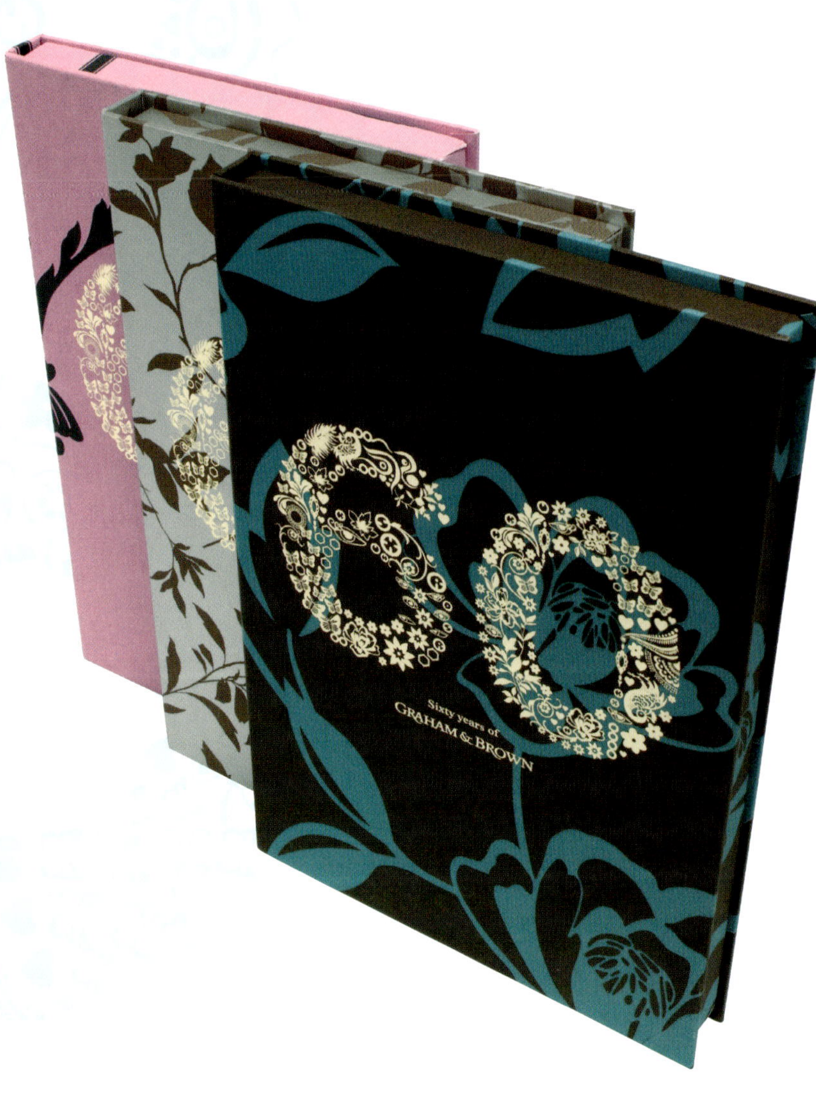

⬆ ➡ Peter and Paul's work is a study in elegance; a very modern take on a traditional theme, recalling the chicest in wallpaper designs, and the most modern graphic techniques. At heart, though, this is an assembly of clip-art icons into a pattern that works equally well as background texture, focal point, and as the substance of the letterforms. This demonstrates how sophisticated, expensive-looking design can be achieved with a few clip-art icons, which might even be derived from a freely available font, and then layered within a simple colorway.

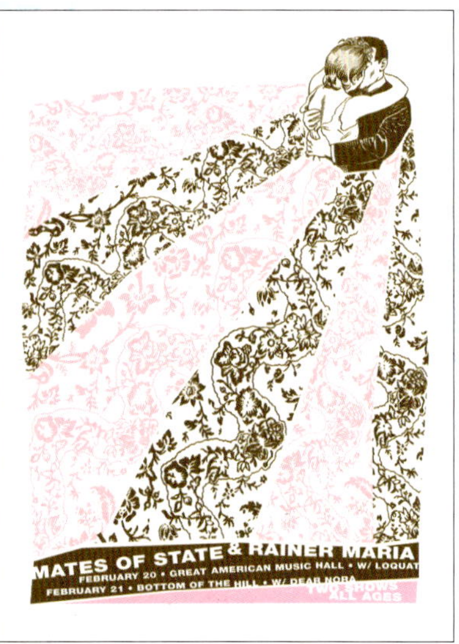

⬅ The Small Stakes floral tribute to Mates of State; floral pattern with overlaid diagonal stripes, topped out by clip-art figures.

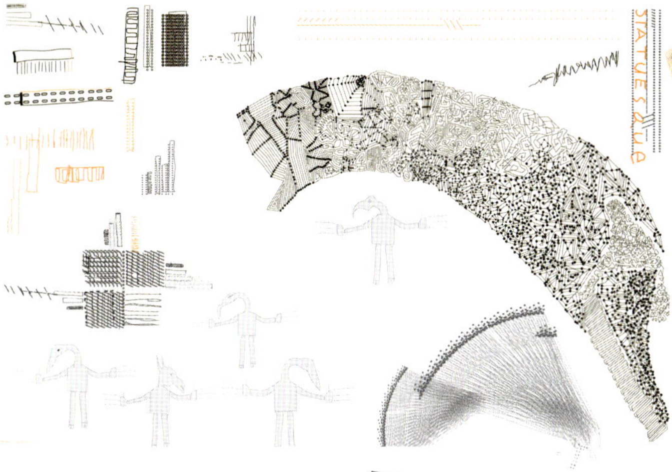

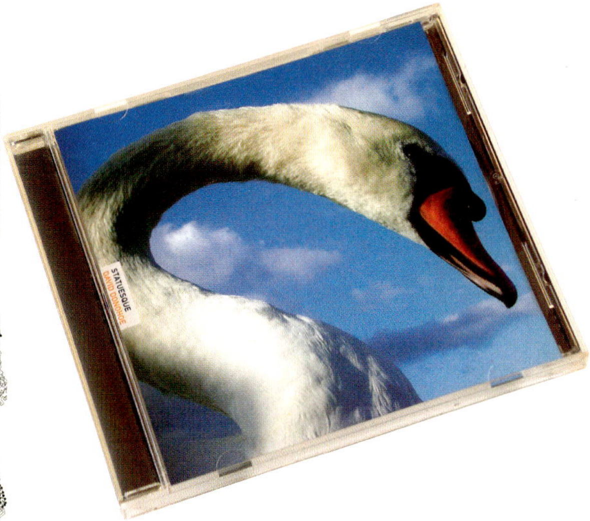

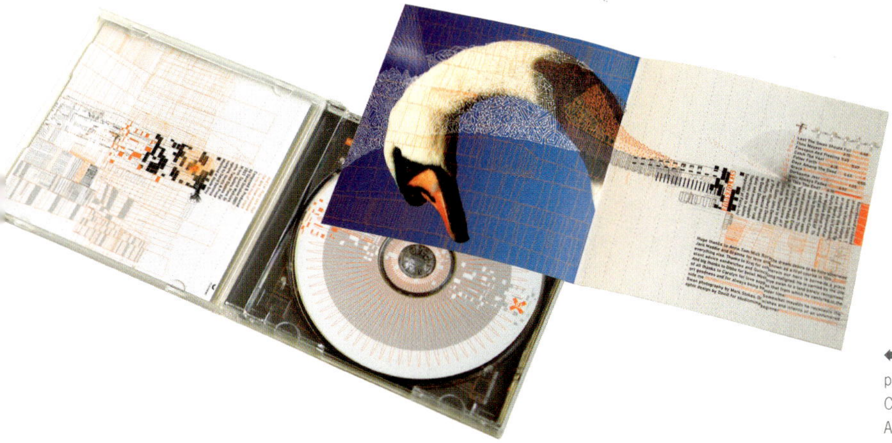

⬅ ⬆ Studiomime takes a source image and fills it with pattern to create a visual unity through the pages of this CD insert, which also ties it in with the label and cover. A good strategy for making the most of one or two strong visual ideas and playing with variations of them through the course of an extended design.

⬇ The Small Stakes presents an unusual combinaton of clip-art elements to create a geometric pattern reminiscent of traditional Arabic and Asian designs.

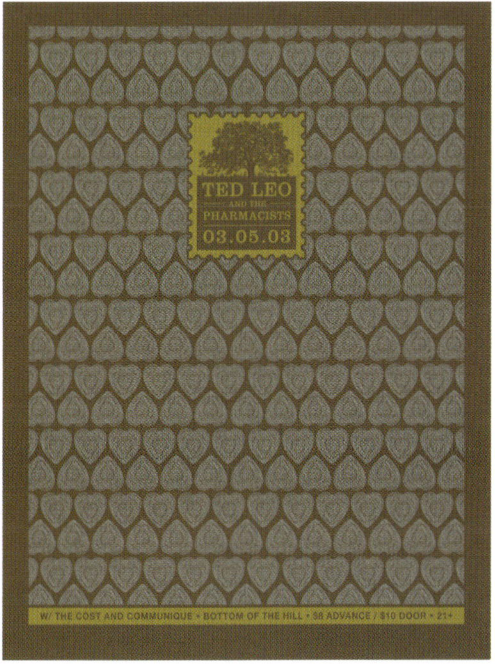

CREATIVE HINTS AND TIPS

— *Take a shape, or create a silhouette, and fill it with a pattern.*

— *Make patterns of your own in Photoshop or Illustrator, and create your own clip art from these to sample and use within a graphic or illustration.*

— *In Photoshop, create an outline or path and fill it with an unusual texture, or with a different image altogether.*

— *Scan old cloth samples and use the close-up image of the fabric as the raw material for a pattern fill.*

— *Add texture or pattern your background fills to make an image jump out from the page or screen.*

— *Create patterns with found decorative elements. Duplicate them, flip them, and layer them to create backgrounds and borders.*

— *Take details from digital photographs, sourcing motifs, shapes, and textures to tile and repeat to form patterns and decorative elements.*

Contrast and filters

Photoshop and programs like it are set up to allow the straightforward application of processes and techniques that in previous decades were largely the preserve of darkroom experts with expensive professional hardware or your local lab.

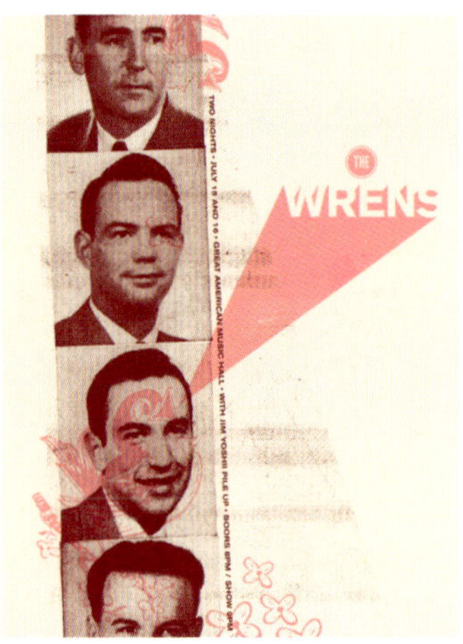

⬆⬇ The Small Stakes illustrate how clip art, texture, and the subtle application of filters and effects can provide striking work, even for limited-budget items, such as flyers and posters for one-off events.

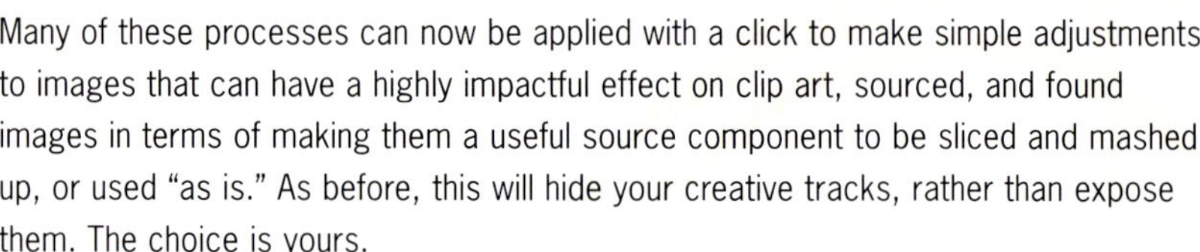

Many of these processes can now be applied with a click to make simple adjustments to images that can have a highly impactful effect on clip art, sourced, and found images in terms of making them a useful source component to be sliced and mashed up, or used "as is." As before, this will hide your creative tracks, rather than expose them. The choice is yours.

CREATIVE HINTS AND TIPS

— *Adjust brightness and contrast to simplify a four-color image, objectify it, and explore its potential as a graphical or mood device, rather than as a photorealistic representation of the object in its original state.*

— *Experiment with Levels to expose the tonal potential of your source material and push it to extremes.*

— *Follow what would normally be your worst instincts by making overt use of all the filters you would normally reject for photographic work—rubber stamp, plaster, graphic pen, halftone pattern, torn edges, and so on.*

— *Exposing obvious, point-and-click working methods such as this can be crass in the wrong hands, but in the hands of a skilled professional they can push the freshness of a brilliant concept to the fore. In some contexts, the very use of such a drop-down menu standard shows you have guts—as long as you can pull it off.*

— *Make your image original. Manipulating images in this way also makes it easier to mix images from different sources, and of different styles, giving them a similar overall look.*

— *Distress them, simplify them, complicate them. Experiment with a whole palette of different techniques—don't be afraid of something simply because it is easy to do. If you can see it, do it.*

— *Equally, don't rely on your Mac or PC. Turn it off and get your hands busy with source material you can touch, cut up, and play with in the real world. It will enrich your digital work beyond compare and put a broader palette of techniques at your fingertips—perhaps even a new direction for your work, or for a difficult brief.*

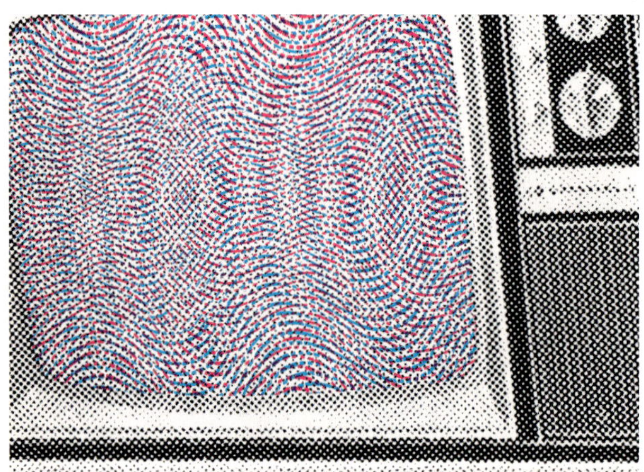

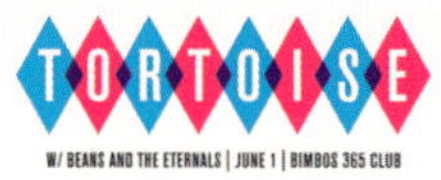

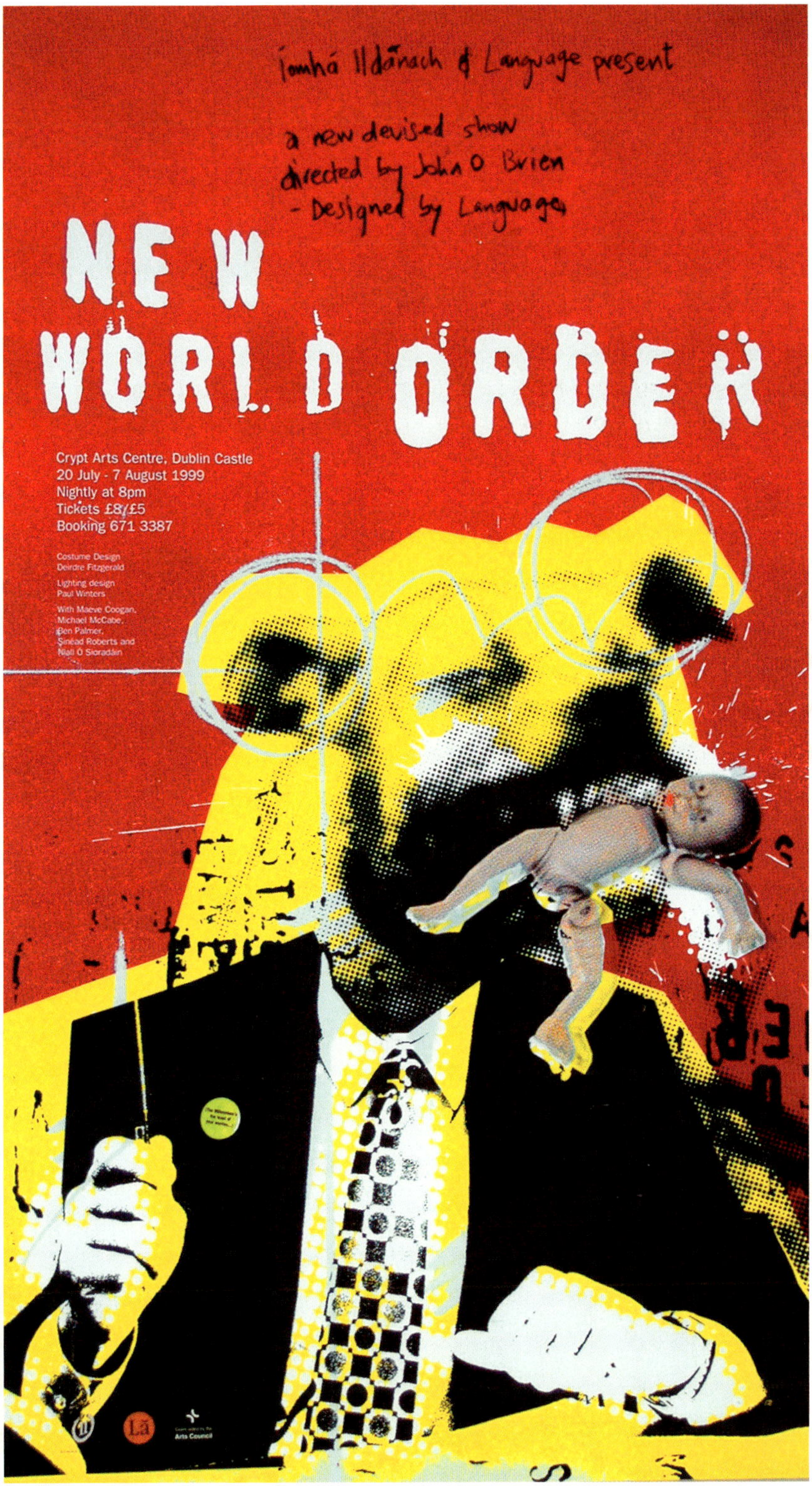

⬆ David Joyce said that in response to the content of the play, *New World Order*, staged by a Dublin theater company, he wanted to create an image that was striking and compelling. The image—inspired by Goya's *Saturn Devouring One of his Children*—was built using a variety of mixed-media techniques, given extra finesse by the application of pushed contrast and posterizing effects.

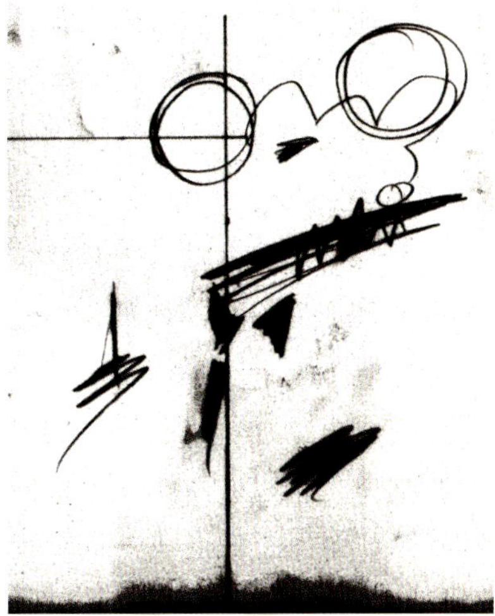

⬆ David Joyce produced these hand-drawn elements on a separate layer and overlaid them on the collage of found and clip images before solarizing the entire image and applying the filter effects.

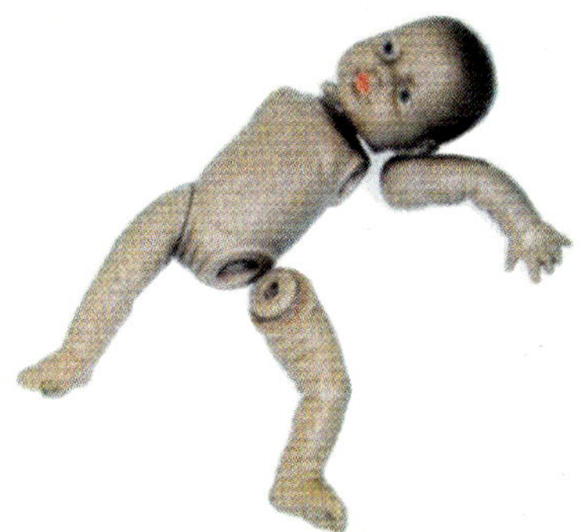

⬆ This is one of the main images sourced by Joyce to be combined into the final image.

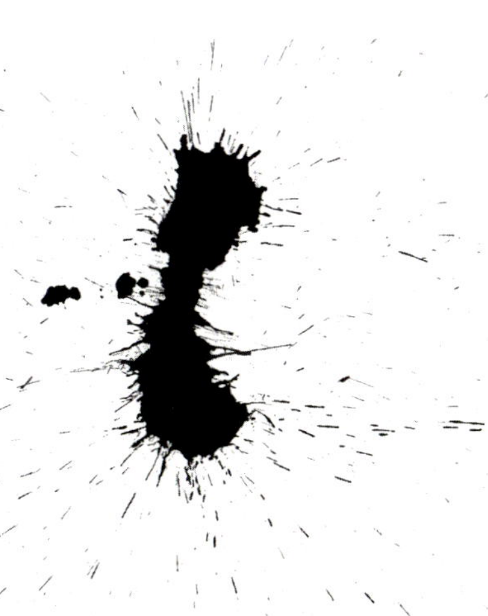

⬆ Joyce placed this ink splash image in one corner of the composition, adding a cartoon-like dash of graphical violence to the image.

Distortion and textures

In the fleeting present, we think that digital techniques remove texture and create a sharp, pixel-perfect sample of the real world, but we swiftly realize looking back (and these days nostalgia travels just as fast as technology does) that every technology we use to capture and edit the real world adds a definitive, characteristic texture to our work, just as film and vinyl does.

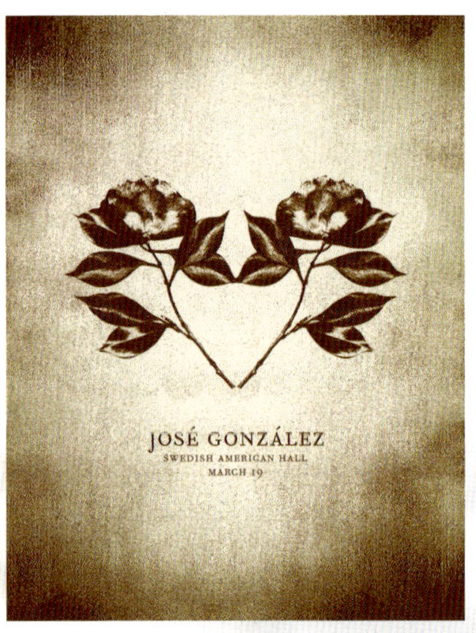

▲ The Small Stakes prove yet again that they are masters of the poster form, using texture and granular effect over their signature clip-art selections to lift this design out of the ordinary and give it real presence and impact.

▼ The Joneses use texture and subverted iconic images to make fun of the printing world, while also showing the potential impact of the printed page.

Musicians go to great lengths to fake the unique sound of earlier digital instruments now that we can hear, in retrospect, that they offered a far from perfect copy of real instruments. Cold and clinical machines? No, their now-obvious texture and lack of realism seems quaint and even charming: something to emulate. The same goes for digital image-making: soon, early digital cameras will be sought-after retro objects whose imprecise, jittery, pixelated sampling quality will become a desirable texture for graphic work, and maybe some photographers.

Cellphone companies are now the world's biggest camera manufacturers, and cellphone cameras have already changed the way videos and photos look, because moving a phone while shooting a video clip or still image creates wildy fluctuating wavy lines and a very imprecise, noisy motion blur. We now proudly share murky images from cellphones printed on letterpaper though a desktop ink-jet, whereas a few years ago, we might have been sharing pristine film prints from our local labs.

Texture is inherent in every image and object, but it is also inherent in every era, or age, because of the media we choose to record the times in which we live. So play with that quality in your work.

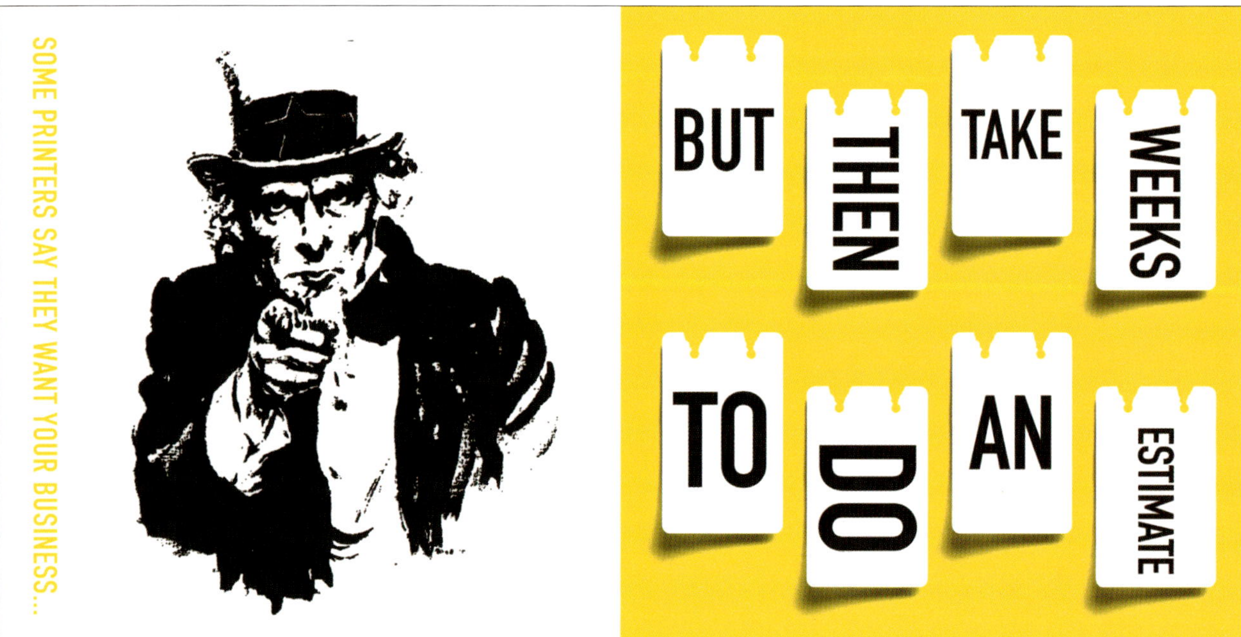

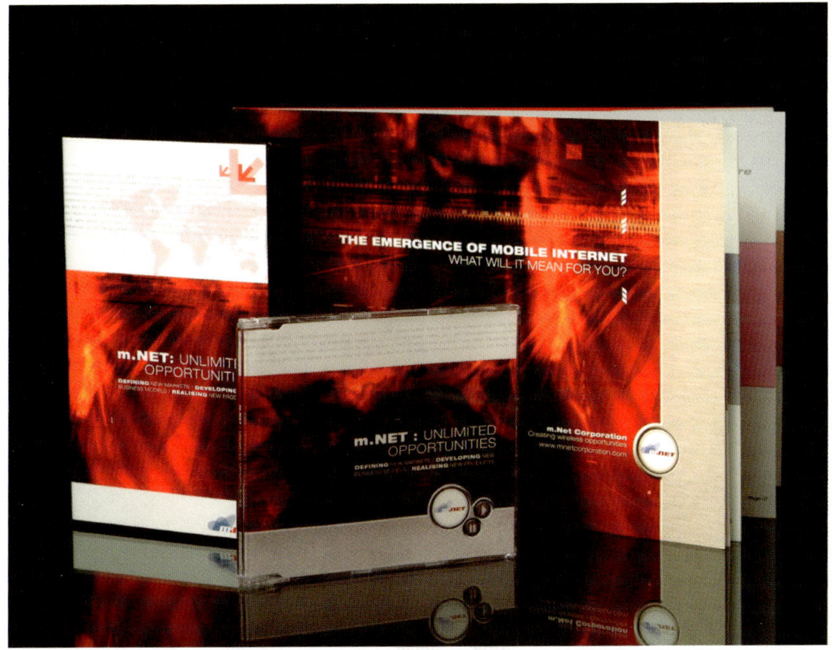

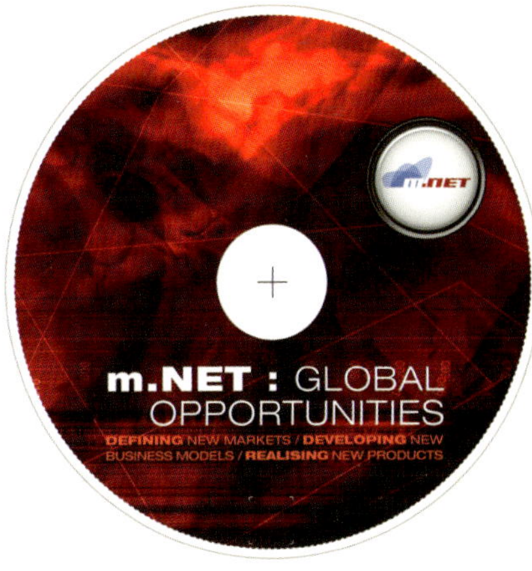

Studio threefiftyseven raise this corporate design package head and shoulders above most others with the intelligent use of texture and manipulated stock shots.

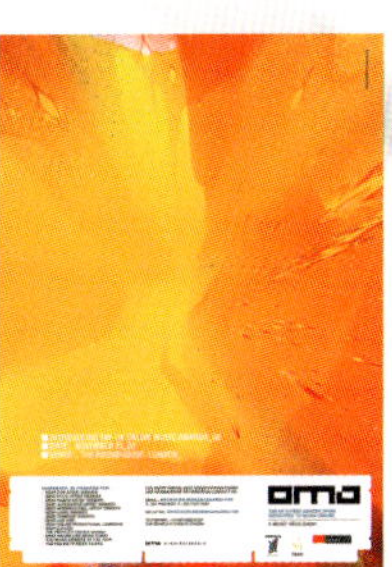

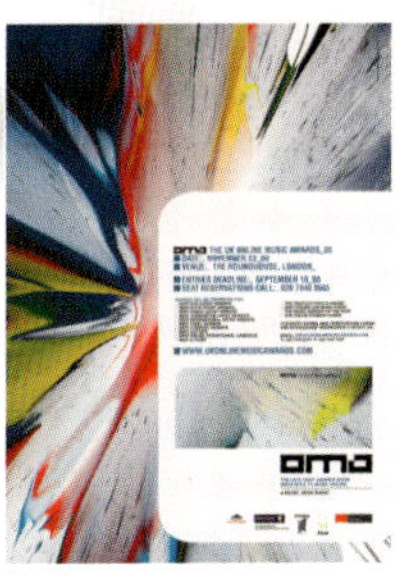

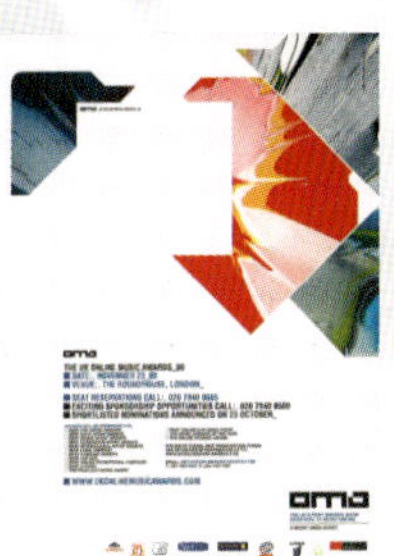

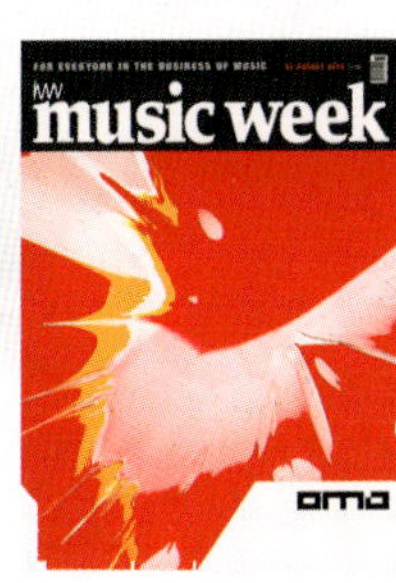

Form studio lives up to its name by distorting widely available images out of all recognition for this series of designs. Any image, it suggests, can be the jumping off point for wild experimentation.

CREATIVE HINTS AND TIPS

— *Adding grain and texture to any given piece of clip art, found image, or graphical element gives it a rougher, handcrafted feel, or adds the characteristic feel of a particular media, technology, or its associated era.*

— *Texture palettes in Photoshop allow you to experiment with a number of different grain types. You can add film grain, photo grain, and so on, giving a fresh image a retro look and removing its shine: now it's just as good as old.*

— *Create textures by sampling elements of found images and graphics and applying them to the whole; also by magnifying key elements. Keep saving downward and see what effect lower resolutions have on image texture. (Keep a copy of the original, higher-res image.)*

— *Import textured or patterned images as backgrounds. This works best with abstract images.*

— *Abstract images can be bought from photo libraries. Alternatively, create your own by photographing abstract textures or patterns, such as rusty metal, pebbles on a beach, or grass. Shoot at night without flash and see what abstract patterns are created by moving lights.*

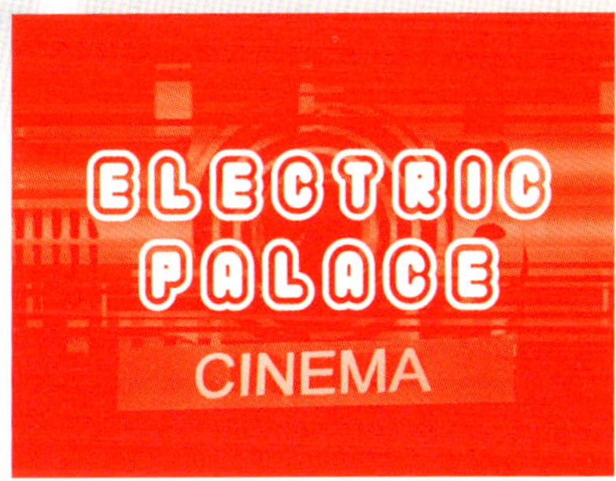

This image by Studio Ink for an independent cinema's brochure has been created by distorting and manipulating a number of images in Photoshop. These have then been layered together to create an abstract background that has a film-like quality.

Cutouts and cutups

The heart of the contemporary collage and photomontage, cutups and cutouts are conceptually rooted in scrapbooking, and in the experiments of the Beat Poets in the 1950s on the one hand, and also in shadow play and theater on the other. To remove a character from its context (to cut him, her, or it out of its background) is to focus on that character, and to invite reintepretation.

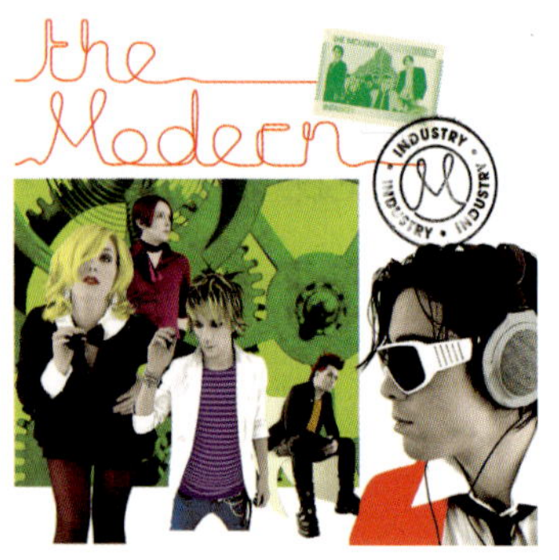

CREATIVE HINTS AND TIPS

— Isolate images by making simple cutouts.

— Equally, create character by making simple cutouts. For example, if you cut one character out of an ancient photograph of a group gathering, and you create a story around that person, give him a name, strip away the anonymity that history has lent him, and supply him with a new contemporary context.

— Cutouts can be done by hand or in Photoshop by drawing around the image with the Lasso tool, or using the Highlight tool if the contrast between background and image is great enough.

— Once cut out, experiment by placing the image on different colored backgrounds, overlapping with other images, duplicating to create patterns, and so on. Use a number of images to build up a composition.

— Look for beautiful or unusual examples of everyday objects; cut them out and keep them, and build up reference collections of mood board raw materials. Being a curator or collector can suggest expertise in a given area, but it can also be about an impulsive or emotional reaction to an image you like—or you may simply be a hoarder! The more you collect and curate, the more you will become attuned to the fine distinctions between images of similar objects.

⬆ Form show that cutting images out of their original context can transform the meaning of even familiar stock shots, clip-art icons, or found imagery.

➡ AdamsMorioka make a design feature out of these cutups and clip image sources, even suggesting a recycled aspect that seems to be a good fit with the Sundance Film Festival's humanistic and budget-conscious credentials.

⬇ Plan-B Studio constructed this piece entirely from cutout clip-art elements, and clipped sourced imagery.

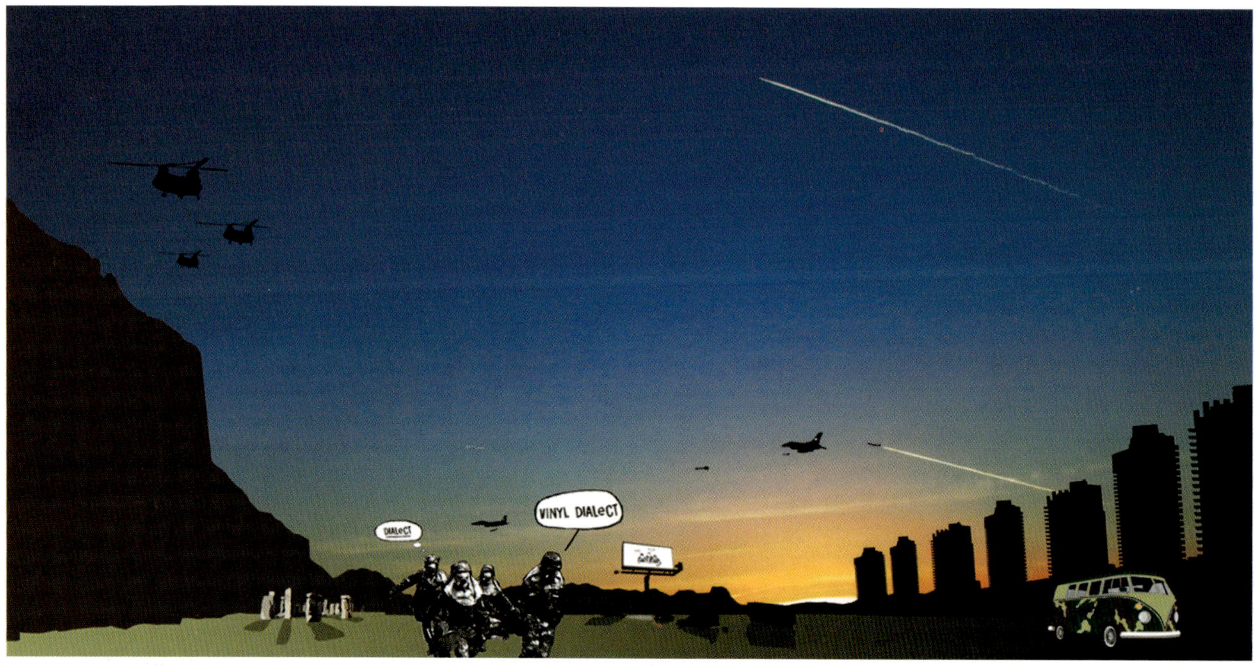

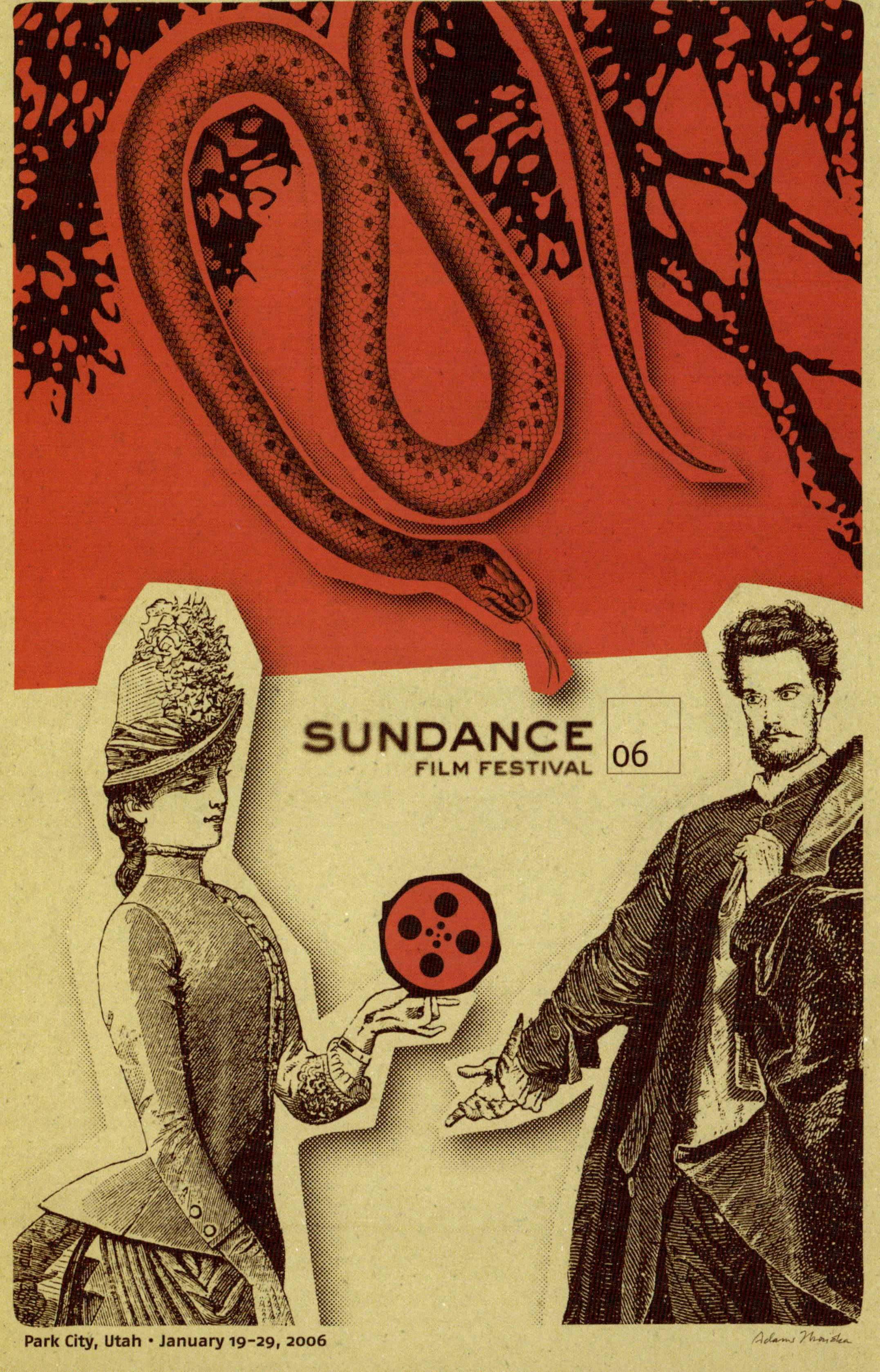
SUNDANCE
FILM FESTIVAL
06
Park City, Utah • January 19–29, 2006

Grouping images

Sometimes just removing images from their original contexts is enough to create something that looks unique. Old found photographs from personal albums and scrapbooks can be used to suggest an idea or get a concept across to a client.

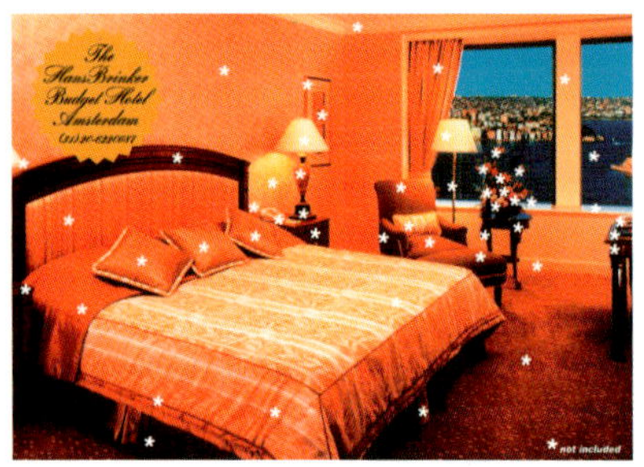

KesselsKramer overlay clip asterisks to pinpoint all of the "luxury" features that are *not* available at this budget, no-frills hotel.

Old images can be cut and pasted into new situations giving them a modern feel, or forming a commentary on some aspect of contemporary life by illustrating it with images from another era—for example, 1950s nuclear families representing a story of contemporary twenty-first century life. Putting together a collection of similar images, or images which share some common aspect, is a statement in itself: the collection is both a group of individual images or objects, and an entity that invites new perspectives and interpretations.

— *Recontextualize the everyday. For example, Absolute Zero° scanned a printed page of numerals set in a particular typeface; blew up the numerals so that the texture of the ink on the printed page was visible; combined the numerals, at different sizes, into a larger pattern, tiled the pattern, and then changed the colorways. The result: a beautiful retro design that was printed as a modern wallpaper and as a decorative motif on a range of crockery.*

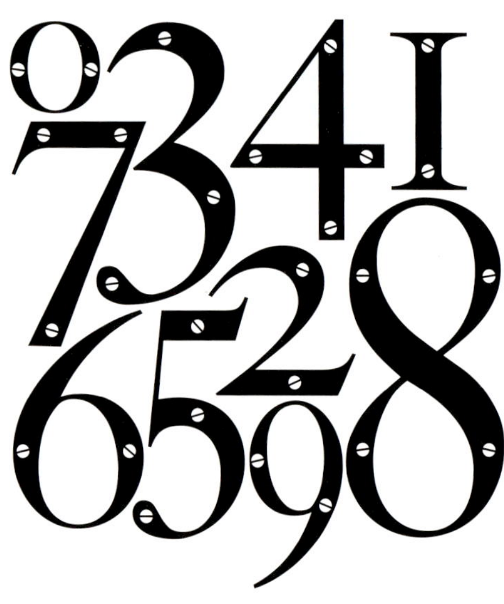

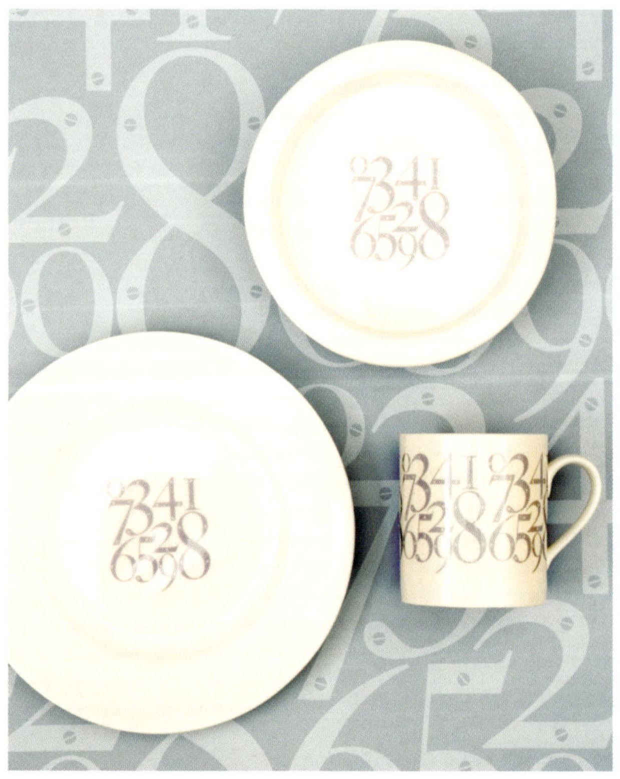

Absolute Zero° grouped together these numerals from the font Big Caslon Medium to create a recurring motif on their wallpaper and crockery designs (right).

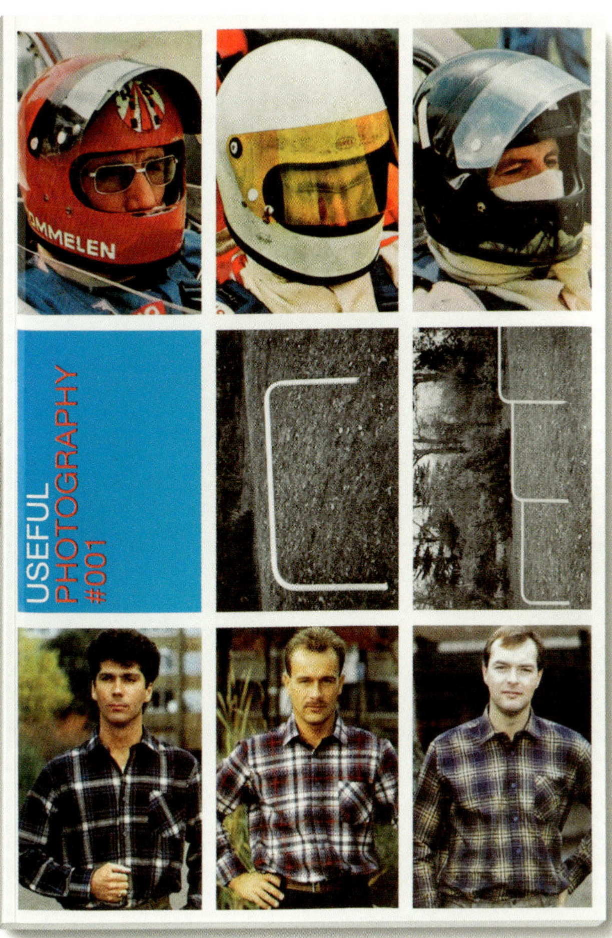

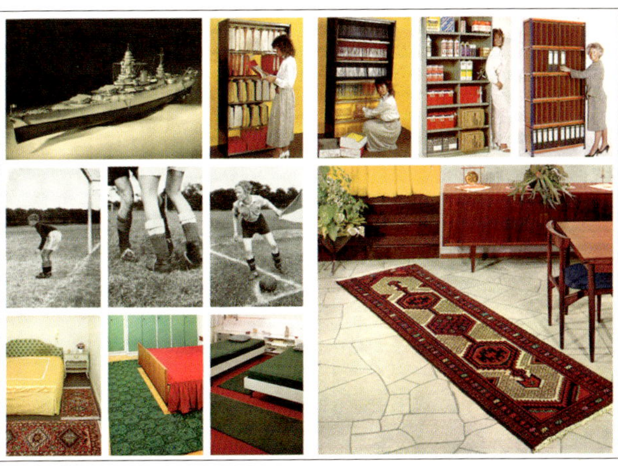

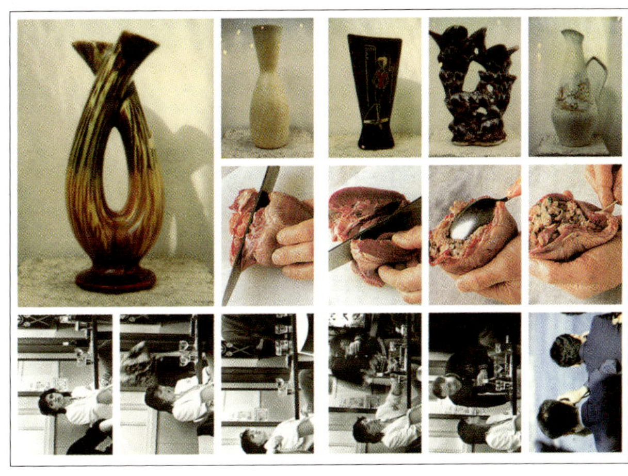

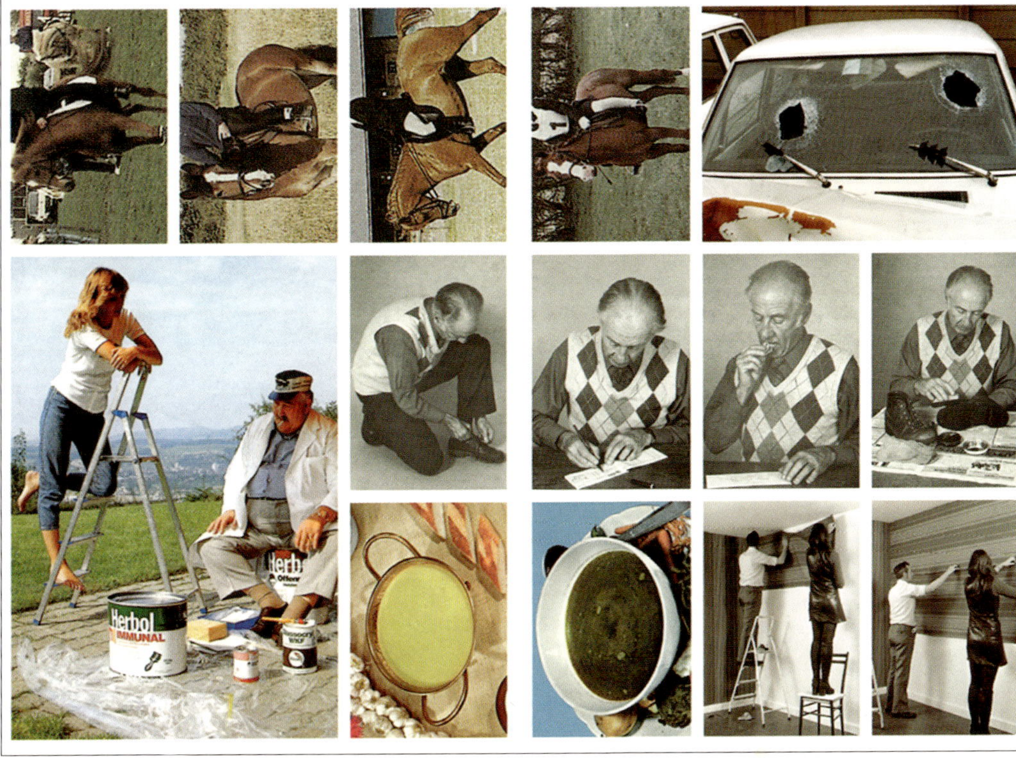

⬅ ⬆ KesselsKramer produced its *Useful Photography* series, celebrating what it calls "more down-to-earth" photography that would normally be ignored until put into the new context of this ongoing magazine series.

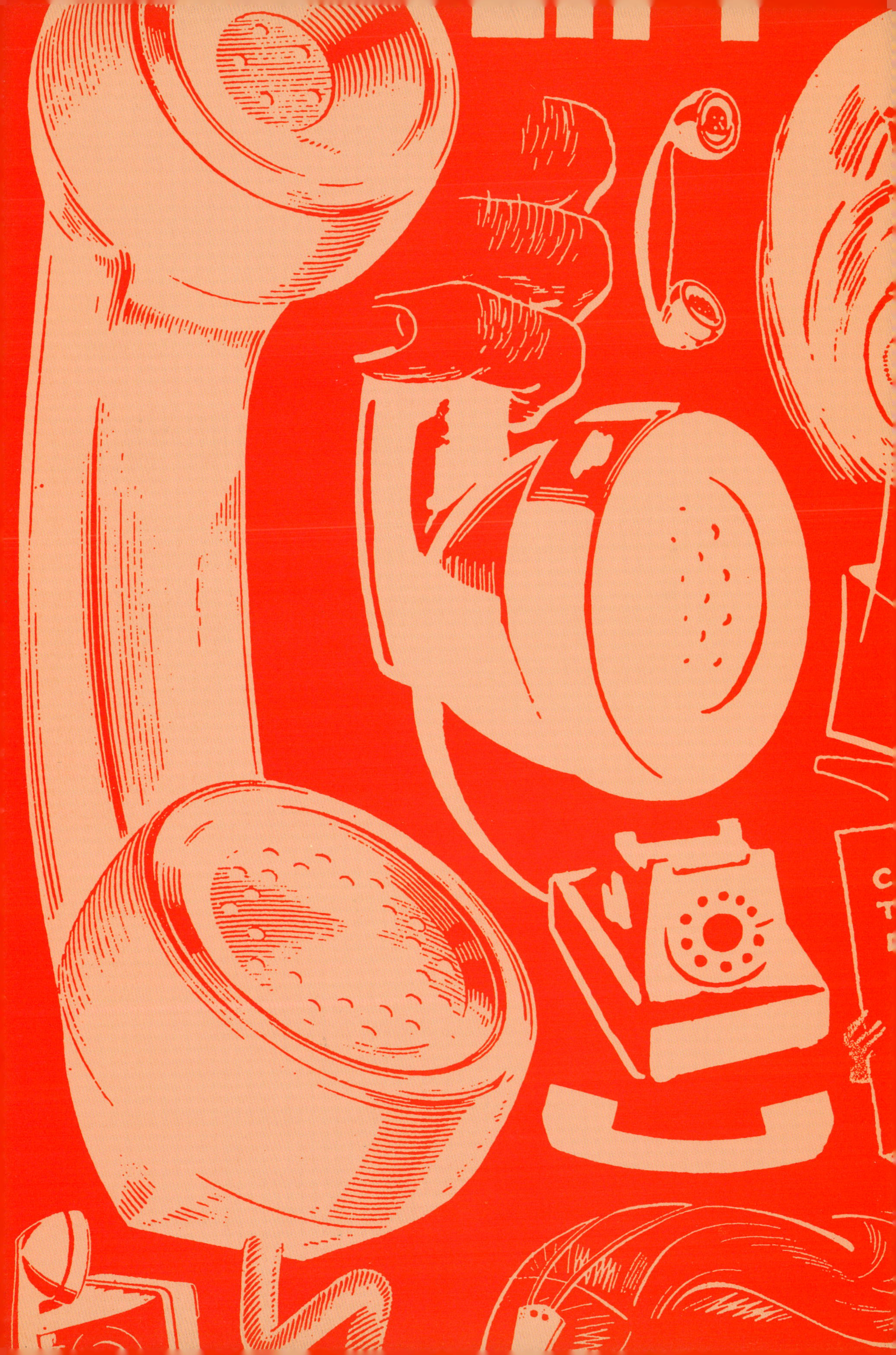

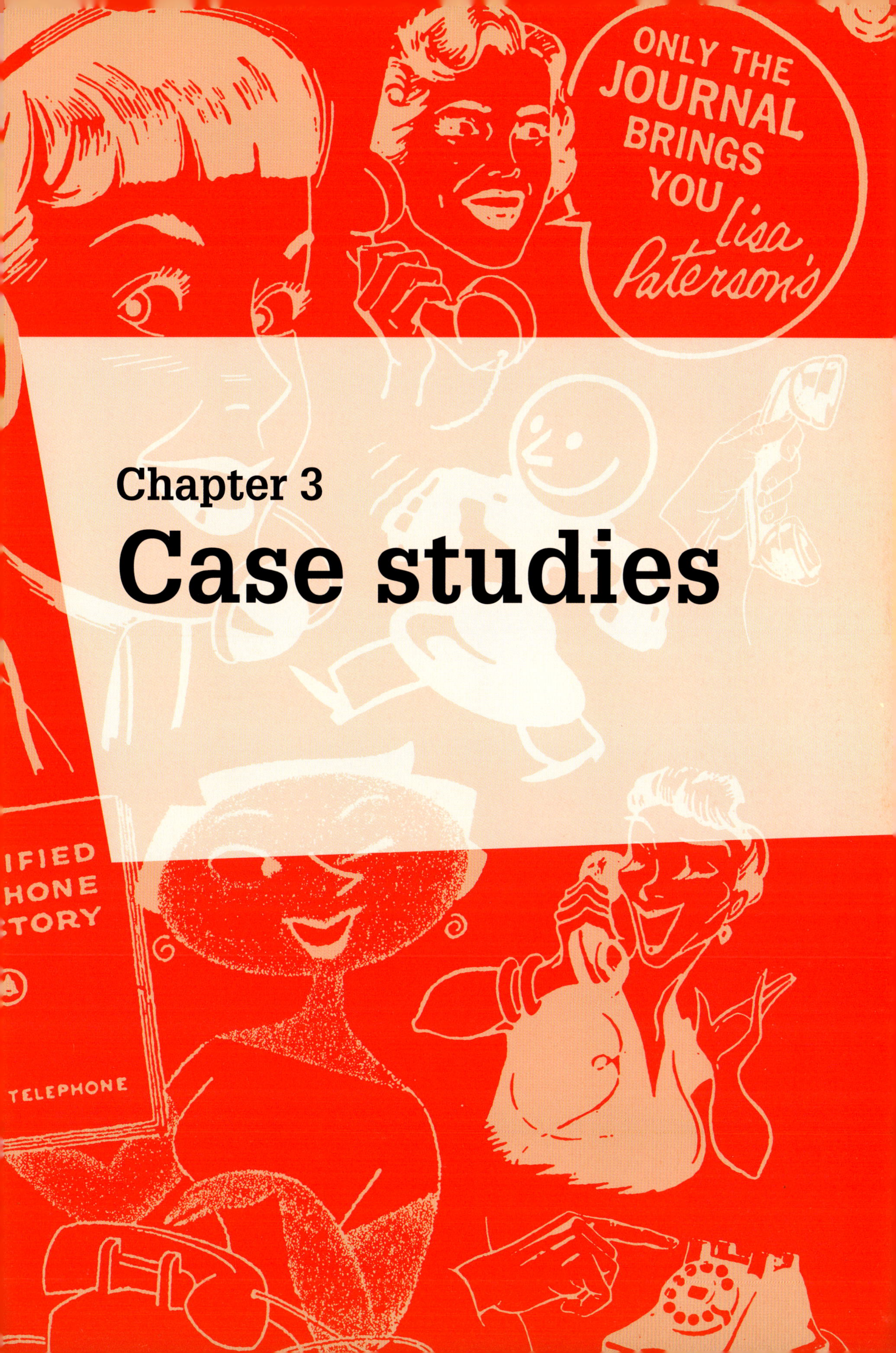

Chapter 3
Case studies

AdamsMorioka

Beverly Hills-based design studio AdamsMorioka would seem to be ideally placed to produce work for Hollywood and the movie industry, and yet it took a very nonHollywood movie mogul, one synonymous with independent American movies, to capitalize on the studio's talents.

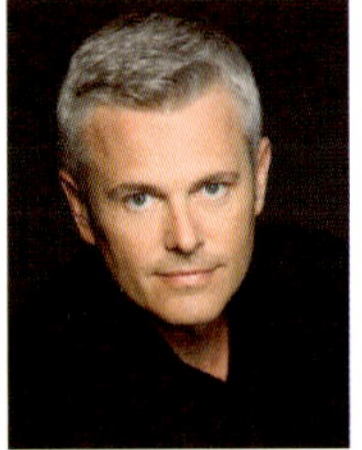

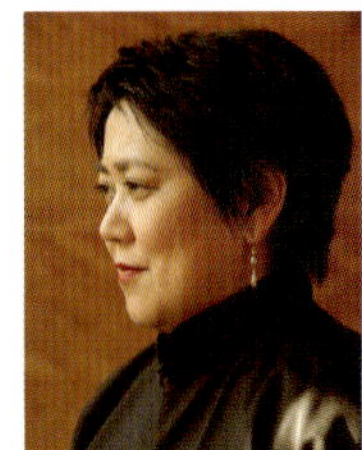

"Without the Sundance Institute, film today would likely consist of one car chase and explosion after another, with no alternative. Since its founding, Sundance has promoted the individual voice," say design duo AdamsMorioka, who were asked by the Institute to design a campaign for a programming block on the Sundance Channel. It soon became clear that this was the tip of the iceberg, they say.

The team explain that they were soon involved with clarifying the voice of all Sundance projects, channels, institutions, and entities, including movie workshops and festivals, various commercial brands, and creating a cohesive tone across multiple groups and leaders. The solution was not in a "Grand Unification Theory," they say, but based on a clear message to be told with dissimilar visual systems—a single, rigid, identity system communicates a corporate structure that is antithetical to Sundance's independent, "frontier spirit," talent-hothousing outlook. A system with a basis in ideas—expressed in a multiplicity of sourced and found imagery—allows for continuing creativity, change, and surprise.

One of the key building blocks of the various visual identities that the team brought to the table was the extensive use of clip-art style imagery, found imagery, and images across a variety of styles that the team researched and downloaded, as well as sought from print-based resources.

If the Sundance Channel is about personal vision, creativity, and filmmaking—built in the complex and enigmatic image of Robert Redford—there was no need for tricky typography, multiple shapes, or avant garde color combinations. Sundance is about ways of seeing.

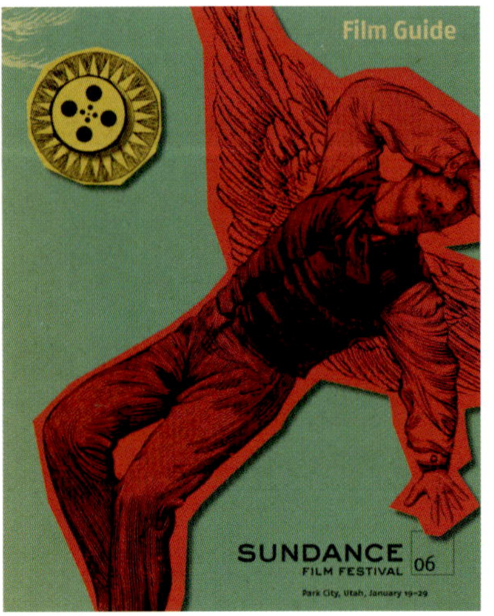

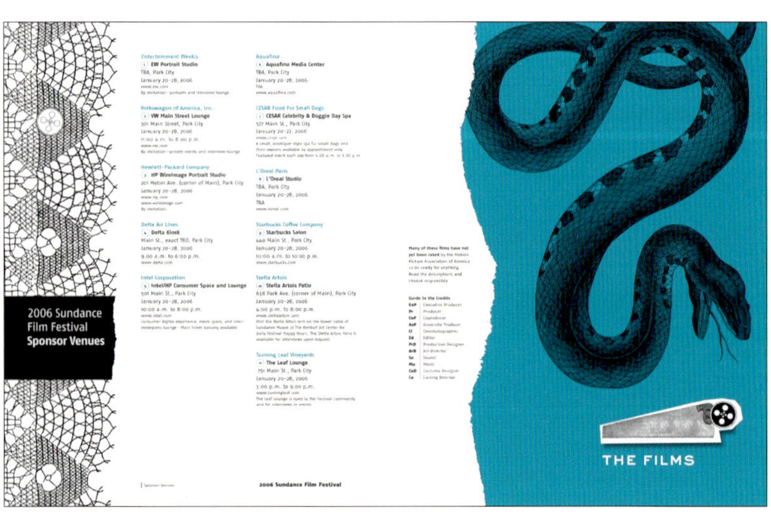

↓ Film Guide for the 2006 Film Festival. The theme of the festival was storytelling. AdamsMorioka used "found imagery to represent major characters," says designer Monica Schlaug.

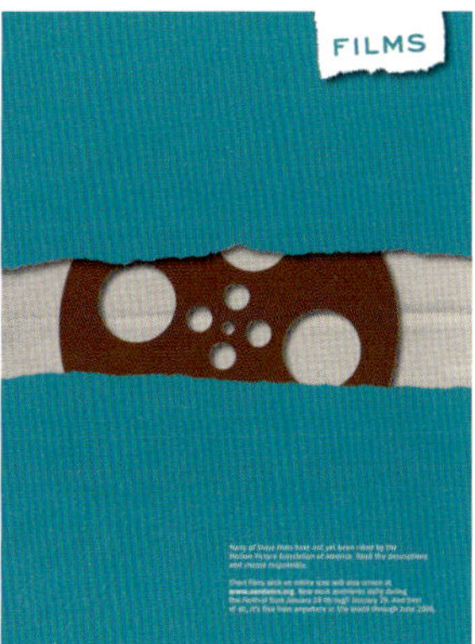

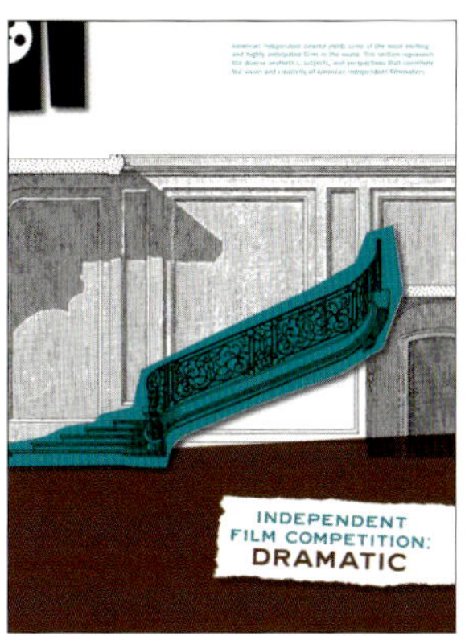

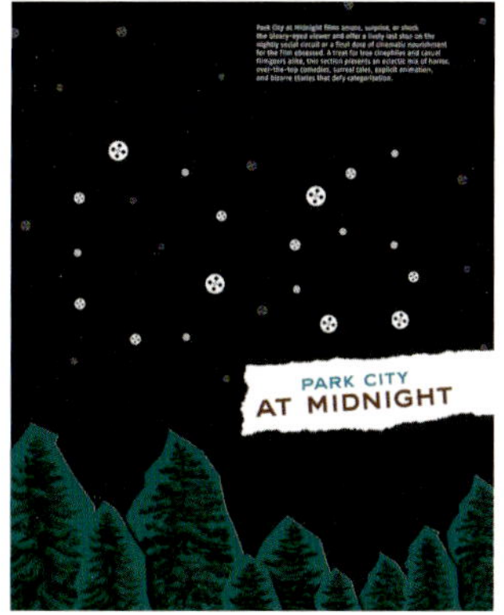

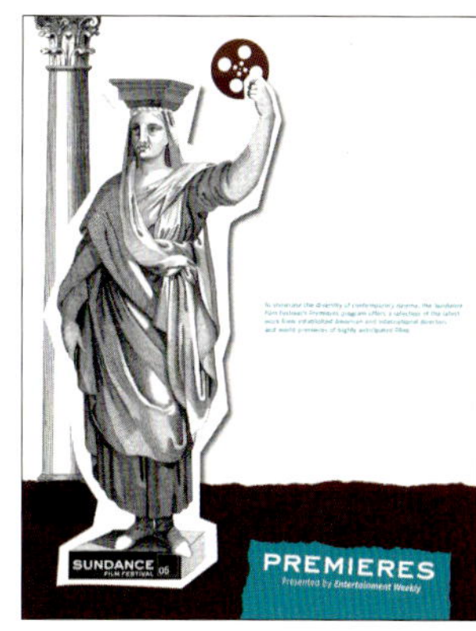

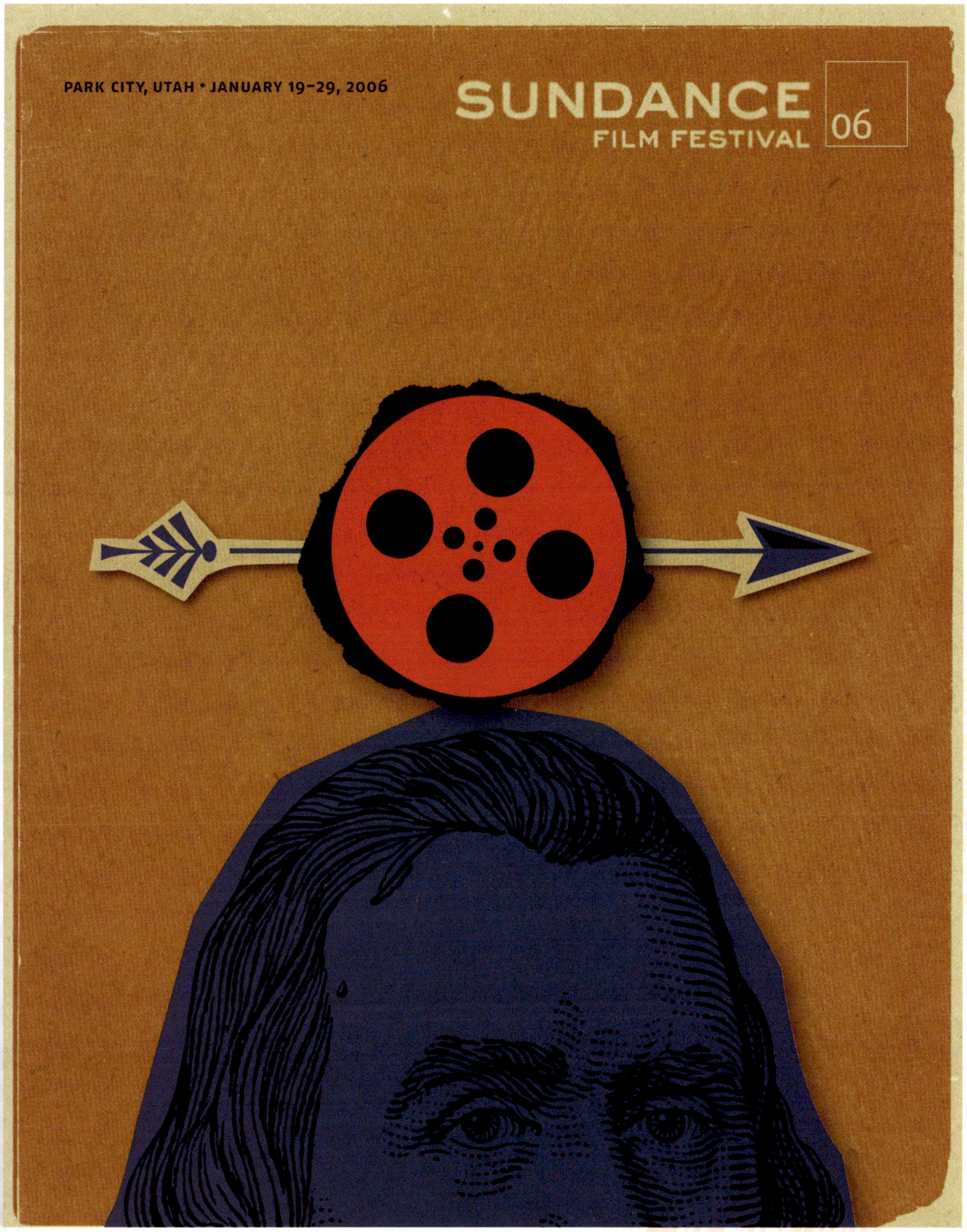

PARK CITY, UTAH • JANUARY 19–29, 2006

SUNDANCE
FILM FESTIVAL 06

Brochure for the 2006 Film Festival. The clip-art design approach allows the run of work to be both consistent and consistently surprising.

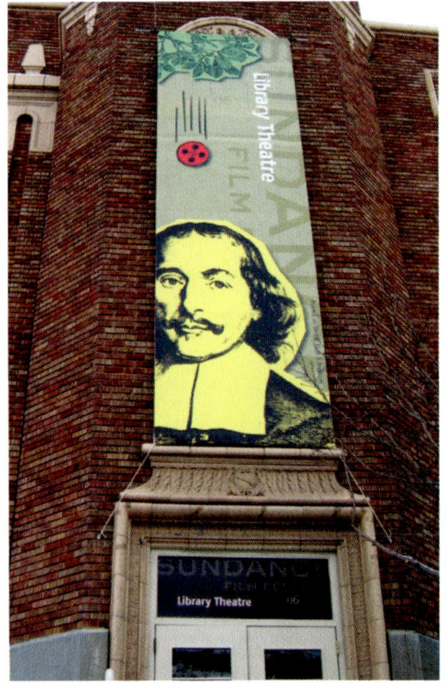

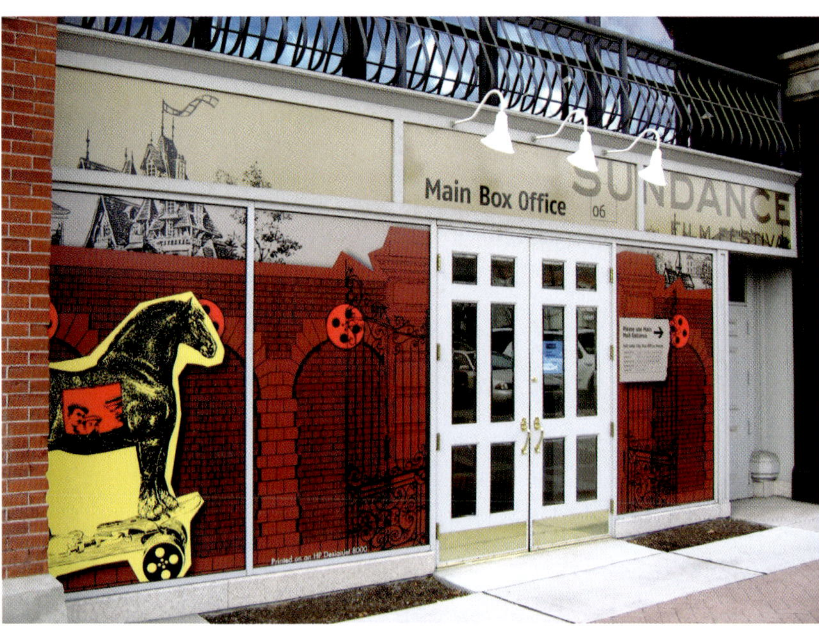

⬆ Even the festival's signage carried the clip art and found imagery theme, creating a powerful unity of design across every aspect of the festival's visual presence.

➡ The use of clip art and a wide range of found imagery was appropriate for a number of reasons: first, it showcased diversity and a multitude of image references appropriate to a showcase of diverse movie work; second, it communicated an event steeped in tradition, and yet also modern and remixed; and third, it cleverly suggested that creativity and sophistication are achievable on a low-budget—something that is at the very heart and soul of independent movies.

For the channel idents, a library of film was created focusing on images that involved "missed moments"—a plane flying overhead, the pattern of water over river rocks, bare feet on fresh grass—details missed by others, but noticed by a filmmaker. Sundance seeks to attract filmmakers and writers who have stories to tell about the world around them, rather than the usual blockbuster approach.

This working regime was extended to Sundance's many print-based promotional items and informational resources, in the form of clip-art style found imagery that, arguably, captures the frontier spirit and brings it back into the Sundance visual identity.

Adams explains the studio's attitude to clip art, sourced, and found imagery in the context of their work for Sundance. "I can't remember not using found imagery in my work," he says. "I'm inspired by other designers, not as in, 'I need to do exactly what Michael Vanderbyl does,' but by their incredible enthusiasm and commitment to creativity. Designers take a beating. Designers deal with subjects that are very close to our clients' hearts, and creativity is very personal. But they still get excited, try new things, and are committed to the culture and society at large. That is remarkable." A good fit with the Sundance ethic, it seems.

Asked to name some of the sources of clip art and found images that he used, Adams says: "The Library of Congress is a great source for copyright-free, no cost images. We also scoured used bookstores for Victorian books and ephemera.

"I have never met a designer who is not a closet collector of something. Whether it's thimbles, Japanese packaging, or rocks, everyone has one collection. Being a collector is just like being a designer; you don't choose to be a designer, it chooses you. You don't choose to collect tin toys, they choose you. I remember Saul Bass' office filled with multiple collections. Every time I visited him it grew, until there was little room to navigate to his desk!"

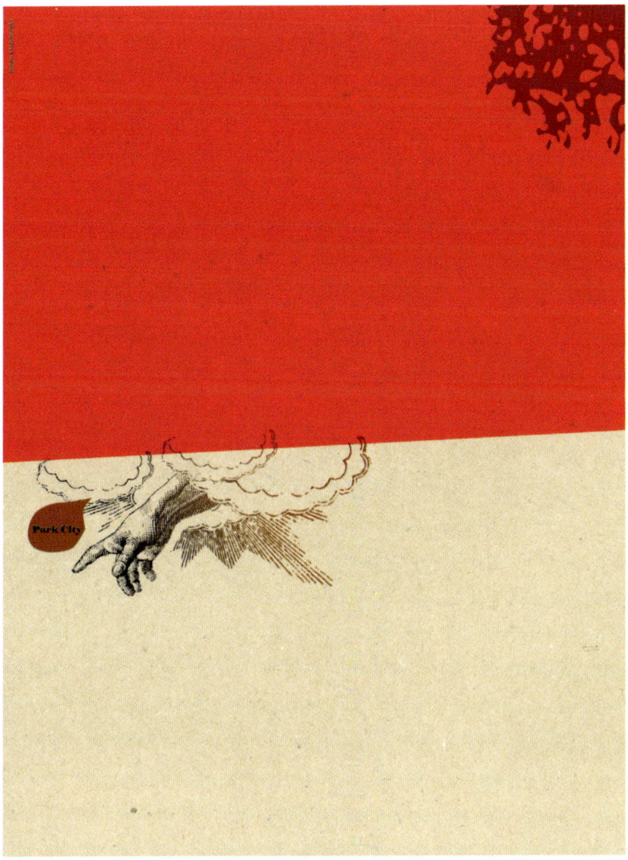

Park City

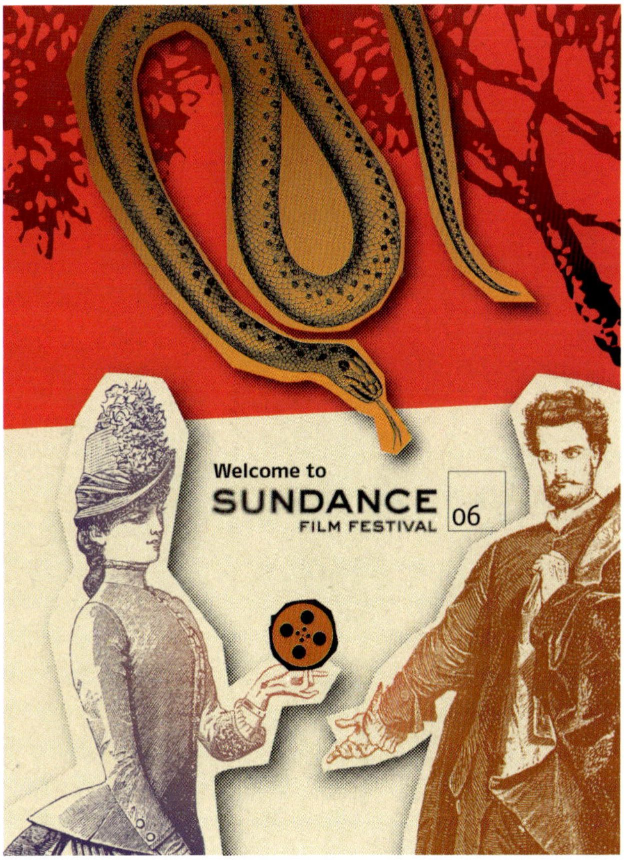

Welcome to
SUNDANCE
FILM FESTIVAL
06

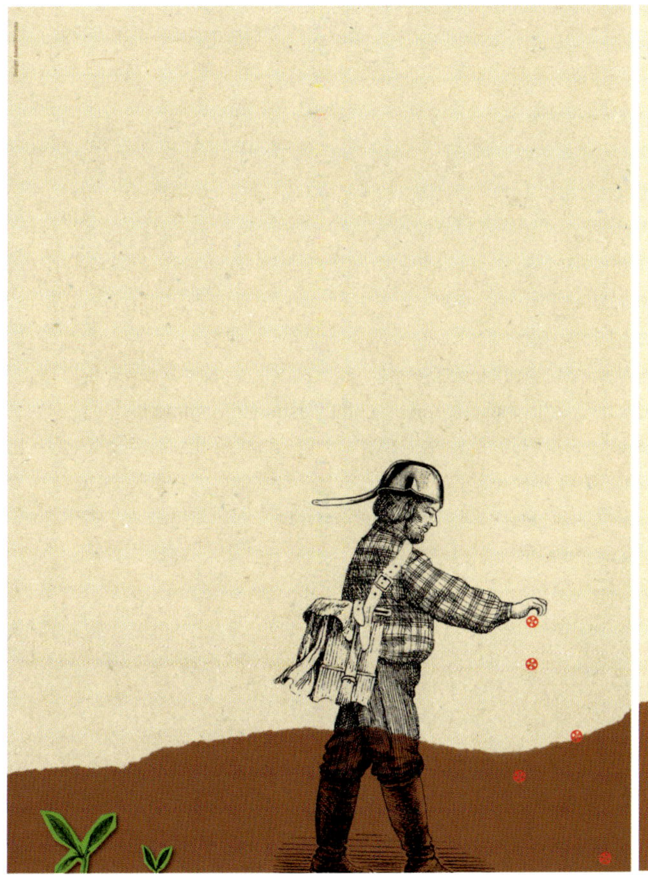

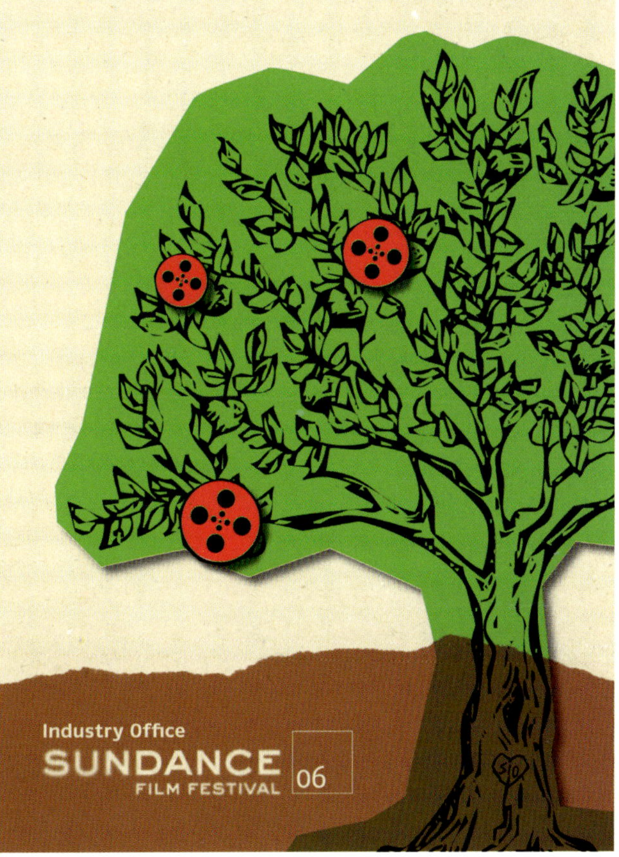

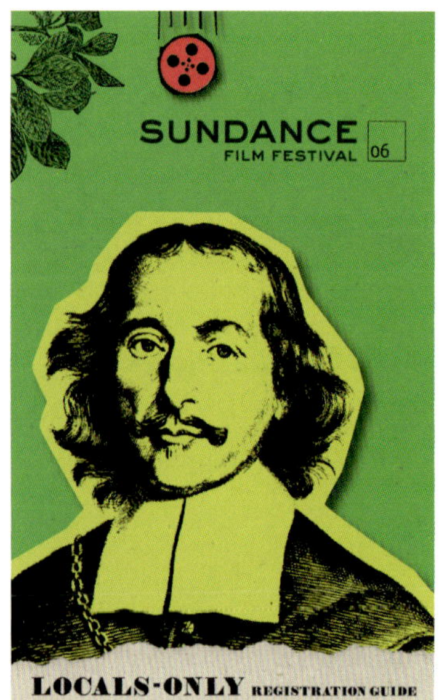

With the collector ethos in mind, do AdamsMorioka build libraries of images to use within their work? "No, each project is unique. I'd rather focus on the project at hand, and if found imagery is appropriate, it is used for that client and no others."

Several issues were uncovered during the Sundance design project. The Sundance Institute's large number and broad variety of activities, programs, and initiatives were unclear to much of its audience, and the audience itself had evolved from the Institute's original filmmaking workshop activities in the 1980s, and was now rather less defined. The design response included clear definitions of audience, values, history, connectivity, and the mediums that the Institute supports.

The festival itself needs to reinvent itself every year, say AdamsMorioka, with annual themes ranging from, in recent years, the frontier spirit to notions of "the West" (i.e. Western culture, not the Wild West), and so creating multiple identities around found imagery, including moving images, is a way to create visual diversity and also longevity in the context of the Institute's ongoing programs.

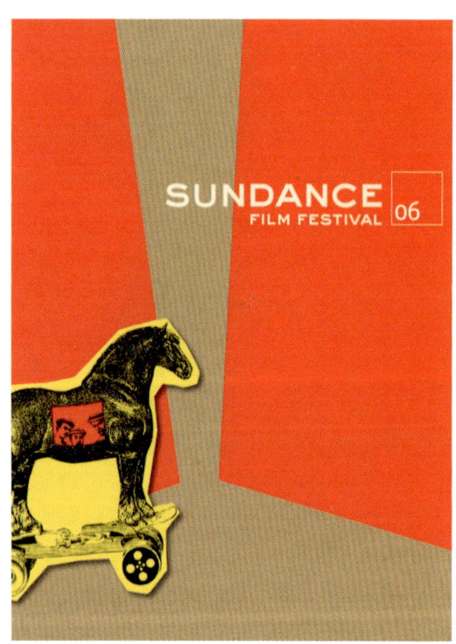

Registration brochure cover. The visual identity was also fun, and suggested that storytelling has a playful, childlike quality, rather than being something cynical and calculated, as so much big-budget Hollywood moviemaking has become.

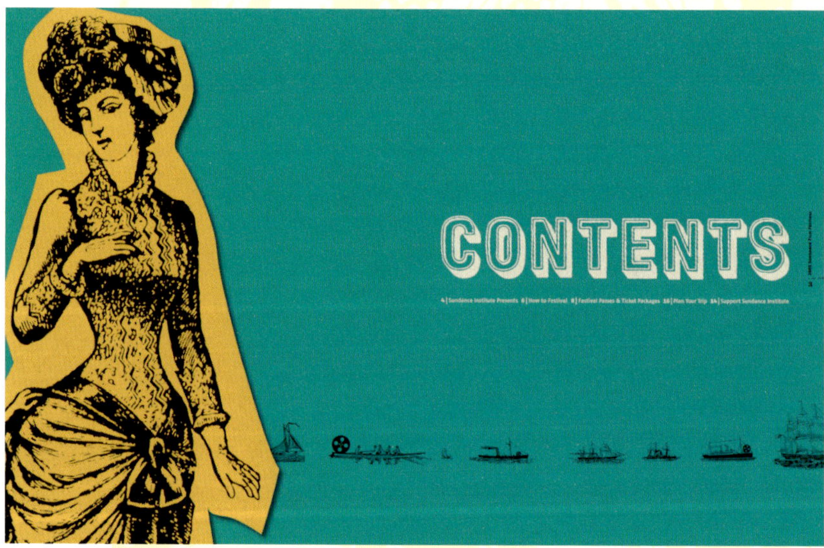

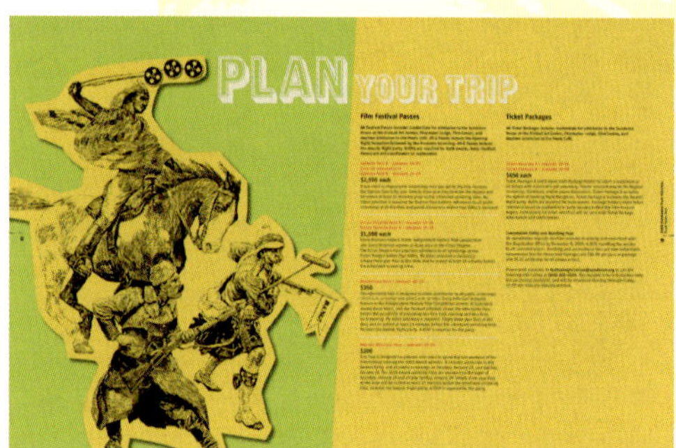

Registration brochure spreads. The remixed clip-art graphics here suggest characters in a cutout, cardboard theater of the type that many storytellers and moviemakers seem to have played with as children. They also take cinema back to its prehistory in shadowplay and puppetry across many cultures.

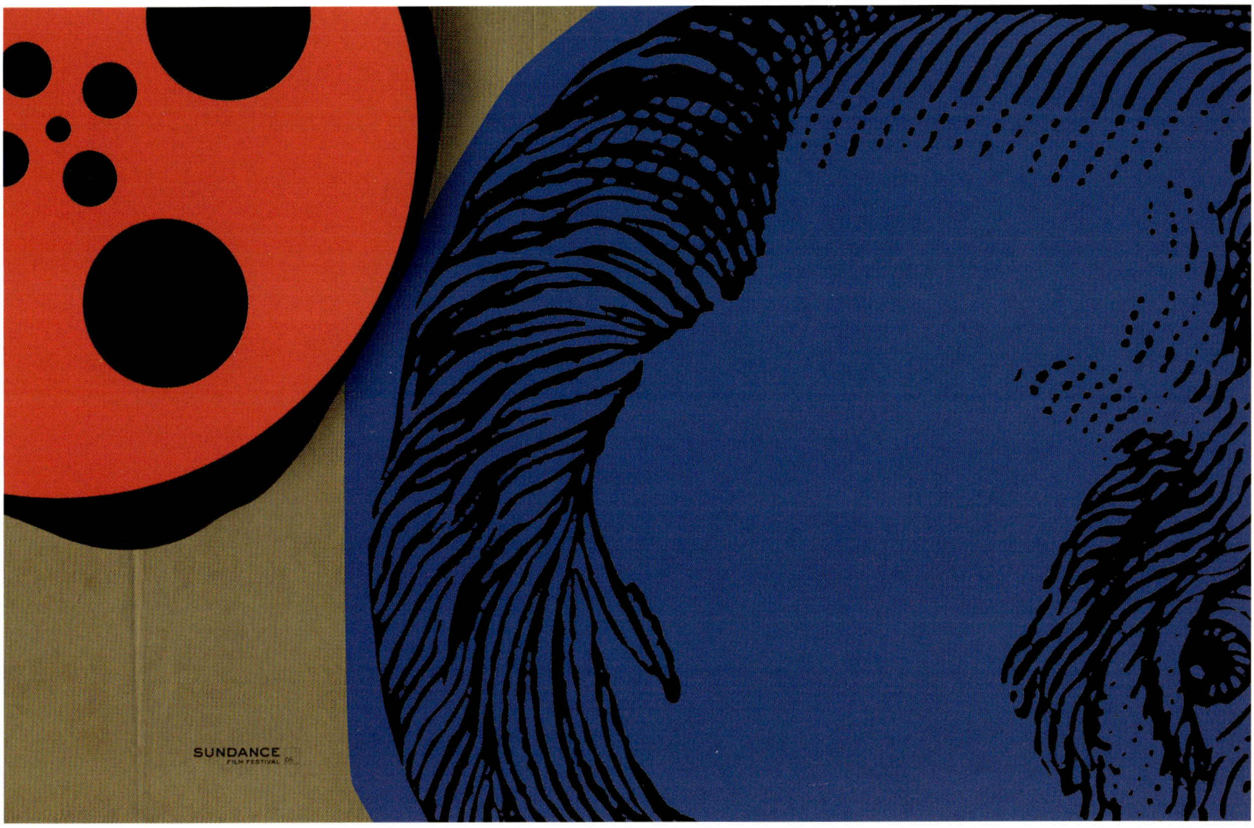

It must maintain the ability to address different ideas and evolve. At its core, however, it must be true to the overarching principles of Sundance. However noble the festival's aims might be, we inevitably live in a culture of sampling and recontextualizing, acknowledges Adams. "We live in a culture where appropriation is second nature. We are barraged with images and sounds constantly. How could anyone in this atmosphere create work that ignores the outside world? We are products of our time and place. Since this time is a pastiche of multiple cultures, ideas, and ways of seeing, we make design in the same way. The work is primarily digital, and ends up as offset litho, websites, or broadcast. We use silkscreen, engraving, and three-dimensional forms to convey an idea."

The studio also uses commercial image banks. "Adobe Stock Photos is a great starting point. There are incredible images to be found. They're not all static images of executives at desks!" Obviously, there are times when the budget for photography or illustration is so low, or nonexistent, that found imagery is necessary. We've also worked on projects with large budgets, and the solution was to utilize found imagery."

The Sundance Film Festival designs are a collaboration between AdamsMorioka, Jan Fleming, and the Sundance Creative Team.

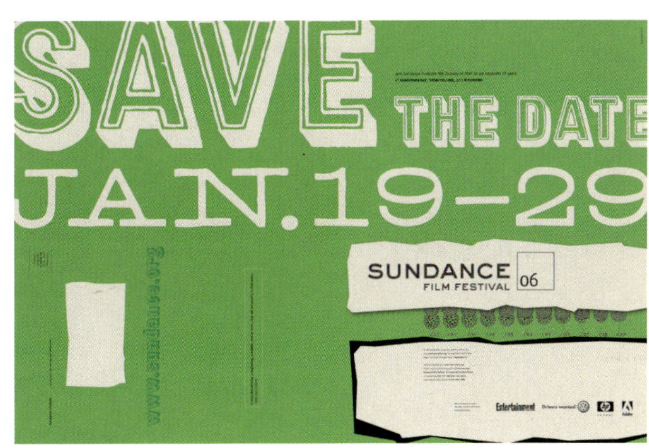

⬆ Save the Date mailer. Advance publicity sets the design theme that is then carried across every aspect of the Sundance identity.

Ashby Design

The histories of graphic design, illustration, and music share many milestones, with a number of classic creative partnerships over the years between musicians and image-makers. Ashby Design is both continuing that tradition and steeped in the history of it in the era of sampling and remixing the sounds and pictures of the past.

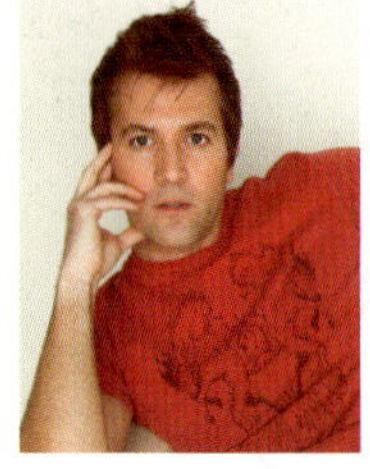

⬆ Studio head Neal Ashby (pictured) and designer Matthew Curry collaborated on the Thievery project.

⬇ ➡ Revolutions and new spins: The Beatles' *Revolver* sleeve design lives on in spirit in Ashby Design's work.

Ashby Design's portfolio includes corporate identities; book, magazine, and editorial designs; print collateral; websites; and advertising. However, it is most closely associated with the music business, notably with dance act Thievery Corporation, and also with the Recording Industry Association of America (RIAA), for whom Ashby produced the now iconic Parental Advisory sticker.

If art is theft followed by collaboration, as the band's name suggests, then Thievery Corporation's mix-and-match, sample-led aesthetic, blended with 1960s-influenced soundscapes and a back-spin on old-school psychedelia, found its perfect partner in Ashby Design's series of album covers. Ashby's work blends sourced/found imagery, clip art, and drawn or assembled graphic elements in a style that is clean, cool, and futuristic, and yet also obviously influenced by Klaus Voormann's line and collage illustration for The Beatles' *Revolver* album, which blended photographs by Robert Whitaker into a monochrome whirl of patterns and forms. Ashby's illustrative work is full of maximalist flourishes, and yet, paradoxically, the design feels minimal thanks to the choice of found imagery, restrained use of color, and tightly controlled forms. Like the band—duo Rob Garza and Eric Hilton—Ashby's principal, Neal Ashby, was educated in Maryland, taking a BS in Advertising Design. Since the late 1990s, Ashby Design and Thievery Corporation have collaborated together on a number of memorable, Grammy-nominated music packages that demonstrate the power of a symbiotic relationship between designers and musicians, as exemplified over the years by such music/design collaborations as Pink Floyd (another influence) and Storm Thorgerson/Hipgnosis, and Joy Division/New Order/Factory Records and Peter Saville.

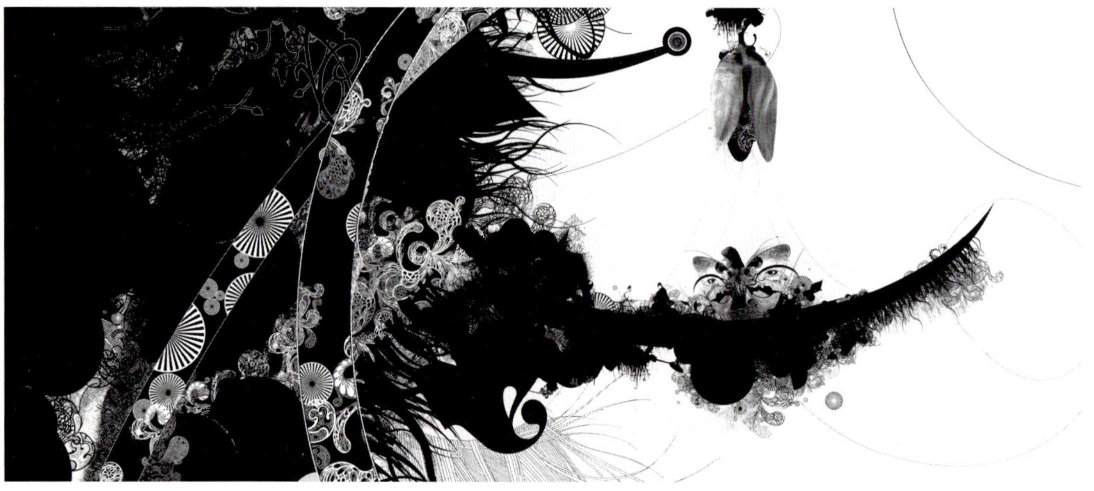

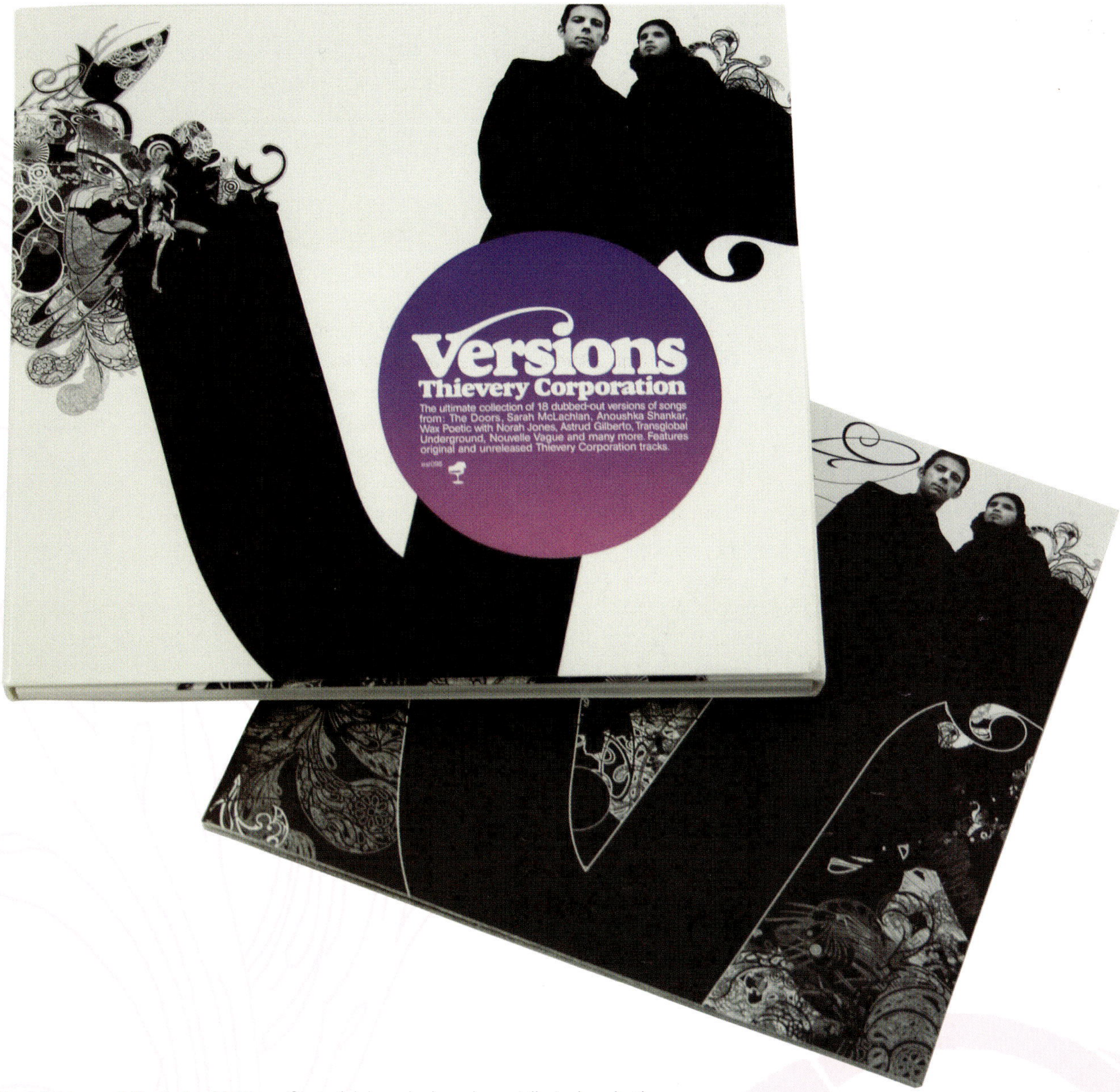

Neal Ashby and illustrator Matthew Curry (ninjacruise) each contributed as both illustrator and designer, blurring the dividing lines between the disciplines—as is so often the case when using sampled elements to release creative intuition. The two handed the story line and digital files back and forth many times, creating enough material to fill a 32-page illustrated book within the CD and vinyl packages.

They also created a promotional poster—including a special limited edition of the poster for sale—along with three different skateboard decks decorated with art from the package. The individual pieces were created using a variety of methods: the hair/grass illustrations were handdrawn using pen and ink and then scanned; photos were taken from various sources, including catalogs and car magazines, and some photography was done by the artists, using friends as models. Textures, including the paisley patterns, were taken from fabric samples from the 1960s. All of these pieces were assembled on layers in Photoshop, and then passed back and forth between the two designers/illustrators, with each adding to the other's version. The poster includes one Photoshop illustration with over 340 layers, and tens of thousands of individual pieces.

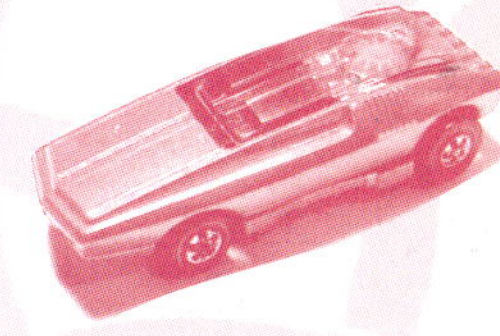

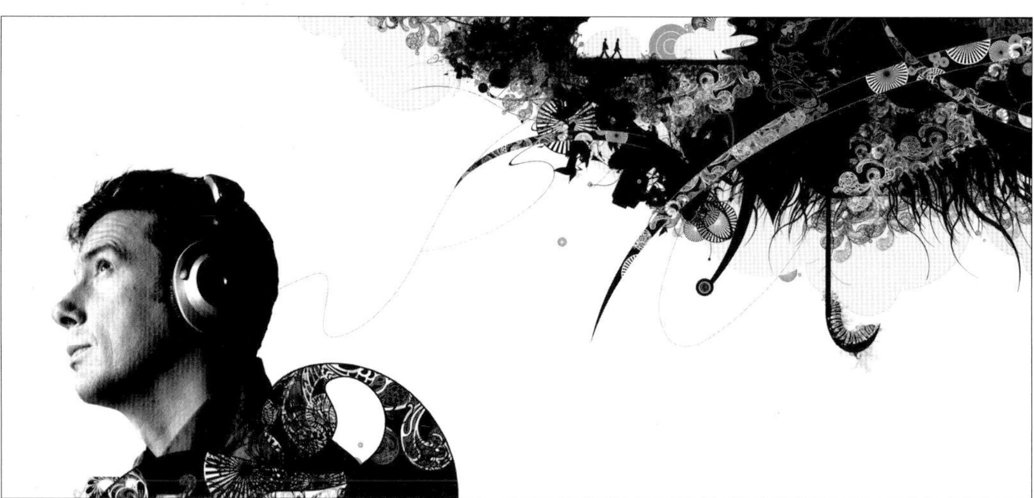

Ashby Design pull off the difficult trick of making bold visual statements that are teeming with life and minute details.

Packed full of influences, riffs, and visual jokes, these designs draw you in and reward both a casual glance and hours spent trying to spot and identify all of the elements.

New-school psychedelia: Ashby Design plays games with our expectations, creating images that suggest psychedelia, while being resolutely monochrome.

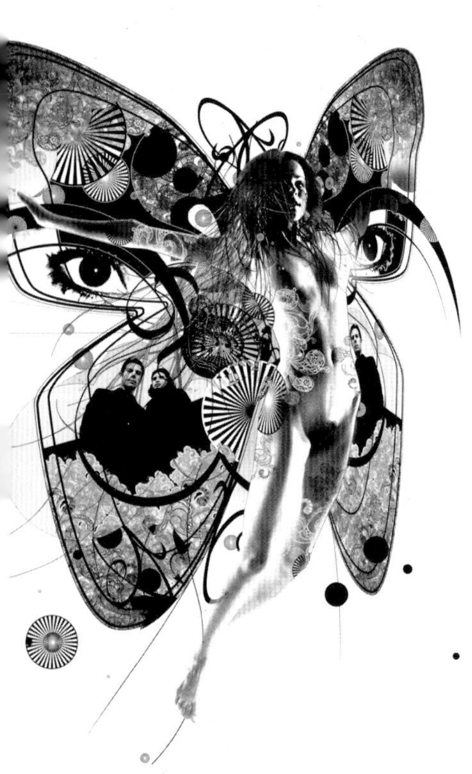

Ashby explains that the work includes both clip art and found images. "Hundreds of individual pieces and parts were collected before the designing began. Photos came from photoshoots of the band, websites, Google searches, Dover copyright-free books, fabrics, old Sears and Montgomery Ward catalogs, and our friends and family. The hair was handdrawn by me, Matt and I drew the grass, and Matt also drew the organic vector shapes in Illustrator.

"Some of the images were left in their original state, such as the loudspeaker pictures, but most were altered in some way. The fairy nymphs, for example, are composites of dozens of pieces: body parts and images of dozens of different women from the web, faces from 1950s–1980s Sears and JC Penny catalogs, wings that were handdrawn and then filled in Photoshop with paisley patterns from Dover clip-art books, as well as old fabric swatches found at flea markets."

After Ashby and Curry designed the package, they wanted to tell the story of the three-month process that led to the final product. The result was an interactive, motion graphics website reusing the same source material and called The Art of Versions (built using Photoshop CS and Flash). The site illustrates a desire not only to walk someone through the process that created art from over 300 individual sources, but also to look ahead to the future of the iPod age, where music packaging will gradually transform into an all-digital format and experience.

For Ashby Design, using found imagery, clip art, and sampling from other sources is as much about looking ahead as it is about acknowledging your creative roots, revealing your processes, your source materials, and your inspirations—true sampling, in other words.

"For the design of The Art of Versions, we knew we wanted to create a real sense of depth within the site, and this was done by making sure all the tools used were complementary to one another," says Ashby. "Once our interface was designed we began breaking down items and graphics in Photoshop making sure the raster images were saved out as transparent PNGs so that each layer would properly interact with the others.

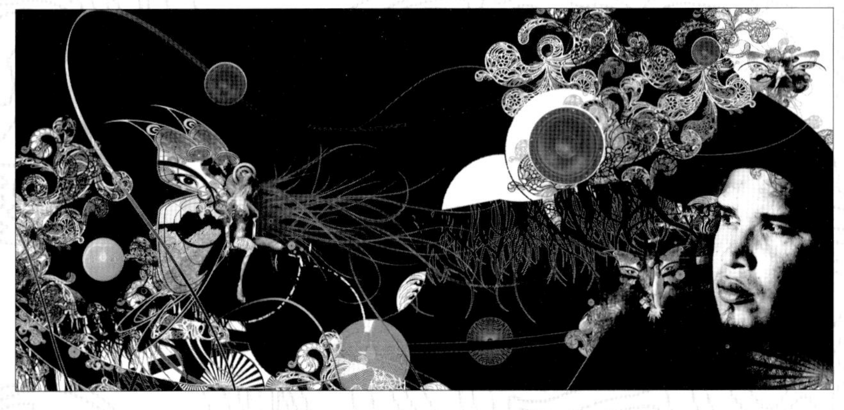

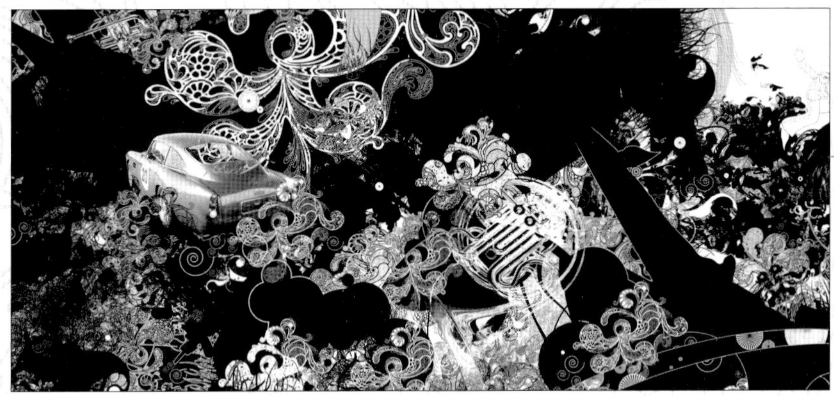

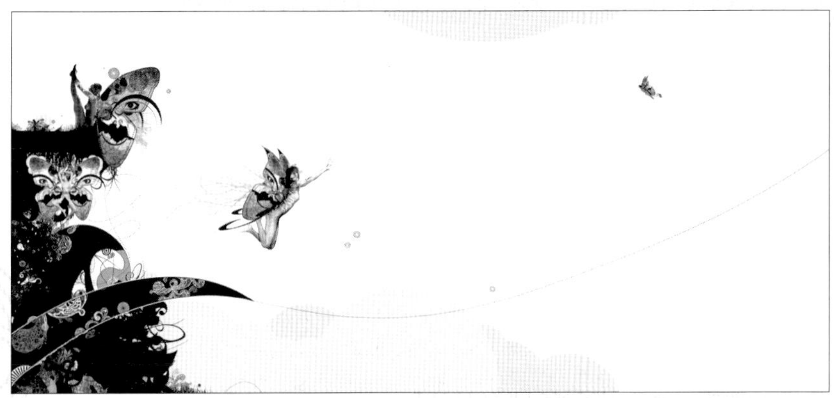

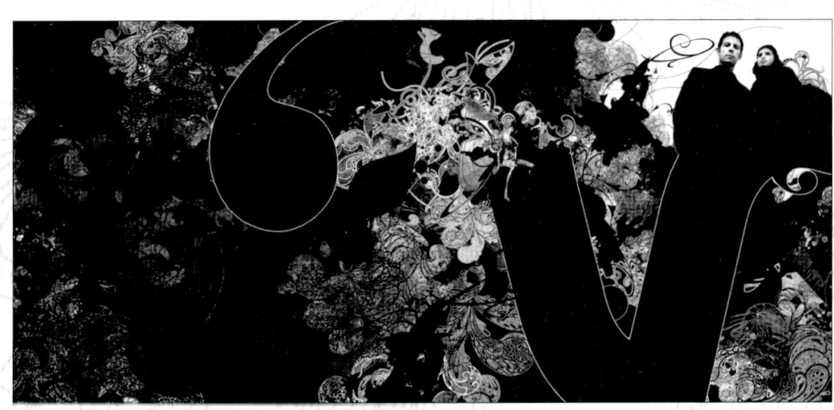

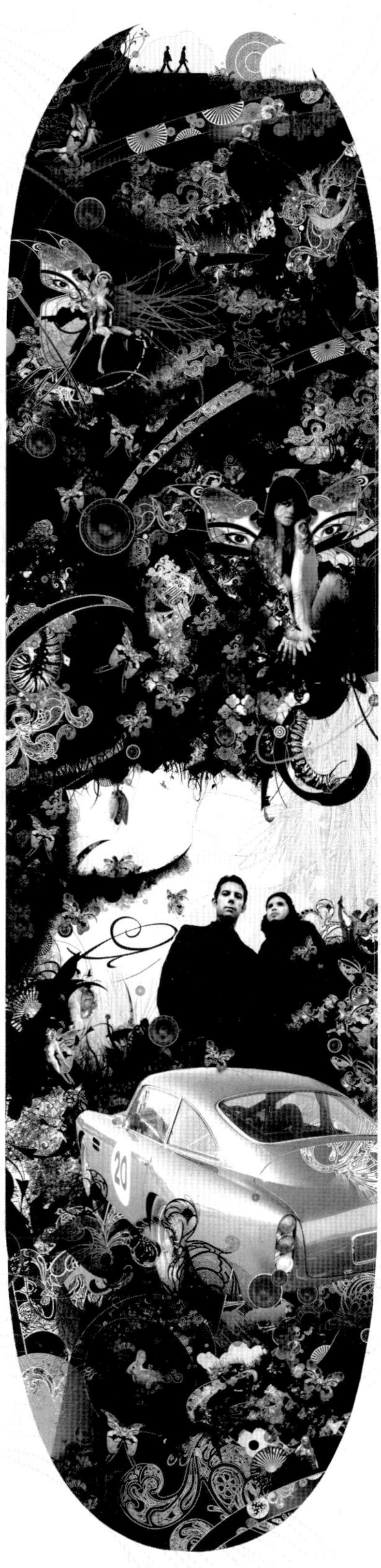

↑ Clip art taken to its apotheosis: perhaps the farthest that a studio can take the use of clip and found imagery; the ambition and the richness of the work are stunning.

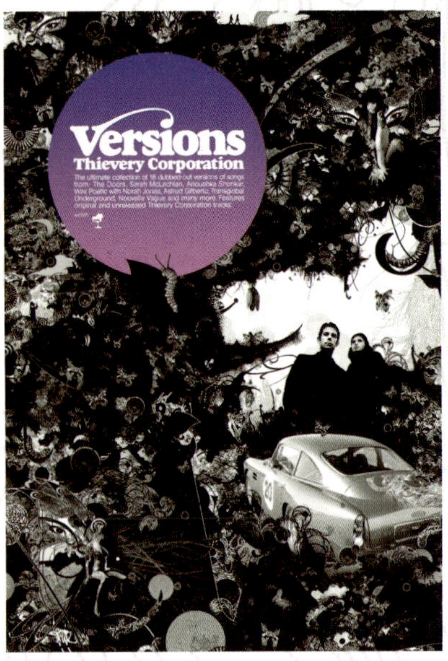

⬆ Just some of the simple clip-art shapes and forms that are merged, layer upon layer, into these almost microscopically detailed worlds.

"Once all the graphics were saved out accordingly, we began rebuilding the interface using several different Flash files to render properly the depth of layering we wanted to create. Once all the Flash movies were in place, we could then go in and start to fine-tune the animations to bring the organic world to life.

"The best example of this can be seen in the building of the intro sequence, where the mood and field of depth are established by having several different movies load into the scene at varying speeds and levels (background/foreground/main interface). The final touch to this intro build is the sweeping movie that builds out our type treatment. The masking technique was accomplished by using six movie clips that were individually timed—then grouped—to create the sweeping effect we desired. This grouping was then condensed into a single movie that we placed like a blanket on top of our type graphic, and converted to a mask layer."

ORIGINAL IMAGES

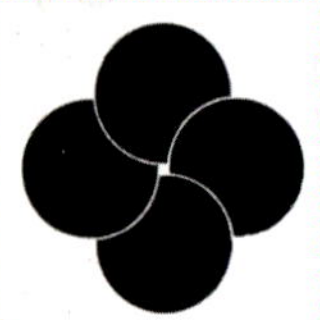
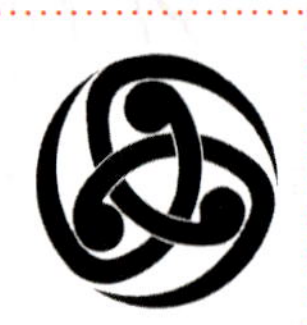
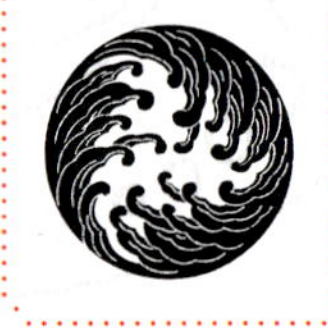
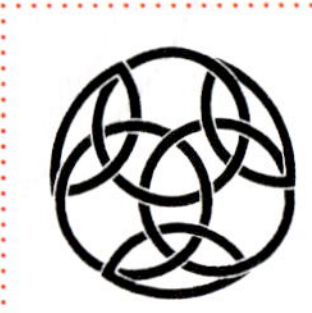
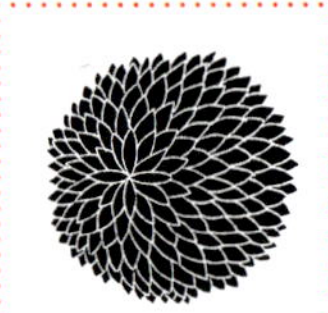
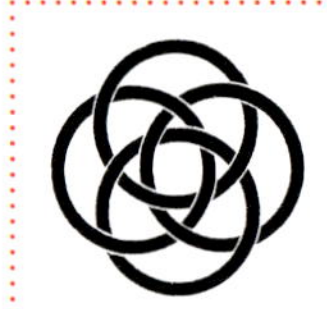
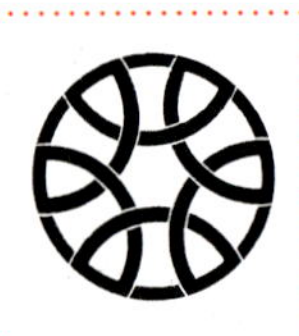
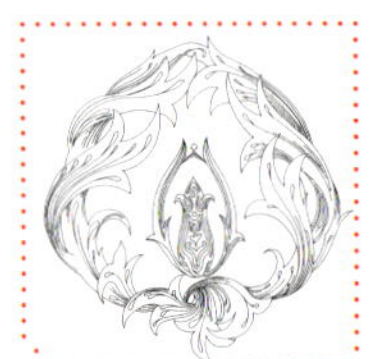
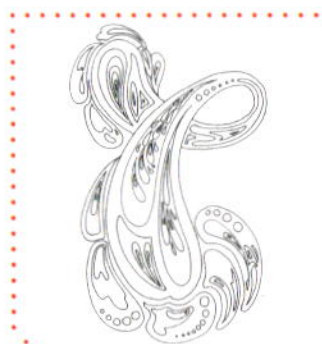
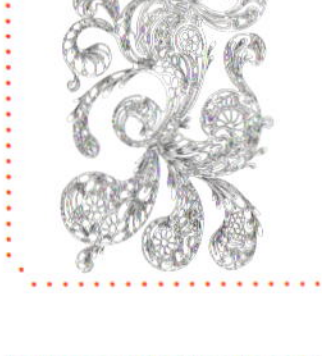
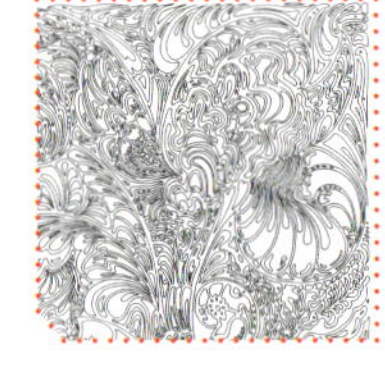
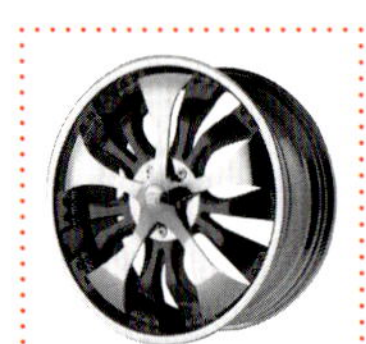
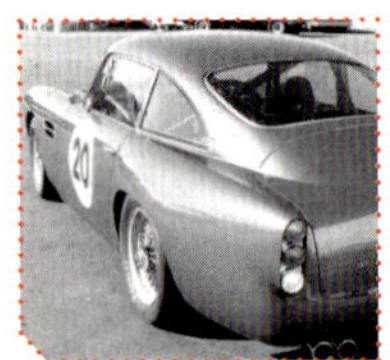
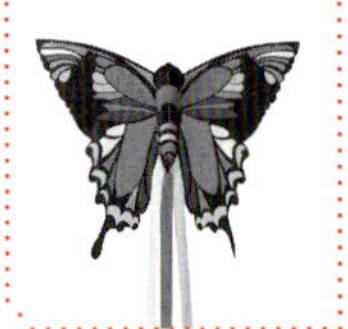
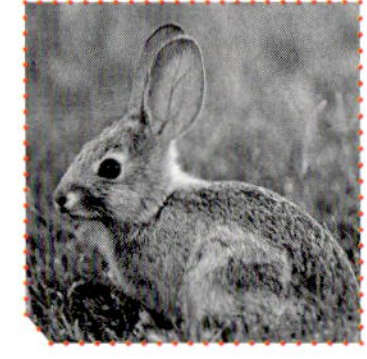
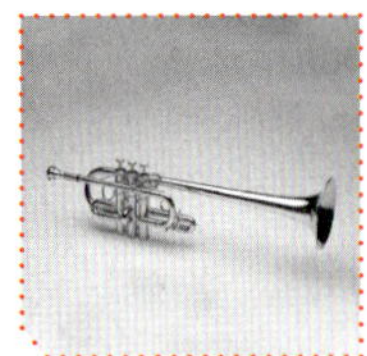
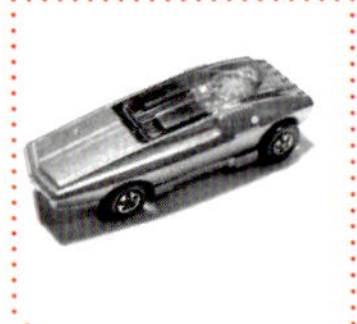
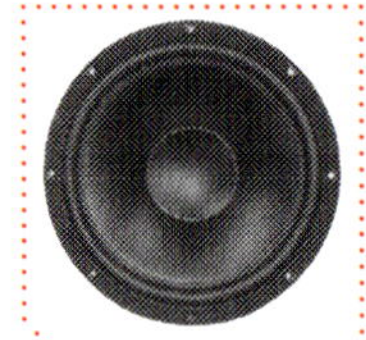
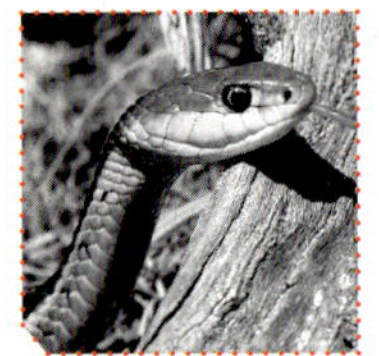
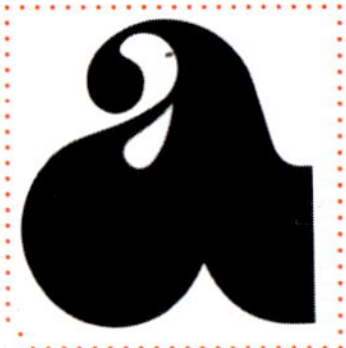

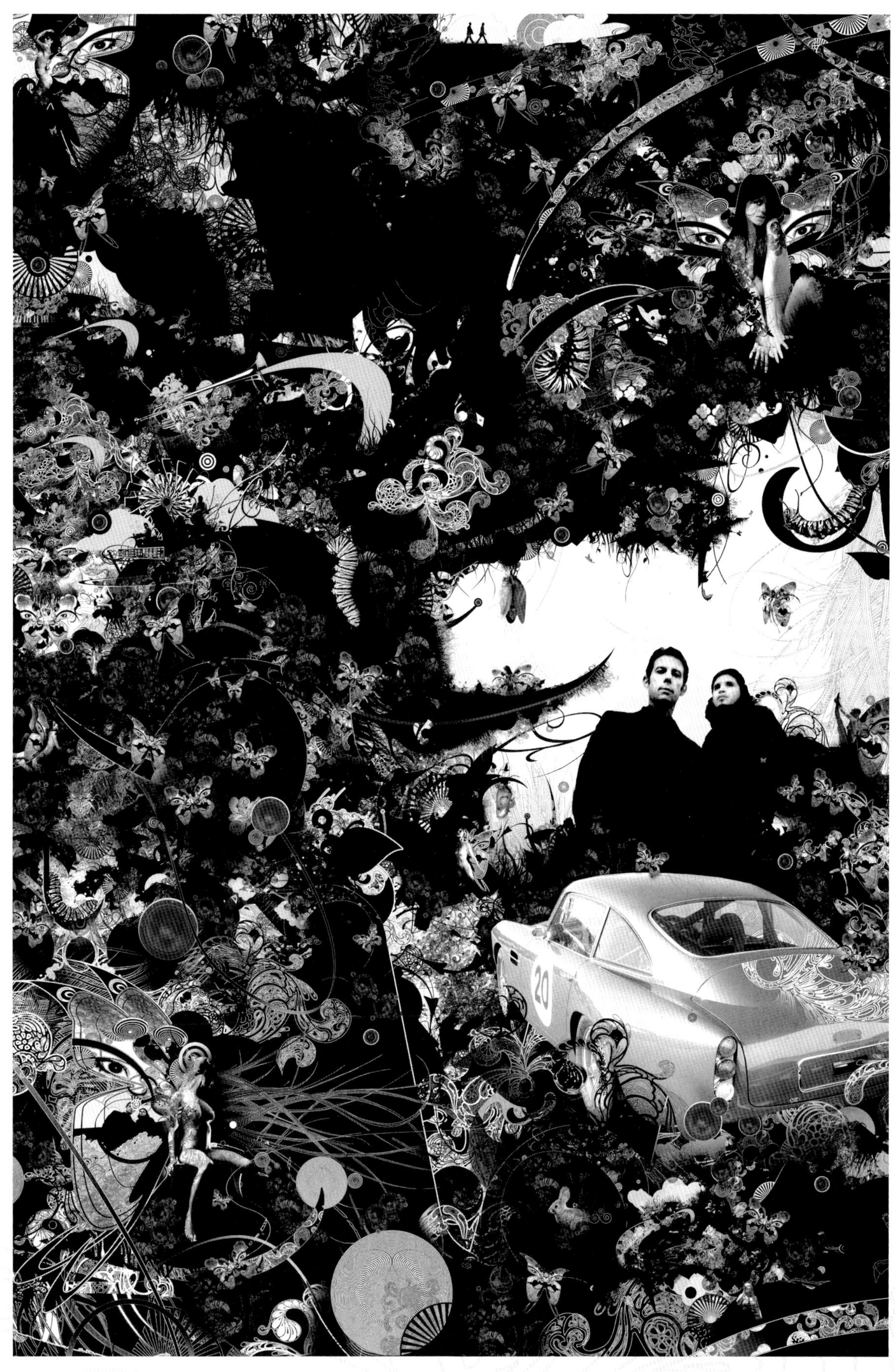

Martin O'Neill

Martin O'Neill has been working commercially since 1994 as a freelance illustrator and is represented by agents in the UK, North America, Japan, and Greater China. Consequently, he works for a wide range of international clients encompassing book publishing, magazine editorials, advertising, design, packaging, and newspaper illustrations. He also regularly exhibits his personal collages and prints and is an associate lecturer at the London College of Communication.

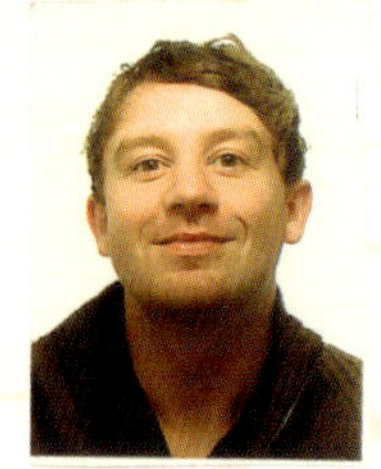

O'Neill's favored medium is handmade collage, in which he amalgamates clip art and self-generated imagery with all sorts of found paper, ephemera, and silkscreen printing. O'Neill has evolved a creative process of his own, and has collaborated with Alex Williamson on spinoff projects that have roots in his haphazard working regime.

Despite his old-school roots, his work is not 100 percent nondigital, and is very much inspired by cutups, sampling, and remixing. He uses computers occasionally to compile images in Photoshop layers; however, he feels that the clean lines of Photoshop assemblies alert the eye to such images' digital origins, and prefers to make collages by hand, which can then be photographed or scanned and still retain something of the texture and flaws of handmade, handcut surfaces.

This process is central to the creation of his work. Over the years he has experimented with handmade image-making processes and has both learnt and invented a wide range of image manipulation techniques that combine methods such as, photocopying, frottage, painting, image transfers, layering, handcut typography, silkscreen, and collage.

Clip art is absolutely core to what he does, and the clips he collects in his burgeoning, chaotic, homemade image bank combine to make a clip-art archive that is as nonlinear and noncompartmentalized as it gets. He thinks the fact that he has continued to experiment with this more analog approach has helped him keep a fresh perspective on his illustration.

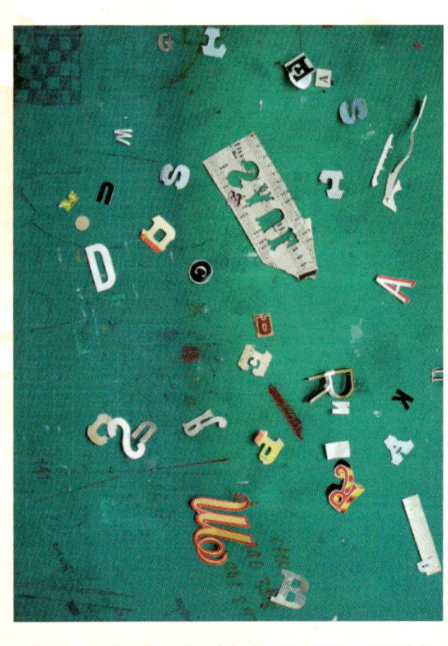

⬆ Workspace or work of art? So involved and painstaking is O'Neill's passion for clip art and collecting that his workspace and his work merge into one and become inseparable from each other.

➡ Notes from overground: the more material he gathers, and the more individual works he creates, the more his portfolio as a whole becomes viewable as one all-embracing work, a museum of the self.

Subsequently, O'Neill gets inspiration every day from various sources. "Working with my archive, I like to keep collage sketchbooks and play around with images, word play, making new connections between the elements in my collection of found material. I like inventing new formats for mini self-initiated projects," he explains.

"Finding junk is a major inspiration. I find that unearthing new, raw collage material, especially from different countries and cultures very inspiring. Whether it is an old annotated photo album in Prague, a disregarded doodled address book in a flea market in Palermo, or even a scrap of cardboard on the beach in Hastings. I'm interested in finding new material and the prospects of manipulating and incorporating that stuff into new works, changing its meaning in some sense," he adds.

A large percentage of the clip art that goes into his images is what he would call "found" imagery. This imagery has been collected over the course of his career and manifests itself in his studio as a secondhand cutout image library, a sort of mutant analog "stock" library, housed in everything from plan chests, multidraw cabinets, and bookshelves to random tins and cigar boxes.

Says O'Neill: "I can usually find or make what I need for an image from this 'library,' but have also built up a list of places where I can go and directly source a particular image, i.e. secondhand bookshops, junk shops, and specialist or professional shops.

"Part of my image library is a collection of my own personal photographs, which include categories like man-made or natural surfaces and textures, type and signage, landscapes and people," he continues. "I make my finished works by combining found

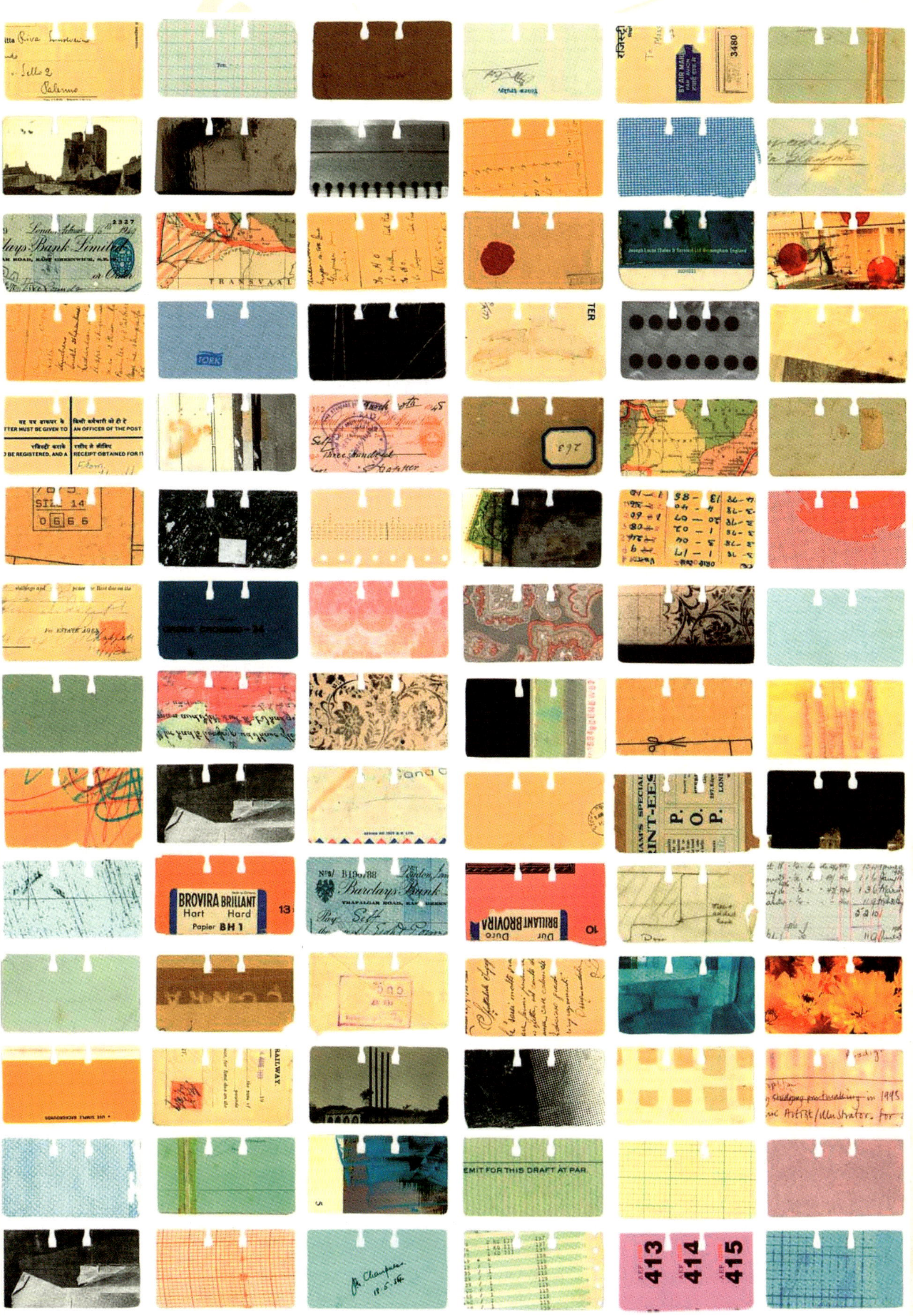

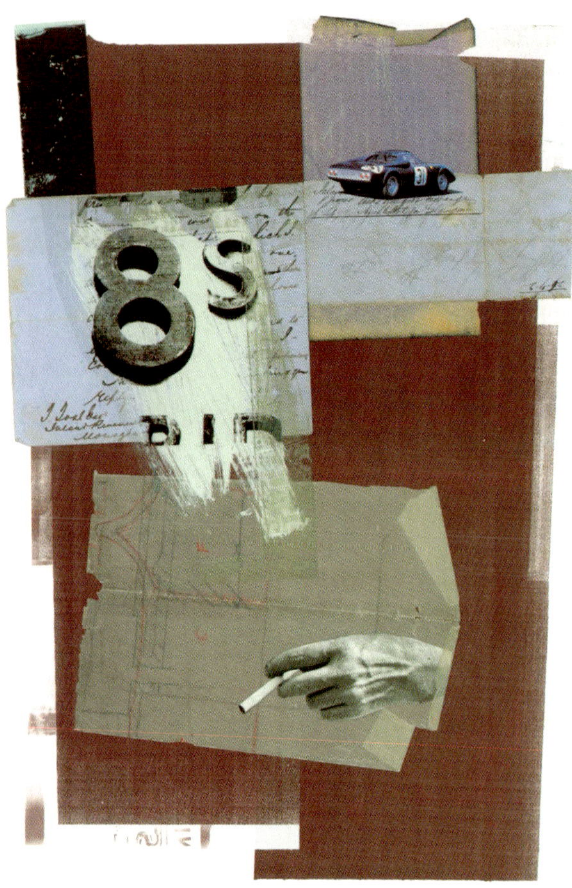

While much of O'Neill's illustration and design work is commissioned, any of his pieces is immediately identifiable and stands alone, and shoulder to shoulder with his others.

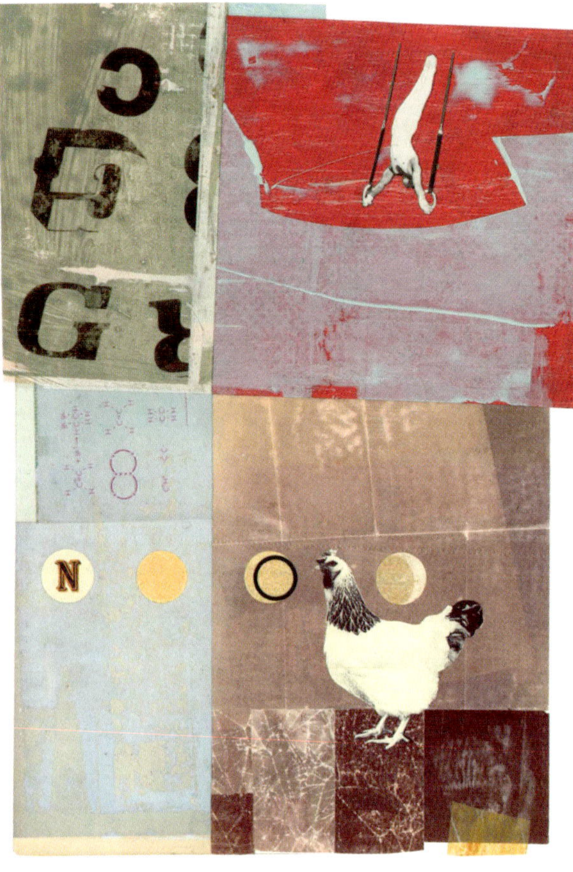

Although O'Neill's source images are culled from many eras and media, it often brings to mind the work of the Beat generation in 1950s America and Europe.

and self-initiated elements; however, all of these components are generally manipulated in some way. On some occasions I am given stock or product images by art directors to incorporate into a piece, something I will treat and manipulate to fit into my illustrative style."

While he avoids using digital means of image searching like Google or stock image sites, and prefers photocopying or photographing something from a physical source, he does occasionally refer to a Dover image book. "I prefer to make a location visit or look through old books and periodicals where I think I'm more likely to find a unique or obscure reference that can add a different dimension to a project. I like a more active approach to image research," he explains.

Also, he likes to maintain an environmental factor in his work. "I recently completed a research project entitled Catalog [with fellow illustrator Alex Williamson] where I explored my collecting, cataloging, and making processes. As a result of this I started to see my studio and its output in a different light. I've begun to see the collection as a piece of work in its own right. The process of selecting and sampling segments of visual culture and taking them out of their context, reinterpreting their meaning, and feeding them back into popular culture through various media is in a sense recycling. I also keep all the offcuts and by-products from this cycle, which go back into the archive for future use. Nothing is wasted."

Sampling is the very nature of his work, and O'Neill thinks it's the actual image selection that's important. "The decisions I make as to what to pick up and keep and what to disregard are central to the success of a particular piece of work. The most unusual element I've ever used was a dead scorpion that I caught creeping up on me in Greece when I was 16. I taped it to a postcard for an ad campaign for advertising agency Publicis."

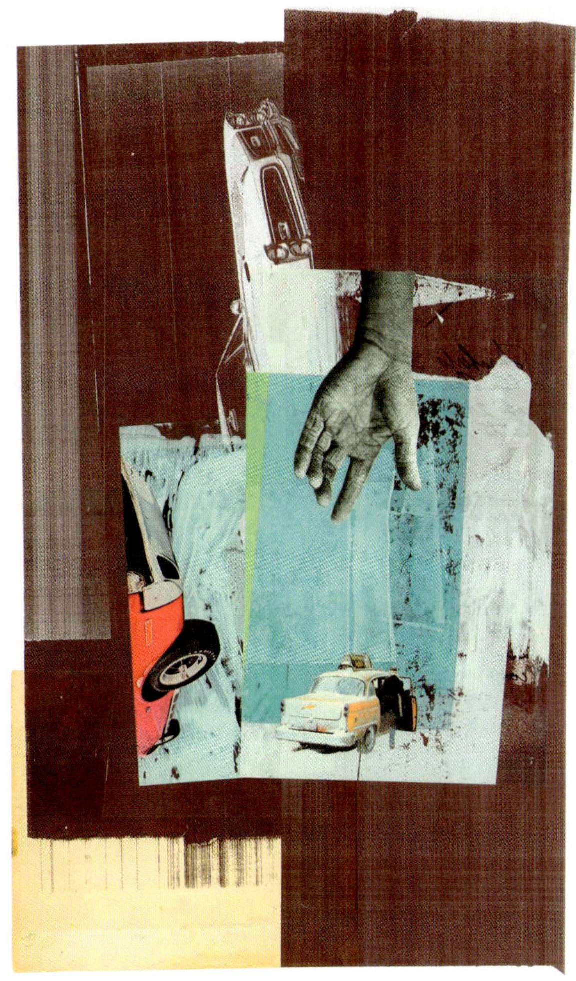

⬆ Once cut out of their backgrounds and original contexts, O'Neill's subjects become characters in a dislocated world, and his images suggest stories and events we can only guess at.

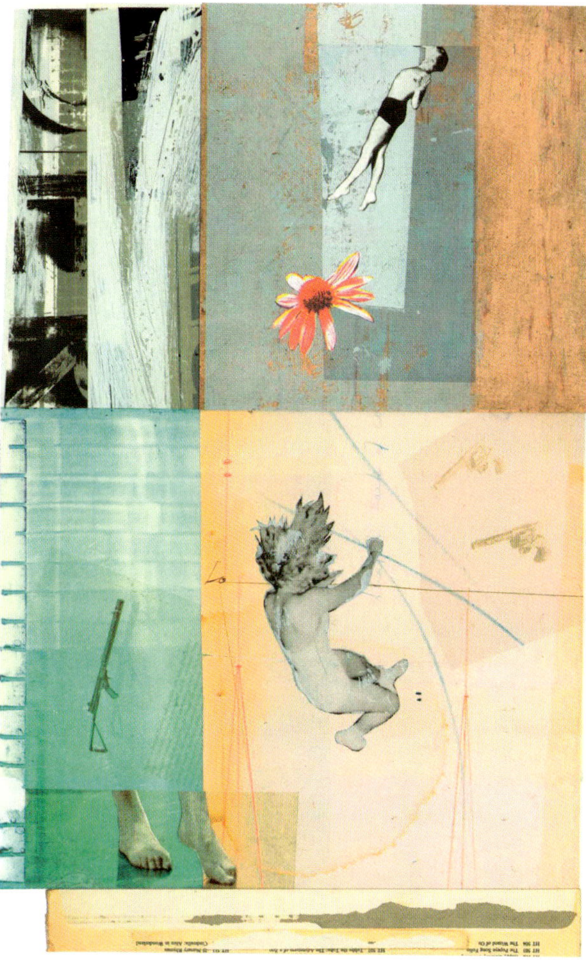

⬆ There is also something Hockney-esque about these swimmers and other characters, and the atmosphere is often warm despite the sometimes chilly, muted color palette.

He continues: "Swapping and changing the context of an element and merging or contrasting it with another unrelated element can add an unexpected and powerful dynamic and create an impact that other methods, such as photography, can sometimes lack."

O'Neill sees that the terms "sampling" and "collage" now have a much broader meaning in the creative industries. "I grew up in the 1980s and 1990s in London where people were experimenting and developing the sampled music genre, something which heavily influenced my early cut-and-paste image-making," he says. "I'm now seeing that sampling culture has spread across the creative and media industries as a whole, examples range from music, poetry, film, pop video, to food and fashion. It seems that sampling and collaging existing sounds, moving images, words, lyrics, and even flavors is now an accepted and powerful means to making messages. As a result, I am also turning my collage techniques to other formats, realizing the same principles of collage can be appropriated to audio. I have created found sound collages echoing the way I create my two-dimensional collages as featured on the LP *Stagefright* produced by artist Leigh Clarke."

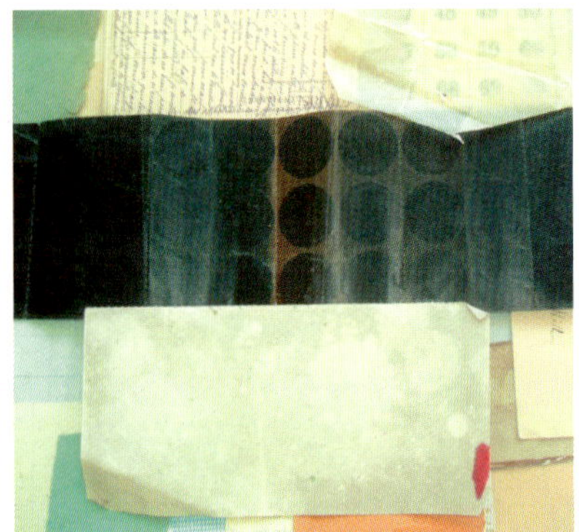

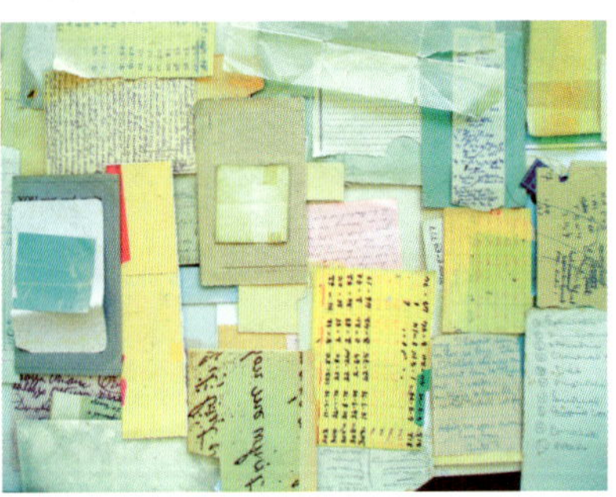

⬆ Some of the source material that went into O'Neill's illustration, opposite, from scraps of paper and notebooks, to pulp comics and other materials. If anything, O'Neill's work is a celebration of paper and ephemera.

➡ The finished work: part film noire, part Weegie-esque crime-scene documentary, designed for a magazine feature about the history of the crime novel.

Guardian Guide cover illustration

The Brief

The brief from Sara Ramsbottom at the *Guardian Guide* was to create a cover image for the "Murder, They Wrote" issue with the lead feature focusing on the history of the crime novel. The brief was very open and the image had to have a dark feel to it without being too morbid.

Research

O'Neill started by sourcing images from a collection of old detective magazines from the early 1960s and also looked in a few of his collage index drawers. One of these is loosely titled "crayons and death," where he has collected cropped images and textures pertaining to crime, death, and general brutality. He also has a collection of newspapers and found some missing persons pages that looked useful.

O'Neill then set about sourcing some interesting textures and other loose collage material that could allude to a noire-like background. Referencing a book on pulp novel covers, he got a feeling of what textures he was looking for. O'Neill wanted something to convey the feeling of a dirty floor that could be in or outside; something monotone, dull, and stained that evoked a crime scene. He looked in his paper texture boxes and found various bits of paper including the back of a 1940s check, a scrap of sunkissed paper with strange disc markings on it, and some old faded fax paper from a box in the studio called "Fax You," containing old, light-damaged faxes.

Development and final image

O'Neill then started to gather these elements together and created a loose composition, resizing, photocopying, and treating the photographic elements, cutting parts away, moving parts around, trying to make visual connections between the elements and creating freeform collage sketches. The component parts were still loose and not stuck down at this stage. Having to work on a few other jobs at the same time, he revisited the image on two occasions, playing with various compositions, adding new elements and new ideas, stripping things back and trying alternative routes. Working with silkscreen, layering, and collage, he came up with two different compositions for the piece. The second image was chosen, with the addition of a blood spot, and was dropped into the template.

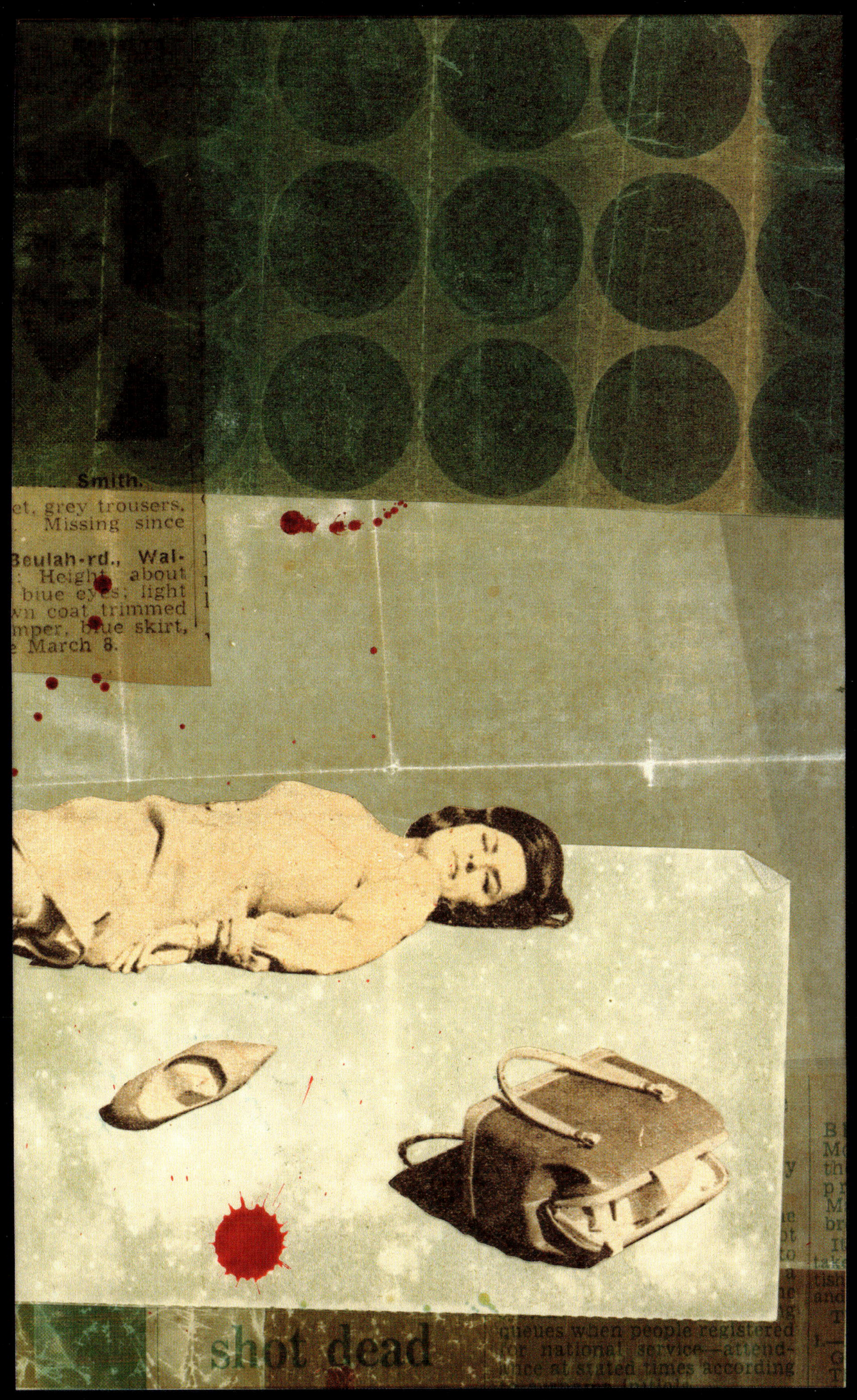
Smith.
et, grey trousers,
Missing since
Beulah-rd., Wal-
Height about
blue eyes; light
wn coat trimmed
mper, blue skirt,
March 8.
shot dead
queues when people registered
for national service—attend-
ance at stated times according

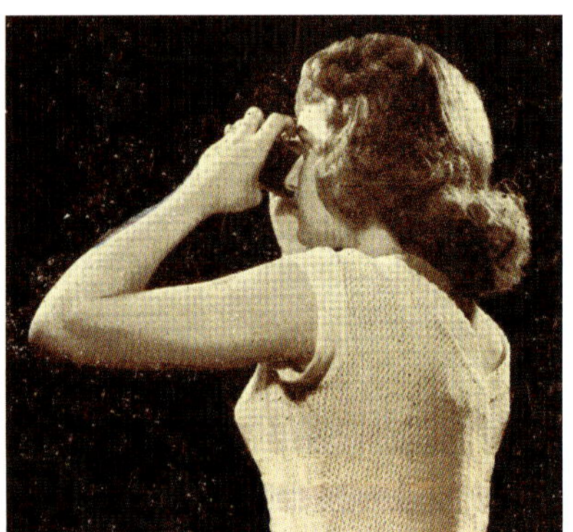

A very literal clip on the theme "looking back" for a retrospective feature about the year's events in the design community.

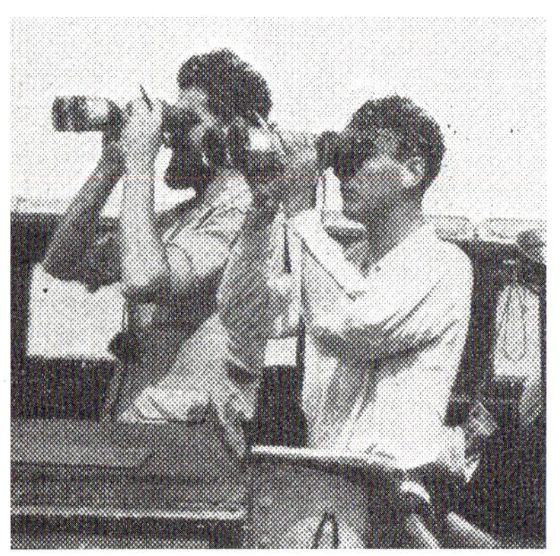

A similar image, here showing that even the most low-fi graphic can be grist to the creative mill when putting together a high-profile commission.

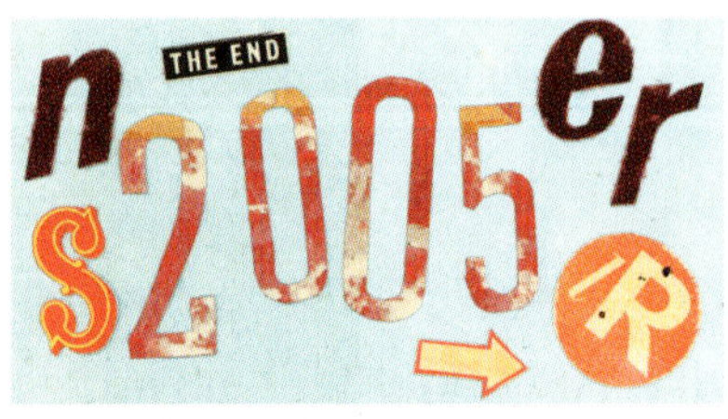

Some of the collection of type clips that O'Neill assembled to include in the final illustration (opposite).

Design Week cover image

The Brief

Design Week commissioned O'Neill to create a cover illustration for the penultimate issue of the year. The feature was a retrospective of events in the design world and the image had to include some sort of visualization of the terms "looking back" or "backtracking." It had to be fairly straightforward and eye-catching as a cover image.

Research

The deadline was tight so O'Neill had to get the main component part of this image quickly. Looking in a box in his studio entitled "Parsley People" (a collection of found images and photographs of people doing odd things), he found a few clip shots of people taking photos and looking through microscopes, including a strong image of a woman taking a picture. He realized that, with a bit of manipulation, it could look as if she was using binoculars, and looking at something. He also thumbed through a set of old encyclopedias where he remembered seeing an image of a few sailors on deck with binoculars. He then started gathering together a selection of loose collage of material that had a feeling of nostalgia and history about it, including opened envelopes, writing paper, and torn letters.

Development and final image

O'Neill changed the hue of the image of the woman by processing it through his color copier and tweaking the color balance, trying to get the right impact and tone for her, as she seemed too old-fashioned in the sepia tone. He cut her out and started to create the collage with an array of component parts that were laid out in front of him. He felt that the image needed something else—some other smaller, more detailed elements and decided that text or type might get the message across of time passing and the months of the year going by, so he handcut some numbers and letters in various typeface styles from different textures and surfaces, like fabric and leather. He also cut some small circles out of diaries, calendars, check stubs, and pieces of paper with dates on. He chose 12, each a small indication to a month in the year. As O'Neill had a lot of fiddly elements to stick down with the image, he ended up doing several compositions, scanning them in each time to save them as he went along. With a few composition changes and the addition of a second figure "looking back," he achieved the final image. O'Neill also created two internal spot illustrations to go with the feature. He glued all the collages down and scanned them ready for print.

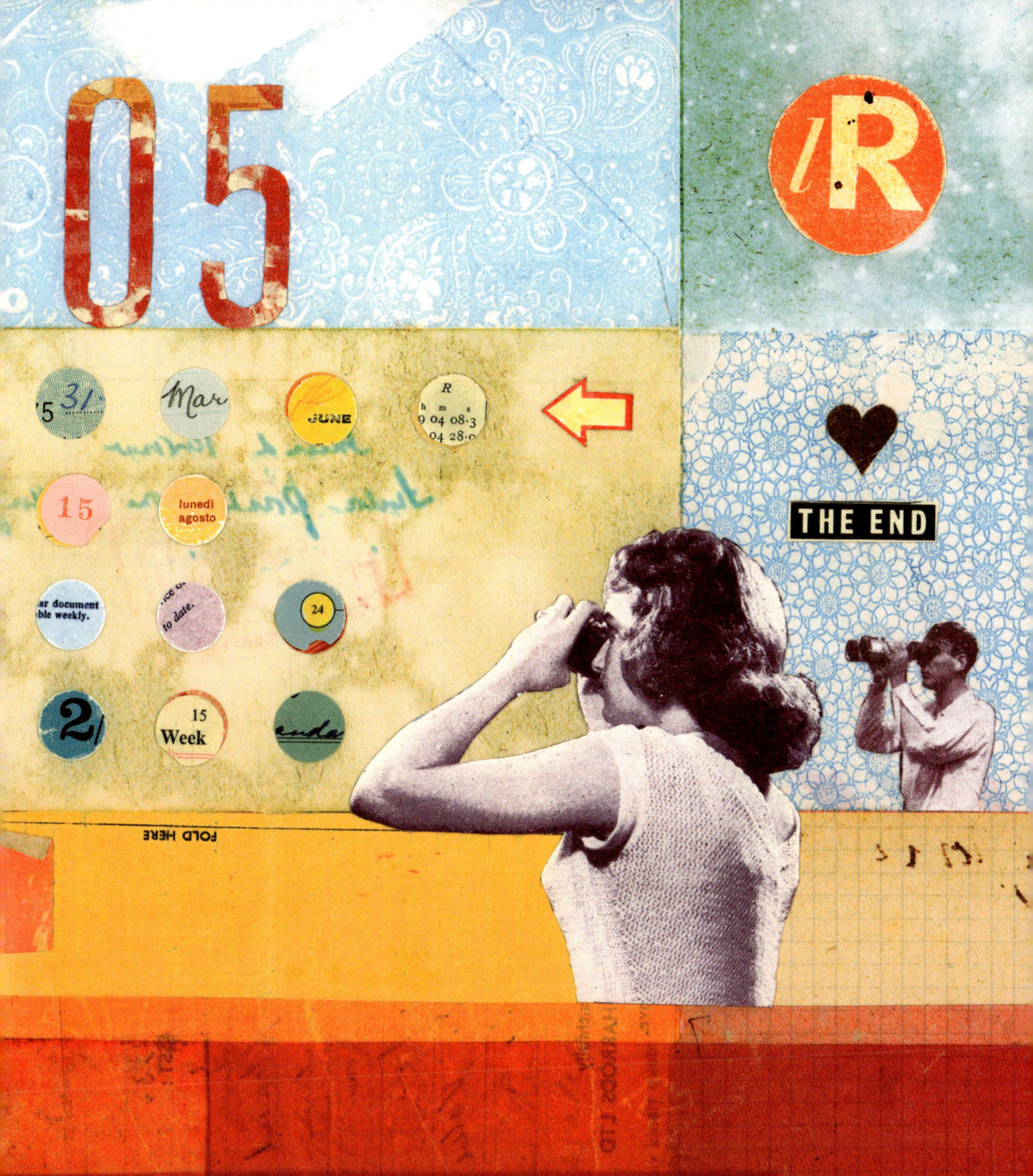
05
Mar
JUNE
15
lunedi
agosto
24
15
Week
THE END

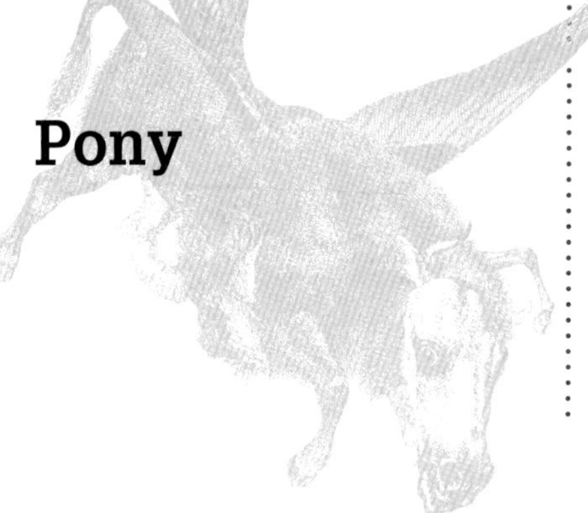

Pony

Just as the roles of designer, illustrator, photographer, art director, and typographer are merging and taking on new combinations of skills, so graphics themselves are morphing into new hybrids of form and function that play on our perceptions of, and relationships with, the past: and with the source clips within each image.

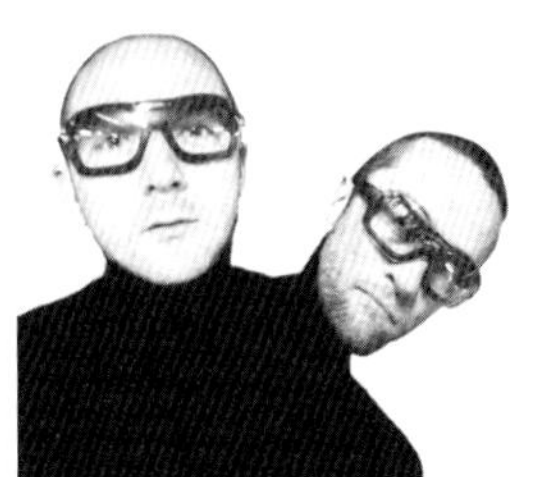

Design consultancy Pony launched in 2000 as a graphics studio producing designs in print and other media. Pony has a keen interest in words, pictures—and the chance of a dance, it seems.

D1ASPORA is a record label that was established to distribute Irish electronic recording artists in America. According to Pony designer Niall Sweeney, the studio's work for the label involved no greater technique than copy, cut, paste, and collage—both digitally and manually using physical art clips.

Sweeney sourced clip-art samples of copyright-free etchings of animal parts and then spliced them together to create new beasts and new beats. The designs played on clichés of mythical Irishness, with riffs on concepts such as bogus histories, human and animal cloning, and the Irish diaspora. In short, the question of identity was what these simple, fun, provocative designs were all about—questions that are no less pertinent to the Irish at the turn of the twenty-first century, of course, than they were decades or centuries ago.

The common element in most dance music since the 1980s has been sampling loops, breaks, and beats to create new forms and genre hybrids, and Sweeney's mashed-up creature designs reflect these obsessions too.

🡇 A menagerie of imaginary beasts for a music project that is all about sampling, cut and paste, and remixing elements of the past.

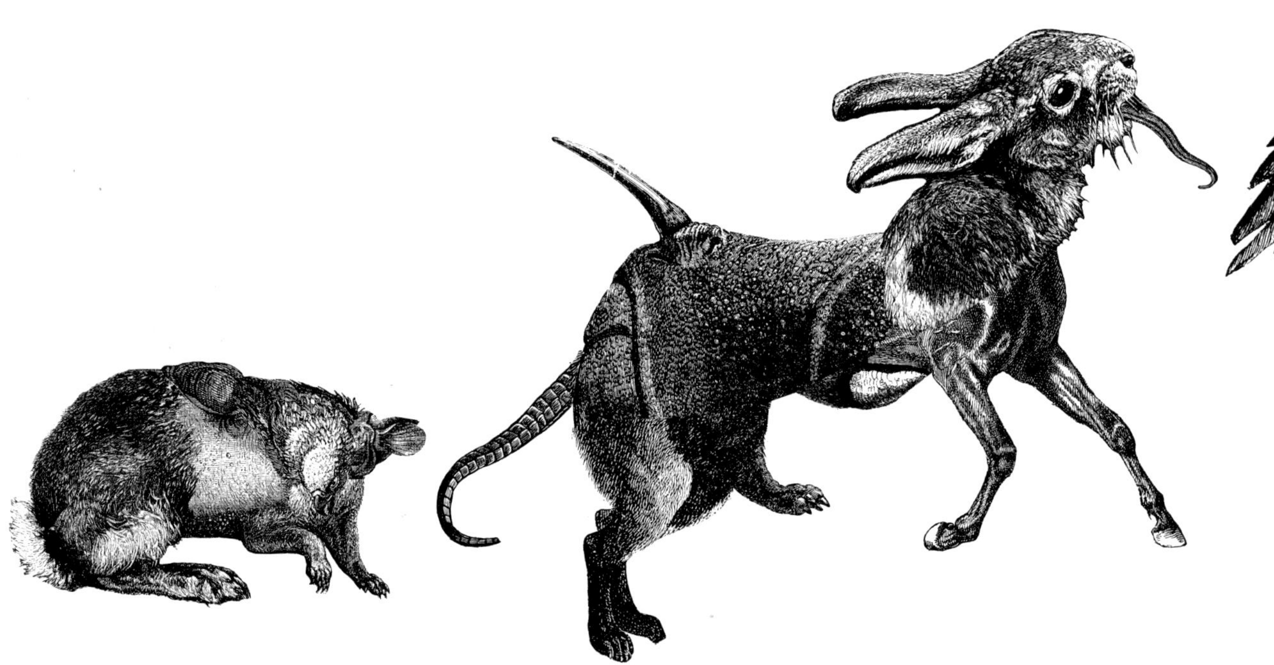

The other aim was simply to create images that looked fantastic, but which were far removed from the design archetypes normally associated with dance music—substituting etching or scraperboard style for the big, blocky, dayglo, smiley mash-ups of most dance graphics. Another impetus behind the designs was that they had to be monochrome due to the limited finances available, so using etchings as source material was the perfect mix of creativity and budget. Sweeney claims to have generated "a whole zoo" of these animals, one of which is put onto the label each time there is a new release. "So the animals are released into the wild too," he says.

"I like the idea of fonts being clip art. Unless you create your own fonts each and every time—which some do," he adds. Sweeney is now working on an identity for a design group using fonts. At one stage, the client's logo was generated by a system that used the font database on any computer as a clip-art source. Each time the logo went to print, the system randomly chose a different font for each letter, which made the logo at once instantly recognizable, while also different each time. "It forced both a nonpreciousness and tidy housekeeping on the part of the company in its font department," he explains, "as the logo relied on whatever fonts were installed in any given computer."

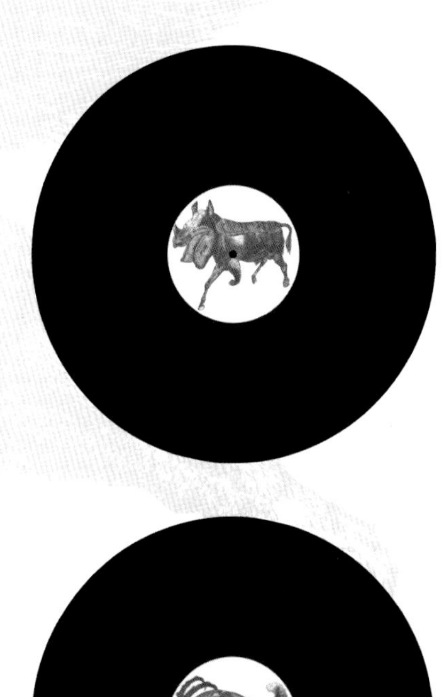

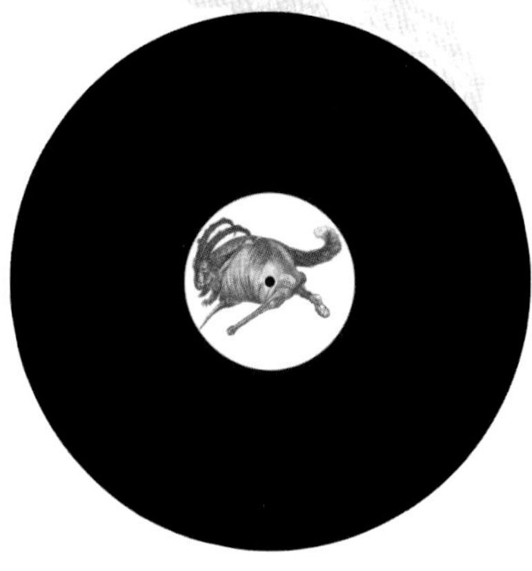

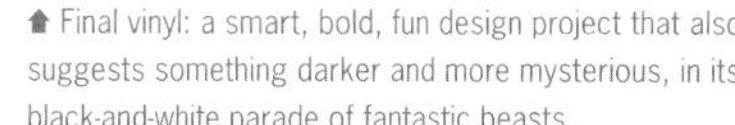

⬆ Final vinyl: a smart, bold, fun design project that also suggests something darker and more mysterious, in its black-and-white parade of fantastic beasts.

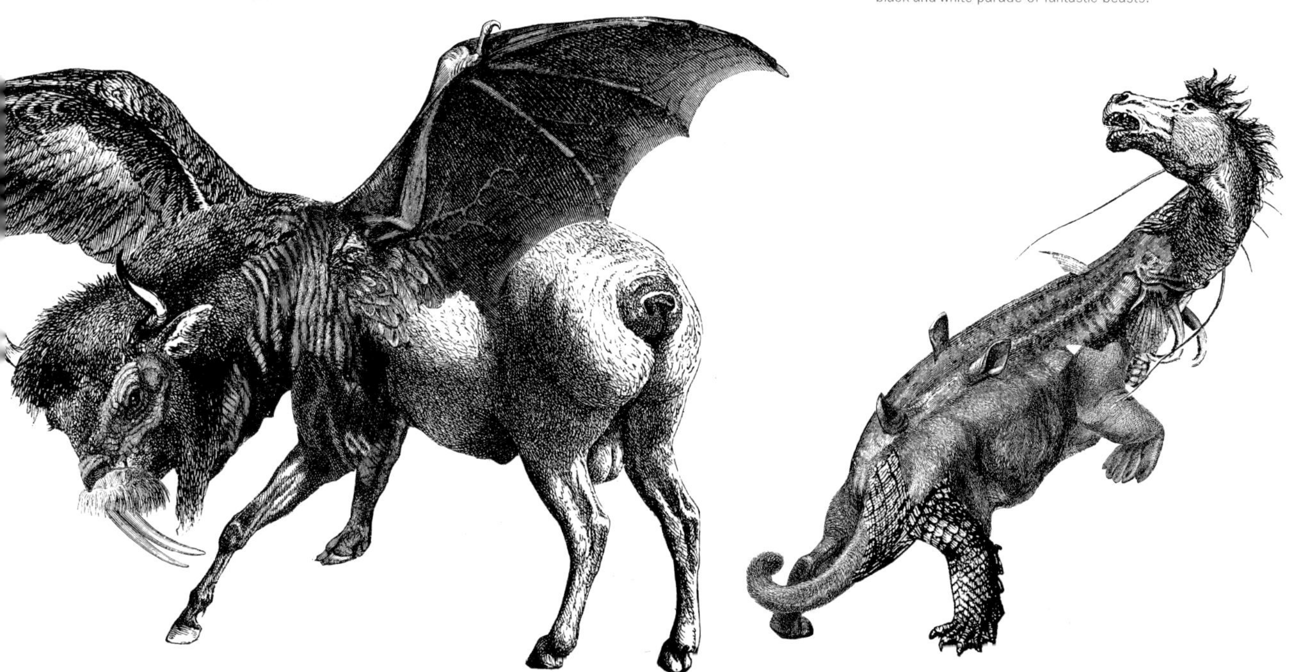

Plan-B Studio

Plan-B Studio is another design team closely associated with creating visuals for music projects, both working for bands directly, and illustrating music features for magazines. Here Art Director Steve Price (pictured) walks us through some of his favorite commissions.

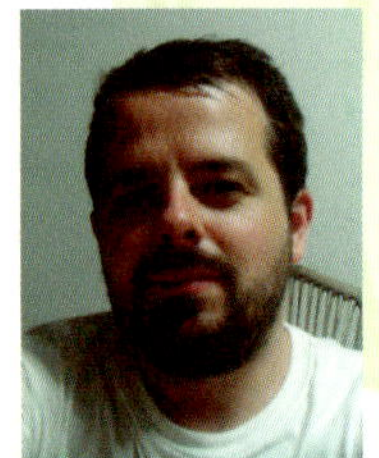

Client: Wall of Sound Recordings
Artist: Vinyl Dialect
Project: CD 8-page booklet/12" inserts

Plan-B Studio was approached by label Wall of Sound Recordings to come up with a range of visuals and packages for hip-hop trio Vinyl Dialect, a relationship that has continued through a number of sleeve designs and other commissions. "This design takes its inspiration from the lyrics, and this single had the lyric 'Playing stonehenge croquet'—an inspiration for any blank canvas! It is a mixture of handdrawn and cut-and-paste imagery with halftone bitmaps, vector stylized drawings, and skyscape images sourced online. There are three characters on the cover, to represent the members of the band. It mixes the brash with the subtle, mirroring the cut-and-paste form of the music."

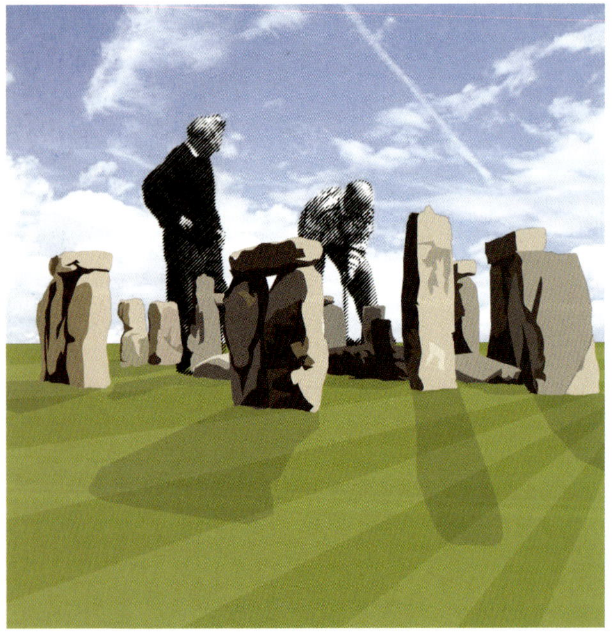

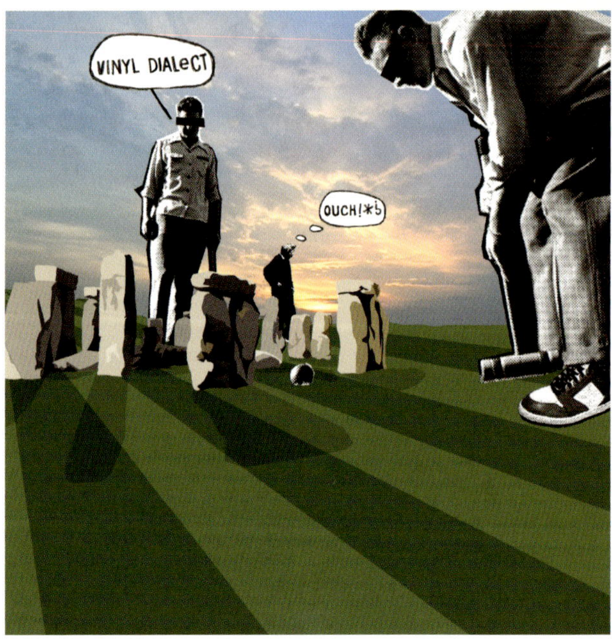

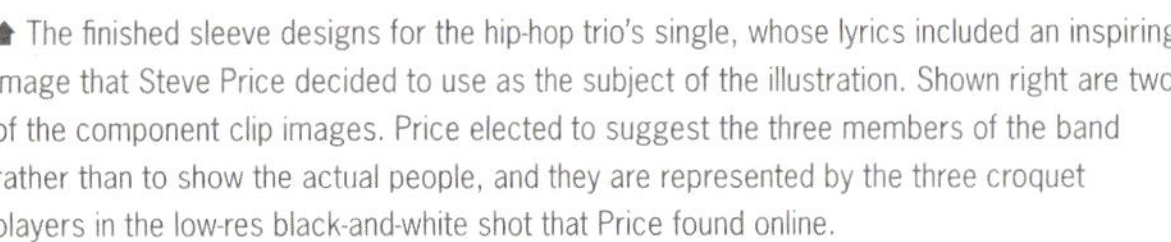

⬆ The finished sleeve designs for the hip-hop trio's single, whose lyrics included an inspiring image that Steve Price decided to use as the subject of the illustration. Shown right are two of the component clip images. Price elected to suggest the three members of the band rather than to show the actual people, and they are represented by the three croquet players in the low-res black-and-white shot that Price found online.

SOURCE IMAGES

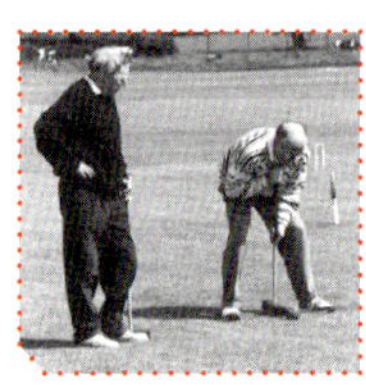

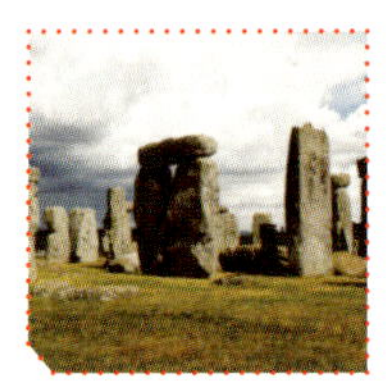

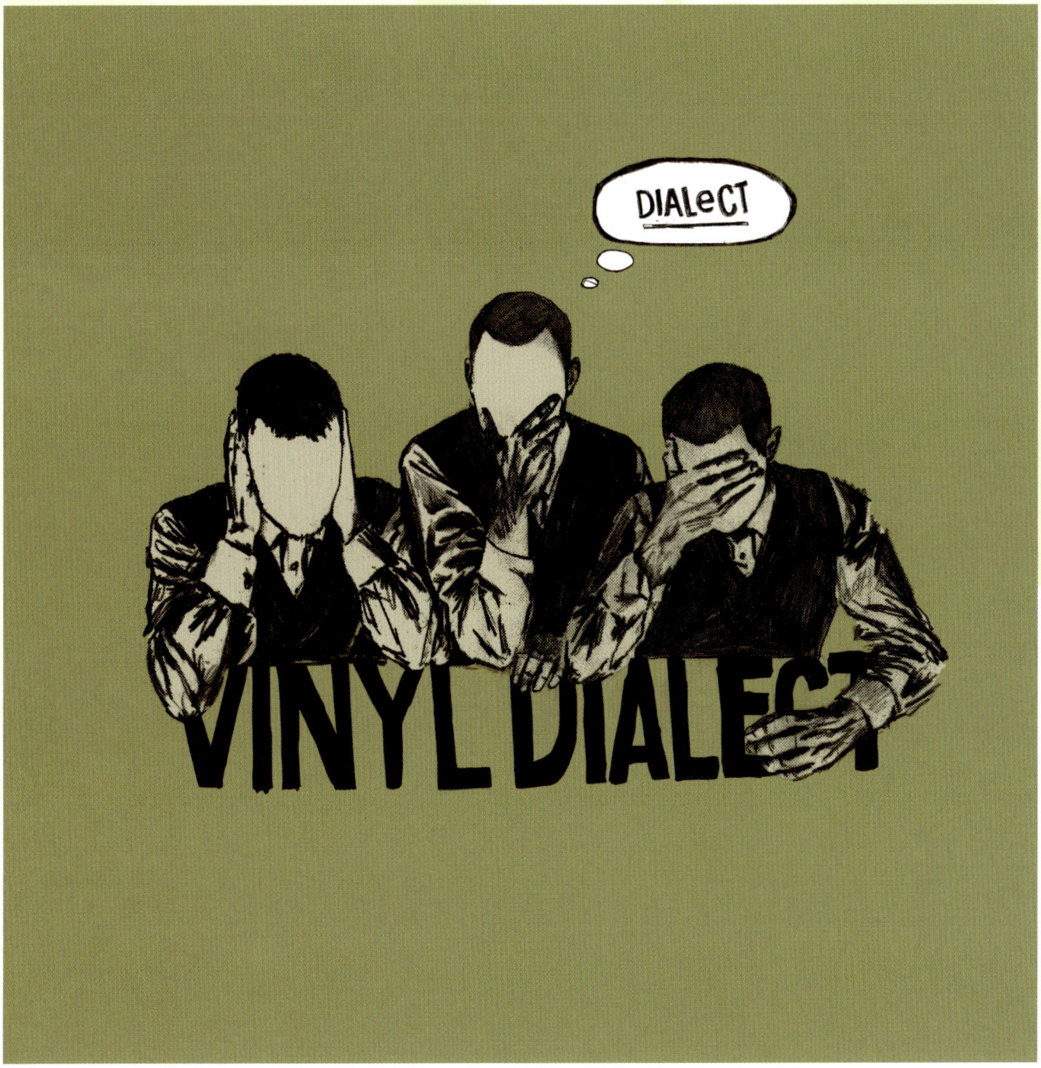

SOURCE IMAGES

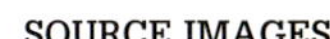

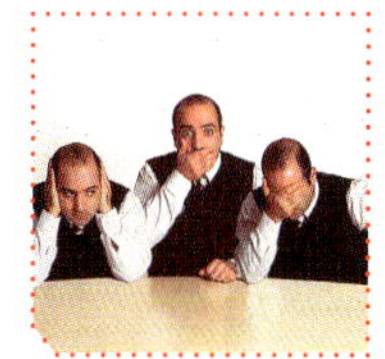

Client: Wall of Sound Recordings
Artist: Vinyl Dialect
Project: CD/12" single

"Wall of Sound Recordings said 'We don't want the band on the cover.' 'Why?' I asked. 'They aren't pretty enough <wink>,' came the response. This was my first discussion with the label when asked to pitch. The album was called *Dialect*, which to me is a simple form of communication. So I came up with the idea of using the proverb 'Hear no evil, speak no evil, see no evil' as a basis for the art direction, handdrawing with a 6B pencil three characters in a pose to suit the proverb. The original image that inspired the illustration was taken from this picture found online. Giving each of the characters anonymous features was also important—it saved on trying to draw their faces and therefore avoid them 'being on the cover.'"

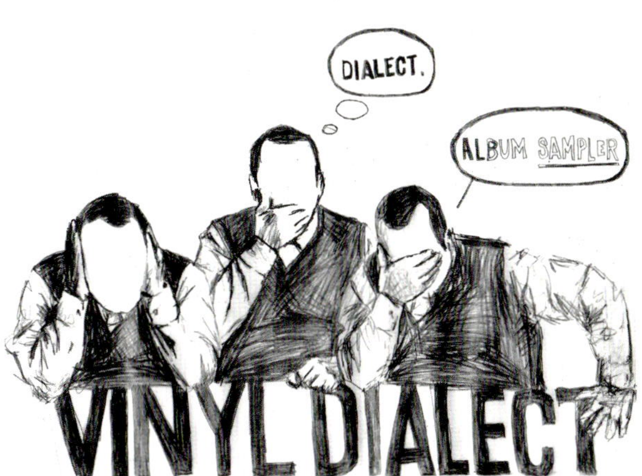

⬆ Clip art as source imagery. Price did not use the clip art he found to represent his conceptual thinking; instead, he used it as a jumping-off point for what became a pencil drawing. This added a handmade touch to a music genre that often stresses power, glamor, and machismo rather than something more considered and light of touch, as here.

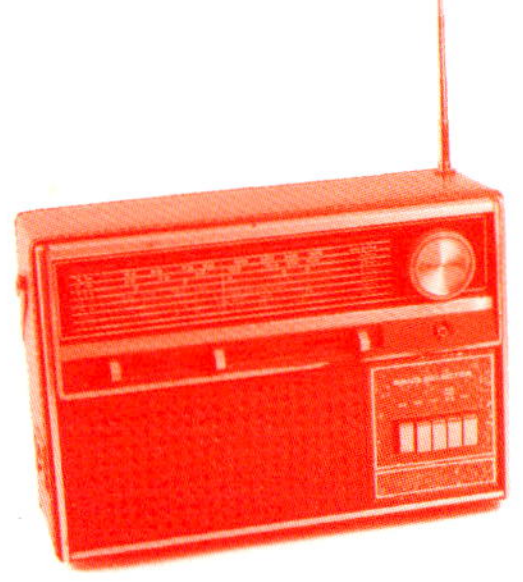

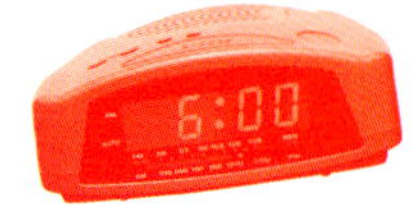

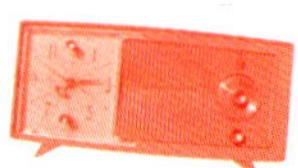

Client: *Radio Billboard* magazine
Project: Magazine illustration

Plan-B has established a strong and fruitful relationship with legendary American music trade magazine, *Radio Billboard*, which produces the official US charts, and its sister titles and supplements. More than most, radio is a medium that has undergone a massive transformation in recent years. Where once it was associated with either elitist, paternalistic broadcasting on the one hand, or underground, pirate, and/or student channels on the other, now the whole industry is in a state of flux as internet radio, digital audio band (DAB), podcasting, mobile networks, media players, and filesharing have redefined the whole idea of what radio means in the twenty-first century. Now that "broadcasting" is potentially in the hands of everyone from the largest multinational corporation to the smallest bedroom-based outfit with the technical savvy to talk to the world, even traditional radio broadcasts can be heard again and again at the listener's leisure as radio escapes its defining limitations of time and scheduling.

To illustrate a feature on radio innovation for the magazine, Plan-B trawled all manner of sources for retro clip-art shots of radios, and also images of space, satellite broadcasting, soundwaves (here sourced from iStockphoto), and microphones. The result is a transformed landscape that recalls Manhattan, power stations, oil rigs, and electrical grids; a post-industrial look at how broadcasters large and small can contact the world using nothing more than the power of the spoken word.

SOURCE IMAGES

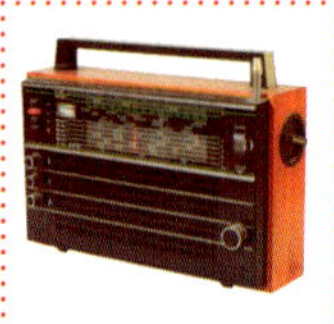

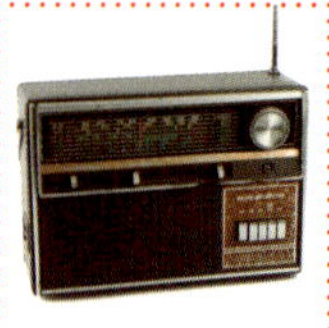

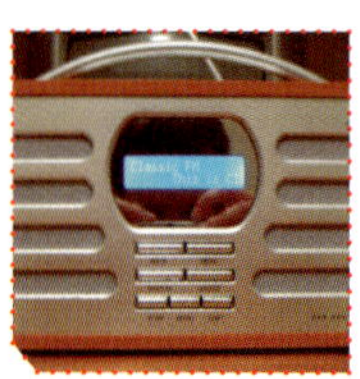

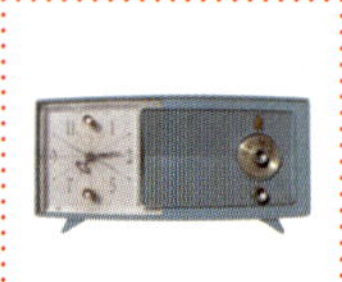

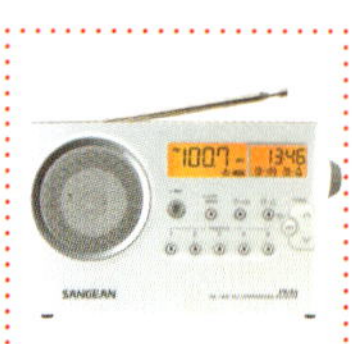

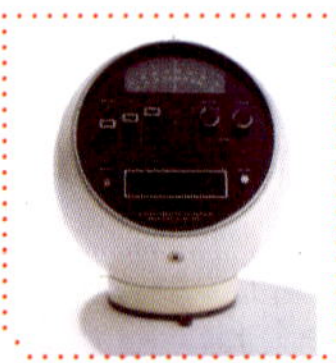

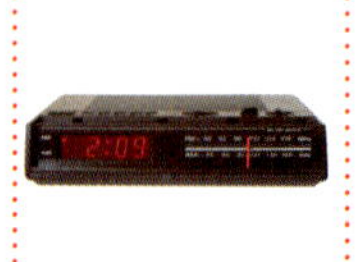

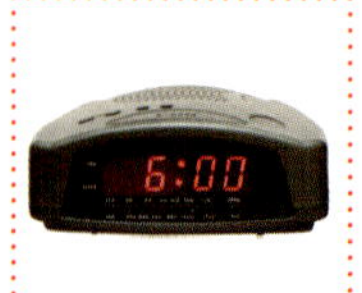

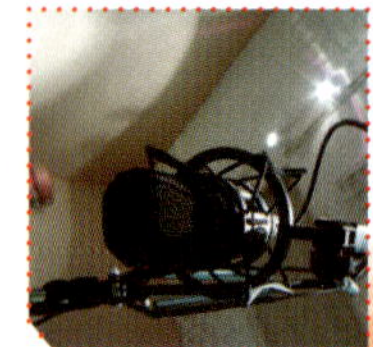

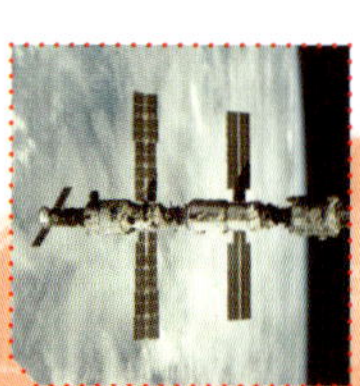

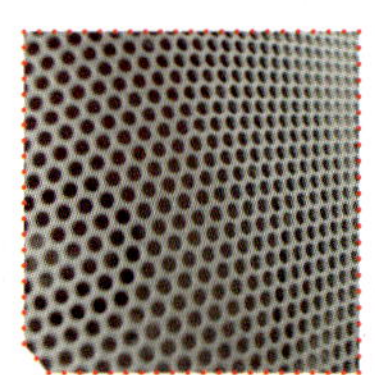

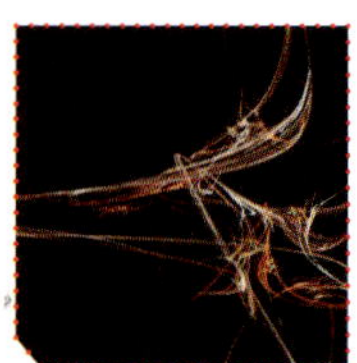

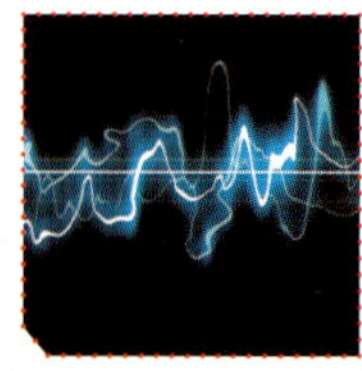

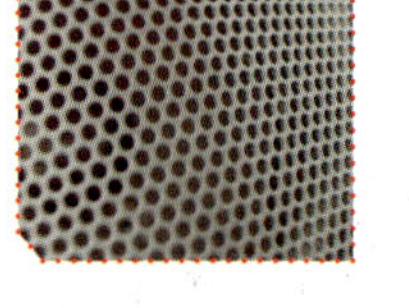

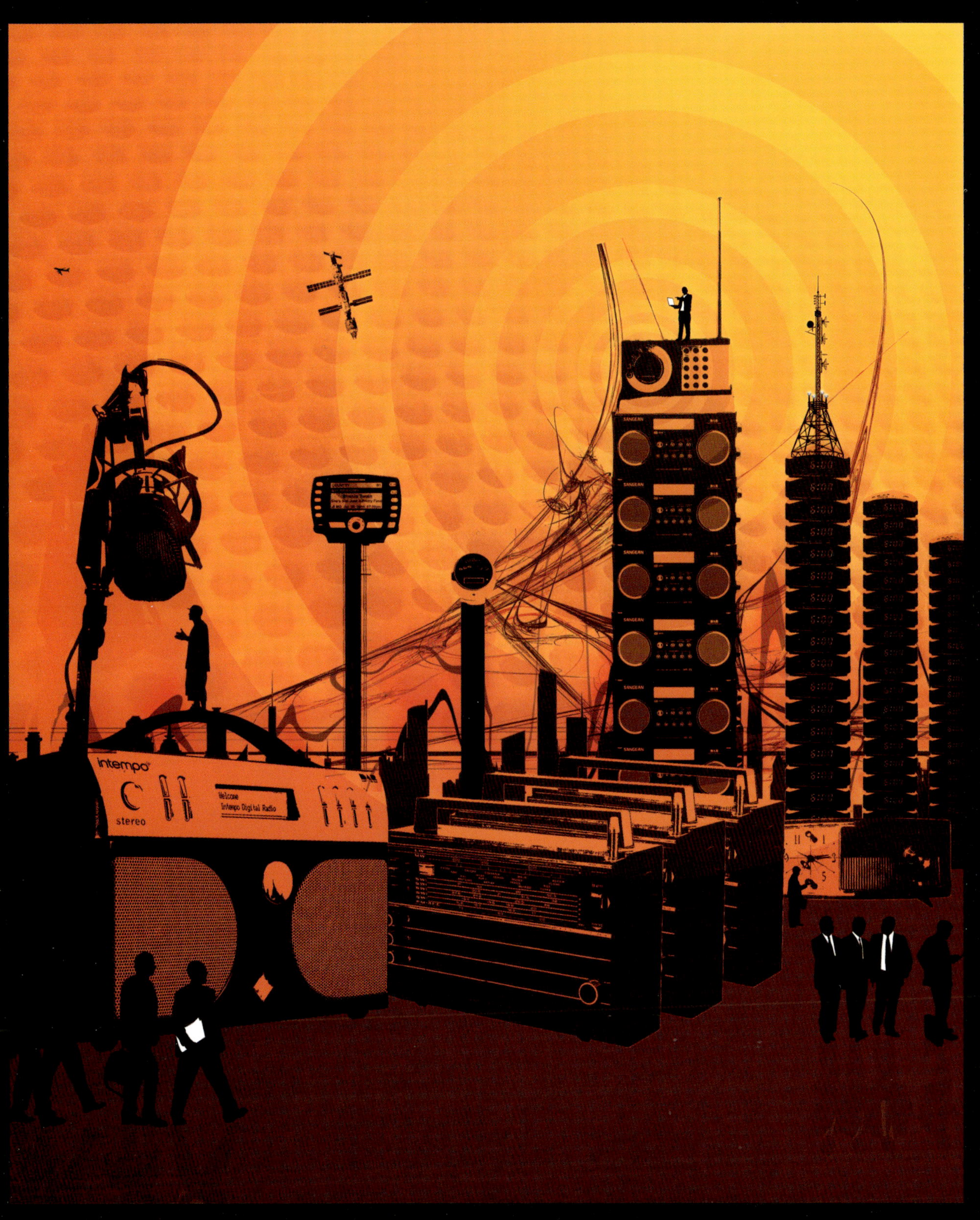
intempo
stereo
Welcome
Intempo Digital Radio
SANGEAN

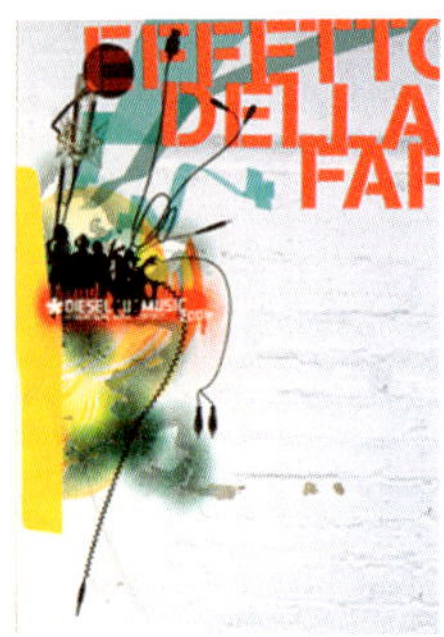

Clip-art forms plug in and connect with the world outside in this graphic superimposed on a wall, like a gig poster in a club or basement music venue.

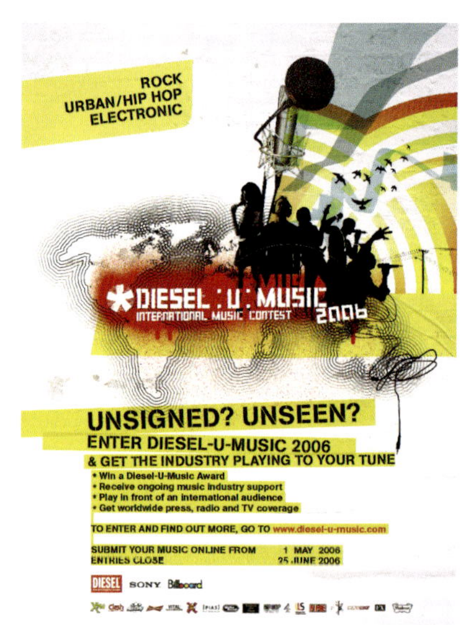

The familiar Diesel branding is here subsumed into the event graphics, in a design that suggests the event is more important than the big brand behind it.

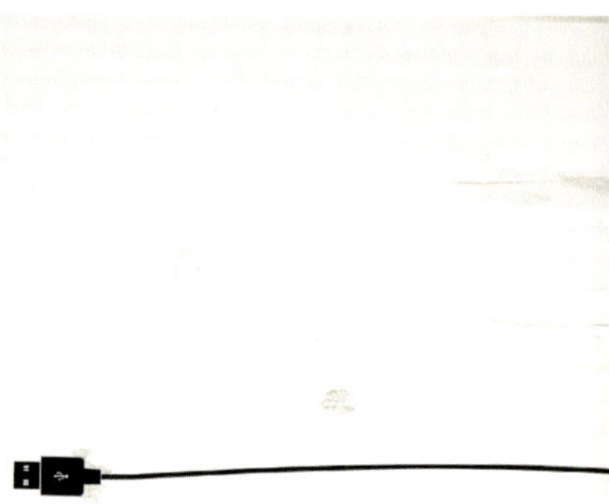

The approach is loose but dynamic, creating the impression of something attainable that might lead the successful entrants into a new and exciting world.

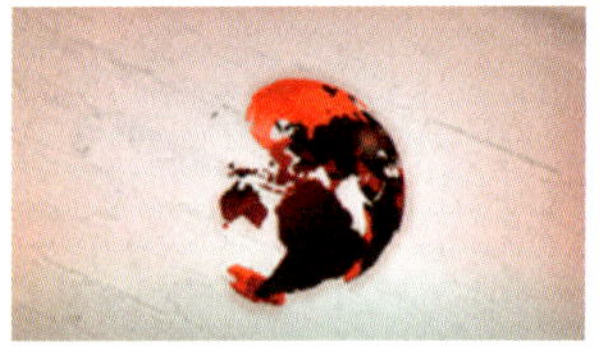
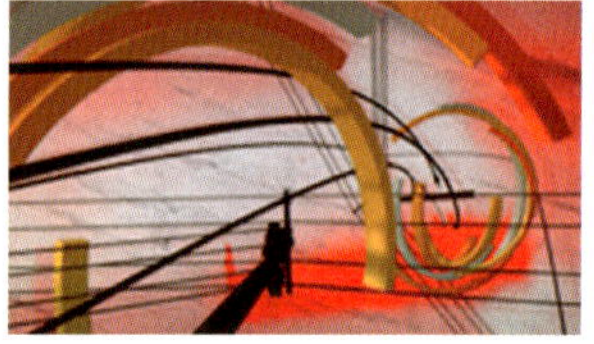
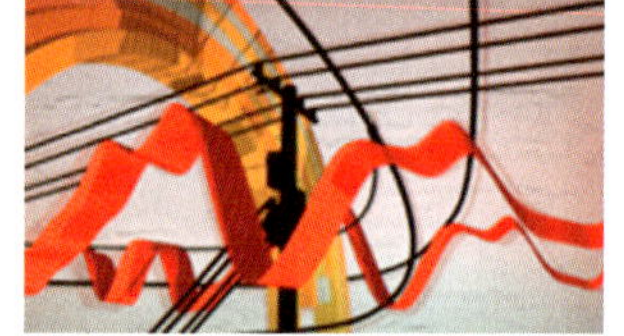
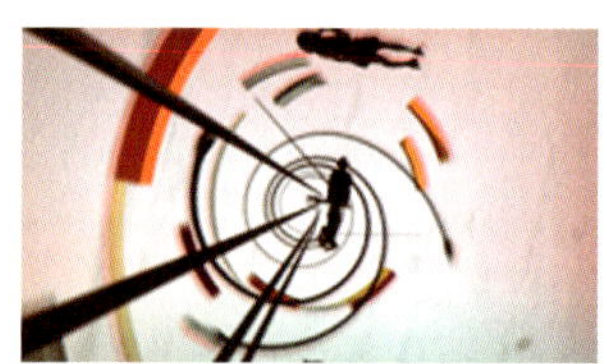

SOURCE IMAGES

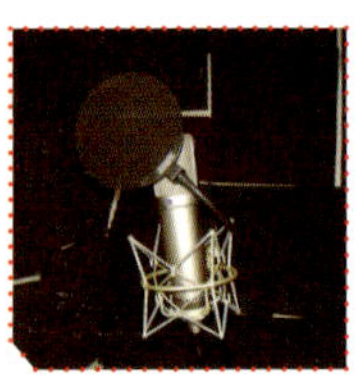
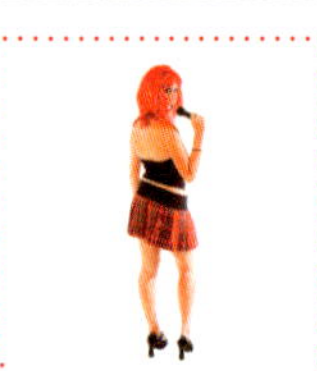
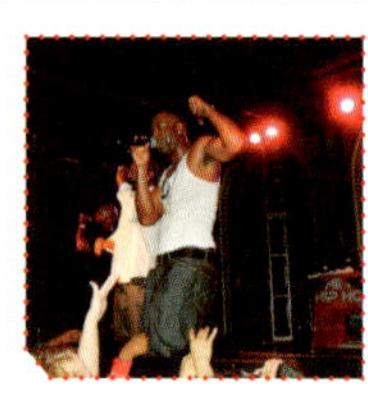
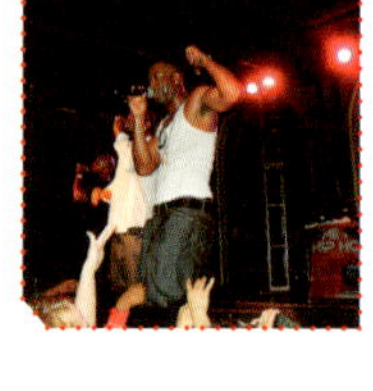
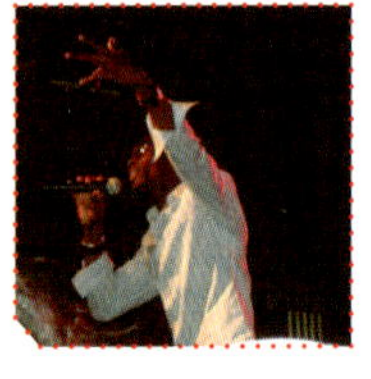
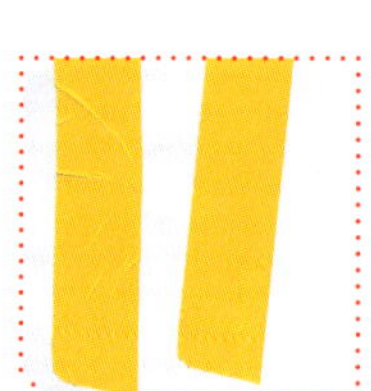
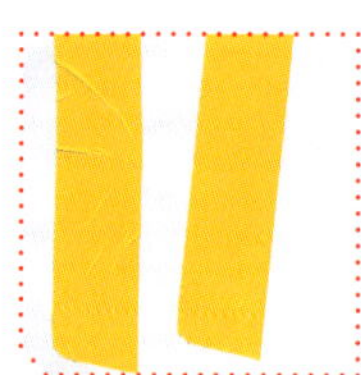
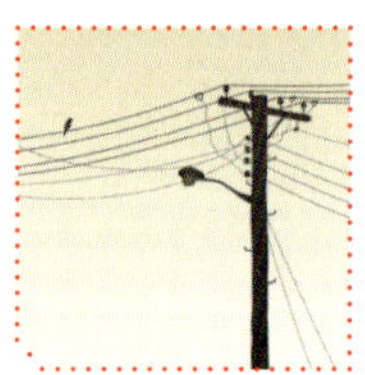

Client: Diesel
Project: Diesel-U-Music 2006
Format: Identity, posters, T-shirts, invites, adverts CD inlays, 24-page fanzine, TV titles

Clothing label Diesel decided to escape its up-market denim tag and find new ways of connecting with its choosy, cash-rich young customers in ways that extended the brand—like this sponsored new-music event. Diesel told Price that they wanted to be “more brave.” Price explains the design: “The illustration, which I created using found imagery and then assembled in Photoshop, pays homage to the various genres of music using intense, vibrant colors, waveforms, headphones, and microphones, all plotted along paths within a cropped landscape. Rather than just purely graphical (as in previous years), or photographic, I developed a more illustrative route to work across all of the platforms.”

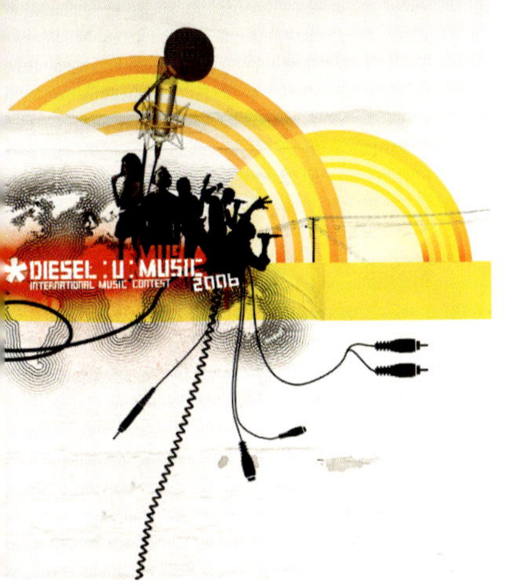

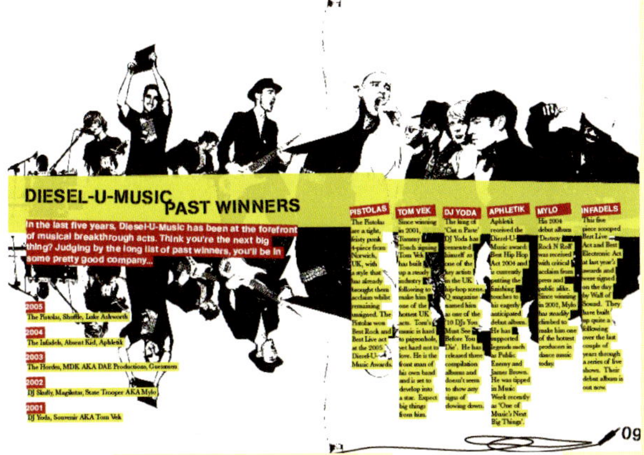

⬆ A roll call of excellence rounds off the campaign that has played fast and loose with the often monolithic Diesel brand, taking it into a new relationship with its customers.

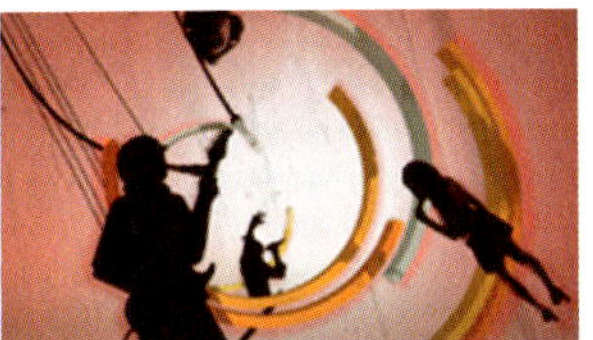

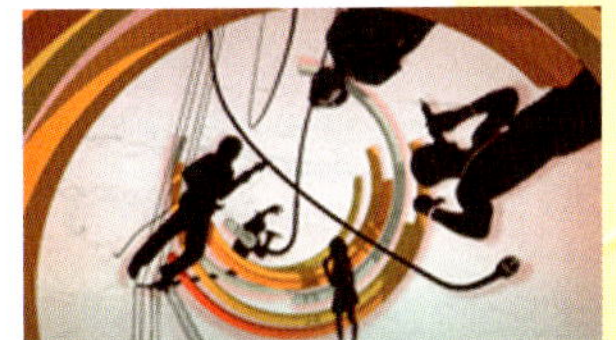

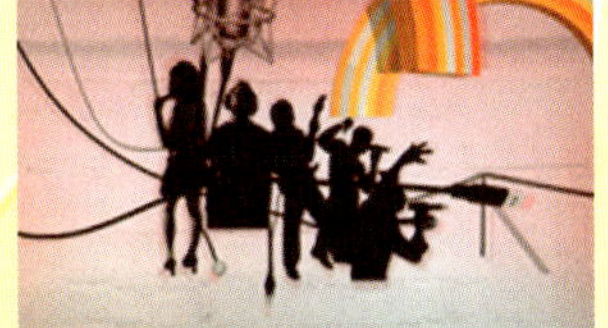

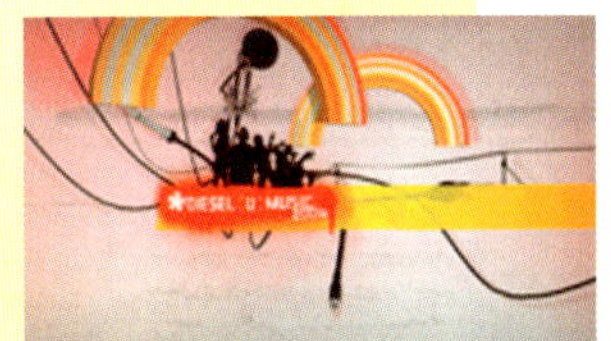

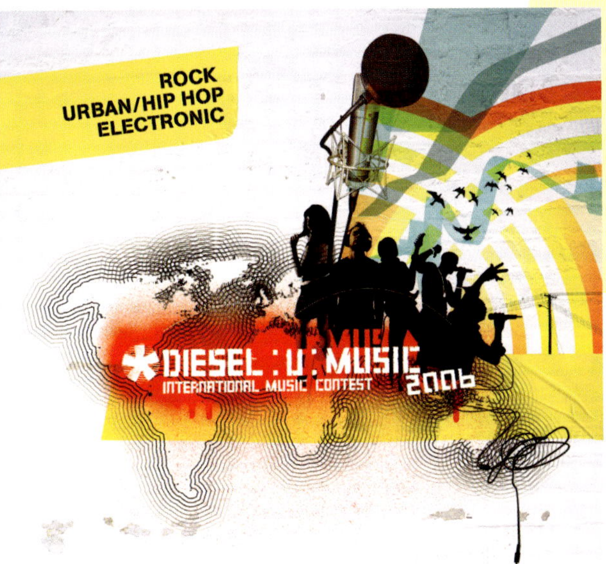

⬆ Plan-B extended the clip-art aesthetic into its motion graphics for a campaign of TV adverts for the new music festival and competition.

⬅ Here Plan-B creates a true mash-up of styles as rock, hip-hop, and electronica all fuse in an illustration that recalls the psychedelic 1960s, black music of the early 1970s, and the new dance explosion of the "second summer of love."

The Small Stakes

Designer Jason Munn of The Small Stakes is rapidly building a matchless portfolio of concert posters for the cream of the indie music and singer/songwriter scenes. His work is beautiful, meticulous, and, although very modern, carries strong echoes of nineteenth-century posters and pamphlets from both the American West and the Victorian music hall.

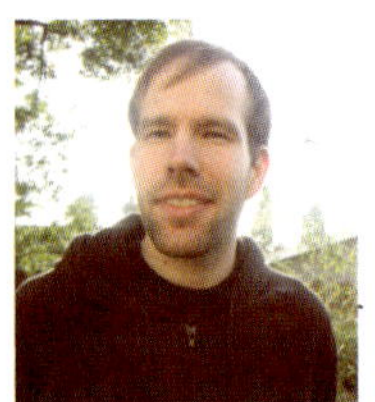

➡ In this poster for Cat Power, the eyes, hand, and background shapes are all image clips sourced from old catalogs and from Xerox copies, which have then been optically distorted using a photocopier in a very hands-on mix of old and new techniques.

⬇ Posters for the bands Death Cab for Cutie and Low, using Dover Books-sourced images collaged in Photoshop. The final posters have then been screenprinted on colored papers to create a look reminiscent of earlier times.

"Pretty early on—even in school," says The Small Stakes' designer Jason Munn (pictured left) when asked when he first began using clip art in his work. "I've used Dover Books, old catalogs and such that I pick up at flea markets. I also use a lot of natural objects that I pick up when I'm out walking, like leaves and plants. But I'm not so organized about it. I'll usually think of an idea and then look for imagery to fit it. I think it's pretty natural for most designers and definitely not easy to turn off for me—I'm always picking up things!"

Munn's extraordinary relationship with the indie music scene has seen him become a one-man factory of gig posters for acts from Cat Power and Low to Death Cab for Cutie, Joanna Newsom, and Kings of Leon. Munn's work is certainly an exhibition-in-waiting for afficianados of the music poster, and could be an investment for anyone astute enough to hang onto the best examples of this most ephemeral of forms.

His techniques vary from piece to piece, although there is clearly a strong seam of continuity in his work—you can spot a Munn in much the same way as you can identify the cutout animation and illustration work of Terry Gilliam, one of the prime movers of clip art in commercial work.

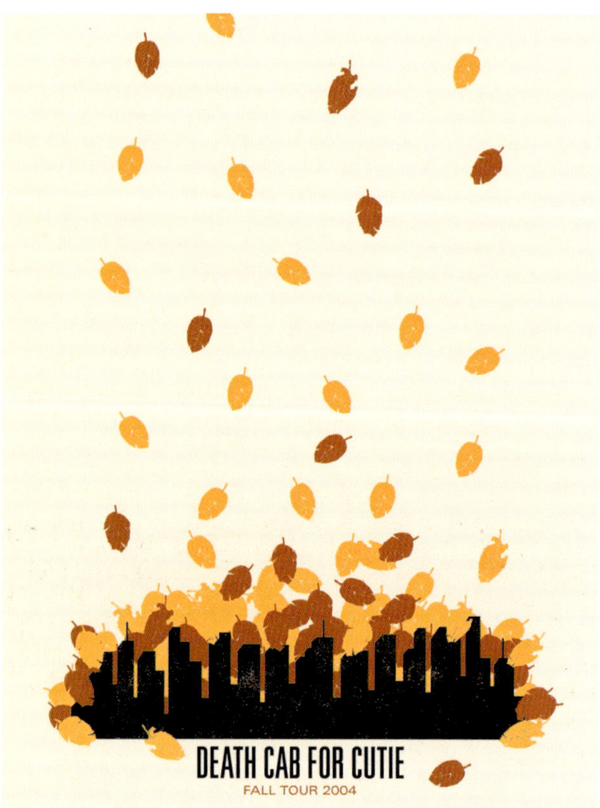

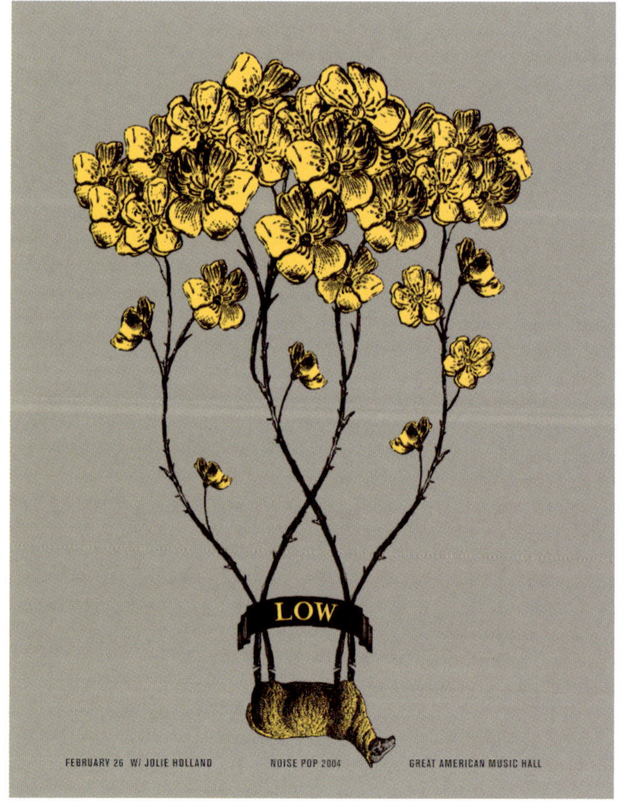

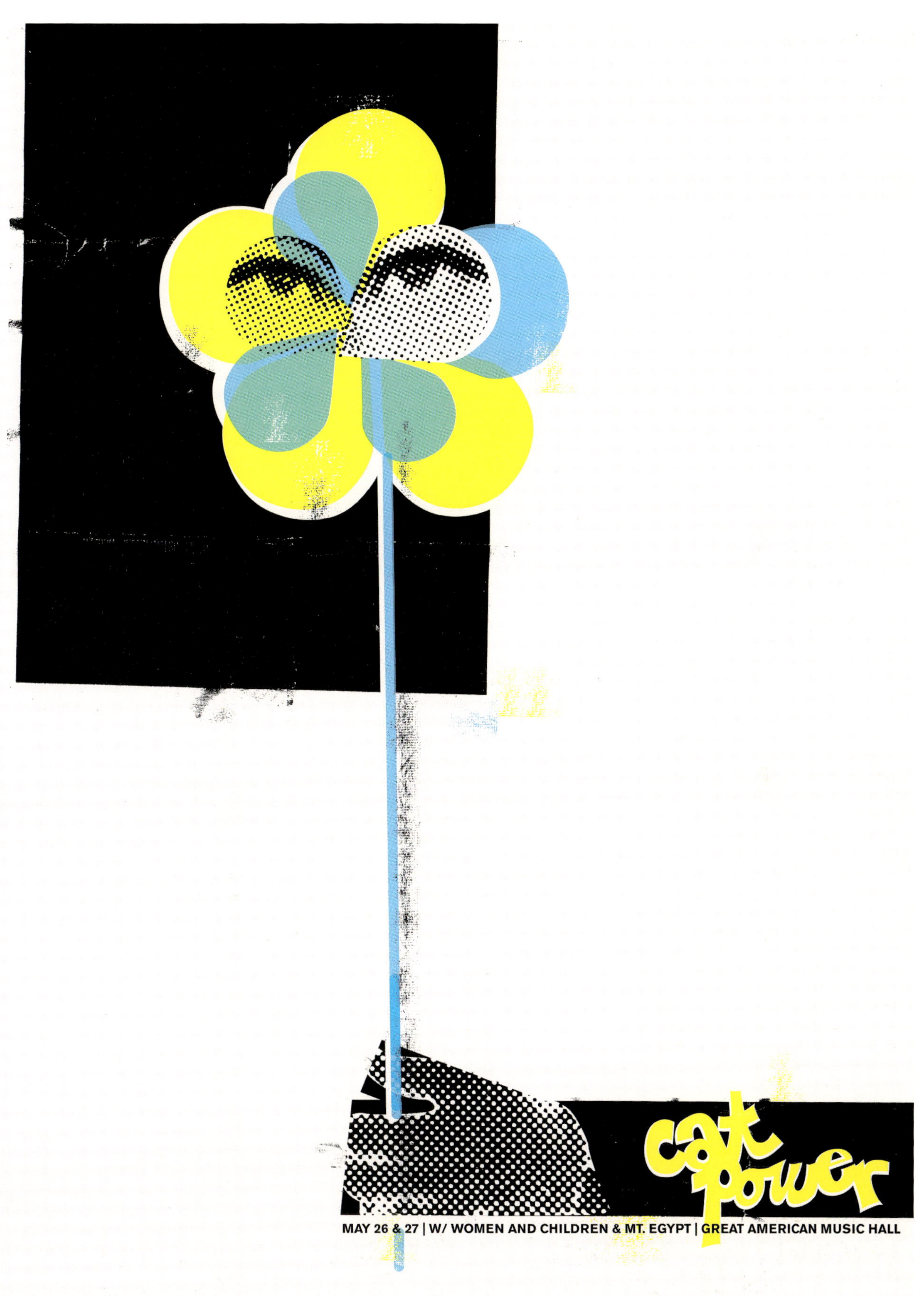
cat power
MAY 26 & 27 | W/ WOMEN AND CHILDREN & MT. EGYPT | GREAT AMERICAN MUSIC HALL

➡ Dover Books images feature prominently in these posters for acts as diverse as Blonde Redhead, Q and Not U, and Sufjan Stevens. Although the designs are very different in conception, many could be part of a series of illustrations from a single book.

His most commonly used source is public domain clip art from the now legendary Dover Books series. "I use source imagery that is easily accessible, and so there may be a chance you'll see that image in someone else's work, but the context could be totally different," he says, adding that he has never yet used commercial image banks.

The instantly identifiable look of a Small Stakes poster is down to a mix of old and new techniques, he explains. "My layouts are mostly done digitally, but my posters are screenprinted after the design/layout is completed digitally."

So given the prevalence of clip art and found imagery in his most public works, are rights and legal issues a potential minefield in the use of it? "They could be; just be fairly smart about how you are using it!" he advises.

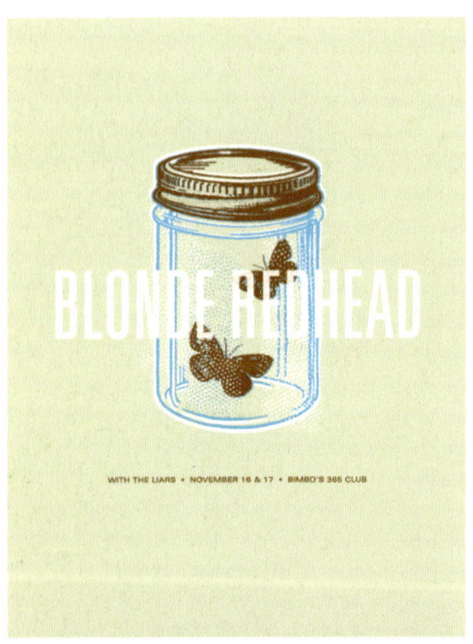

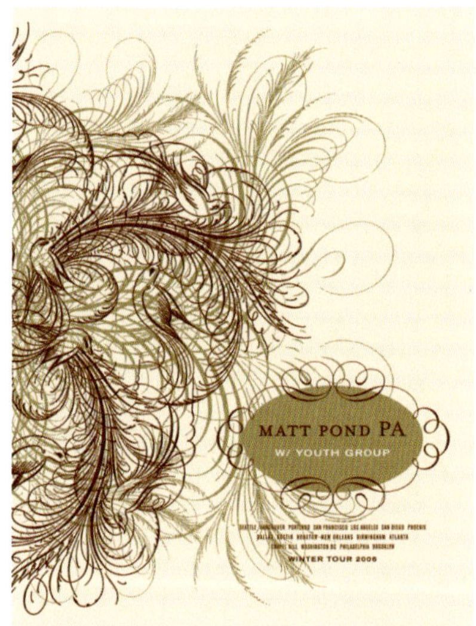

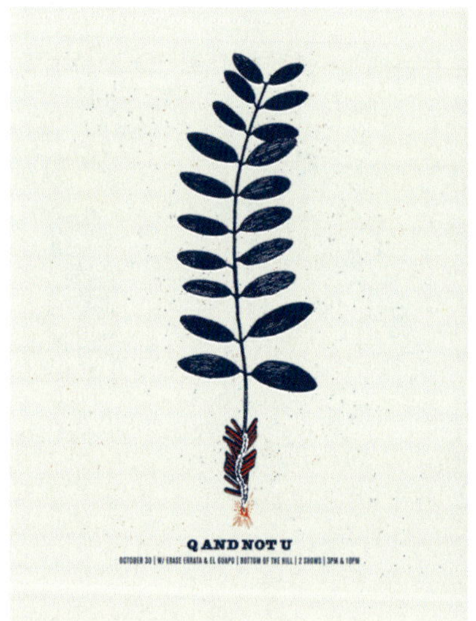

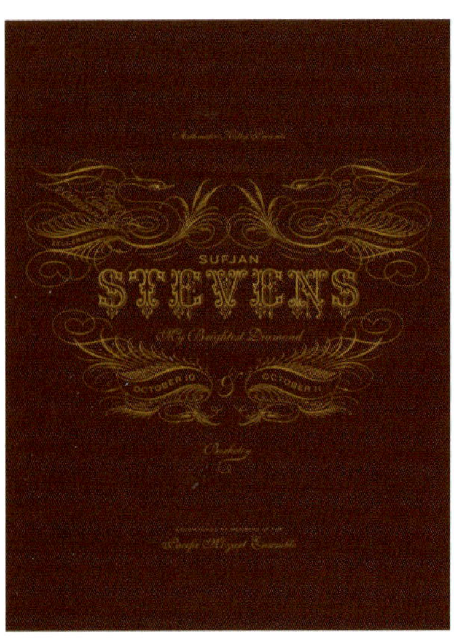

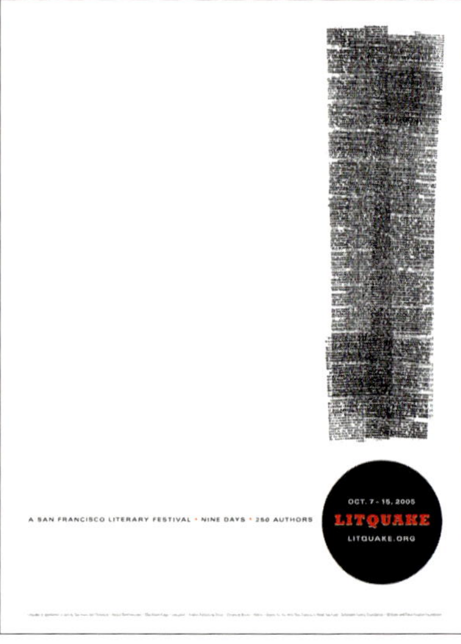

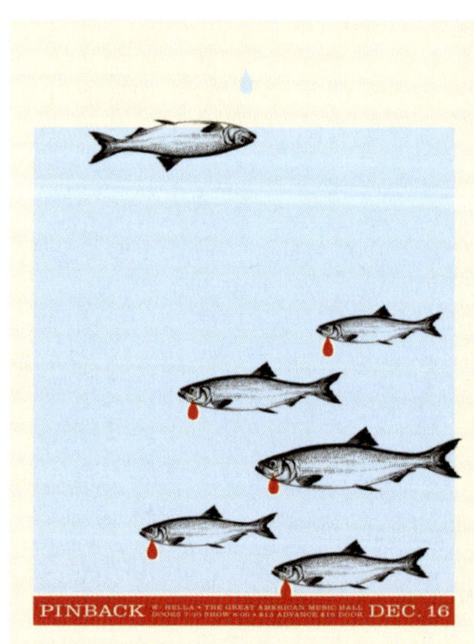

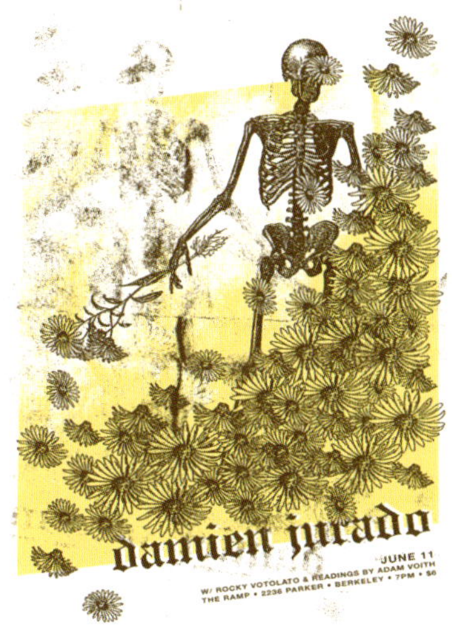
damien jurado
JUNE 11
W/ ROCKY VOTOLATO & READINGS BY ADAM VOITH
THE RAMP • 2236 PARKER • BERKELEY • 7PM • $6

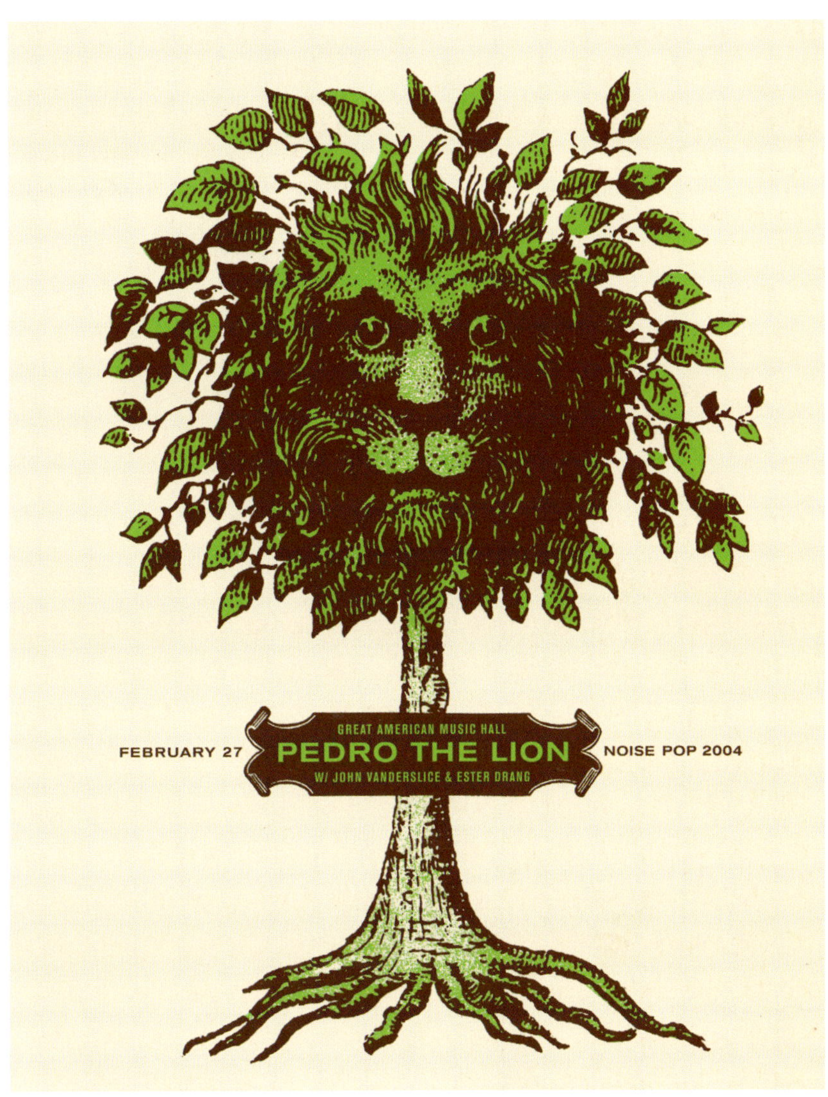
GREAT AMERICAN MUSIC HALL
FEBRUARY 27
PEDRO THE LION
NOISE POP 2004
W/ JOHN VANDERSLICE & ESTER DRANG

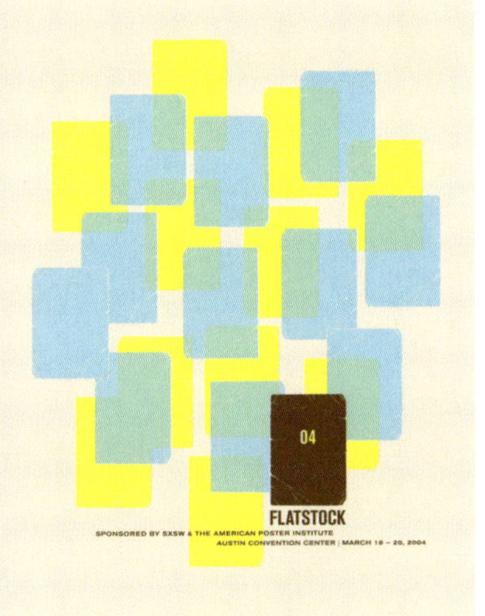
04
FLATSTOCK
SPONSORED BY SXSW & THE AMERICAN POSTER INSTITUTE

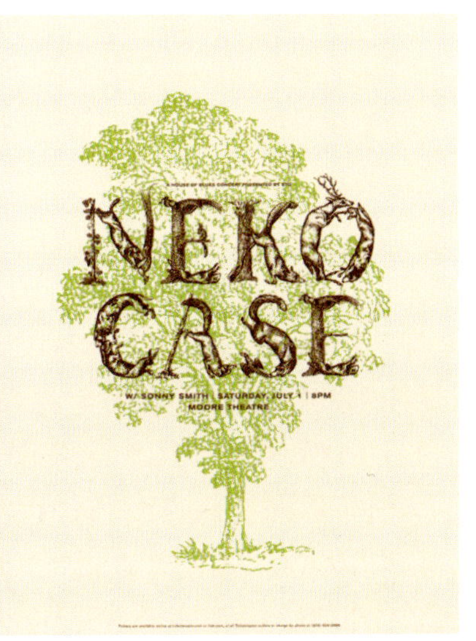
NEKO
CASE
W/ SONNY SMITH | SATURDAY, JULY 1 | 8PM
MOORE THEATRE

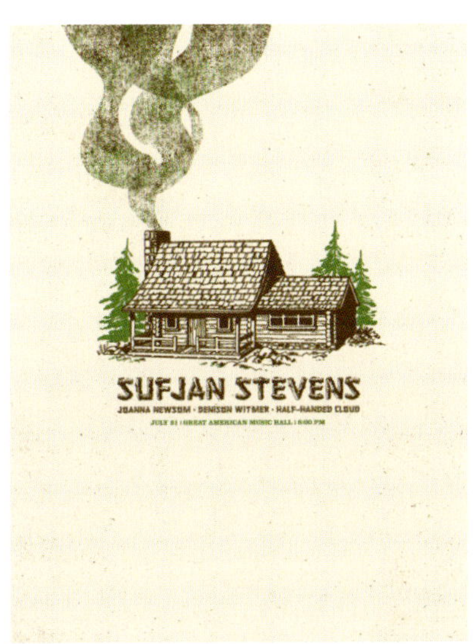
SUFJAN STEVENS
JOANNA NEWSOM • DENISON WITMER • HALF-HANDED CLOUD

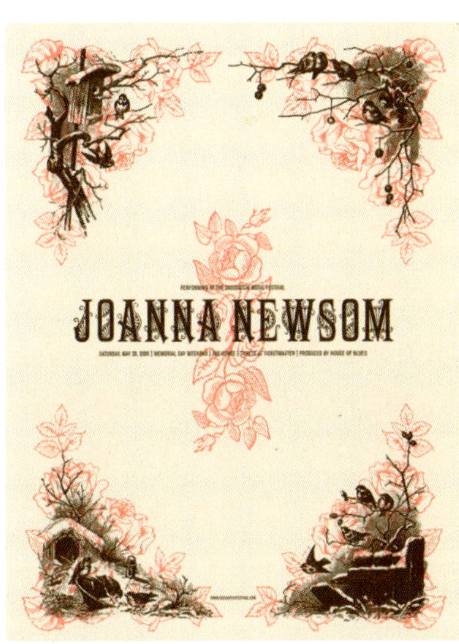
JOANNA NEWSOM

Russell Warren Fisher

Designer and illustrator Russell Warren Fisher uses clip art and found imagery to meditate on the passing of time and to preserve details that are often overlooked and forgotten.

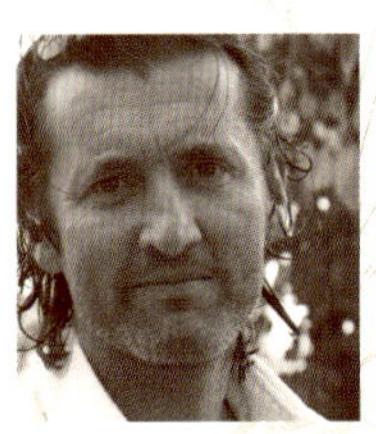

Russell Warren Fisher is one of the best examples of an image-maker who uses found objects and images in a subtle, almost ornate way, to create not haphazard cut-and-paste assemblies that recall Modernist experiments with type and image, but delicate and minimal works that respect the origins of the images themselves.

For example, *Printed Matter No. 1* (a title that suggests an ongoing study of form and function) is what he describes as "an expermental print project using found objects," carried out as a collaboration between himself, Park Lane Press, and Ripe Digital. It is a 16-page piece, with self covers. "Throughout the project," he says, "I sourced dead insects and decaying paper-based matter to montage as new works." The source material was found in his garage and his sketchbooks, and then assembled in layers in Photoshop. As such, the work is a study of decay and the passing of time, but also a study of nature's fleeting beauty in a medium that will itself also decay.

It is perhaps not surprising that these are the same preoccupations of many designers, illustrators, and artists who are as much image collectors and curators as they are image-makers; there is something about the desire to collect and catalog ephemera that suggests a desire to hang onto the past to preserve it and then analyze its meaning for the present.

➡ The cover of *Printed Matter No.1*, Fisher's experimental print project that explores the beauty and decay found in his immediate environment.

⬇ Details from the same print project, focusing our attention on the eerie beauty of the insects he finds near his place of work, seeking to hang onto moments that pass almost too swiftly for the eye to see.

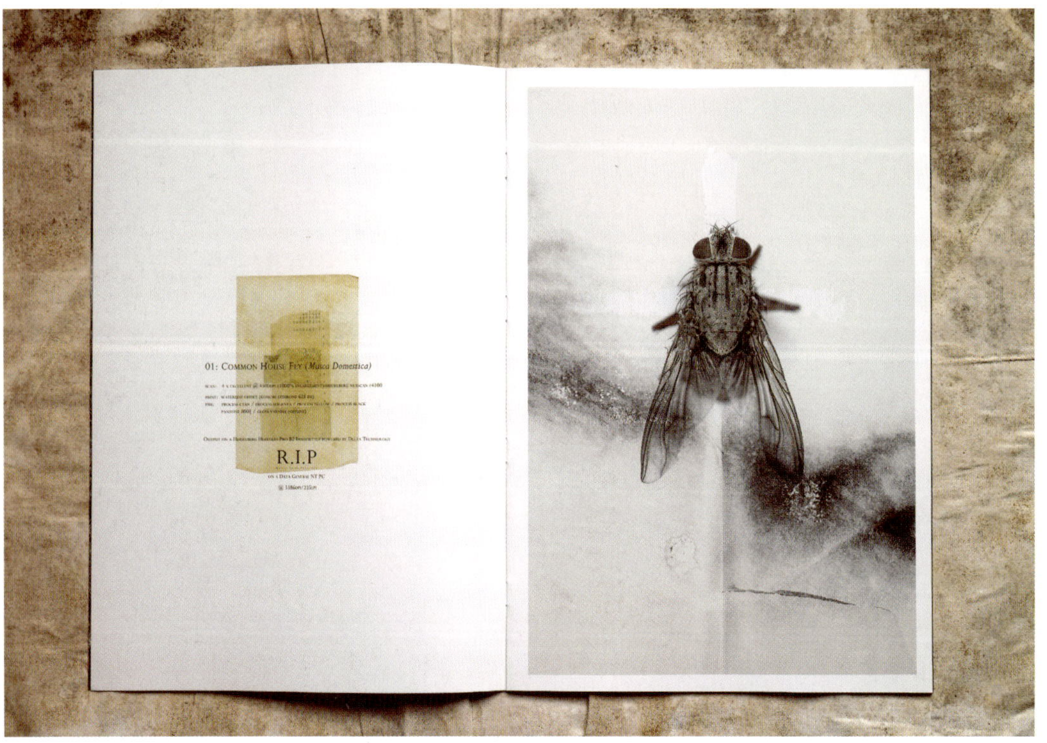

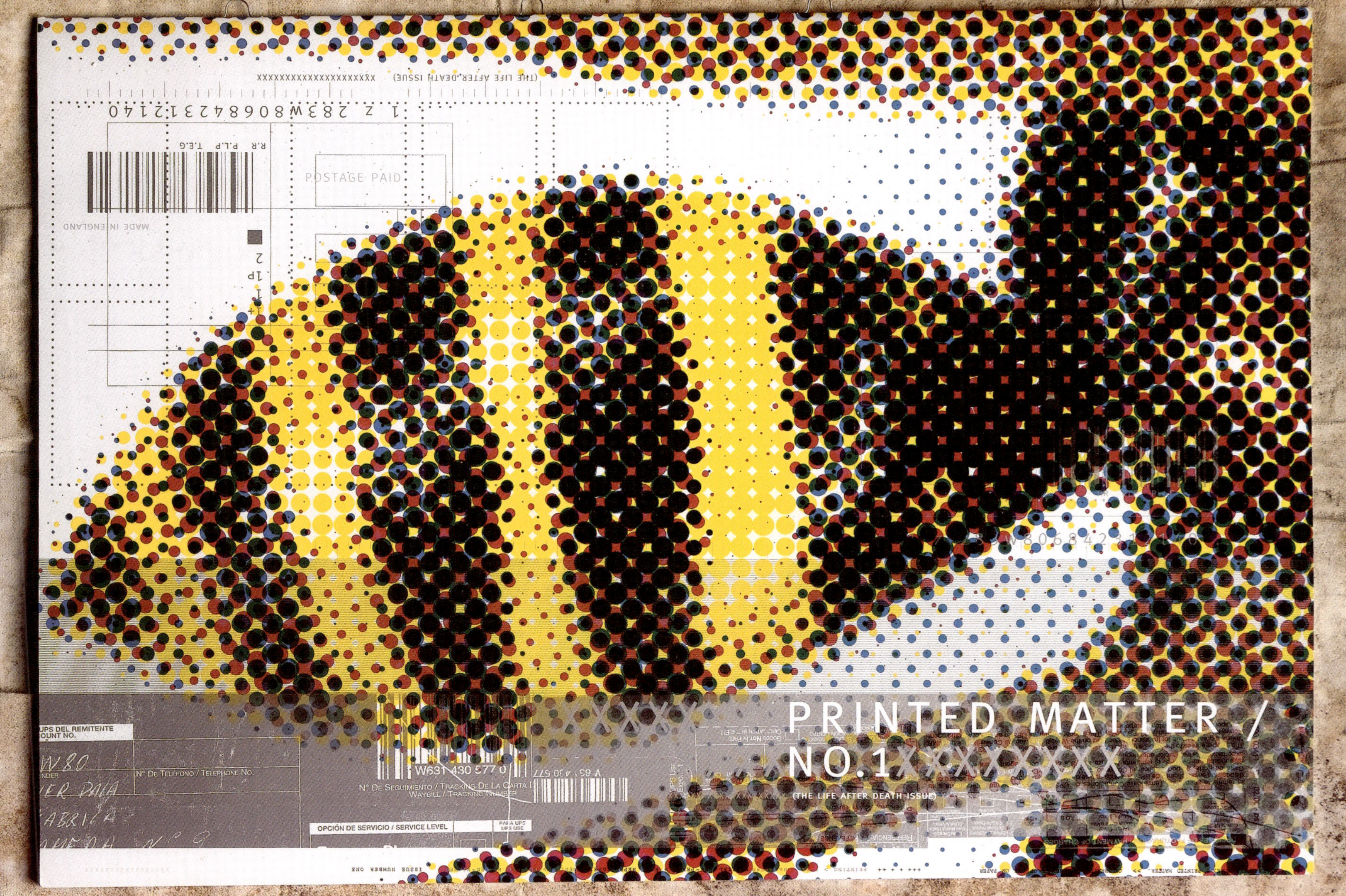
PRINTED MATTER /
NO.1
(THE LIFE AFTER DEATH ISSUE)
POSTAGE PAID
MADE IN ENGLAND
OPCIÓN DE SERVICIO / SERVICE LEVEL

Russell Warren Fisher

Fisher explores this passing of time in many of his works, such as his booklet for the theater group Theatre du Complicité, which celebrates their "journey," to use his word, from their small beginnings to being an international force. Again, for this work, he trawled personal sketchbooks and found objects, along with junk shops and antique markets, and then combined his discoveries with images supplied by the group.

For The English Group, Fisher designed a launch brochure for a new shop, Tiggy Twilight, once again sourcing images for the project from his sketchbooks, along with old manuscripts. This desire to unearth and preserve the past in order to explain the present is the strongest theme in a portfolio of work set apart by its originality and elegance in a world of cut-and-paste that, at its worst, is often noisy, samey, and bereft of emotional impact.

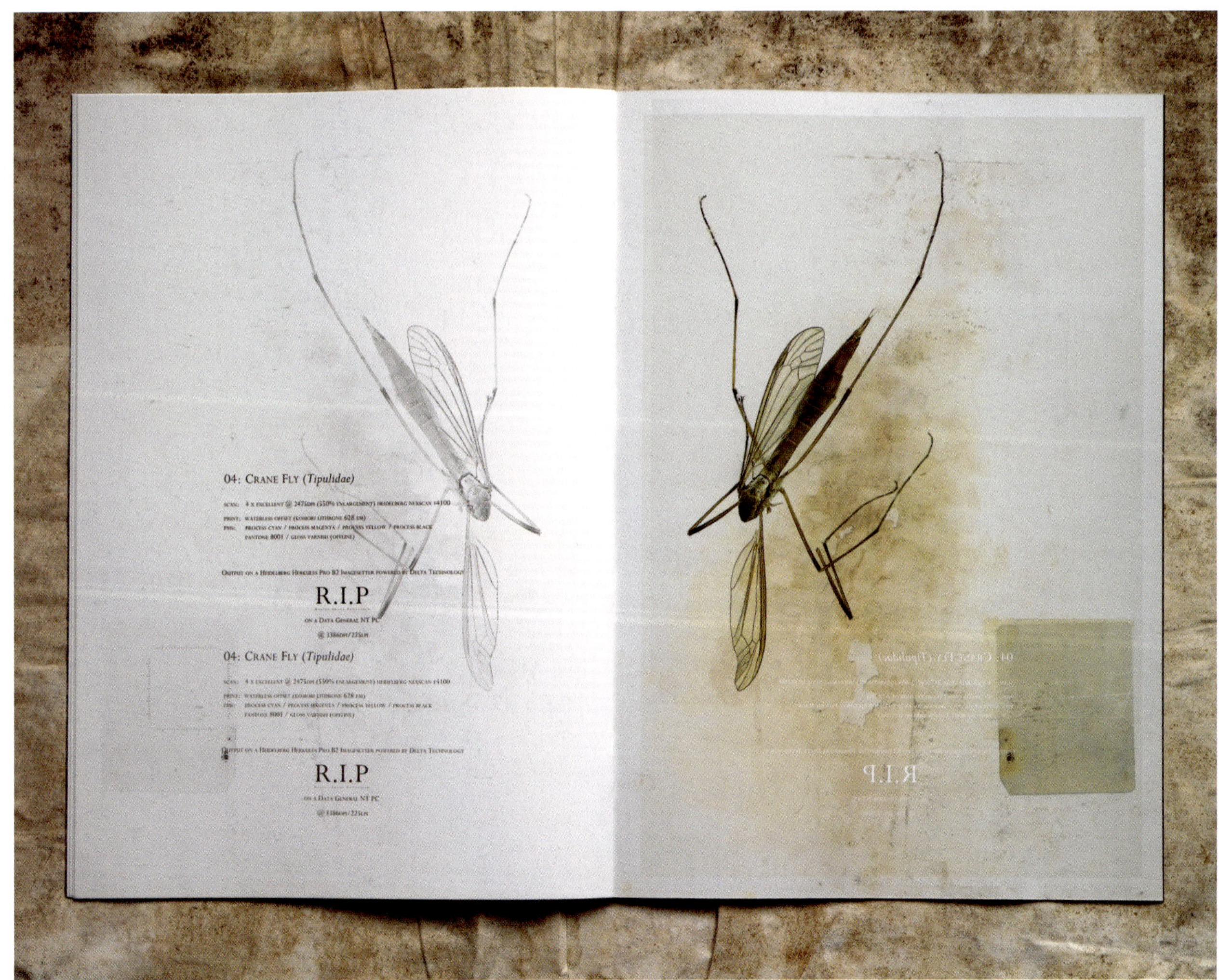

➡ Fisher's print work uses images pulled from dozens of different sources.

⬇ Fisher says "rest in peace" to even the smallest and, apparently least significant lifeforms, here magnified so we can appreciate the beauty of their forms.

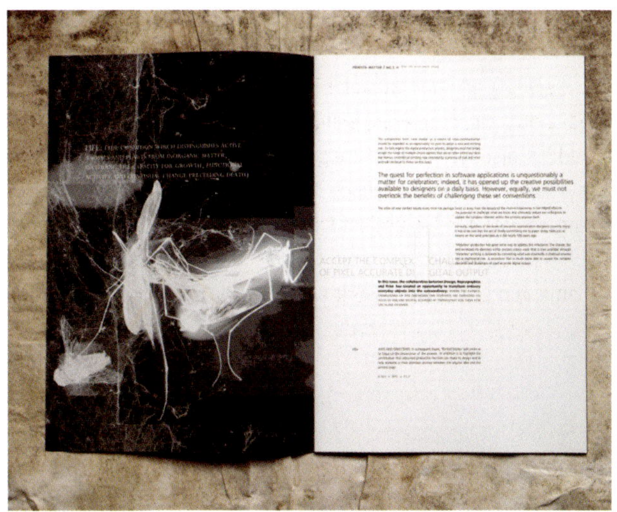
The quest for perfection in software applications is unquestionably a matter for celebration; indeed, it has opened up the creative possibilities available to designers on a daily basis. However, equally, we must not overlook the benefits of challenging these set conventions.

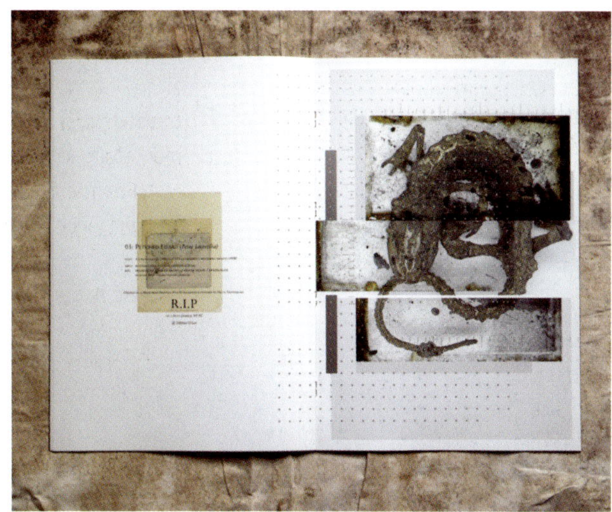
R.I.P

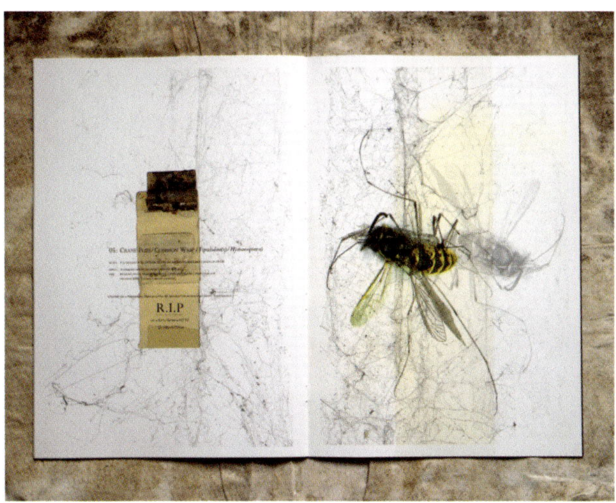
R.I.P

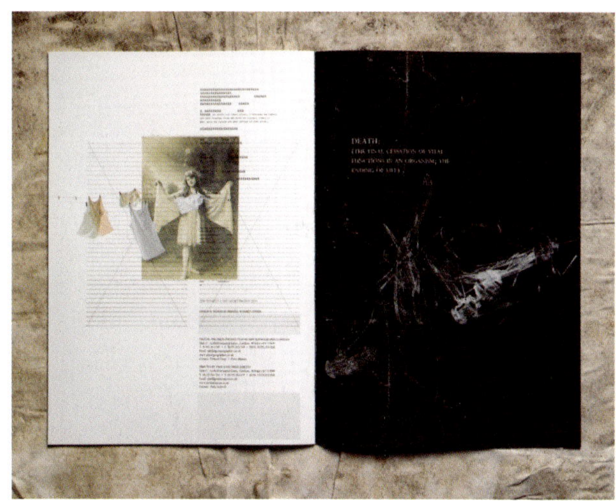
DEATH:

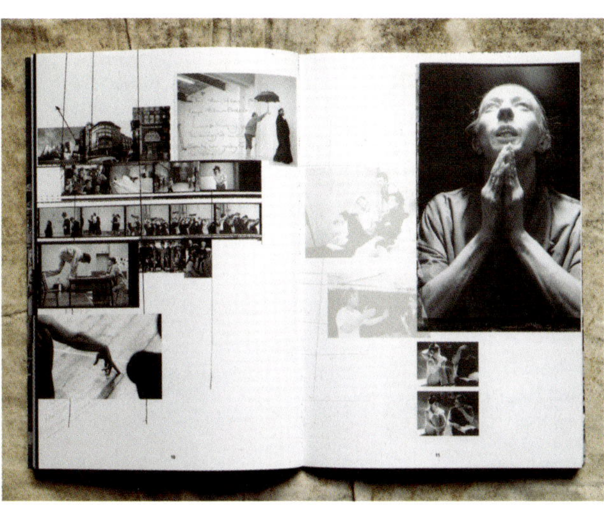

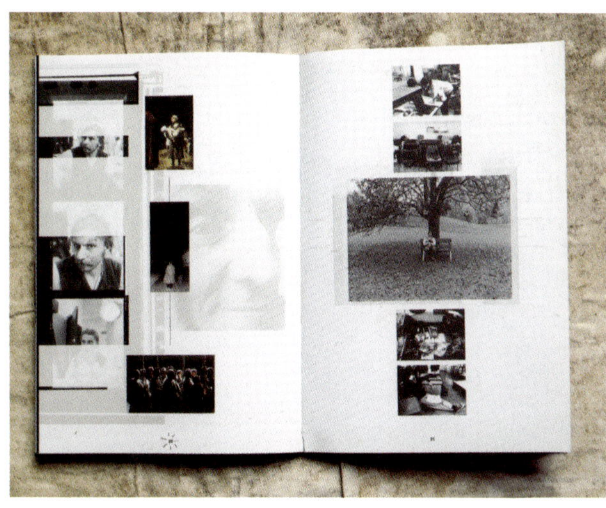

UMS

India is growing in every field of industry, and graphic design and illustration are no exceptions. The UMS design studio in Mumbai typifies this surge of creativity and dynamism, with a series of bright and highly entertaining book projects that transform often dry subject matter into bold and inspiring examples of publication design.

UMS has put together a series of stunning book designs, using clip art and mixed media to create some truly elegant and transfixing design packages, often with a strong social message or conscience. For example, for an event and conference exploring the value of social entrepreneurship in India (pictured here) Design Director Ulhas Moses says, "The concept was to show growth in society and how a small seed can be sowed by an individual entrepreneur, and how a small vision can grow into a large movement and create social change. The [clip art] growth motif has been used in the inner pages of the book, while also being printed on several pages in concentric circles, on textured stocks to emphasize the 'grassroots' feel."

For a book design and illustration for the International Student Awards (ISA), run by the British Council, Moses explains that a single found image of a child was scanned and modified as the basis for a series of images of different children from around the world, by blending the original scan with found images of different types of clothing and then colorizing the images in Photoshop, or modifying their hue and saturation. "Found images of clothing have been digitally manipulated in Photoshop," he explains, "and textures have been added and the color changed to create the many children. The entire image has then been color toned using Color Balance."

Perhaps the most ambitious of the studio's recent book design projects has been a 358-page book design, layout, and illustration commission called *Children of the Balwadi.* The book documents children's education in Mumbai, and the images have been sourced from these children's own books and craft projects. Says Moses: "The

↓ → Mandala-like clip-art patterns dramatize the idea that growth and new life begin with the smallest seed—in this case, an idea, for this publication looking at the vital importance of entrepreneurship in India, which day by day drives ever greater economic growth in this dynamic part of the world.

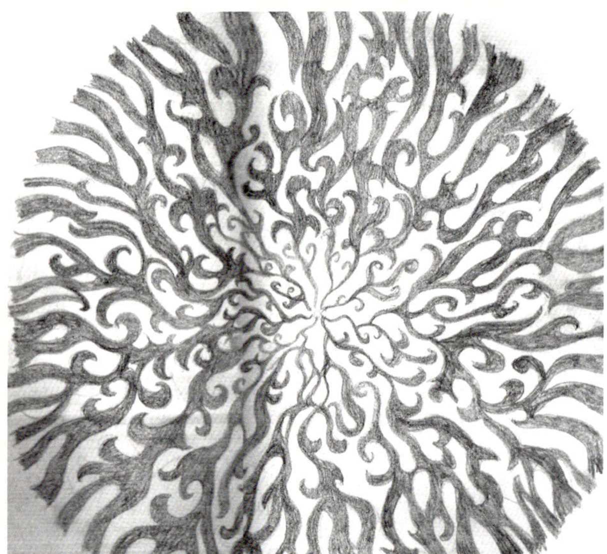

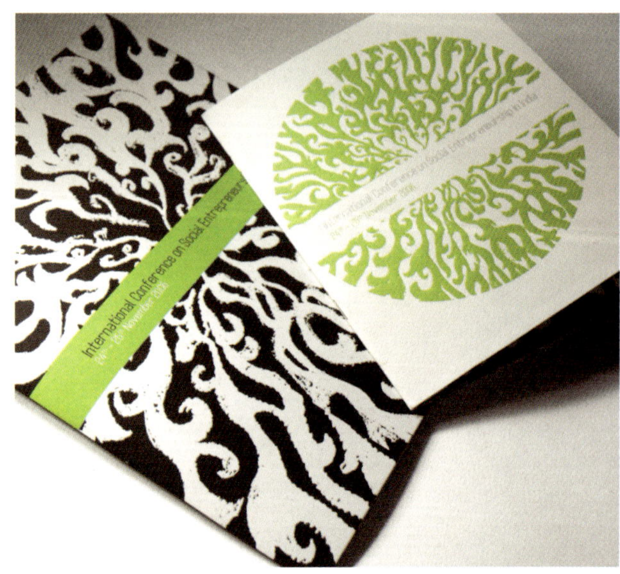

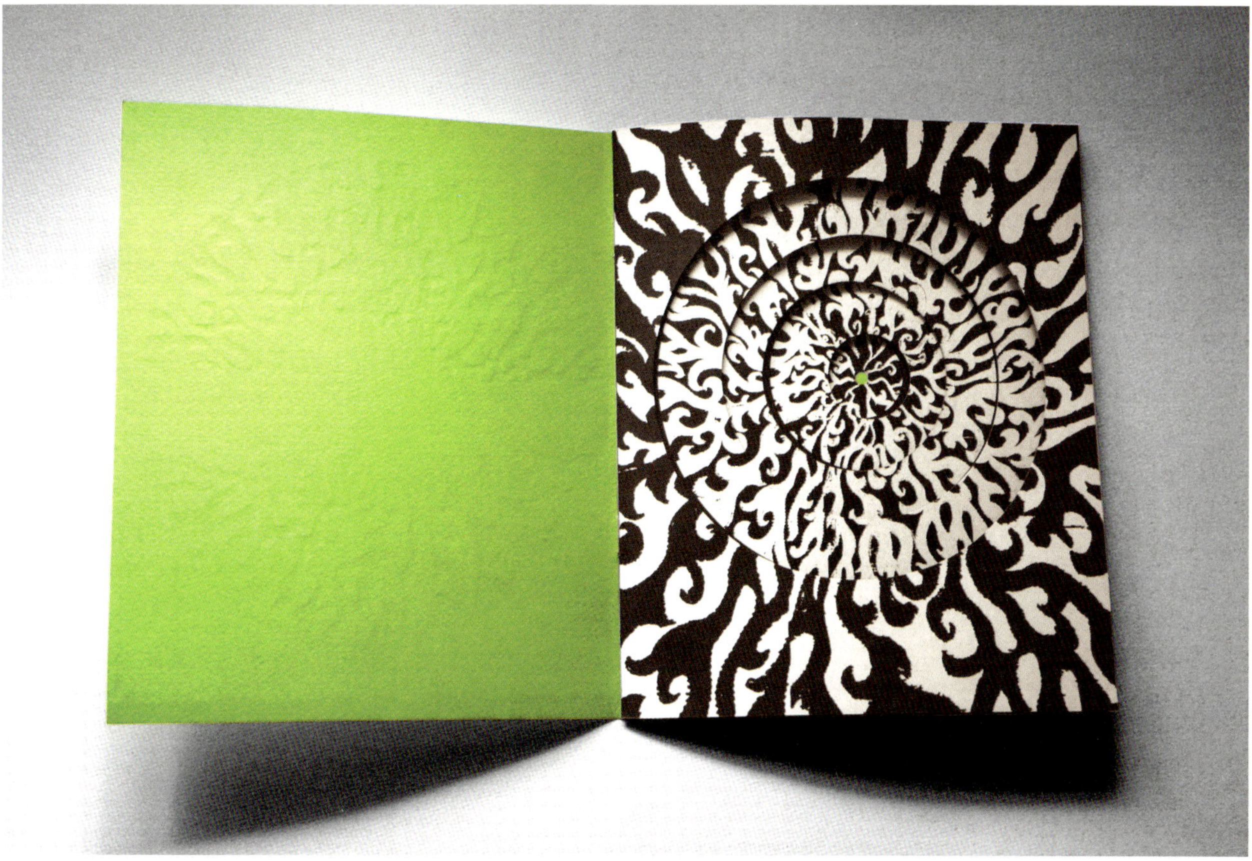

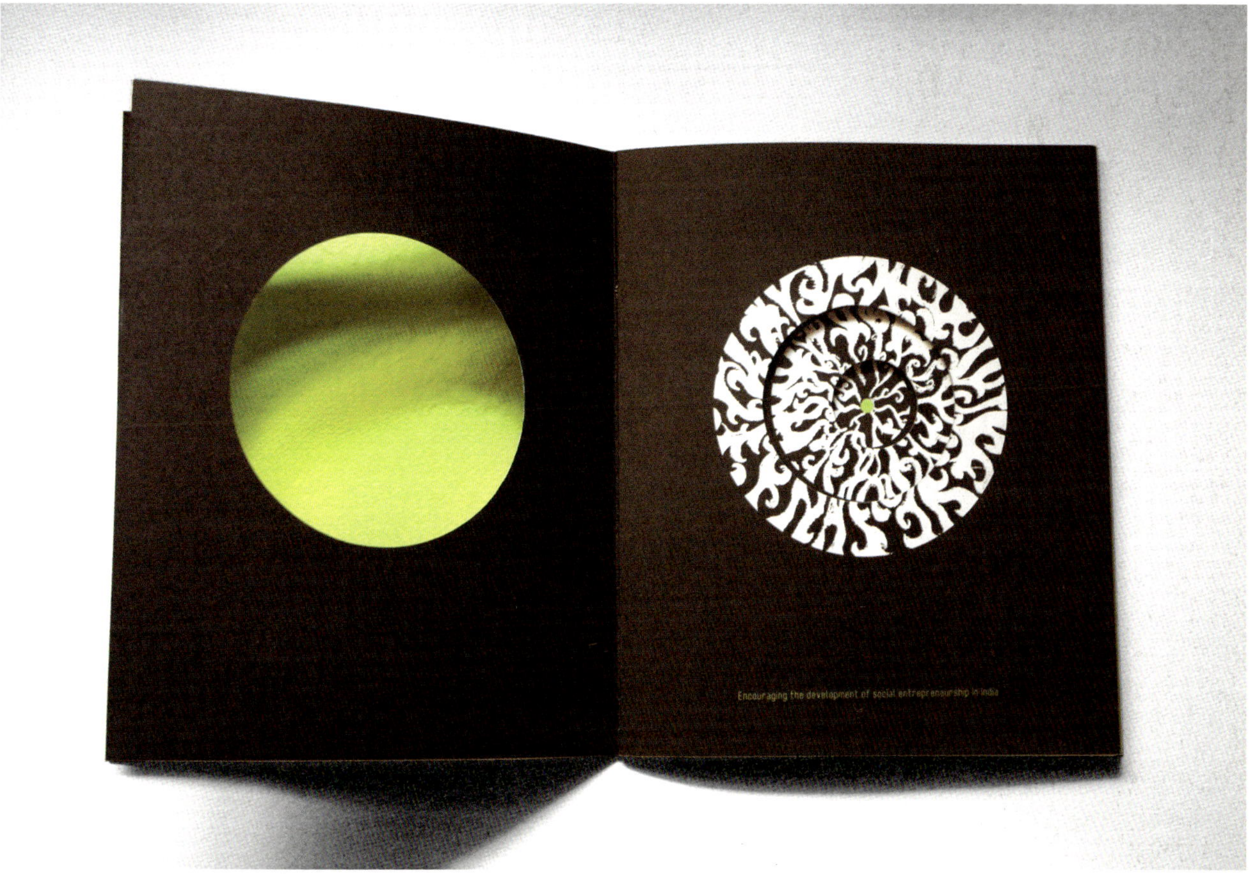

Encouraging the development of social entrepreneurship in India

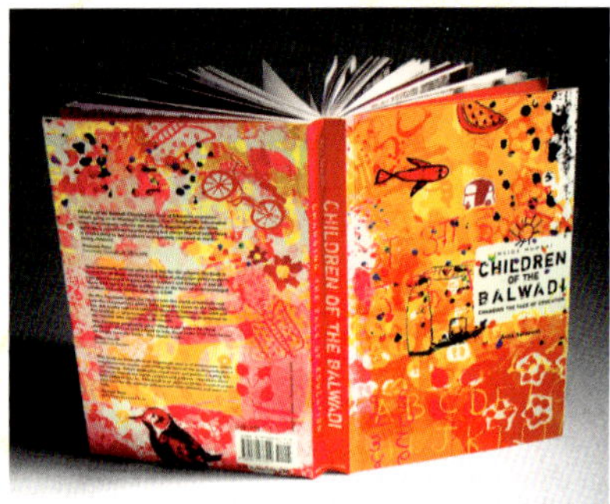

⬆ *Children of the Balwadi*: an eye-catching book package produced using children's own images as source material that was then sampled and remixed to create this truly inspiring study of what can be achieved in education among sectors of society often overlooked in India's booming economy.

imagery is derived from chalk drawings, crayon scribbles, paint splashes on folded paper, and leaf and vegetable prints that have been scanned in and digitally manipulated to form the final compositions for the illustrations."

Once the raw images had been scanned and imported into Photoshop, says Moses, "Using Levels, some images have been made more 'graphic' with a vector look; others have been scaled and repeated to form patterns. Color toning using adjustment layers have been stacked with blending modes and opacity applied to create a digital collage."

Of the title, Moses explains that it refers to a specific education system in Mumbai; a very basic education given free to children of what he calls "economically backward" sections in society. "This book is probably the first attempt to document this form of education, and busy, bright, energetic collaging has been used to show the vitality of the children." The project was carried out by UMS for the International Center for Ethnographic Studies in the US.

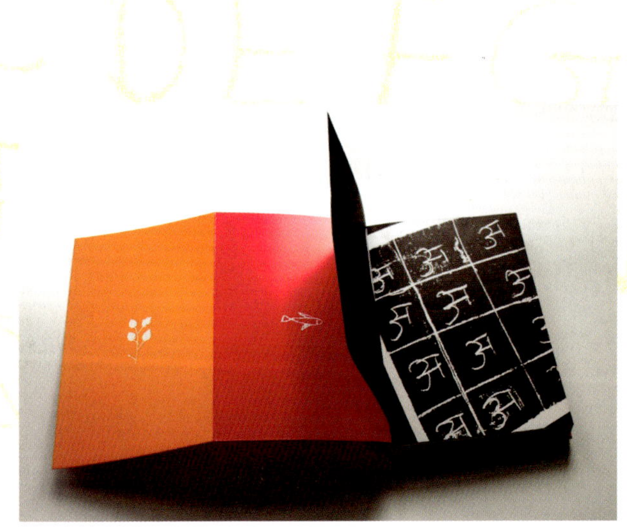

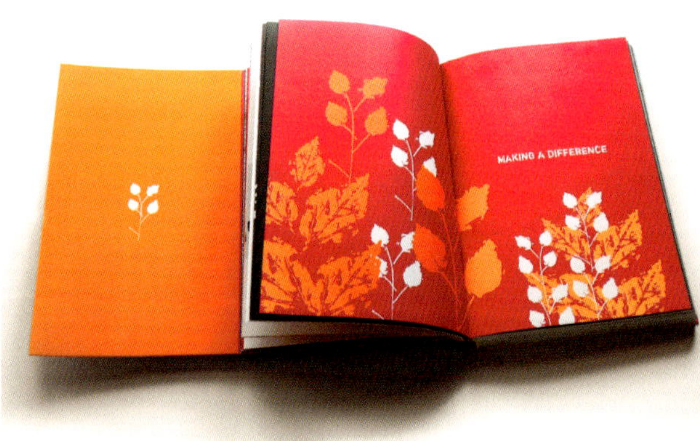

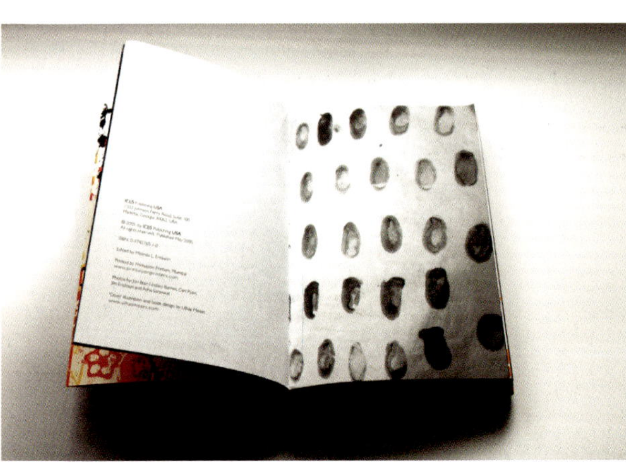

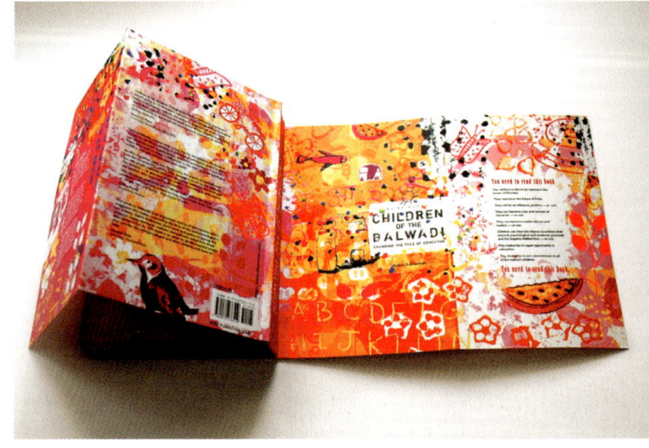

SOURCE IMAGES

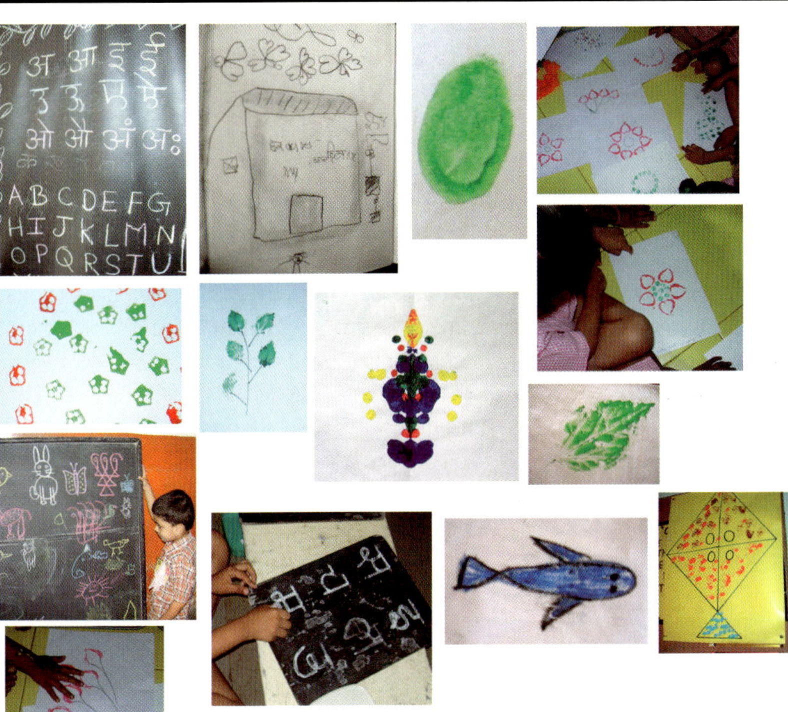

◆ A selection of the original children's drawings and scribbles that were then given a whole new lease of life by being combined into a colorful, complex, lively digital collage throughout the course of a lengthy book.

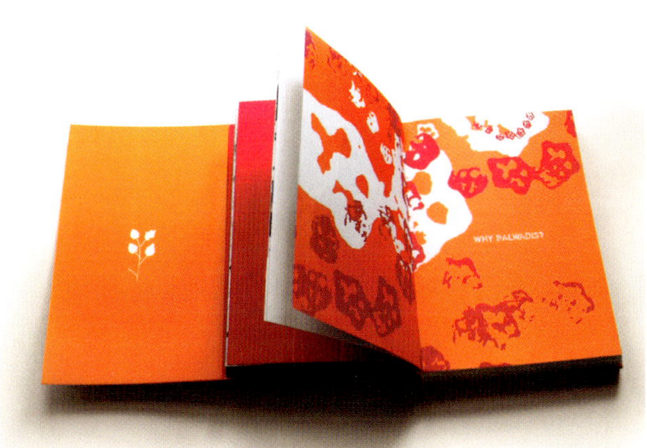

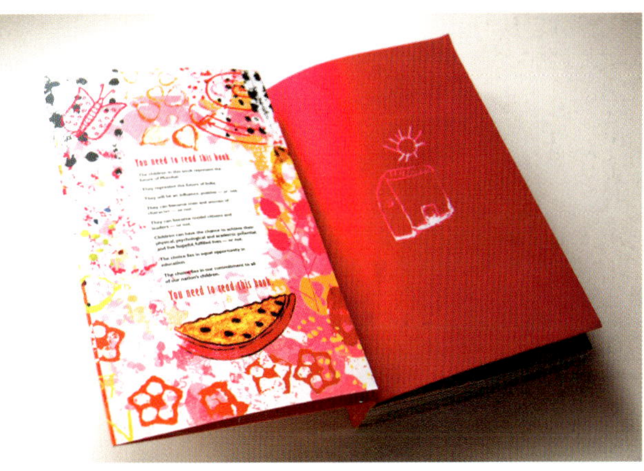

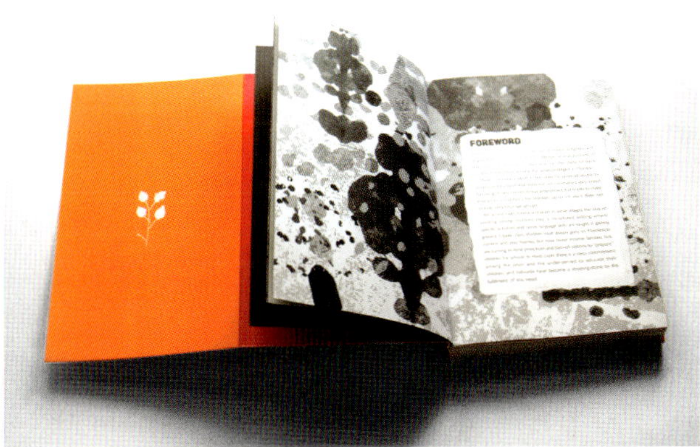

◆ ◆ Subject matter that could perhaps have been dry and academic—an ethnographic study of the education system—has become something much richer and more entertaining, strongly underlining what can be achieved with some inward investment.

Kanardo

We've shown that clip art and found imagery is to design and illustration what the break beat, loop, and sample are to music: raw material to be remxied and recontextualized in ways that doff a cap to the original sources. So it should be no surprise that, for one designer at least, clip art has taken a step closer to music by becoming a live performance.

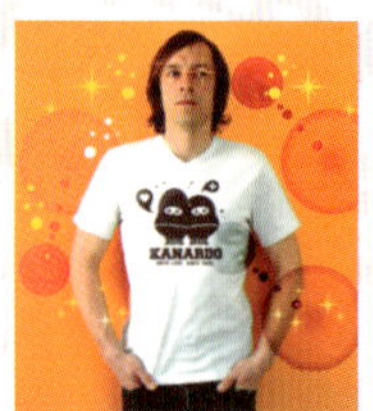

Francois Verdet (Kanardo) was approached by graffiti writer CartOne to do a live performance with him at the De la Break party in 2005. Kanardo explains what happened: "The promoter of the party usually uses a rabbit as a logotype, so we decided to 'draw' a giant rabbit on a wall using thousands of cheap clip arts sourced from free fonts downloaded at a popular font website."

The final work, Rabbit, was 9.8x9.8ft (3x3m) in size and composed of more than 5,000 clip arts and font characters. "We printed over 5,000 vector patterns on vinyl sticky paper and used these to 'draw' the rabbit," says Kanardo. "At the beginning [of the performance], people could not understand what we were doing. And they came back to us all night long to try to guess what we were drawing—and finally discovered the rabbit at 4am. The performance was a total success!"

Whatever the merits of this particular giant rabbit—a popular theme with culture-jammers and displaced youth since *Alice's Adventures in Wonderland*, by way of *Harvey*, *The Matrix*, and *Donnie Darko*—Kanardo's piece nevertheless proves that clip-art culture, sampling, and remixing are moving ever closer together, and once disparate creative streams are merging into one, with often unexpected results. And as we've said before, why not have fun with it and don't ask too many questions.

➡ A giant map of the word, perhaps? The performance piece at an earlier stage puzzles the club crowd.

⬇ The rabbit takes shape from thousands of clip-art characters and glyphs, sourced free from dafont.com.

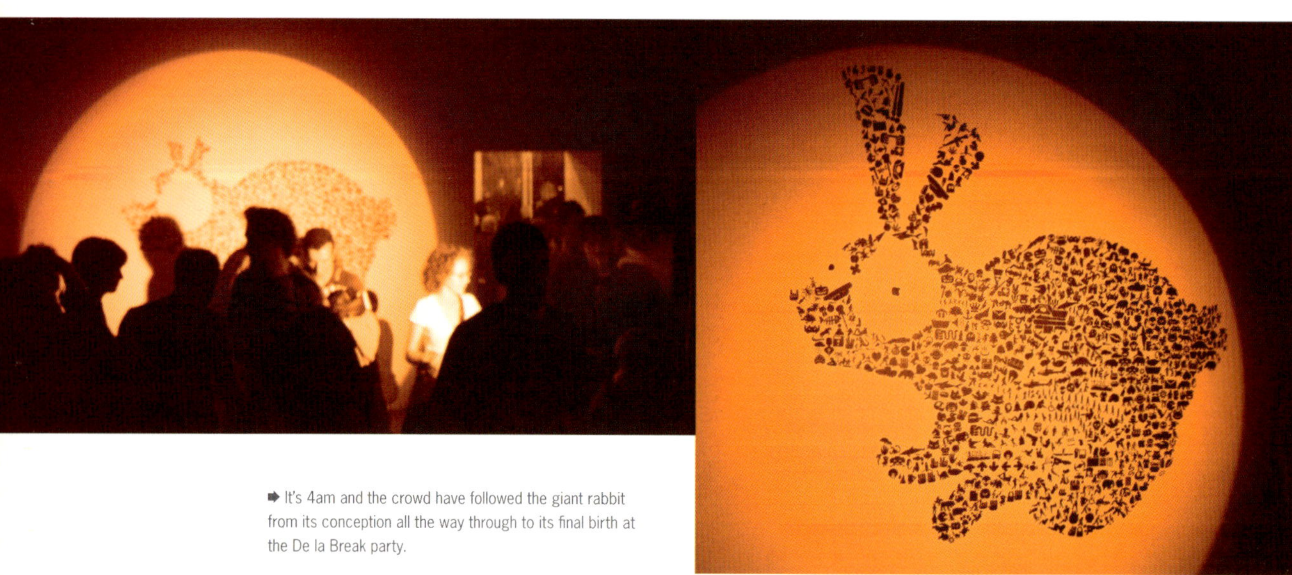

➡ It's 4am and the crowd have followed the giant rabbit from its conception all the way through to its final birth at the De la Break party.

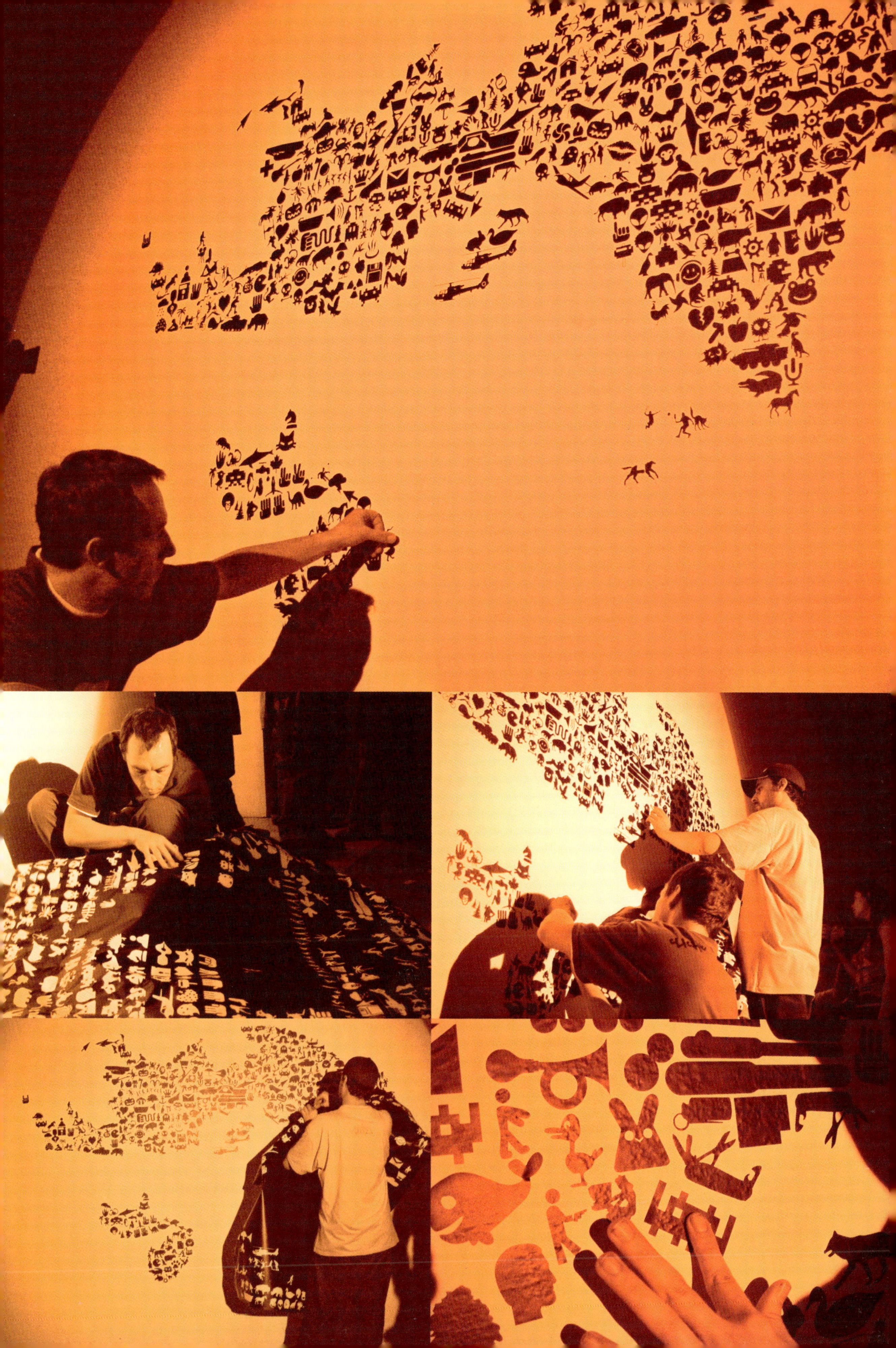

Sean Tejaratchi

Crap Hound's Sean Tejaratchi cuts pictures out of old books and sticks them in new ones to sell. It says much about today's copyright laws that good, old-fashioned scrapbooking should be seen as a radical idea.

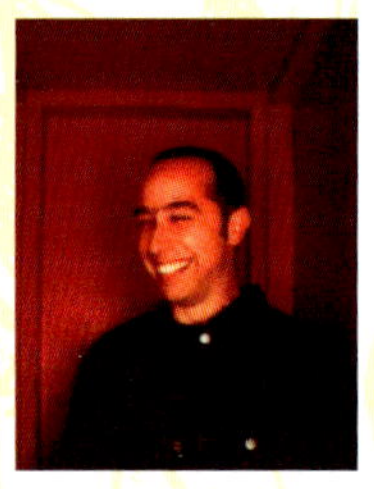

⬇ ➡ Examples of Tejaratchi's legendary clip-art zine *Crap Hound*.

Designer and editor Sean Tejaratchi has gained near-legendary status among designers, samplers, and other creative people who see sharing and idea exchange as the only worthwhile capital. This is partly because of his association with that bane of the copyrighted world, music collective Negativland, but mainly for his clip-art zine, *Crap Hound*. "*Crap Hound* is a picture book for discussion and activity," says the Zine Wiki at zinewiki.com, quoting one of the issues illustrated overleaf, whereas Tejaratchi himself now describes it as "a zine of found and stolen popular imagery." In other words, *Crap Hound* consists of page after page of themed collections of high-contrast, monochrome clip art from vintage catalogs, advertising, obscure books, and found ephemera—what Tejaratchi describes as "printed matter from around the world, mostly the US. Color images and grayscale were clarified and converted to high contrast."

In among some of the massed clip-art collections are the occasional satirical essays and observations on cultural appropriation. Out-of-print issues are in high demand, and recently *Crap Hound* has returned, being published in newly minted reprinted editions by Reading Frenzy/Show and Tell.

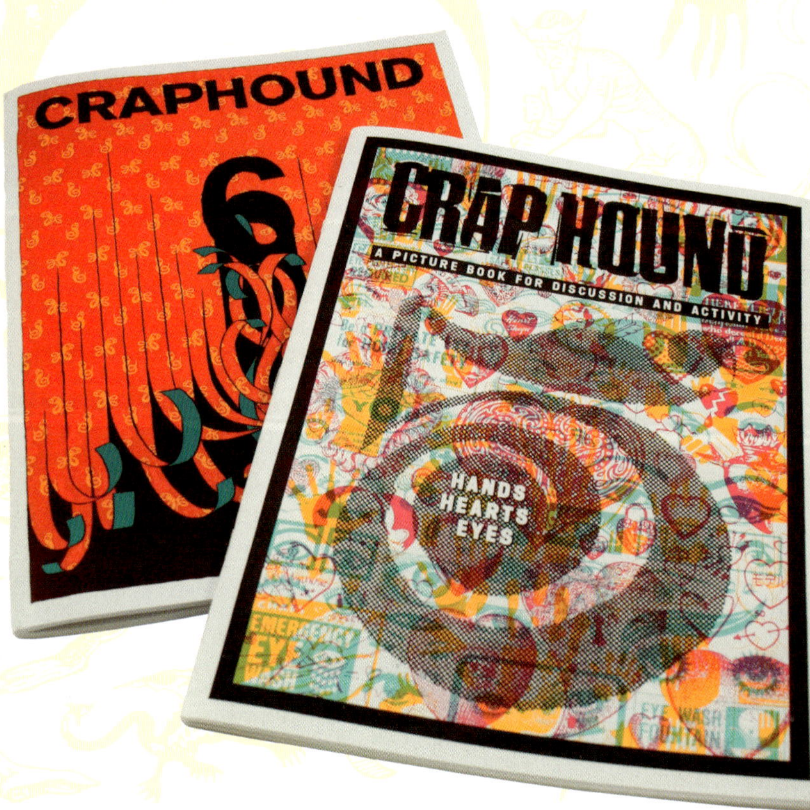

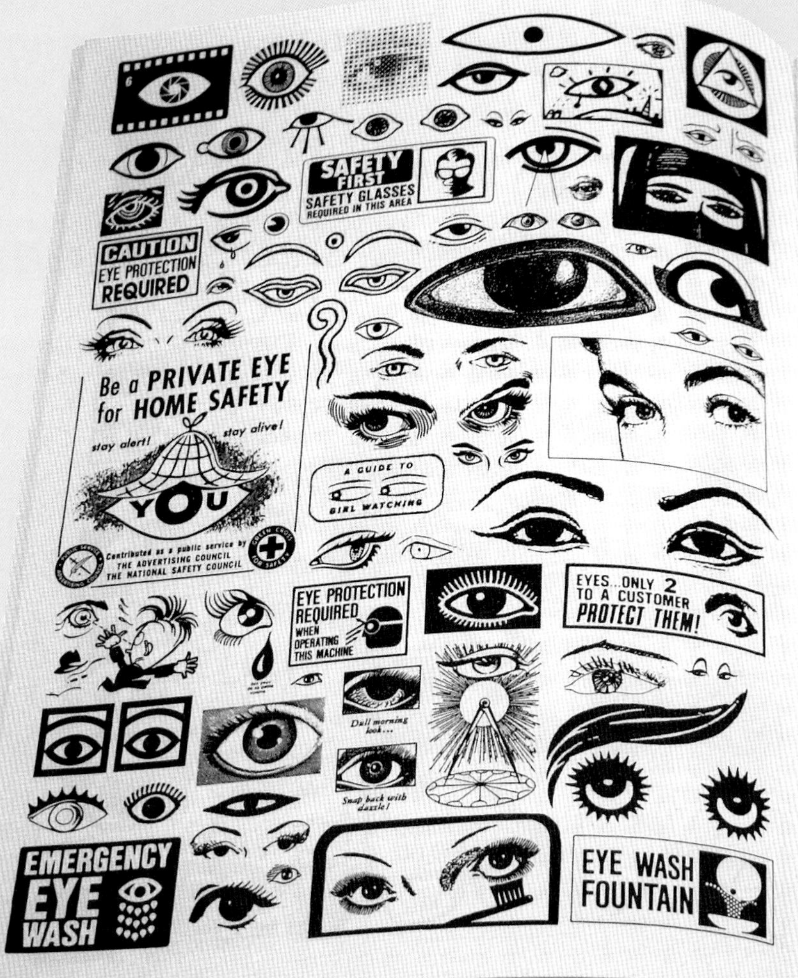
SAFETY FIRST
SAFETY GLASSES
REQUIRED IN THIS AREA
CAUTION
EYE PROTECTION
REQUIRED
Be a PRIVATE EYE
for HOME SAFETY
stay alert!
stay alive!
YOU
Contributed as a public service by
THE ADVERTISING COUNCIL
THE NATIONAL SAFETY COUNCIL
A GUIDE TO
GIRL WATCHING
EYE PROTECTION
REQUIRED
WHEN
OPERATING
THIS MACHINE
EYES...ONLY 2
TO A CUSTOMER
PROTECT THEM!
Dull morning look...
Snap back with dazzle!
EMERGENCY
EYE
WASH
EYE WASH
FOUNTAIN

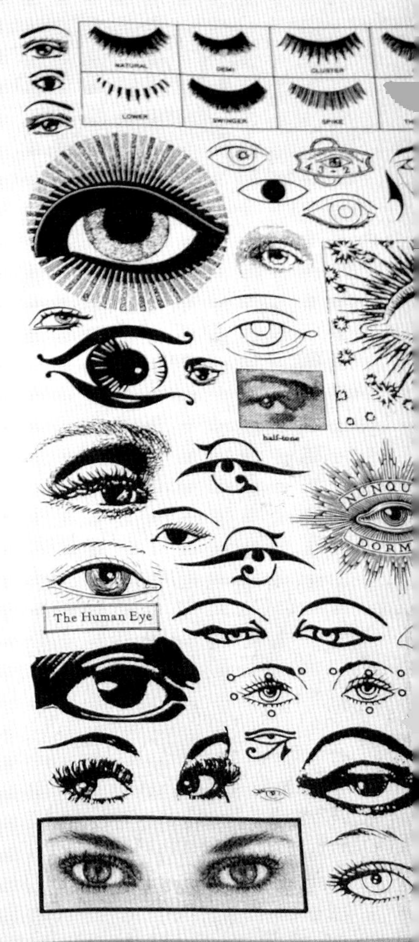
The Human Eye

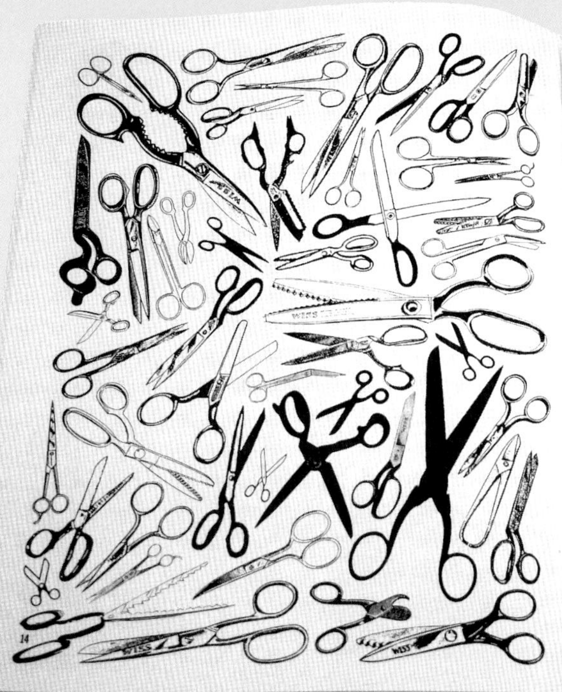

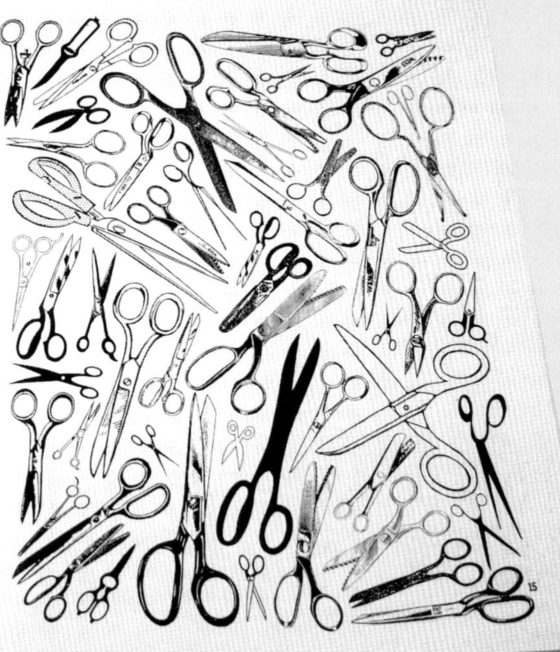

➡ Some of the much sought-after and collectible issues of *Crap Hound*, some of which are now being reissued. Sex, kitchen gadgets, demons, lovehearts, and scarey clowns are all clipped and cataloged in the legendary zine.

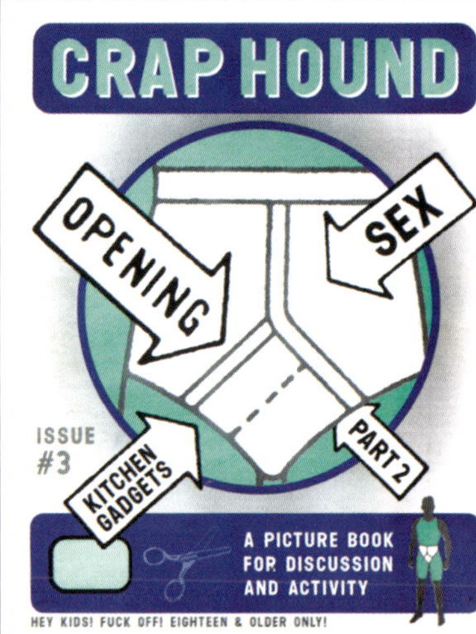

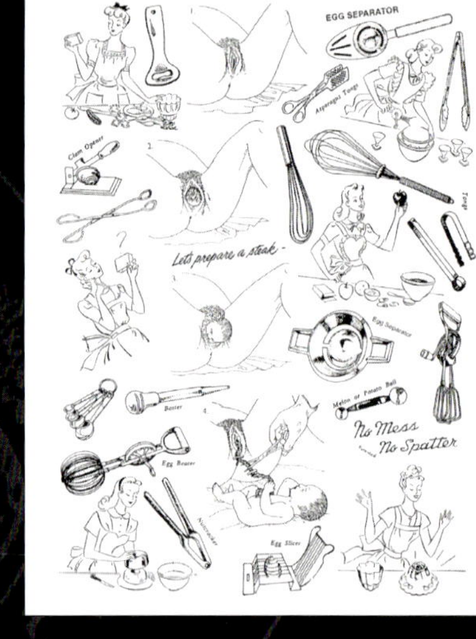

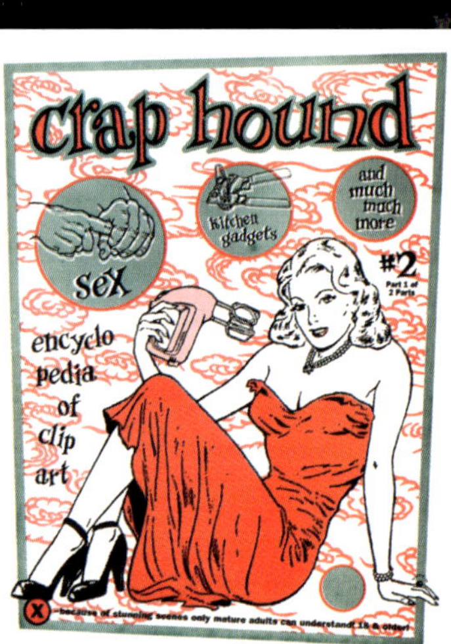

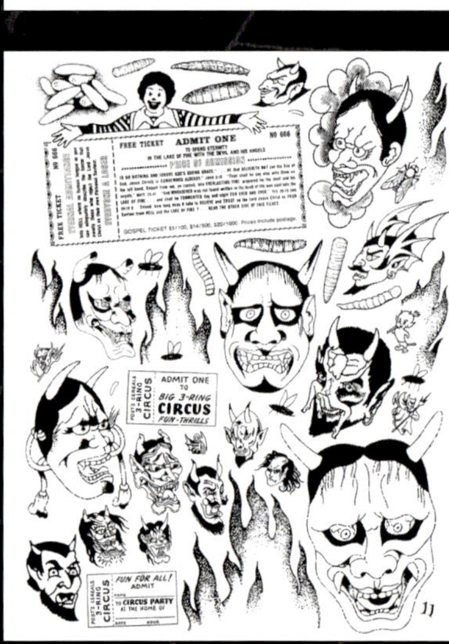

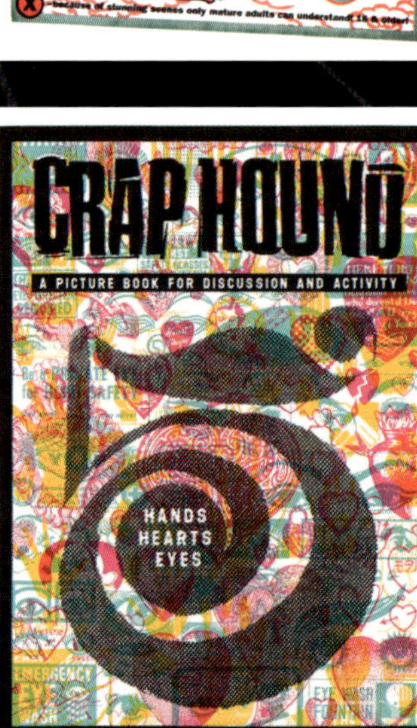

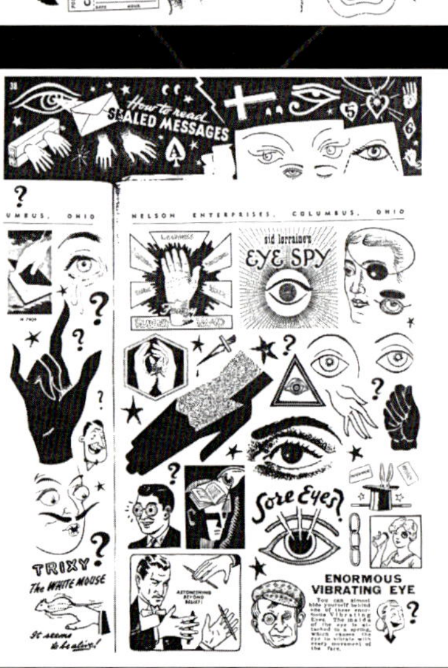

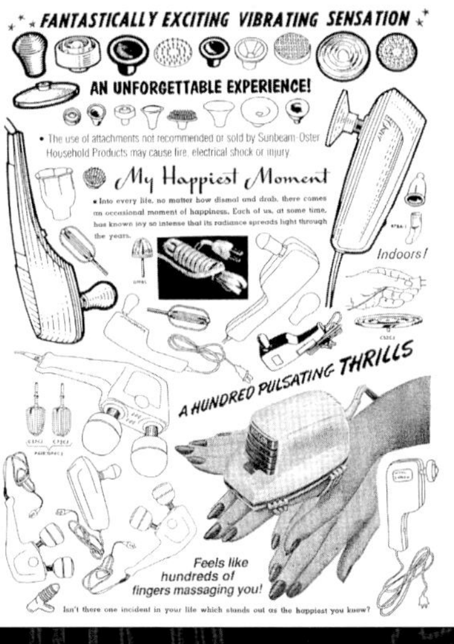
FANTASTICALLY EXCITING VIBRATING SENSATION
AN UNFORGETTABLE EXPERIENCE!
The use of attachments not recommended or sold by Sunbeam Oster Household Products may cause fire, electrical shock or injury
My Happiest Moment
Into every life, no matter how dismal and drab, there comes an occasional moment of happiness. Each of us, at some time, has known joy so intense that its radiance spreads light through the years.
Indoors!
A HUNDRED PULSATING THRILLS
Feels like hundreds of fingers massaging you!
Isn't there one incident in your life which stands out as the happiest you know?

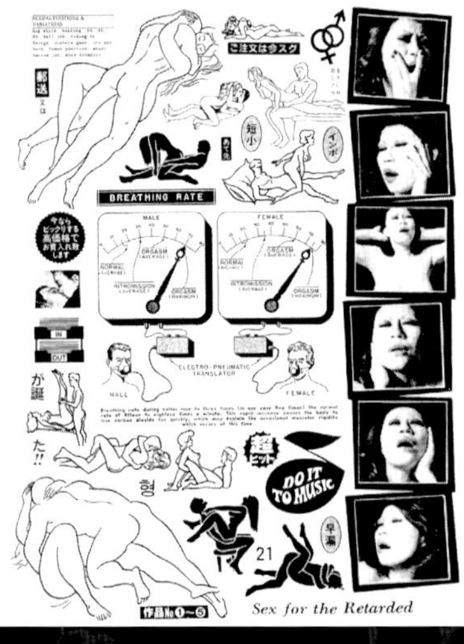
ご注文は今スグ
BREATHING RATE
MALE
FEMALE
ORGASM
ELECTRO-PNEUMATIC TRANSLATOR
DO IT TO MUSIC
21
Sex for the Retarded

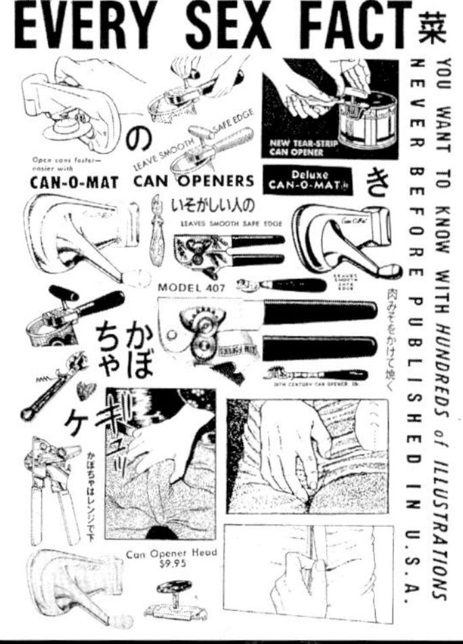
EVERY SEX FACT
YOU WANT TO KNOW WITH HUNDREDS of ILLUSTRATIONS
NEVER BEFORE PUBLISHED IN U.S.A.
CAN-O-MAT
CAN OPENERS
Deluxe CAN-O-MAT
NEW TEAR-STRIP CAN OPENER
LEAVES SMOOTH SAFE EDGE
いそがしい人の
MODEL 407
かぼちゃ
Can Opener Head $9.95

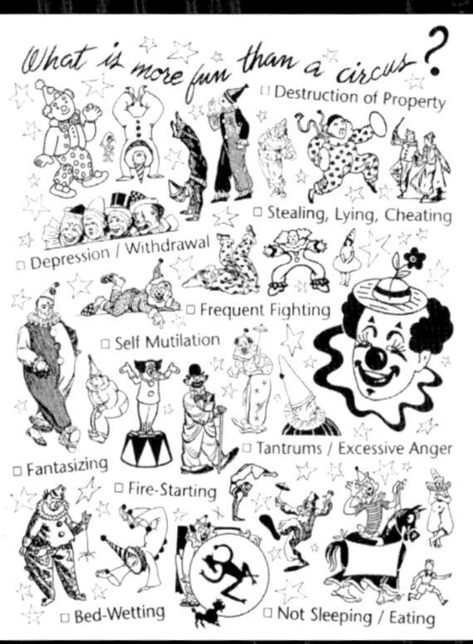
What is more fun than a circus?
☐ Destruction of Property
☐ Stealing, Lying, Cheating
☐ Depression / Withdrawal
☐ Frequent Fighting
☐ Self Mutilation
☐ Tantrums / Excessive Anger
☐ Fantasizing
☐ Fire-Starting
☐ Bed-Wetting
☐ Not Sleeping / Eating

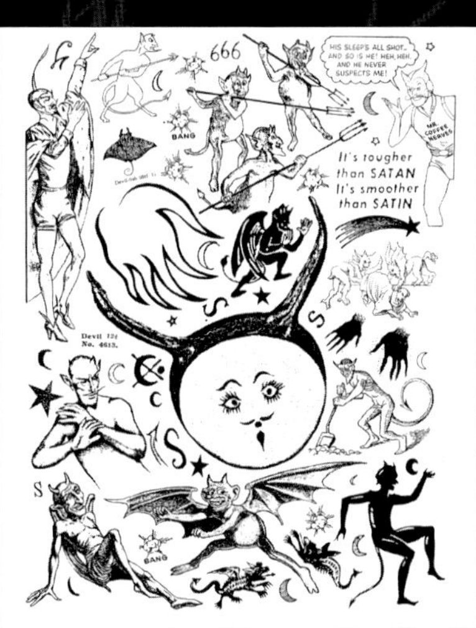
666
HIS SLEEP'S ALL SHOT... AND SO IS HE! HEH, HEH, AND HE NEVER SUSPECTS ME!
It's tougher than SATAN
It's smoother than SATIN
BANG
Devil 12c No. 4613.

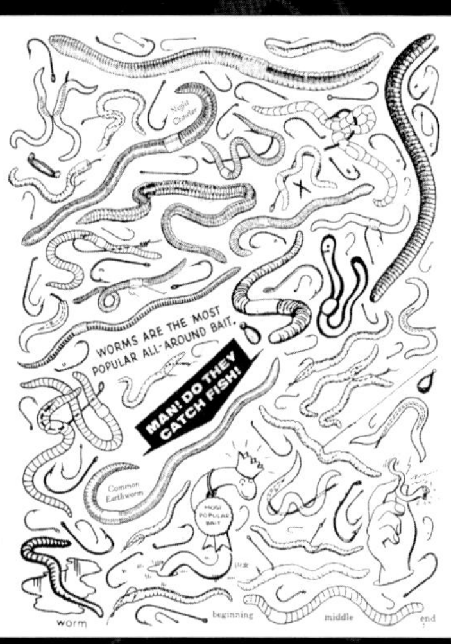
WORMS ARE THE MOST POPULAR ALL-AROUND BAIT.
MAN! DO THEY CATCH FISH!
Common Earthworm
worm
beginning
middle
end

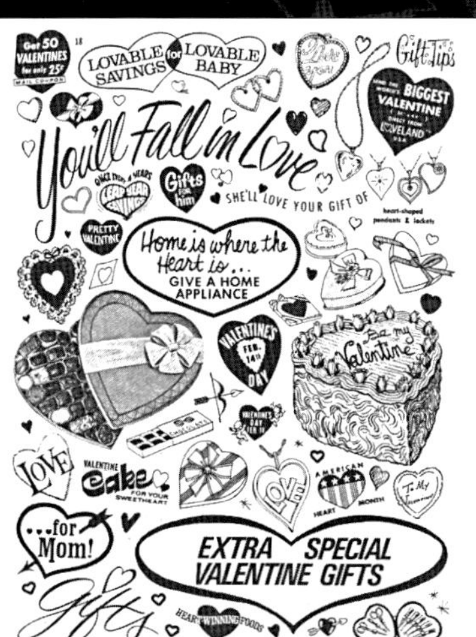
Get 50 VALENTINES for only 25¢
LOVABLE SAVINGS for LOVABLE BABY
Gift Tips
BIGGEST VALENTINE
You'll Fall in Love
Gifts for him
SHE'LL LOVE YOUR GIFT OF
PRETTY VALENTINE
Home is where the Heart is...
GIVE A HOME APPLIANCE
VALENTINE'S FEB. 14th DAY
Be my Valentine
LOVE
Valentine cake FOR YOUR SWEETHEART
...for Mom!
EXTRA SPECIAL VALENTINE GIFTS
Gifts

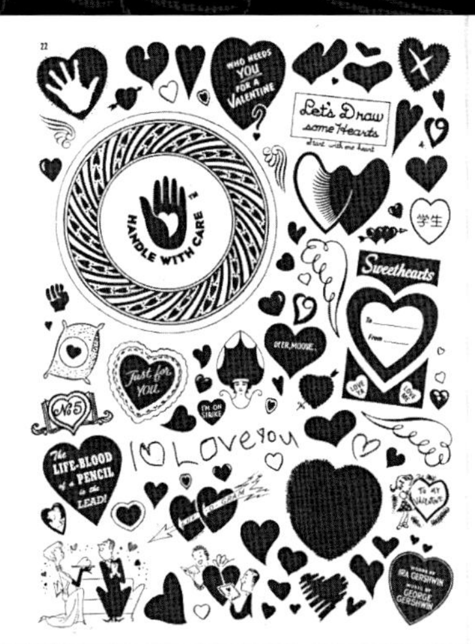
WHO NEEDS YOU FOR A VALENTINE
Let's Draw some Hearts
HANDLE WITH CARE
Sweethearts
学生
Just for You
No5
The LIFE-BLOOD of a PENCIL is the LEAD!
I Love you

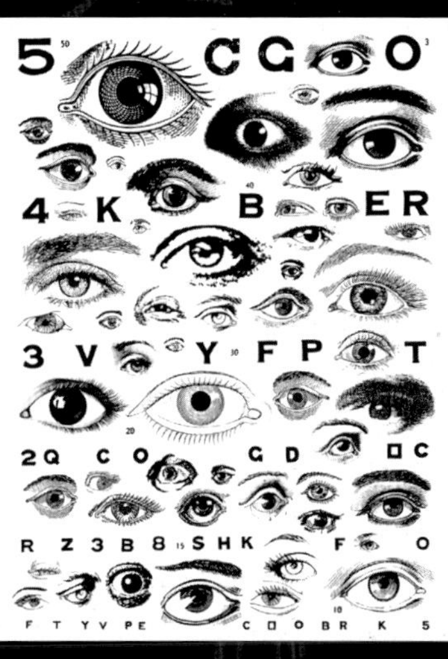
5 C G O
4 K B ER
3 V Y F P T
2Q C O G D ☐ C
R Z 3 B 8 S H K F O
F T Y V P E C ☐ O B R K 5

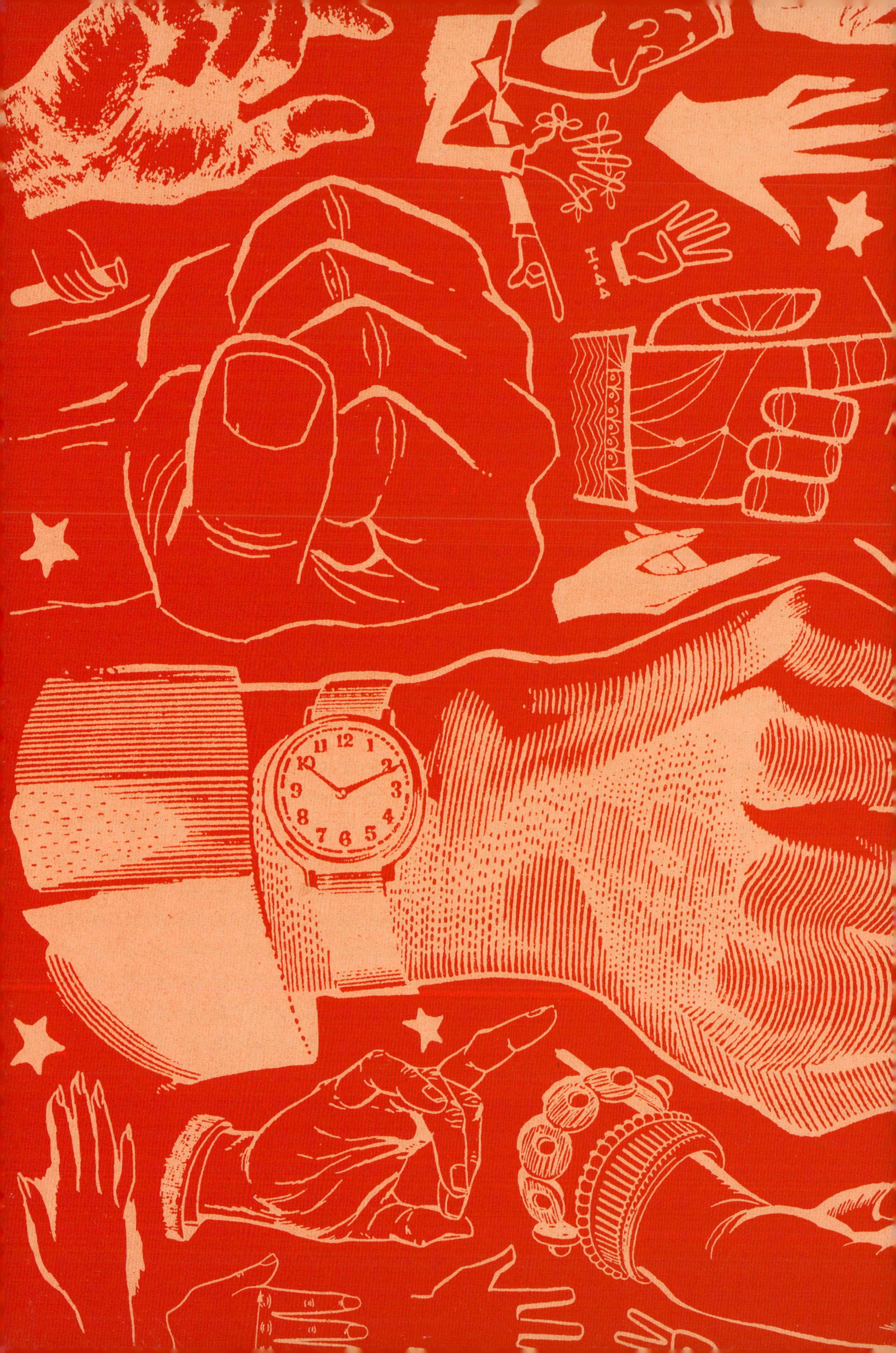

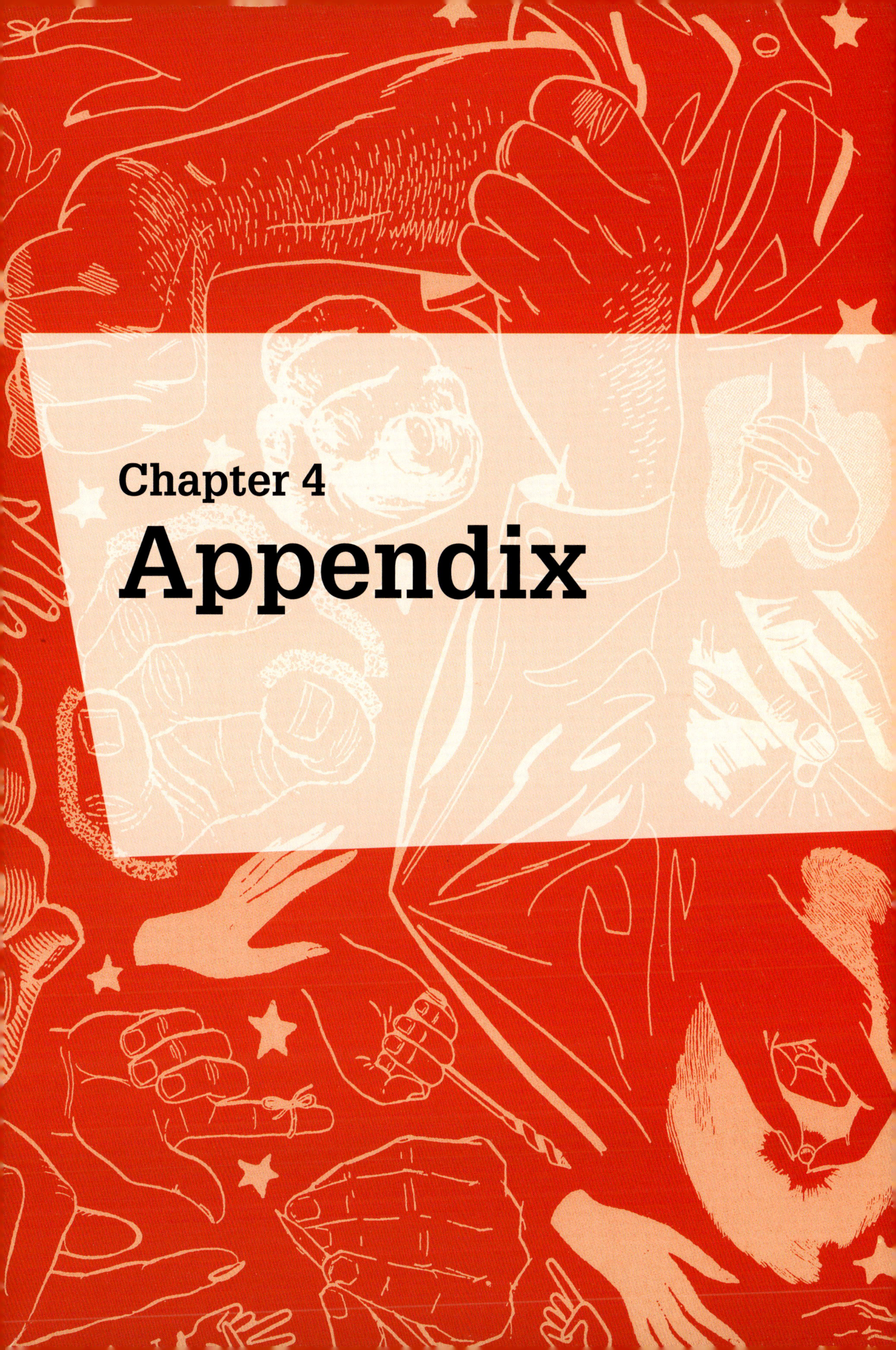

Chapter 4

Appendix

Directory

Read me!

Reader, please note: any print publication can only offer a snapshot at a moment in time of online resources and clip-art sites. This is by no means a complete listing, but rather a concise selection of what is on offer.

In places, we have listed the URLs of certain types of commercial image banks that offer similar types of services; in others, we give you more detailed descriptions of sites that either offer something new, supply work in the public domain, or which typify a particular approach to image gathering in the commercial arena. In a handful of cases, we have included mini case studies.

Neither the authors nor the publishers vouch for the quality, nor the content, of any of the websites listed here. We have endeavored to present a selection of royalty-free and/or public-domain image resources, but many of the sites in this directory are commercial, paid-for image banks or subscription services, while others offer images that are free to use within certain markets or for certain purposes.

It is the responsibility of readers to check licensing restrictions and terms of use with copyright owners in every case. Inclusion in this directory is not a sign that any given site is necessarily a source of free imagery for designers and illustrators, or that it can or ought to be used in this way. We do not endorse using copyrighted work outside of the terms the copyright owner has set.

We have endeavored to check each URL, but again, sites appear and disappear very quickly, so some links may be broken or incorrect.

We have tagged a lot of the sites Free (F), Royalty Free (RF), or Public Domain (PD), together with further guidance where necessary. These denote how some sites describe themselves, or have been described. Unmarked sites are either paid-for/commercial enterprises, contain a mix of images, have images of unknown or untested provenance, or which are listed at reader discretion. Some of these sites may include free or public-domain imagery.

Please note that "free" and "public domain" are not the same thing: any image may be offered free of charge, but the copyright may remain with the creator; similarly, some public domain images are free, while the use of others may entail paying a convenience fee to the hosting organization.

In every case, it is your responsibility to read any licensing restrictions—in the self-publishing, social media, blogging age, some claims for images being free, royalty free, or in the public domain may be wrong, or even malicious, and so their listing as such here is not definitive.

Whatever you use this listing for, I hope there is much here to surprise and entertain you and to divert you from the mainstream toward some fresh creative avenues.

Chris Middleton

Introduction

Here is an alphabetical selection of the millions of clip art and other image sources available on the internet, chosen by the authors to reflect the variety of work in this book. Some are excellent, and others are not, so we have reviewed each of the sites featured here.

The listing is not divided by subject area, as we decided that too many of the sites cover a range of topics and host too many different types of media for any subject division to be meaningful.

Some of our featured websites are collections of clip art, public-domain images, Creative Commons-licensed works, old photographs, centuries-old printed ephemera, line drawings, scans from out-of-print books, maps, flags, historical documents, "copyleft" (not traditionally copyrighted) works, and so on—while others are simply useful URLs or search tools for designers.

Some of the sites are intended for educational purposes, or are hosted by public, educational, or even government institutions.

Copyright issues

While the original source images may be long out of their original copyright, a company or institution may own a more recent copyright, so caution is advised. Some works come into a new copyright period if they are reformatted—for example, by being digitized from an original print. Images do not need to be registered to be considered under copyright; once a work is in a fixed medium, it is automatically copyrighted for a set period of time, unless the owner waives that right.

Copyright laws are in a state of constant flux, and the prevalence of digital download services has persuaded many aging copyright owners who are still alive, such as some artists and musicians, to press for an extension to the standard copyright period, which in the US varies (see right) and in the UK, for example, is generally accepted to be 50 years.

US copyright reference table

Work	Protected	Term
Created 1/1/78 or after, the effective date of the 1976 Act that eliminated common law copyright	When work is fixed in tangible medium of expression	Life + 70 years (or if work of corporate authorship, the shorter of 95 years from publication, or 120 years from creation)
Published before 1923	In public domain	None
Published from 1923 to 1963	When published with notice	28 years + Could be renewed for 47 years, now extended by 20 years for a total renewal of 67 years. If not so renewed, now in public domain
Published from 1964 to 1977	When published with notice	28 years for first term; automatic extension of 67 years for second term
Created before 1/1/78, but not published	1/1/78, the effective date of the 1976 Act that eliminated common law copyright	Life + 70 years

Copyright/royalty free and "free"

Many online image sites describe themselves as "royalty-free" resources, but some of these remain expensive subscription services where you pay for usage, not for copyright, while others are institutional sites hosting public domain images, and which nevertheless charge for the convenience and service.

Royalty free can be indicative of a robust business model: you, the designer or illustrator, pay the publisher for the right to use the image, but the publisher has already paid the image creator a flat fee for the picture. The creator wins if only 10 people download the image, but loses if ten thousand people do.

Subscription sites are cost-effective if you plan to download hundreds of images during your subscription period, or you may choose to purchase a CD or DVD of images for a one-off fee, after which you are free to use the images in a commercial context whenever you choose. In these cases, you have bought the right to use the images, not the copyright of the images.

Most commercial image resources allow you to download a low-res comp or positional, or provide you with a watermarked preview image. For print purposes, the site owners (and copyright holders) assume that these are usually too low-res for reproduction, and so oblige you to download a paid-for high-res version.

Other sites are free, but it is worth remembering that the word "free" can have two meanings online: first, zero cost; and second, unfettered (i.e. not locked up) by big-business licensing restrictions. This means that some sites that describe themselves as free may still charge nominal fees for usage. Others are free for private, non-commercial, or educational use, but charge a fee for commercial reproduction. This throws down the gauntlet of honesty to you.

There are a growing number of very low-cost image banks online, which not only make available broad ranges of clip art, stock photography, vector graphics, icons, and other imagery for as little as a few dollars per picture, depending on usage restrictions, but they also allow creative people to upload images of their own, for which they will receive a fee per download.

These can be very cost-effective if you only intend to use a handful of images. Such image exchanges also allow creative people to set up their own "cottage industries" and trade pictures with like-minded people.

Beyond these, several sites are genuinely free, in every sense, for commercial print and web uses, perhaps supported by advertising or other traffic-related revenue and add-on services—or simply because the site owners believe in the free flow of knowledge and information on the web. We have included these wherever we have found them, and strongly recommend some of them.

Again, free does not denote public domain; you may still have to credit the creator of the image, who retains the copyright.

If you are seeking something very esoteric, then the answer probably lies in a search of your own. If so, it is often best to do a web search in Google, or your preferred search tool, using the search term plus phrases such as "public domain," "free," "copyleft," or "royalty free," rather than doing a Google Image search.

A word on resolution

It is surprising that many people do not understand that a crisp, clean, detailed image onscreen does not translate into a crisp, clean, detailed print. It is all down to the size of the image and its resolution—web (computer monitor) resolution is 72dpi, whereas print is usually upward of 300dpi. That said, scaling down a very large 72dpi image can lead to an acceptable resolution in print, if it is reproduced relatively small. View "Actual Pixels" in Photoshop to see the actual dimensions of all continuous-tone/raster/pixel-based images.

Although an accidental by-product of the way that monitors display pixels and light, this anomaly has both enabled and sustained the business model of all online still-image publishers as it prevents most screen-resolution images being ripped for print.

The exception is the vector image. These can be rescaled up or down with no loss of quality. To work on them in Photoshop, or another pixel-editing package, the image first has to be rasterized (turned into a bitmap).

Enjoy surfing around these links.

Free
Royalty Free
Public Domain

123 RF
www.123rf.com

Over 800,000 low-cost, royalty-free images (at single-digit prices), with some introductory offers. Images are mainly in a high-quality stock-shot style, but with a fair degree of variety, including some good clip-art graphics, shapes, patterns, and icons. Also here are some atmospheric graphic works, textures, details, and conceptual/abstract images, together with some more creative image crops than are usually found on stock-photography sites.

3D Science
www.3dscience.com/3D_Science_Clip_Art.php
A link to some clip-art resources hosted by this three-dimensional science artwork and diagram site.

A9
a9.com/-/company/opensearch.jsp
Not a clip-art site at all, but a promising search tool that is itself in an open format under a Creative Commons license. Like some others, it incorporates the results from many search engines. Recommended by some of the designers featured in this book.

Action Links
www.action-links.com/clip/misc/index.htm

Useful free site of icons and mini web graphics for action links, buttons, and so on, all in GIF format at web resolution.

Alamy
www.alamy.com
Traditional, glossy image-bank site that allows downloads of comps, but is a paid-for gallery site. Has offices around the world.

All Free Backgrounds
www.allfreebackgrounds.com

Free downloadable and savable backgrounds, graphics, and image elements, mainly for web applications, but usable in some print projects. Images are designed to tile. Also a useful site for other aspects of print and web design, principally for enthusiastic amateurs.

Amazing Textures
amazingtextures.com/textures/index.php
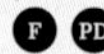
A texture library with hundreds of free textures to download, including high-resolution textures, images, backgrounds, wallpapers, and texture maps. Includes a collection of tiled textures.

Ancient Egyptian Clipart
atschool.eduweb.co.uk/trinity/projects/egypt/clipart.html
Links to a variety of clip-art resources about ancient Egypt, including photo galleries, patterns, line drawings, papyrus art paintings, and so on. Check with each link for attribution and the copyright status of images.

Art Renewal Center
www.artrenewal.org/asp/database/contents.asp
PD (with caution)
Site hosted by self-styled online museum, the Art Renewal Center (ARC). Images include the works of thousands of

often overlooked realist painters, some of which may be in the public domain, among much academic debate. Provenance unclear, so check with the site's owners.

Association for Science Education
www.ase.org.uk/cgi-bin/imageFolio/imageFolio.cgi

The Association for Science Education image gallery, mixing photography and clip art in a variety of subject areas, including dinosaurs, energy, icons, insects, the environment, and so on.

Backgrounds Archive
backgroundsarchive.com

Thousands of public-domain images organized by category, color, and brightness.

Big Stock Photo
www.bigstockphoto.com

The usual glossy mix of stock photos and mood/conceptual illustrations for fans of the "Mr and Mrs Lilac-Sweater with their family" school of image-making.

Brooklyn College, Chinese Studies
acc6.its.brooklyn.cuny.edu/~phalsall/images.html

Chinese cultural images including maps, divinities, art, people, customs, archaeology, and historical illustrations.

Burning Well
www.burningwell.org

A variable collection of "donated" images from around the world, but like any such site, it has a serendipitous element whereby someone's poor image, in its own right, might furnish you with just what you are looking for. Debatably, a poor-man's flickr, it is nevertheless worth a search. Categories include: activities, animals and bugs, cityscapes, landscapes, objects, people, plants, and textures. Of these, textures, plants, and objects may yield the most useful image elements for print or web work.

Business Clipart & Photos
www.bizart.com

An unpromising page that may include one or two unexpectedly useful art clips among all the brightly colored, cartoony "business" graphics, which are presumably aimed at home-business websites.

Canadian Illustrated News
www.collectionscanada.ca/cin/index-e.html

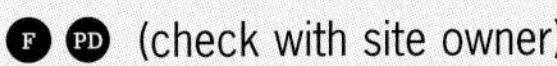

The *Canadian Illustrated News* site is a selection of almost 4,000 images of people, places, and events across Canada and from around the world taken from the popular nineteenth-century magazine. The *Canadian Illustrated News* was published in Montreal by George Desbarats from 1869 to 1883, and was notable for its innovative use of halftone photographs. Potentially a goldmine for image-clippers.

Cepolina Photo
www.cepolina.com

Over 5,000 public domain photos from Europe, the US, and Asia.

Chinese Clip Art
www.in4mation.org/clipart.html

Fascinating and useful, but not extensive, Chinese clip-art resource, including folk art, calligraphy, glove puppetry, paper cutting, craft, opera facial makeup, painting, patterns, and other images. Many of the images have been cut out. Worth a look, particularly for the calligraphic and mask-like facial makeup clips.

Classroom Clipart
classroomclipart.com

Free resource of thousands of image clips, illustrations, icons, and photographs at screen resolution, in a very broad range of categories and subcategories, from animals to weather, via other educational topics.

Coolclips
www.coolclips.com

Cartoon-style icons clip-art site, of the variety that might suit business PowerPoint presentations, school projects, and light-hearted websites. That said, some of the work is superior within the limits of this largely hackneyed genre. All media previews displayed at CoolClips.com are available royalty free at screen resolution, and are for your personal enjoyment, says the site. The images included here, and derivative images from them, are not public domain, and cannot be redistributed without the written permission of the publisher. High-res images may be available.

Cool Notions
www.coolnotions.com/PDImages/PDImages.htm

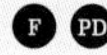

This website includes links to online galleries of various public-domain imagery from old books, magazines, and a variety of ephemera. A mixed bag of monochrome line drawings, engravings, book plates, and color illustrations, some of which are unusual and worth a look.

Copyright Free Photos
www.copyrightfreephotos.com

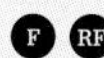

Relatively small collections of free photos of animals, buildings, technology, nature, and places. The copyright (royalty) free photos available on this site have been made available free of charge for web design, graphics, backgrounds, printed images, desktop wallpaper, and screensavers, says the site owner who may be a private photographer. Low key and overtaken by larger, more ambitious sites.

Corbis
pro.corbis.com

One of the big-five, major-league photography sites, focusing on top-quality photojournalism, and commanding large fees for its collections of often exclusive images. Has over one hundred million images and serves more than 50 countries worldwide. Corbis is controlled by Bill Gates, suggesting a lucrative if very old-economy view of the world.

Creative Commons
www.creativecommons.org
search.creativecommons.org
commons.wikimedia.org
www.flickr.com/creativecommons
commoncontent.org

Many images

As we have seen, Creative Commons offers a new and promising licensing framework for digital media, whereby sharing and, often, free use is encouraged within certain boundaries that also acknowledge the rights of the creator. You can support this model by searching for images of any kind (and other digital works for multimedia projects) that have been released under Creative Commons licenses.

The Cyclopedia of Puzzles

www.mathpuzzle.com/loyd/

Rather ineptly scanned pages of the entire contents of a 1914 book of puzzles. Worth flicking through the numerous scans as there are some excellent, and potentially clippable, period line drawings and diagrams.

David Dailey Public Domain Images

srufaculty.sru.edu/david.dailey/public/public_domain.htm

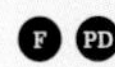

Some quality scanned etchings and line drawings that are claimed to be public-domain images, including animals, insects, machines, plants, reptiles, agriculture, and architecture, taken from old books, dictionaries, and encyclopedias. A potential favorite if you can work with the resolution of the featured works.

The De Rienzi Gallery

www.mapsouthpacific.com/engravings/index.html

In 1836, M.G.L. Domeny de Rienzi's *Océanie ou Cinquième Partie du Monde* was published by Firmin Didot Frères in Paris, France. Domeny's prints of Polynesia are available here.

Digital Vector Maps

digital-vector-maps.com

Download royalty-free, editable vector maps in Adobe Illustrator and PDF format.

Digital Vision

www.digitalvision.com

Creative, stylized, and conceptual royalty-free stock shots. Has offices in Europe, the US, and the UK. In 2007, Digital Vision became part of the ever-expanding Getty Images family of sites.

Discovery Education

school.discovery.com/clipart

One of several schoolchild-friendly clip-art resource with a mix of black and white and color downloadable art clips, including animations, for print and web. Although many of the graphics are very "children's book" in style, most avoid the most garish "greetings card" aspects of many of the self-styled clip-art sites. Part of the Discovery Channel.

Dover Books

store.doverpublications.com

Many images RF

This book publisher has become a byword for print-based clip-art resources and is well known for its reprints of classic works of literature, classical sheet music, and public-domain images from the nineteenth century. Dover also publishes an extensive collection of mathematical, scientific, and engineering texts, as well as numerous books in niche interests such as the history of science or the history of furniture design and woodworking. Recommended by several of the designers whose work is featured in this book.

eBay

www.ebay.com / .co.uk / .fr / .de (etc.)

The online auction giant is the designer's and illustrator's secret best friend; it's an invaluable research tool, and puts an ever-changing world of imagery at your fingertips.

Every minute of the day, new auction items come online. Among them, obviously, are popular items such as vintage postcards, photographs, and prints, but also just about any object you can imagine—and a great deal more besides. So, if you are seeking images of memorabilia, vintage toys, machines, magazines, catalogs, posters, vehicles, signs, musical instruments, furniture, furnishings, and so on, then use the sellers' images as a reference tool.

In many cases the seller might be happy to send you a high-res photograph of whatever is on sale, as the image may not be of sufficient resolution for print production, except perhaps as a background texture, or as a deliberately low-fi graphic. Alternatively, you could trace the image within your drawing package and produce a derivative work—entirely at your own risk. For online graphics, the resolution is what you see (72dpi). As with all of these suggestions, copyright responsibility rests with you and we do not encourage using images without permission.

eBoy
www.eboy.com
hello.eboy.com/eboy
Homepage of the legendary pixel-art collective, eBoy, with a broad, ever-expanding range of its beautiful, detailed, early-game-art-influenced illustrations, information graphics, fonts, and icons—together with more than a handful of robots, monsters, spaceships, and cityscapes. eBoy's work often pokes fun at the digital, pixel-based age, while being enthusiastically rooted within it. Impossible to look at a lot of this work and not crack a smile.

Edin Photo
www.edinphoto.org.uk/0_ENG/0_engraving_-_0.htm
Engravings, postcards, and so on of Edinburgh, Scotland. Please check with the copyright owner of some images.

Edupics
www.edupics.com
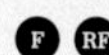
Something of an unexpected gem and highly recommended: behind the unpromising front of this extensive free clip-art resource targeted at children are some good and potentially useful high-res monochrome line drawings and clips within such categories as animals, art, buildings, environment, health, people, families, religion, traffic, toys, and the like. For example: line drawings of Hindu deities, naïve drawings of family groups, and even a good selection of complex Mandala patterns and geometric shapes, which would be a boon to any designer. Among them is a more predictable mix of cartoon-style clip art and color work, but there is much here to recommend the site if you explore it.

Exploring Florida, Le Moyne Engravings
fcit.usf.edu/florida/photos/native/lemoyne/lemoyne.htm
Ⓕ (check with site owner)
Nineteenth-century engravings of Florida from the Le Moyne collection, including details of old ships and drawings of Native Americans and early French explorers. Check with copyright owner.

Featurepics
featurepics.com/PhotoCommunity/Photo-Galleries-Links.aspx
Ⓕ (in many cases)
The Featurepics Photography Directory—see Open Image Suite for images that can be used free, with appropriate credits, and which can also be cropped and resized. A very useful portal to the work of many image-makers. Do read the terms and conditions carefully.

First People
www.firstpeople.us/FP-Html-Clipart/Native Clipart_pg1.html
F (web usage)
Potentially good, but frustrating, Native American clip-art resource, including arrowheads, Kachina dolls, and baskets (some beautiful patterns and circular images here). However, the images are small and of screen resolution, and therefore only useful on websites. If you require high-resolution images you need to contact the site owners. The page is part of the First People Native American/Canadian Indian information portal.

flickr
www.flickr.com
www.flickr.com/groups/publicimages
www.flickr.com/groups/public
www.flickr.com/creativecommons
Some images F RF
flickr is to photography what YouTube is to video and MySpace is to self-publishing. Like them, it also hosts groups and communities of interest around subjects and styles of photography. flickr has manifold attractions. First and foremost, it is a burgeoning site where millions of people post their own photography, from "me on vacation" shots to photojournalism and political activism. However, it is also a matchless and unpredictable resource of abstract imagery, patterns, and mood board inspiration and provocation.

The reason for this is that contributors can tag their images in any way they choose, using as many or as few tags as they wish, and so searching for terms such as "circles," "red," "rage," "cool," "classic," etc., will throw up a variety of often stunning and unexpected results. This self-tagging system means that flickr is an excellent resource for brainstorming ideas and formulating new creative strategies and directional concepts—far better for creative work than simply doing a Google search, which will give you a more pedestrian and obvious set of results. flickr will present you with as many new creative options and choices as there are people posting their work on the site. An excellent resource for kick-starting new thinking—and perhaps sourcing and encouraging new talent from the amateur community.

Try the links listed here for images that you are free to use under whatever restrictions (if any) have been set by the creator—such as giving them a credit if you use the image, or not being able to use the image for derivative works without prior permission.

Florida's Educational Technology Clearinghouse
etc.usf.edu/clipart/index.htm
F (restrictions apply)
Free clip art for teachers and students from Florida's Educational Technology Clearinghouse. Over 25,000 pieces of monochrome, engraving-style clip art, in categories such as birds, botany, people, ships, machines, and air transportation. Check terms of usage.

Fontmonster
www.fontmonster.org
Cool and ever-changing site with downloadable fonts and clip-art graphic collections for Mac and PC, designed by the likes of Dave Luscombe, Ivan Philipov, Sebastien Theraulaz, Stefanie Koemers, and the Freewave Collective, who sell DVDs through the site—such as one Freewave collection that has more than 4.5GB of clip-art and font material.

Fotolia
www.fotolia.co.uk
Buy professional stock photographs, clip art, vector graphics, and so on, for relatively little financial outlay. Also sell your work through the site for a percentage of any downloads. Similar to iStockphoto.

Fotosearch
www.fotosearch.com

Royalty-free galleries. Like many such sites, you can search for royalty-free images and clips, but in fact these still incur a significant fee. However, purchase a CD of multiple images with a one-off payment and you can use them free within fairly broad agreements. Fotosearch includes work from hundreds of collections and image libraries, including: American Spirit Images, Asia Images, Bilderlounge, Birch Design, Comstock, Digital Vision, fStop, Gourmet Images, Illustration Works RM, ImageShop by Corbis, John Foxx, Map Resources, National Geographic, Photodisc, Retna, Time Image, Toons4Biz, and Zefa Royalty Free.

FreeFoto
www.freefoto.com
(for noncommercial use)
FreeFoto has over one million images and counting, at the time of going to press, and these are organized into more than 3,000 categories. FreeFoto says it is the largest collection of free photographs for private noncommercial use on the internet. This claim is impossible to substantiate, but it is certainly a sizable resource. The site is free to private noncommercial users and offers images for sale to others. Prices start from just $30 for internet use with up to 11¾ x 16½ in (297 x 420mm; A3) 300 dpi versions also available. Freefoto is one of the suppliers to Yotophoto.

Free Images
www.pachd.com/free-images

Growing collection of well-categorized, royalty-free stock photos.

Free Photo Bank
www.freephotobank.org
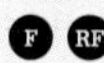
Thousands of Creative Commons licensed pictures of variable quality, but worth a look.

Free Photos
www.freephotos.se

Small personal photographic collection dedicated to the public domain. Images are viewable large. Some clippable material here, perhaps.

From Old Books
www.fromoldbooks.org

Images of the remains of ruined castles, deserted abbeys, old manor houses, mansions, and stately homes; also engravings, woodcuts, and pictures of old England and Wales; symbols, photographs, and clip art; pictures of old books, and much more, scanned, prepared, and published by Liam Quin. There are also RSS and ATOM feeds.

Geek Philosopher
geekphilosopher.com/MainPage/photos.htm

Free-to-use stock photos. The collections are small, but of generally high quality, within categories such as people, buildings, events, texture and paper, nature, food, animals, and art/music.

Getty Images
www.gettyimages.com
Certainly one of the big-five, major-league photography sites, focusing on top-quality photojournalism, and commanding large fees for its collections of often exclusive images, with offices based around the world.

If you become part of some of these galleries' paid subscription services, you can have relatively low-cost access to a selection of the images, which is worthwhile for high-volume commercial customers.

Gimp Savvy
gimp-savvy.com/PHOTO-ARCHIVE
F RF PD (restrictions apply)
Copyright-free, browsable photo archive of more than 27,000 free photos and images, which are in the public domain. The images and photos found come from a number of sources, including: the National Aeronautics and Space Administration (NASA), the National Oceanic and Atmospheric Administration (NOAA), and the US Fish and Wildlife Service (FWS)—each of which is represented elsewhere in this listing.

The site says that the photos are copyright-free, but some restrictions may still apply. Specifically, people have a legal right to privacy, and the use of their likeness for commercial advertising typically requires their consent—a "model release" form, in other words. So, if a person is identifiable in any image, a model release must be obtained before using the image for commercial purposes.

As a rule of thumb, if a photo is sufficiently modified so that people are no longer recognizable, it may be OK to use. Final responsibility for the fair use of the images found on this site is yours.

The use of any of the agencies' official emblems to implicitly or explicitly endorse any product, organization, policy, or agenda is prohibited.

Gode Cookery
www.godecookery.com/clipart/clart.htm

An excellent collection of medieval clip art pulled from various period sources, most notably woodcuts of the fifteenth and sixteenth centuries. These pictures are all in JPEG format, and in many cases are very large. Includes borders, people, animals, creatures and beasts, biblical scenes, decorative letterforms, and so on.

Graphic Maps
www.graphicmaps.com/clipart.htm

Monochrome and full-color clip-art continents, flags, globes, outline maps, and world images. Any clip art featured on these webpages may be used without written approval online or in any document/publication, although the site requests a link or credit.

Industrial Design Centre
www.designofsignage.com/application/symbol/hands
www.designofsignage.com/application/symbol/railway
www.designofsignage.com/application/symbol/building
www.designofsignage.com/application/symbol/hospital
www.idc.iitb.ac.in/resources/signage.html

Excellent public signage symbols clip-art resource provided by the Industrial Design Centre (IDC) at the Indian Institute of Technology (IIT) in Mumbai. Within various categories, this site provides free downloadable and universally recognizable international information graphics, for buildings, hospitals, transportation systems, building site safety, and so on.

Inmagine
www.inmagine.com

Two million royalty-free images, including vector and continuous-tone images, clip art, and so on. Tends toward "catalog" style, traditional stock gallery stuff.

iStockphoto
www.istockphoto.com

Good to average quality vector graphics, clip-art graphics, icons, stock photography, and video graphics, combined with a decent search engine and a low-cost (single-digit) pricing model per image. If you search the site for such tags as "wings," "gadgets," and so on, you are often presented with a page of *Crap Hound*-style clip-art images and icons, in vector format, alongside the more predictable stock shots.

The site encourages commerce: purchase the appropriate number of credits, and then download high-res images (vector illustrations come in a package of different editable formats) at various sizes until your credit runs down. A bonus is that anyone can upload images using their account and receive a fee per user download, which brings some of the benefits of sites such as flickr, both in terms of the expanding numbers, and of the occasionally esoteric nature of some of the images. Many designers use the site and pretend not to.

Japanese Clip Art
www.rr.em-net.ne.jp/~sfweb/index-e2.html
"Cliparts (sic) of ancient Japan." Mostly greetings card-style, naïve cartoon graphics, including animated GIFs. Probably not one for the design professional.

John Leech Archive
www.john-leech-archive.org.uk
F PD (contact site owners)
John Leech sketch archives from 1841 to 1864 from the satirical *Punch* magazine, including line drawings and Victorian cartoons. The page states they are out of copyright and believed to be public domain. The site requests charitable donations.

Jumpola
www.jumpola.com
A "big list of links" will take you to thousands of resources for designers and illustrators.

Jungle Photos
www.junglephotos.com
F (check with site owners)
Hundreds of images and information pages on animals, plants, people, textiles, patterns, crafts, scenery and more, from Central and Southern Africa and the Amazon Rainforest. Images are not in the public domain, but art teachers and students can use set numbers of images free, with permission from the site, which welcomes commercial approaches.

Karen's Whimsy
karenswhimsy.com/public-domain-images

One of the best stylized historical clip-art resources on the internet. Karen's Whimsy is a collection of clip art and public-domain imagery, sourced by Californian artist Karen Hatzigeorgiou from high-resolution scans of pre-1923 books, magazines, postcards, catalogs, and other print ephemera. This treasure trove is essential viewing for any reader of this book.

Included among these are silhouettes, line drawings, scraperboard pictures, engravings, cutout paper dolls, maps, animals, flowers, alphabets and alphabet graphics, seasonal clip art, Victoriana, patterns, fashions, architecture, printable frames and borders, and even graphics such as signing symbols for the deaf.

Says the artist: "You are free to use them in your artistic endeavors, either privately or commercially. My only request is that you not sell or give away the images themselves, either individually or as a collection. I spend a lot of time searching for and buying the source material, scanning, fixing, and editing the images, and then putting them on the web. By respecting these simple terms of use, you allow me to continue providing wonderful artwork that would remain hidden between the covers of these books, decayed from age, or tossed into landfills."

A link or footnote back to her page would be appreciated, she says. Of her own work, the artist says it "intertwines text and imagery in an interesting way… [and] integrates the written word with textured surfaces containing vintage images and layers of paper, paints, and embellishments. What started out as a small gift to people viewing my artwork has become a huge labor of love."

The artist is a member of ISABA, the International Society of Altered Book Artists (alteredbookartists.com), artists who make creative use of any book, old or new, that has been recycled by creative means into a work of art, "rebound, painted, cut, burned, folded, added to, collaged in, gold-leafed, rubber stamped, drilled, or otherwise adorned." Art or sacrilege? You decide. Any listing of the contents found on this site only touches on the riches stored here, so spend some time looking through the collection—which, not surprisingly, errs on the side of a nineteenth-century window into the world, whether the art clips are monochrome line works or full-color illustrations and paintings. As clip-art source material, however, it is hard to imagine a superior site for images of a certain look and feel.

Select listing:

Animal life (including animal clip art, prehistoric mammals, cave paintings, butterfly clip art, bird drawings, horse clip art, pictures of insects, reptiles, cat clip art, dog clip art)

Ocean life (including ocean animals, seashells, mermaids, sailing ships)

World religions (including Christian images and Hindu gods)

Ancient past (including Greek, Roman, Egyptian, Aztecs, hieroglyphics, Persia, Babylon, cuneiform, Phoenicians, Assyria, Chaldeans)

Music (including music clip art, string instruments, brass instruments, woodwind, percussion instruments)

Paper crafts (including paper dolls, paper doll patterns, Christmas craft patterns, circus clip art)

Occasions and holidays (including birthdays, St. Patrick's Day, 4th of July, weddings, Valentine's Day, Easter, Christmas, Thanksgiving, winter scenes)

Flowers (including spring clip art, flower parts, flowers by color, mushrooms, ferns)

Vintage images (including women, Victorian children, vintage fashions, vintage hairstyles, hats, historical costumes)

Text and languages (including alphabets)

Decoration (including clip-art borders, decorative borders, floral frames)

Kids Click!
www.kidsclick.org/psearch.html

Aimed at children in education, this is nevertheless a useful resource for searching trusted image sources for sometimes free or public-domain images, from UNESCO to the Smithsonian, via NASA and AMICO (The Art Museum Image Consortium).

The Librarians' Internet Index
lii.org

Not a clip-art or image site specifically, but an index and filter of trusted reference websites, including a variety of image sources and libraries, some of which may be in the public domain.

Library of Congress, Advertising
memory.loc.gov/ammem/collections/advertising

Fascinating clip-art and information resource website covering the emergence of advertising in the US between 1850 and 1920, including rare images of early print advertisements. Some images can be viewed at 150dpi. A good reference source and a clippings goldmine.

Library of Congress, American Memory
memory.loc.gov/ammem/index.html
PD (in many cases)
American Memory is the main gateway to rich primary source materials relating to the history and culture of the US. The site offers more than seven million digital items from more than 100 historical collections. See some of the subjects or try the Collection Finder. Collections include: African American history, architecture and landscape, environment and conservation, cities and towns, culture and folklife, government and law, immigration, literature, maps, Native American history, performing arts and music, sports and recreation, religion, war, technology and industry, women's history and Presidents. Some images are in the public domain, but many are not. Click on "Photos and Prints" and check the Copyright and Restrictions section for each collection.

Library of Congress, Printed Ephemera
memory.loc.gov/ammem/rbpehtml/pessay.html

Covering US print ephemera (posters, broadsides, pamphlets, and so on), from 1600 until the turn of the twenty-first century.

Library of Congress, Prints and Photographs
www.loc.gov/rr/print

Online collection of the Prints and Photographs Reading Room of the American Library of Congress, including many rare collections of early or historical photographs.

Logo Design Web
www.logodesignweb.com/stockphoto

Small but growing free stock photos site released by one photographer, including some useful, well-taken images. Credit the photographer, please.

Matton Images
www.matton.com
Mid-priced image gallery, with a fair selection of less traditional "image gallery" shots, some of which appear to have clipping paths.

Microsoft Office Clip Art
office.microsoft.com/en-us/clipart/default.aspx?lc=en-us

Microsoft clip-art resource for Office-related work. More than 150,000 free images and sounds, says the company. Bill Gates also controls image giant Corbis, but Microsoft has to pay to use its images, apparently.

Morgue File
www.morguefile.com

Not, as the name might suggest, a gallery of gore and the macabre, but a slick, high-quality, and completely free searchable image library where images are dowloadable at high resolution for commercial use with the originators' permission. Images include a broad mix of subjects and styles, from photojournalism and mood imagery to textures, shapes, objects, patterns, and abstract shots. Searches typically discover hundreds of matches. "This website follows in the tradition of the world wide web. It is dedicated to the proposition of free thought and exchange," says the site's owner. While images are available at zero cost, they are not in the public

domain, and some of the image-makers encourage dialogue and feedback. Recommended. A project originally set up by designer and illustrator Michael J. Connors: www.mconnors.com.

Mr Donn
www.mrdonn.org/clipart.html
Privately made portal containing links to a large but mixed bag of clip-art sites and resources, ranging from cartoon-style graphics to ethnic and regional sites. Worth clicking through all of the links, as you may turn up a diamond among the dayglo dross and detritus.

NASA
grin.hq.nasa.gov
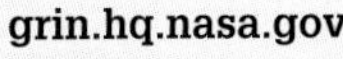
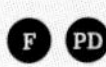
Top-quality, free, high-resolution public-domain images from NASA covering space exploration and research, moon landings, astronomy, galaxies, planets, and the like. Excellent stuff, provided by "Great Images in NASA" (GRIN). Also try:
nix.nasa.gov
www.nasa.gov/gallery/index.html
www.nasa.gov/gallery/photo/index.html

National Atlas
nationalatlas.gov
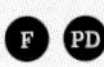
Lots of GIF maps of the US, such as congressional district maps, all in the public domain.

National Library of Medicine
www.nlm.nih.gov/hmd/index.html

History of Medicine at the National Library of Medicine. Most, but not all, of the exhibitions are in the public domain. Clicking on "Metadata" near the bottom of the page will generate a popup window with information that includes rights usage for each page.

National Oceanic and Atmospheric Administration
www.photolib.noaa.gov/search.html
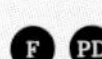
Searchable, rich, public domain photography resource of the National Oceanic and Atmospheric Administration (NOAA) in the US, with thousands of free images of the natural world and the oceans. The site has modest aims: "The NOAA collection spans centuries of time and much of the natural world from the center of the Earth to the surface of the sun." Images are of excellent quality and high-res downloads are available by clicking on the relevant links. Credit must be given to NOAA unless otherwise stated.

National War College Military Image Collection
www.ndu.edu/nwc/nwcCLIPART/NWCclipart.html
Gung-ho, flag-waving US site of military images, designed for personnel assigned to an institution called the National War College. Ignoring the bellicose tone, the site has images of badges, medals, posters, maps, US presidents, international leaders, and military hardware—together with foreign military images that are listed as "Russian" and "Other Than Russian"—an intriguing glimpse into the twenty-first century military psyche! All are frustratingly small and for web usage only.

Nature Gallery
www.cohsoft.com.au/NatureGallery/action/thumbs
F (check with site owner)
Photographs of animals, birds, and more. These images are not in the public domain, but photographer Ann Jessel may allow art teachers and students to use her images in the creation of works of art and for presentations.

Netdiver Magazine
www.netdiver.net
Not a clip-art resource, but one of the best and most well-kept secrets for professional designers and illustrators. This beautifully designed portal showcases the best in new design and illustration work, with dozens of new links and new work in photography, design, illustration, video, and animation every week. Well worth adding to your bookmarks or favorites—and more likely than not to point you toward a new image resource or emerging talent. Run by people with good eyes and ears.

New York Public Library Digital Gallery
digitalgallery.nypl.org/nypldigital/index.cfm
F PD
An excellent, largely free service from the New York Public Library (NYPL) offering hundreds of thousands of digital images of historical materials from the Library's original, rare and specialized holdings. Included are artworks; fine prints; manuscript illuminations; maps; photographs; stereographs; printed ephemera, such as menus, postcards, posters, and trade cards; rare illustrated books; and other picture formats. Periods range from the middle ages to the twentieth century.

NYPL provides free and open access to its Digital Gallery and images may be freely downloaded for personal, research, and study purposes. Although many images are in the public domain, the library charges a convenience fee for commercial usage.

Old Book Illustrations
www.oldbookillustrations.com
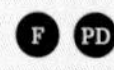
Highly recommended and wonderful site for designers and illustrators packed full of downloadable images, such as engravings, etchings, and line drawings scanned from old books. Particularly worth a look are the sections on characters, science and technology, and ornaments, all of which contain a wealth of clip elements that cry out for a new context. Searchable by keywords.

Open Photo
openphoto.net
F RF (in many cases)
High-quality image gallery, including clip art, stock photography, fine-art photography, and so on, contributed by several thousand image-makers. Creators can assign their own licensing terms. For example, some works are available on an "Attribution/Share-Alike" license, which means you can use the work free if you credit the creator, while others specify that derivative works are not permitted, or that commercial usage is forbidden. Well worth browsing the collections, which include both stock shots and thematic, mood, and conceptual pieces.

Pagan Public Domain Clipart
www.angelfire.com/pa2/sacredspiral

Unusual site containing dozens of original Pagan artworks along the lines of Goddess imagery, runes, stars, witches, birds, peace signs, Ankhs, suns, dragons, and so forth, together with patterns, textures, silhouettes, Celtic circles, symbols, and borders. Images are fairly small and in a variety of media, but many are monochrome line works. "Dedicated to the public domain" by the artist.

PA Photos
www.paphotos.com
Formerly EMPICS. The image bank of the Press Association. One of the big-five, major-league news photography sites, focusing on top-quality photojournalism, and commanding large fees for their collections of often-exclusive images.

PD Photo
www.pdphoto.org
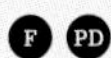
A personal mix of public-domain travel and location photos for commercial uses, websites, school projects, articles, adverts, and so on. Unless something is marked as being something other than public domain, you can assume it is free to use, says the site's owner and photographer Jon Sullivan.

Phillip Martin Clip Art
www.phillipmartin.info/clipart/homepage.htm
Very much the old-school definition of clip art. A collection of jokey, cartoon-style graphics, covering a mix of seasonal events and ancient civilizations, presumably aimed at schoolchildren.

Photographic Libraries
www.photographiclibraries.com/search.php
A handy image search facility that allows you to search filtered selections of websites, for image types such as free photos and clip art, fine art, posters, prints, graphics, stars and celebrities, student galleries, and various stock categories. Worth your time.

Photos
photos.com
Expensive subscription site for a familiar mix of professional royalty-free imagery, clip graphics, conceptual photos, and so on. Worth considering if you plan multiple downloads over time. Sites such as iStockphoto offer similar quality on a low-cost credits system, while the Stock XCHNG and others offer a comparable service free. Full marks for the URL, which surely picks up a lot of traffic.

PicFindr
www.picfindr.com
Helpful search tool that trawls the web and the "free-stock photosphere" for stock imagery that is free to use commercially.

Pics4Learning
www.pics4learning.com

Another child-friendly image library for teachers and students. The collection consists of thousands of images, in dozens of categories, that have been donated by students, teachers, and amateur photographers, and includes clip art in a variety of styles, photography, illustrations, cartoons, and much more.

Project Gutenberg
www.gutenberg.net/catalog

The Project Gutenberg site features thousands of digitized books, only a few illustrated, but the number of illustrated books increases from week to week. There may be thousands of public-domain images here as the collection grows.

Public Domain Images
www.pdimages.com

Paid-for public-domain image site, covering vintage and historical imagery in many categories.

Public Domain Photos of Spain
publicdomain.photopress-spain.com

Photo archive containing a collection of free, public-domain images and photos of Spain.

Reuters
www.reuters.com/pictures
One of the big-five news photography sites, being part of the Reuters international news agency. You need to register to view the full catalog of regularly updated images.

Rex Features
www.rexfeatures.com
Arguably also one of the big-five, major-league news photography sites, focusing on top-quality photojournalism and celebrity shots, and commanding large fees for exclusive images. Not as extensive a library as Reuters or Getty, for example, but it does include some rarer or less familiar images, which makes it an often-fascinating port of call. Register to see anything bigger than thumbnails (unlike Corbis and Getty Images, which watermark their images).

Ruid
www.ruid.com
F (check with copyright owners)
Free image-hosting and sharing site.

Show and Tell Publications
readingfrenzy.com
Site of Show and Tell Publications, publisher of the most recent issues of Sean Tejaratchi's *Crap Hound* zine, among other alternative publications.

Shutterstock
www.shutterstock.com

Large royalty-free subscription service. Includes clip-art devices, heraldic crests, and so on, alongside more traditional royalty-free image library fare.

Stock XCHNG
www.sxc.hu
F RF (restrictions apply)
Highly rated by many professional designers and illustrators, Stock XCHNG is a free-to-use image library and exchange, with hundreds of thousands of images available online via a good search engine.

Images include the usual mix of high-quality stock shots, illustrations, and abstract or conceptual pieces, along with clip-art patterns, icons, borders, and so on, which frequently appear within searches such as "circles" or "flowers" (rather than "borders"). Think outside the box in your searches.

You have to register with the site to get large previews and high-res downloads of the otherwise watermarked thumbnails. The pictures are available to use free online or in print publications, such as books or promotional items.

There are some restrictions—such as on physical items for print-on-demand or resale (eg mugs, mousemats, T-shirts, and so on); and for one-off printed works for resale, such as prints, or where an identifiable person within the image might be seen as promoting a product or service. Extended licenses are available.

Subscription clip-art sites
coolarchive.com
www.allfree-clipart.com
www.barrysclipart.com
www.clipart.com
www.clip-art.com
www.clipartconnection.com
www.graphicsfactory.com
www.myclipart.com
Subscription services and portals featuring mainly low-grade, full-color cartoon-style clip art, of the wedding invitation and birthday cards variety, together with animated GIFs, textures, fonts, moving clip art for cellphones, and so on. Many of these sites are

segmented by clip art, vinyl-ready images (for signage), photos, web graphics, three-dimensional clip art, illustrations, fonts, and sounds/ringtones. Full marks to the companies for purchasing the URLs. Some of these sites are fronts for Jupiter Images, which also owns www.comstock.com.

Teaching Politics
teachpol.tcnj.edu/amer_pol_hist/index.htm

A collection of over 500 public-domain images of American political history. Browse the collection by era—from the eighteenth century through to the twentieth—or search for a specific image within categories such as maps, civil rights, suffrage, abolition, buildings, and Presidents.

Training Reference
www.trainingreference.co.uk/free_pictures/index.html

Small but helpful free-to-use gallery of images covering subjects such as animals, flowers, sky, snow, trees, etc.

University of Maryland, Public Domain Links
www.umuc.edu/distance/odell/cip/links_pubdomain.shtm

Useful set of mainly US links concerning public domain legal issues and copyright debates, for anyone interested.

University of Pennsylvania, African Studies Center
www.africa.upenn.edu/Face_Masks/menu_Face_Mask.html

(check with site)

One page from the University of Pennsylvania multimedia resource archive for its Africa Studies courses. This page includes a number of clip-art GIFs of tribal masks. The page also includes a number of links to other pages that include clip-art images of flags, maps, and other images.

University of Washington Libraries, Fashion Plate Collection
content.lib.washington.edu/costumehistweb/index.html

(check terms and conditions carefully)

This image collection includes original fashion illustrations from 1806 to 1914 from some of the leading style journals of the time. Scans are of high quality, but in some cases resized downward in terms of their physical dimensions. Read the detailed copyright notes carefully.

US Air Force
www.af.mil/photos

Free US Airforce photography site with high-res, often good-quality downloads of airplanes, helicopters, natural disasters, space, people, and so on. Most US governmental sites are very good at providing free image resources.

US Department of Agriculture
www.ars.usda.gov/is/graphics/photos/

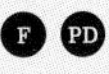

Useful image gallery hosted by the US Agricultural Research Service, which means lots of (often creative and high quality) stock photographs and illustrations of food, crops, plants, animals, and field research. They encourage feedback, but it is not mandatory, and 300dpi downloads are available within each page. Some potential here for illustrators and designers.

US Fish & Wildlife Services

www.fws.gov/pictures

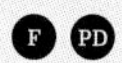

Invaluable resource of clip-art images, illustrations, and photographs of fish and wildlife from the US Fish and Wildlife Service. These images are in the public domain, and you are free to use them. There are hundreds of images online, and thousands more to come, say the site owners. Included are hundreds of detailed monochrome line drawings of dozens of species, which are available as both screen-res previews and high-res TIFFs. The site requests that you credit the named illustrators or photographers.

Veer

www.veer.com

"Elements for creativity." A commercial photography, illustration, and motion graphic service, including stock shots, rights-managed and royalty-free imagery. The site hosts content from providers such as: Canopy, CSA Archive, CSA Mod Art, CSA Printstock, CSA Snapstock, Gallerist, Graphistock, Index Stock, SIS, Alloy, Digital Vision, fStop, image100, ImageZoo, PhotoAlto, Photodisc, Spots, Stockbyte, and Visual Language. Any of these are worth checking out.

Vintage Pixels

www.vintagepixels.com

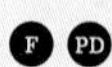

Large, free database of historical photographs. Pictures are high-res and free to use, and the site allows people to share their old archived photos. You can download images for print, or use them in graphic designs and illustrations at no cost. You need to register with the community to get access to the high-res files, but you can preview medium-sized screen versions and positionals.

Vintage Postcards

www.vintagepostcards.com

Self-explanatory and mainly US site for serious collectors. Scans of cards are listed by category, including, among many others: advertising, Art Nouveau, Art Deco, aviation, baseball, circus, Disney (beware of lawyers!), glamor, military and propaganda, music and dance, ocean liners, photography, social history, teddy bears, the *Titanic*, women's suffrage, and more.

Wikipedia

www.wikipedia.org

www.wikimedia.org

There are numerous public-domain images and clip-art resources available via the global phenomenon that is Wikipedia, the user-editable online encyclopedia. As it is a resource that changes by the second, more may be added (or taken away) at any moment, so it is worth doing a Wiki search for "public-domain images," or the tag "PD," rather than searching for, or within, the category you are researching first of all.

Many of the PD image galleries within Wikipedia, for example, contain regional or national image archives, and as such, can be an invaluable image resource of people or places pictures.

However, a more serendipitous resource within the PD galleries might be general categories such as "Author died more than 70 years ago public-domain images," which can throw up a whole world of random riches, such as playbills, posters, old newspapers, transportation images, sepia postcards, paintings, and so on. These are not the most searchable resources, however.

As a first port of call, try: **en.wikipedia.org/wiki/Category:Public_domain_images.** Alternatively, go to Wikipedia's "parent" site **wikimedia.org/**, which includes a variety of other online projects as well as the well-known user-editable encyclopedia. For Creative Commons-licensed images within Wikimedia, go to: **commons.wikimedia.org**

Wise Gorilla
www.wisegorilla.com/clipart.html

Very useful portal including clip art across a very broad range of categories, including Africa, buttons, birds, Chinese symbols, flags, hieroglyphics, icons, Japanese art, meteorology, optical illusions, signs and symbols, science (including the Periodic Table), currencies, and so on. The images vary in quality, but many—such as the ones at **www.wisegorilla.com/images/african/african.html** (West African signs and symbols)—are invaluable reference images that you can cut and paste into patterns, borders, graphics, icons, illustrations, and so on. Well worth a detailed trawl for the original gems among the rather less useful vector drawings.

WP Clipart
www.wpclipart.com

Browsable public-domain clip art optimized for use in word processors and home/office ink-jet printers. Includes galleries such as: **www.wpclipart.com/flags/index.html** (several hundred flags, with countries listed alphabetically, together with US State flags, historical and other flags, such as some entertaining Copyleft and Pirate flags. All in PNG format).

Yale University, Beinecke Library
beinecke.library.yale.edu/dl_crosscollex/

Yale University's Beinecke Rare Book & Manuscript Library's online collection of digital images. Most may be public domain. 90,000 images from rare books and manuscripts. Search by keyword.

Yotophoto
yotophoto.com
Some images 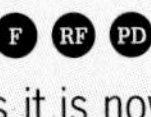
Yotophoto says it is now indexing well over a quarter of a million Creative Commons, public domain, GNU FDL (open source), and other "copyleft" images. It indexes images in the public domain, or which are available for free usage under various forms of copyleft licensing. Essentially, Yotophoto is a portal to a variety of image resources that supply free digital material. As such, it is a constantly changing source of imagery, from traditional and predictable stock shots to more esoteric and surprising sources. Search and see.

Youworkforthem
www.youworkforthem.com
An intriguing, clever, if slightly self-conscious design portal that offers professional designers a range of high-quality, downloadable clip graphics, including emblems, silhouettes, symbols, illustrations, patterns, "botanicals," and ornaments, together with stock images (and video clips), typefaces, and Photoshop-compatible brush collections. Many of the clip-art products are relatively low cost and available in packs—for example, $25 for 25 royalty-free graphic flourishes, ornaments, and patterns. Like many such services, the site is at the heart of a blogging community of users and designers. You can search by keywords within this slightly counterintuitive site. For example, searching for "circles" brought up a set of original Charles and Ray Eames textiles patterns for stationery ($12.99), a profile of Henk Elenga, a collection of 16 royalty-free vector graphics, a collection of Neo Japanese graphics, and an interpretative overview of the Central European Avant Garde. A good piece of web publishing and showmanship, though, as it says "try this" and "look here," which is what the web is for.

Featured designers

Aboud Sodano
www.aboud-sodano.com

Absolute Zero°
www.absolutezerodegrees.com

AdamsMorioka
www.adamsmorioka.com

Nicole Andujar
www.nicoleandujar.com

Archizen Creative
www.archizencreative.com

Ashby Design
www.ashbydesign.com

Beta Design
www.marianabukvic.com.br

Erich Brechbühl
www.mixer.ch

Byboth
www.byboth.com

ChixInk
www.chixink.com

CityAbyss
www.cityabyss.com

Coast Design
www.coastdesign.be

compoundEye
www.compoundeyedesign.com

Corridors of my Mind
www.corridorsofmymind.com

Form
www.form.uk.com

Fullblast
www.fullblastinc.com

Joe Maguire Design
www.joemaguiredesign.com

The Joneses
www.thejoneses.co.uk

Kanardo
www.kanardo.com

KesselsKramer
www.kesselskramer.com

LAKI 139
www.laki139.com

Martin O'Neill
www.cutitout.co.uk

Peter and Paul
www.peterandpaul.co.uk

Plan-B Studio
www.plan-bstudio.com

Pony
www.ponybox.co.uk

Raidy Printing Group
www.raidy.com

Red Design
www.red-design.co.uk

The Small Stakes
www.thesmallstakes.com

Studio threefiftyseven
www.threefiftyseven.com

Studiomime
www.studiomime.com

Tom Varisco Design
www.tomvariscodesigns.com

Traffic Design Consultants
www.traffic-design.co.uk

UMS
www.ulhasmoses.com

Wiretrap Studios
www.wiretrapstudios.com

Index

Chris Middleton:
I would like to thank everyone at RotoVision, especially Jane Roe for all of her patience during the long and complex gestation of this book, and Luke Herriott for all his work sourcing designers and work from around the world and curating the visual material in this book. I would like to dedicate this book to Stu, who has, in a very different way, also been very patient and supportive during the long hours of a busy few months, and without whom I wouldn't be anything like as happy.

Luke Herriott:
I too thank everyone at RotoVision, especially Jane Roe, Tony Seddon, and April Sankey for their support during this project, and Chris Middleton for the endless hours he spent pulling this book into shape. I'd also like to thank all those talented and creative designers who have contributed such inspiring and innovative work along with insights into their techniques and methods of creating it. And of course, my wife Rebecca and our wonderful children Dylan and Pearl who make everything so worthwhile.